DALLAS
FORT WORTH
and the METROPLEX

#1 GUIDE TO ADDISON • ARLINGTON • FARMERS BRANCH
GARLAND • GRAND PRAIRIE • GRAPEVINE • IRVING
MESQUITE • NORTH RICHLAND HILLS • PLANO • RICHARDSON

ROBERT R. RAFFERTY AND LOYS REYNOLDS

Gulf Publishing Company
Houston, Texas

TEXAS MONTHLY GUIDE TO DALLAS, FORT WORTH AND THE METROPLEX

Copyright © 1997 by Robert Rafferty and Loys Reynolds. All rights reserved. This book, or parts thereof, may not be reproduced in any form without permission of the authors.

Printed in U.S.A.

Gulf Publishing Company
Book Division
P.O. Box 2608 □ Houston, Texas 77252-2608

10   9   8   7   6   5   4   3   2   1

Library of Congress Cataloging-in-Publication Data
Rafferty, Robert.
    Dallas, Fort Worth, and the metroplex : the biggest, best, and most comprehensive guide to one of America's most distinctive and diverse metropolitan areas / by Robert Rafferty and Loys Reynolds.
        p.   cm. — (The Texas monthly guidebooks)
    Includes bibliographical references and index.
    ISBN 0-87719-318-5
        1. Dallas Region (Tex.)—Guidebooks.   2. Fort Worth Region (Tex.)—Guidebooks.   I. Reynolds, Loys.   II. Title. III. Series.
    F394.S213R34   1997
    917.64′28120463—dc21   97-17067
                                                         CIP

Printed on Acid-Free Paper (∞)

*To our wonderful grandchildren: Allyson,
Amber, Brice, Daniel, Ernest III, Ian, Jacob and
Jacob, Jason, Nicole, Read, Robert, and Sarah.*

CONTENTS

ACKNOWLEDGMENTS

Details. DETAILS. DETAILS!

A guidebook is only as good as the completeness and accuracy of its details, which is why we are deeply indebted and want to acknowledge many people for their help in gathering and verifying the thousands of details in the listings in this book.

In general, we'd like to thank the executives and staffs of the various convention and visitors bureaus, and city tourism, parks, and economic development departments for their invaluable professional assistance and enthusiastic help.

In particular, we want to offer an extra-special thank you to the individuals listed below who went far and beyond the call of their duties to ensure that our research was complete and accurate.

Addison—Mary A. Rosenbleeth, public communications manager; Greg Pynes, director, visitor services

Arlington—Judy Everett Ramos, director of communications, Arlington Convention and Visitors Bureau

Dallas—Greg Elam, vice-president, communications, Dallas Convention and Visitors Bureau; Cheryl Lewis, director of public relations, Dallas Convention and Visitors Bureau

Farmers Branch—Michael W. Woody, group/convention sales manager

Fort Worth—Mona Gandy, director of communications, Fort Worth Convention and Visitors Bureau

Garland—Cara Harting, director of community relations; Shirley McGuire, community relations department

Grand Prairie—Kristina Thompson, director of communications, Grand Prairie Convention and Visitors Bureau

Grapevine—John R. Meyner III, director of communications

Irving—Maura Allen Gast, director of communications, Irving Convention and Visitors Bureau; Diana K. Pfaff, communications coordinator, Irving Convention and Visitors Bureau

Mesquite—Terry McCullar, director of visitors service, Mesquite Chamber of Commerce

North Richland Hills—Anna Riehm, marketing and research coordinator, Economic Development Department

Plano—Jana Carmichael, marketing manager, Plano Convention and Visitors Bureau; Areva Moore, convention services coordinator, Plano Convention and Visitors Bureau

Richardson—Lucia Arrant, vice-president, Richardson Convention and Visitors Bureau Texas Association of Convention and Visitors Bureaus; LaRue Ersch, director, TACVB

And, of course, at Gulf Publishing, we want to start by thanking the many nameless copy editors, graphic artists, designers, and other publishing professionals who did the grunt work of putting out this guidebook. And, going further up the feeding chain at Gulf, our editors: Claire Blondeau, who agreed with us that there was a need for a guide to the Metroplex as a whole and got our project approved; Tim Calk, our book editor, who shepherded the manuscript through the intricate process of converting it from manuscript to published pages; B. J. Lowe, the editor-in-chief, who guided the Texas Monthly Guidebook Series to its place of honor among regional guidebooks and gave his *imprimatur* to this monster project; and John Wilson, director of sales, who's going to put this book on the travel book best-seller list.

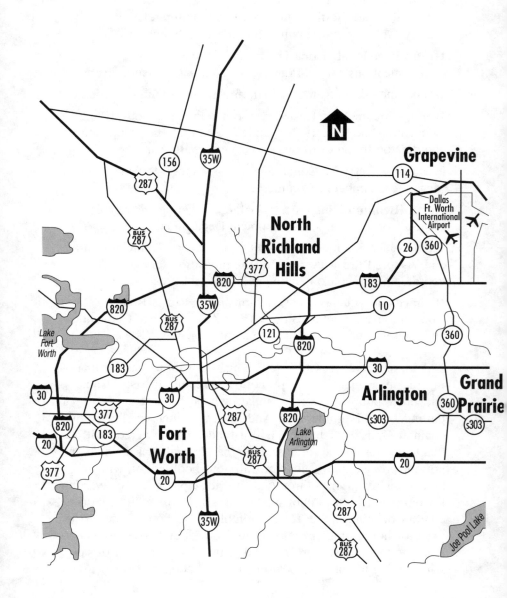

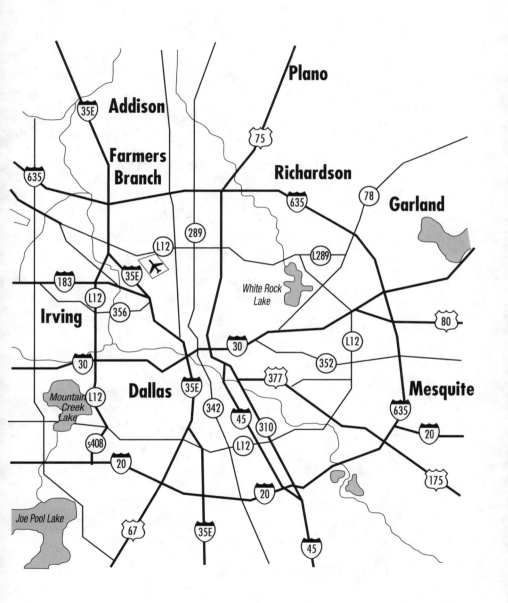

READ THIS FIRST AND GET YOUR MONEY'S WORTH FROM THIS GUIDE!

Why that shouting title for what's really the Introduction?

Because most guidebook users, eager to get into the details about their destination, skip over anything with a mundane title like Introduction; or, for that matter, any other sections in the front of the book that might delay getting right to the heart of the matter.

Unfortunately, if you skip this part you'll be missing some crucial guidelines that will help you squeeze the most out of the listings.

You don't have to read it all right now. Just skim through this section, so you'll know what's here. Then, if you need the details later, you'll have a good idea where to look.

WELCOME TO THE METROPLEX

For years there was no love lost between Dallas and Fort Worth. In the early days, for example, a Dallas newspaper helped establish the feud by claiming that Fort Worth was so dead a panther had been seen sleeping unmolested in the main street. Fort Worth never forgave that insult and after that the two cities became bitter rivals in everything. It's said that the feelings were so strong that, rather than eat in a Dallas restaurant, Fort Worth publisher Amon Carter brought his own sack lunch with him when he had to be in Dallas on business.

Over those years the prairies between the two cities gradually filled as new cities were formed with names like Arlington, Irving, and Grand Prairie. More small cities were formed on the outskirts of the two big towns. Cities like Garland, Mesquite, and Richardson grew up around Dallas, and North Richland Hills by Fort Worth. These cities grew and grew and soon it was hard to distinguish where one ended and the next started. Most of these cities tried to stay neutral in the feud, but if they couldn't they leaned toward the view of the big city nearest to them.

Then, in 1965, Dallas and Fort Worth buried the hatchet, agreeing to build an airport between them that would serve the entire region. The Dallas/Fort Worth International Airport proved to be the missing link needed to pull together all the disparate cities in the area and consolidate them into one gigantic Metroplex.

But it wasn't called that just yet. That name didn't come about until several years later when the North Texas Commission, a sort of regional chamber of commerce, was looking for a catchy advertising slogan that would help lure northern businesses and industry to move to the region once the D/FW airport was opened. After several tries, an ad agency exec dropped a few letters from the words Metropolitan Complex and came up with the magic term "Metroplex." It was catchy and caught on—at least with the North Texas Commission and many businesses.

Today, it's fairly well established in Texas that if you talk of the Metroplex you're talking about the Dallas/Fort Worth area (although many Texans don't realize how many other cities there are in the Metroplex besides those two biggies). But don't expect it to be recognized elsewhere. Ask a travel agent to book you a flight to the Metroplex or get you a hotel room in the Metroplex and you'll probably get a blank stare.

Be that as it may, when you decide what you want to do in this Metropolitan complex, it'll usually be more convenient for you to ignore the boundaries between the complex of interlocking cities and think of it as the whole—the Metroplex—instead of the parts. True, you will have to know the address and which city you want to go to; just don't think of the city boundaries as walls. It's also true that to bring some order to this guidebook we've broken it up into its city parts; however, by using the Metroplex map as your guide you can cross our paper borders as easily as you can on the ground.

SOME METROPLEX STATISTICS AND FASCINATING FACTS

To most of the rest of the world, the stereotypical Texan is a braggart. Like many other stereotypes, this one is false. Residents of the Metroplex don't brag. It just sounds that way when they tell the truth about their amazing complex of cities. Following are just a few statistics and facts to prove this.

D/FW Airport has a land mass larger than Manhattan Island. Now #2 in the number of take-offs and landing of all the airports in the U.S., D/FW is projected to be #1 in a few years.

While the population of the Metroplex area is around 4,000,000, it is the least densely populated metropolitan area in the world.

Dallas, by itself, with a population of over a million, is the seventh largest city in the United States and the second largest in Texas.

The Metroplex:
• Is the top visitor destination in Texas both for leisure and business travel.
• Is the # 2 convention area in the U.S.; second only to Chicago.

- Is the third largest film production center in the United States.
- Is third in the U.S. in the number of industrial company head-quarters.
- Is the home of the largest wholesale merchandise mart in the world.
- Has more shopping centers per capita than any city in the U.S.
- Has more restaurants per capita than New York City (more than 5,000 in Dallas alone), including the only AAA five-diamond restaurants in Texas.
- Has two of the top-ten-ranked hotels in America and the only U.S. hotel in the top ten in the world.
- Has the only AAA five-diamond hotel in Texas and as many AAA four-diamond hotels as any city in the nation.
- Has teams in all major professional sports: baseball, basketball, football, soccer, and hockey, plus rodeo.
- Has major tracks for horse racing and NASCAR auto racing.
- Is home of the largest state fair in the country.
- Has the tallest ferris wheel in the country.
- Has a major amusement-theme park and the country's largest water-theme park.
- Has the world's largest equestrian sculpture and the world's largest bronze monument.
- Is the home of the world's largest honky-tonk.
- Has three of the largest concert hall organs in the country.
- Is the home of one of the largest permanent flea markets in the country.
- Has two major zoos.
- Has more than thirty museums ranging in theme from art to baseball to sewing machines.
- Is home of one of the largest wine festivals in the U.S.
- Is home of the largest arts district in the county.
- Offers more live music every night than Nashville, and not just country and western but everything from blues to symphony.

There's lots, lots more, as you'll see as you skim through this book. What it adds up to is there's truly something for everyone in the Metroplex. So use this guidebook to find your something, and ENJOY!

HOW IS THIS GUIDE ORGANIZED?

As simply as we can make it. Or, in this computer-age, as user-friendly as we can make it. Basically, the thirteen cities we covered are listed alphabetically by city.

The *Dallas/Fort Worth Metroplex,* as the name implies, is a conglomerate of cities tightly bunched together. Dallas and Fort Worth are the largest and anchor the Metroplex on the east and west. But if you're heading for Six Flags you'll be going to Arlington, to see the Cowboys play you have to go to Irving, to taste Texas wines you head for Grapevine (where else?), for horse racing it's Grand Prairie's Lone Star Park and . . . well, you get the idea. It's truly a Metro-complex.

We considered writing this book as just one monstrous city guide, forgetting all about the city boundaries—most of which you may never know you crossed. However, in our visits we found that each of these cities, large and small, has its own distinctive character. Although they are just minutes apart, for example, the ambiance of Mesquite is vastly different from that of Addison. And, each also has its own separate convention and visitors bureau, chamber of commerce, or city office to help visitors with specific information for that city.

Admittedly, a few of the smaller Metroplex cities are really just bedroom communities, pleasant places to live, but with little to interest visitors that would warrant a special trip. Which is why we decided to concentrate on giving you in-depth coverage of those cities that offer the most to you, whether you are a tourist or a business visitor. These are: Addison, Arlington, Dallas, Farmers Branch, Fort Worth, Garland, Grand Prairie, Grapevine, Irving, Mesquite, North Richland Hills, Plano, and Richardson.

THINGS CHANGE

It took a long time to research, write, edit, print, and distribute this book. In the meantime, things have been changing. Restaurants, for example, are notorious for changing their names and management, menu, hours, or—even worse—closing down. Museums change hours or admission fees. Attractions burn down and new ones open up. Prices go up or (rarely) down. In other words, all we can tell you is that the information in this book was as current as we could make it at the time it went to press.

If you use a listing for a restaurant and find it's no longer there, or your lodgings don't have all the amenities cited, or the museum is closed on Monday when we said it was open, please try to be understanding.

To help you avoid any inconvenience caused by changes, we've included telephone numbers in the listings whenever possible. A call before you go might save you a little irritation, especially if you have to travel any distance. Remember, however, phone numbers change, too. (While we were researching this guide, for example, the phone company changed area codes.) If you have trouble reaching a listing, check the phone book or call information or the local visitors bureau.

WHAT'S IN THIS GUIDE—AND WHAT'S NOT

It would take a book thicker than a Dallas phonebook to list all the attractions, museums, restaurants, hotels/motels, and all the other places of interest to visitors to the cities in this guide. Therefore, our goal was not to tell ALL, but to give you a solid sampling of the best to get you started on your visit. Once started, you can get more free information from the listed local visitors bureau or city office, the local newspaper, your hotel concierge or hotel/motel staff, or a dozen other local sources. They can help update you on what we did list as well as discover the places and/or events of particular interest to you that space limitations forced us to omit.

If you think we really goofed by omitting your favorite place or event, or you find any errors in this guide, we'd like to hear from you so we can consider your comments for the next edition. Write us: Robert Rafferty and Loys Reynolds, Texas Monthly Guide to the Dallas/Fort Worth Metroplex, c/o Gulf Publishing Company, P.O. Box 2608, Houston, TX 77252-2608.

HOW TO READ THE LISTINGS

Each city's listings begin with the name of the county in which it is located, the best rounded-off estimate of the city's current population, and its telephone area code.

Where a listing gives the days open, a dash (–) between days means "through," including both days. For example, "Monday–Thursday" means "Monday through Thursday."

To make it easier to find the listings, each city's listings are broken down under the category headings that follow.

FREE VISITOR SERVICES

These are visitors bureaus and other organizations that will provide you with free information and answer your questions about their city or area. Each listing includes the address and phone. Unless otherwise noted, these offices are usually open regular business hours Monday–Friday.

PUBLICATIONS

These are local newspapers and magazines that regularly include schedules for theaters and current events, restaurant reviews, opening hours for attractions, and other information that gives you the up-to-the-minute details. Some of these you'll have to buy, but several of the weekly newspapers that highlight local entertainment news are free and widely available.

COMMERCIAL TOUR SERVICES

Tour companies and other organizations that offer commercial tours.

INDUSTRY TOURS

Tours of businesses or industrial plants. Most of these are free, but check to see if there is a minimum age or other restrictions on who can take the tour.

SELF-GUIDED TOURS

Driving and/or walking tours you can take on your own. Most of these help squire you around neighborhoods that are of special interest.

BIRD'S-EYE VIEW

The best places to get a panoramic view of the area.

HISTORIC PLACES

Whether you are a history buff or just curious about our heritage, there are several places that give you a glimpse of what life was like in the Metroplex in the past. Many of the listings are historic homes that are still private residences. If this is the case, it's requested that you just walk or drive by and not bother the residents. Not included are the many city and state historical markers and plaques attached to walls of historic buildings and set up on roadsides near historic sites. Each of these tells a story of a piece of local history, and most are worth the time it takes to stop and read and think about the lives of those who came before us.

MUSEUMS AND PUBLIC ART GALLERIES

The Metroplex has a wealth of museums. Almost every city has at least one. The great ones are comparable to the best in the nation. Others are little gems well worth your time. To get the most from your museum visit try to avoid weekends, which are usually crowded, especially if there's a major exhibit going on. Always ask about free tours or lectures. At least get a floor plan and/or any free brochures that you can use to guide yourself around. If it's a large museum, don't try to do it all at once. Plan on taking a break in some quiet place, perhaps; if there's a café, you can relax over lunch. If you live in or near the Metroplex and plan to be a regular visitor to a particular museum, look into a membership that may pay for itself in discounts on admission or other perks. If you want inexpensive souvenirs, the museum gift shop will probably have postcards with reproductions of the exhibits.

SPECIAL GARDENS

City botanical gardens and a few other gardens of special interest.

OUTDOORS

A selection of city parks, lakes, and other places where you can enjoy the greatness of the outdoors in this metropolitan area.

COLLEGES AND UNIVERSITIES

For non-student visitors college and university campuses are often relatively undiscovered treasure houses with a long list of facilities and events open to the public. These may include art galleries, museums, historic buildings, concerts, plays, film and lecture series, festivals, and major sports events that range from basketball and football to intercollegiate rodeos. Parking is a problem at many schools, so, when available, listings include information on visitor parking.

MUSIC AND PERFORMING ARTS

Theater, dance, and music are alive and robust in the Metroplex. Dallas and Fort Worth, of course, offer the widest possible variety; however, many of the smaller cities have a surprising medley of offerings ranging from community theater to symphony orchestras. There are also many cultural arts groups that sponsor touring shows and celebrity concerts. These listings, which barely scratch the surface of what's going on, include both specific music and performing arts organizations and the places, like theaters and civic centers, that host these events.

FAMILY FUN AND KID STUFF

Special places for kids of all ages.

SPORTS

Listings offer a wide variety of both spectator and individual sports available to visitors. These range from major professional sports to golf, tennis, and jogging. Most intercollegiate sports are open to visitors and, occasionally, college sports facilities are open on a limited basis for the use of non-students. These are listed under each individual school. If your favorite sport or activity isn't listed or you need more details, contact the local visitors bureau, the local parks and recreation department, or the colleges and universities.

OTHER POINTS OF INTEREST

This is sort of a catch-all category for places of interest to visitors that don't fit exactly into any of the categories listed above.

OFFBEAT

And now for something completely different . . . listings under this heading don't fit any of the other categories because they are truly unique.

ANNUAL EVENTS

Every community celebrates one or more annual events that have a distinctive flavor. Many of these are just one-day affairs that really don't warrant a long trip. For this reason, we've used two rules to select what to list under this category: (1) the event must last at least two days and (2) it must draw visitors from out of the immediate area. Listings don't include specific dates because these usually change from year to year. For the exact dates and details call the number in the listing or contact the local visitors bureau.

SHOPPING

According to the Dallas/Fort Worth Area Tourism Council, there's more shopping available in the Metroplex than in New York City. True or hype, with 36 malls and hundreds and hundreds of shops there's plenty of evidence to support this claim. The city of Dallas alone can truthfully boast it has more shopping centers per capita than any other U.S. city, plus it lays claim to being the home of America's oldest shopping center, Highland Park Village.

When Neiman Marcus opened its "exclusive woman's ready-to-wear store" in 1907, it put Dallas on the national fashion map. Since then, many national and international retailers have moved in to offer a variety of fashion alternatives that would impress the most discerning and experienced shopper. Among the major names in retailing that have come to the Metroplex are Macy's, Stanley Korshak, Marshall Fields, Lord and Taylor, Tiffany and Co., Chanel, Calvin Klein, Polo/Ralph Lauren, Sak's Fifth Avenue, Nordstrom, Rodier Paris, and Haggar Apparel Company. In addition, Plano is the headquarters of the retail giant J.C. Penney's. As a result, the Metroplex—with Dallas as its heart and hub—is considered one of the nation's top retail and wholesale centers.

A Metroplex shopping spree is not limited to high-end merchandise. In addition to flea markets and trade fairs, in full swing every weekend somewhere in the region, Metroplex shoppers have embraced discount retailing with a passion. From local manufacturer's sample sales to national and regional discount chains offering brand names at off-retail prices, there is a palette of tastes for all shoppers. To rephrase a popular song, "If you can't find it here, you won't find it anywhere."

If you are attracted to pursuing discount shopping, you'll want to check out the Grapevine Mills Value Mall. When fully developed, this mega-mall will be the home of a slew of outlet shops, off-price retailers, catalogue stores, and discount merchandisers. It is expected to be an attraction in itself, perhaps drawing as many as 16 million visitors annually. You also might want to get a copy of *The Underground Shopper Dallas/Fort Worth* (Great Buys Press, Carrollton, Texas, about $10) at almost any Metroplex bookstore. This handy paperback, which has been published annually for about a quarter of a century, is the most comprehensive and detailed guide to this form of shopping we've found.

If shopping is your #1 priority, when you come to the Metroplex and you want to get to it quickly, you might want to try one of the many commercial tour services that offer shopping tours. Contact the Dallas or other Metroplex city convention and visitors bureaus for lists and recommendations.

Even if shopping is not high on your visit agenda, it's nice to know where there is a good mall to satisfy your basic needs, so we've listed a selection of the biggest and/or best. (You can find the others in the Yellow Pages.) In addition, here and there we've listed a few specialty shops we found that are different from the run-of-the-mill stores found in every city. Hours are not given unless they vary from the normal shopping hours in that area.

DINING OUT

If you enjoy dining out, the Metroplex is your Mecca. There are thousands of restaurants of every type and every price range, so all we can offer is a sampling in each of the cities. These should get you started. Once you're there, you can check various sources to find the restaurants to fit your taste and budget. The alphabetical listings in each city give the basic details on each of the sample restaurants with notes on type of cuisine, prices, credit cards accepted, and other information that will help you make your selection for each meal.

Like to try a fine dining restaurant, but the prices scare you off? Try it for lunch when prices may be as little as half those at dinner. The lunch entrees probably will not be the most expressive examples of the chef's talents, but almost always are a fair sampling of them, and you'll enjoy the same ambiance and service, and have much less anxiety when the check comes.

The keys to listing a restaurant in our sample were simple: Cleanliness was a given and ambiance was a factor, but most important was that the food was well-prepared, enjoyable to eat, and lived up to the promises on the menu. It didn't matter if it was a gourmet restaurant or a cafe or barbecue place, high or low priced, if it delivered in full on its promises and the meal was a pleasure, it made the listing. If it promised and didn't deliver, it didn't make it.

In general, fast food restaurants and major chain restaurants are not listed because most travelers know of them and can look them up in the phone book.

Finally, although not listed, cafeterias are a major part of the eating-out scene here. There are several cafeteria chains that do a superior job of providing convenient, well-prepared meals at reasonable prices. One chain we found especially favored and consistently recommended by residents is Luby's. But all the cafeterias offer a welcome alternative to fast food and high prices, especially for families, and are worth a try.

Because exact prices are hard to keep up with, the following $ symbols are used to indicate the approximate cost of a typical dinner (or lunch, if dinner is not served) for one person, exclusive of drinks, tax, and tip. If two symbols are used, it indicates the price spread of the entrees on the menu.

$ = Under $12
$$ = $12 to $30
$$$ = Over $30

The symbols for credit cards accepted are:

AE = American Express
DC = Diners Club
DIS = Discover
MC = MasterCard
V = VISA
Cr. = All major credit cards
No cr. = No credit cards accepted

THE TASTES OF TEXAS

You can find just about any type cuisine you like in the Metroplex, but for the real taste of Texas you should try barbecue, chicken-fried steak, and Tex-Mex food. All are hearty, tasty, and inexpensive.

Barbecue

They say Texans will barbecue anything, including the old tires off their Cadillacs, but to most Texans barbecue means beef. Beef brisket, shoulder clod, or some other cut cooked slowly for hours and hours in a pit over mesquite or hickory or another wood carefully selected by the cook. Of course, barbecue pit operators realize that some people have strange and uncultivated tastes, so to keep these people from going into a frenzy, the pitman may smoke up some pork ribs, or sausages (often called "hot links") or some other such thing. Some heretics say that barbecue is a way of cooking and it doesn't matter what meat you use. But the real Texas barbecuer knows this is just not so. His heart and soul remains with his beef, which is served moist with side dishes of potato salad or beans or coleslaw.

Chicken-Fried Steak

This is just what the name says. An inexpensive steak—round steak is probably top-of-the-line here—beaten until it's tender, then coated with a batter, fried like chicken, and served with a cream gravy made from the drippings. A good chicken-fried steak should be tender and the crust light and crispy. It's so well-known in Texas that many restaurant menus merely list it as CFS. Unfortunately, it's becoming harder and harder to find a good CFS because more and more restaurants are succumbing to the convenience of the frozen packaged version, which too often tastes like the box it came in. But there are still chefs out there who care enough about their customers to do it the old-fashioned way. They may be hard to find, but they're worth the looking.

Tex-Mex

The Metroplex abounds with restaurants serving all types of ethnic food from Czech to Greek to Vietnamese. One of the most popular, of course, is Mexican. But Mexican restaurants serving authentic Mexican dishes from interior Mexico are rare. What you are more likely to find is a derivative made to please Texan taste and known affectionately as Tex-Mex. It's different, it's delicious, but you should know it bears only a distant relationship to real Mexican cuisine.

The names of Tex-Mex dishes are invariably in Mexican or Spanish, so here's a rather loosely translated short list of some of the names you should learn to recognize to get you started ordering Tex-Mex (or real Mexican, if you should be so lucky).

al carbon: charcoal grilled
arroz: rice
cabrito: kid (young goat), usually cooked on a spit over a fire
carne: meat
cerveza: beer, the preferred beverage with Tex-Mex
chile: spelled with an "e" refers to peppers—a wide variety from mild to sinus-cleaning—used in Tex-Mex cooking
chili: spelled with an "i" (also called a "bowl of Texas Red") is a stewlike dish of meat, onions, herbs, and spices, and, of course, *chiles* that may be mild or hot enough to require an asbestos mouth. There's a major on-going war among *chili*-lovers as to whether it should be made with beans or not. Try them both and make your own choice. We're not enlisting in that war.

chorizo: spicy pork sausage
enchilada: a rolled soft *tortilla* filled with cheese, chicken, or
    other fillings and a *chile* sauce
fajitas: marinated and broiled or grilled strips of beef skirt (a term
    now corrupted, like barbecue, to include marinated grilled
    chicken strips and even grilled shrimp strips)
guacamole: a mashed avocado salad usually made with onions
    and *chiles*
huevos: eggs
jalapeño: a hot, green *chile* that is used in many dishes
migas: eggs scrambled with pieces of corn *tortilla* and sometimes
    with *chorizo*
picante: spicy hot
pico de gallo: a spicy side dish usually made with hot *chiles,*
    onions, and cilantro
pollo: chicken
queso: cheese
taco: usually a U-shaped corn *tortilla* deep-fried and filled with a
    variety of fillings limited only by the cook's imagination
tamale: corn dough spread in a corn husk, topped with a meat fill-
    ing, rolled, and steamed (don't eat the husk!)
tortilla: corn or flour dough flattened like a pancake, cooked on a
    griddle or steamed and used like bread, both for eating as
    a pusher, to soak up the sauce, or rolled into a sandwich
    you fill from your plate.

CLUBS AND BARS

We're more selective listing clubs and bars than any other category because we don't want to steer you wrong nor waste your
time. These open and close and change format so frequently that
the listing may be outdated, at the least, or even dead by the time
you want to go there. In an attempt to avoid this, we tried to list
only those places that have a history of permanence.

If you want more in the way of nightlife, look in the local entertainment newspapers listed under Publications.

LODGINGS

Finding a place to live is usually high on the priority list when planning a trip. To make this hard choice as easy as possible for you, we've included information on just about everything you might want to know to find lodgings that fit your price range, your lifestyle, and your expectations.

Lodgings are listed in two places. Only the basics are listed under the city it is in. Use this as a cross-reference to the section titled LODGINGS in the back of the book. There you'll find each listed alphabetically by area within the Metroplex and the details on each of the sample hotels/motels or bed and breakfasts, and fine points on everything from rates to facilities and services that will help you make your selection of where to stay.

Even though our lists in the Lodging section are extensive, there are so many hotels and motels in the Metroplex that, once again, all we can give is a sample.

SIDE TRIPS

Occasionally we'll suggest making a trip to some place of interest outside the cities we cover. The suggested side trips are rarely more than an hour's drive and usually well worth your time and effort.

SYMBOLS USED IN THIS BOOK

The symbols that follow are used throughout the book.

WHEELCHAIR ACCESSIBILITY SYMBOLS

Under recent laws most public buildings and many business buildings are now accessible to the mobility impaired who must use a wheelchair, and there is an increasing number of tourist attractions that offer facilities for them as well as reserved parking. The following symbols are used in all appropriate listings to indicate wheelchair accessibility. And sometimes we'll add a note to clarify a symbol.

W In general, this place is accessible to persons in wheelchairs; at least one entrance is wide enough and there are no more than two steps. However, not all facilities (rest rooms, etc.) are accessible.

W+ This place and all its major facilities, including rest rooms, are accessible.

No symbol indicates this place is either not accessible or accessible with great difficulty.

RESTAURANT PRICES

The following **$** symbols are used to indicate the approximate cost of a typical dinner (or lunch, if dinner is not served) for one person, exclusive of drinks, tax, and tip. If two symbols are used, it indicates the price spread of the entrees on the menu.

$ = Under $12
$$ = $12 to $30
$$$ = Over $30

LODGINGS ROOM RATES

The following **$** symbols are used to indicate the approximate rate for a double room (two persons in a room) for one night. If two symbols are used it indicates the spread between the lowest and highest priced double room. For details see the **LODGINGS** Section.

$ = Under $80
$$ = $80 to $120
$$$ = $121 to $180
$$$$ = $181 to $250
$$$$$ = Over $250

HINTS TO MAKE YOUR VISIT MORE PLEASANT

What's the weather like? What should we wear? How do we get around?

Here are a few basics to answer those questions.

WHAT TIME IS IT?

The Metroplex is in the Central Standard Time Zone (one hour behind the East coast and two hours ahead of the West coast). Daylight Saving Time is in effect from the last Sunday in April to the last Sunday in October.

WEATHER

There's an old saying in Texas that if you don't like the weather, wait a few minutes and it'll change.

The pleasant weather of spring comes early to the Metroplex, the summer is hot and humid, and fall comes late. Winter is usually from late November or December through February or early March. So, if weather is one of the main considerations for your trip, spring and fall are the choice periods.

WHAT TO WEAR WHERE

As in any major cosmopolitan area, dress depends on what you're doing. For business, you can't go wrong with a business suit, at least for your first business visit. If your plans include hitting some of the fancier big city restaurants with a dress-up policy, or selected events, like a first night, women should have some dressy clothes and men will need a jacket and tie. Otherwise, casual dress is fine.

Dress for the season and the weather. Heat is the major factor in what to wear during the late spring, summer, and early fall and that's when natural fibers, like cotton, serve best, remembering that air conditioning is a way of life here so even during the hottest days of summer it's comfortable indoors.

You'll need some warm clothes for the chilliest winter months—layering works well—otherwise, sweaters and a lightweight coat should get you through most of the cool periods in late fall and early spring.

GETTING TO THE METROPLEX

If you're not driving yourself, you can get there by plane or bus. You might check on trains, but when this went to press the passenger train to the Metroplex was just about as extinct as the dinosaur.

The **Dallas-Fort Worth International Airport** (D/FW for short) is the main airport served by both domestic and foreign airlines. It's the world's second busiest airport with about 2,600 passenger flights daily (and with new runways open and under construction, it's in the running for #1). Larger than the island of Manhattan, the airport is located halfway between the two cities for which it is named. You'll need to get a bus, taxi, a shuttle van, or rent a car to get to your chosen Metroplex destination.

All the passenger facilities at D/FW are located along a central north-south highway, called International Parkway. This leads to Highways 114 and 635 on the north and 183 and 360 on the south.

Metroplex Area Average Rainfall and Temperatures

	Average Rainfall in Inches	Average Fahrenheit Temperature	Average Celsius Temperature
January	1.31	56–35	13–2
February	1.97	59–38	15–3
March	2.34	68–46	20–8
April	3.88	75–55	24–13
May	4.36	83–63	28–17
June	2.91	91–71	33–23
July	2.23	95–74	35–24
August	2.23	95–74	35–24
September	2.94	88–67	31–19
October	3.00	79–57	26–14
November	2.20	67–46	19–8
December	1.92	58–37	14–3

Note: Temperatures are averages. In mid-summer it is not unusual for the temperature to reach 100°F and mid-winter temperatures often drop below freezing.

DFW AIRPORT

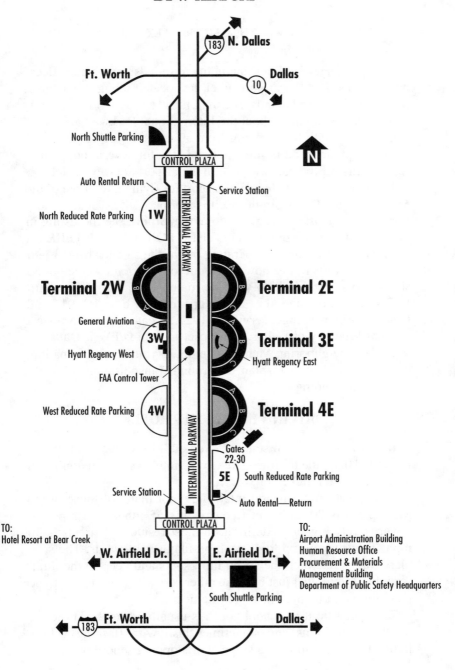

For information on available parking at DFW International Airport telephone 972/574-PARK.

Terminal Parking   Infield Parking

All the passenger facilities, including terminals, rental car offices, parking lots, and the airport hotel are located along this central parkway. (For more details, see map.)

Two things to know about the International Parkway are: (1) it is a toll road with fees ranging from 50 cents, if you're just passing through, up to $2 if you enter and stay for several hours; and (2) all exits off the parkway within the airport are to your left.

In addition to being the major airport for flying into or out of the Metroplex, the D/FW airport itself is worth a visit as an attraction. For details on what to see and do at the airport, see the listing in the city of GRAPEVINE under OTHER POINTS OF INTEREST.

The only major airline operating out of the smaller **Love Field** is Southwest. Its routes now reach out to major cities in about 23 states. Love Field, which was the major airport in Dallas until D/FW was built, started as a military training base in 1917 and began its first passenger service in 1927. Located in the northwest corner of the city of Dallas, it is closer in than D/FW if Dallas or one of the neighboring Metroplex cities is your final destination, but you'll still need to plan on ground transportation to get to where you're going.

DRIVING IN THE METROPLEX

If you're from out of state, or even out of the area, you should know and obey the following Texas driving laws so you don't ruin your visit with a ticket, or worse.

The speed limit on rural interstates (not many of those in the Metroplex) is 70 mph. On freeways it's 55 mph, unless posted lower (rarely higher). The limit on most residential streets is 30 mph. That may go up to 45 mph on major boulevards. The simplest way is to watch the speed limit signs and keep to the limit. And don't think that just because other cars are speeding past you that you won't be the one to get the ticket.

The speed limit in school zones is usually 20 mph. These are marked with signs and sometimes also with flashing yellow lights. It's illegal to pass a stopped or stopping school bus.

Drivers and front seat passengers must wear seat belts and infant seats are also required by law.

Highway traffic has the right of way and is <u>not</u> required to yield to entering traffic. Exiting traffic has the right of way on access roads.

It's legal to make a right turn on red, after a stop, unless otherwise posted. (Watch for the signs.)

It's illegal to consume alcohol while operating a motor vehicle.

Texas has a mandatory automobile liability insurance law. If you're stopped for any reason you may be required to show proof of liability coverage. If it's your car, make sure you have proof. If you rent a car, make sure you're given proof to carry in the car.

GETTING AROUND WITHOUT A CAR

It used to be that a car was essential to getting around anywhere in the Metroplex, and overall, a car may still be the best way to go. Now, however, you have some options if you'll be staying entirely in the downtown sections of Dallas or Fort Worth. In those cases, you can take a reasonably priced private shuttle or your hotel's free shuttle to and from the airport (both D/FW and Love Field) and in the downtowns of those two major cities use public transportation to get around.

Public transportation? I never use public transportation!

Well, maybe you should in those two downtowns where you may find driving a car more of a hassle and parking more expensive than taking advantage of their public systems.

This is particularly true in Dallas where the new, speedy, clean, and inexpensive Dallas Area Rapid Transit (DART) Light Rail system has a station every few blocks in the downtown area and is pushing steadily out toward points north and south, hooking up with the good DART bus system. There are also low-fare special buses that run downtown with routes that are oriented to where visitors want to go (See Dallas.) And in Fort Worth, "The T" operates free buses throughout the downtown area (See Fort Worth).

If you are driving a car, and you're not familiar with the streets, you can help yourself avoid getting into a hazardous driving situation, as well as help your peace of mind, if you take the time to check out where you're going on a city map before you start. To help you find places, we've included a simple map of each city. These aren't as detailed as a city road map, but they do show the main streets and, where appropriate, we've included directions in the listings citing these main streets.

If you're driving without a capable map-reading co-pilot, it'd probably make the trip easier for you if you write the travel directions on a self-stick notepad and paste it on your dash or steering wheel where you can see it easily when you need it. Or record the directions on a pocket tape recorder you can play back as you need them.

ALCOHOLIC BEVERAGE LAWS

The legal drinking age and the legal age to purchase alcoholic beverages is 21.

Under Texas local option laws, where alcoholic beverages (beer, wine, or liquor) may be sold or consumed is decided by the vote of the people within a city or other political division. This means that in the Metroplex you'll find a hodgepodge of designated "wet" areas, where alcoholic beverages can be sold, and "dry" areas where they can't be sold. The exact rules vary. Sometimes in a dry area restaurants and clubs can sell alcoholic drinks and sometimes you can only get an alcoholic drink (no carry-out or package sales) in a private club. Fortunately, it's not hard to become a club member because the law allows most restaurants that serve drinks to sell individual annual memberships for a fee of about $2 or so. Hotels/motels in dry areas usually give automatic memberships to guests if they have a private club.

Because of city boundaries, in some places in the Metroplex, you may find a wet area on one side of a street and a dry area on the other.

We've tried to include a "wet" or "dry" notation in the introduction to each city in this book. But, these can change, so if being in a wet or dry area is important to you, ask before you settle on where you'll stay and go.

SOME FINAL NOTES

Don't think you're back in the Old West if you see a sign on an entrance door that reads: "State law prohibits carrying a handgun on these premises." Texas is one of many states that issues permits for citizens to carry concealed handguns. However, it also has laws that prohibit those citizens from carrying a handgun into many places.

Most prices in listings do not include taxes. As a visitor, you can expect to pay at least two types of taxes: sales and hotel or bed tax. The sales tax in the various Metroplex cities hovers around 8% and the hotel or bed tax ranges from about 11% to 13%.

In an emergency call 911 for police, fire, or ambulance.

ADDISON

DALLAS COUNTY • 10,900 • AREA CODE 972

Although first settled in 1846, in an area once called Peters Colony, it wasn't until the St. Louis Southwestern Railroad arrived in the early 1880s that it grew into a village. Then it was another 20 years before the town became known as Addison, named after Addison Robertson, who later became the community's postmaster.

While the main role of many of the smaller cities in the Metroplex is to serve as residential bedroom communities for Dallas and the other major business cities, the 4.5-square-mile town of Addison can list itself as one of those business centers. Its bedroom aspect consists of only about 11,000 residents, while, on workdays, its daytime business population jumps to around 75,000. That small residential population is a major reason the town can boast that it has more restaurants (well over 100) per capita than any city west of the Mississippi. Addison's restaurants can seat over 17,000 patrons at one time, close to twice the number of residents. Its "restaurant row," originally developed to service the daily workday influx, has become a large draw for after work and weekend diners from Dallas and other Metroplex cities.

A major contributor to the expansion of both business and restaurants occurred in 1975 when the residents held an election under the local liquor option laws and voted the town "wet." Its

26

ADDISON

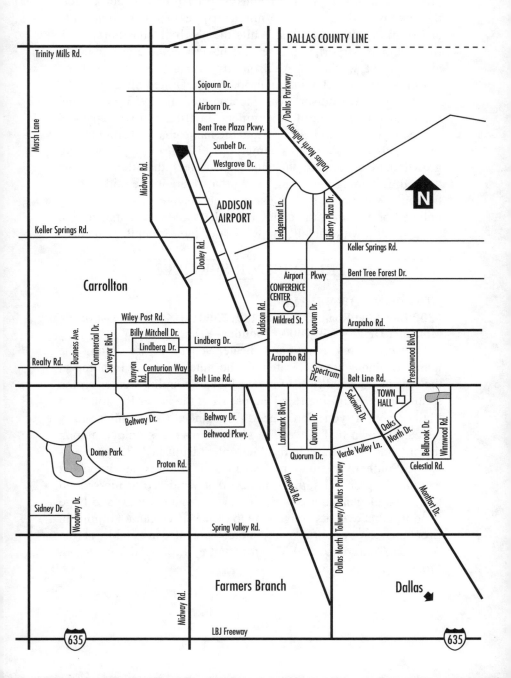

DALLAS COUNTY LINE

Trinity Mills Rd.

Marsh Lane

Midway Rd.

Sojourn Dr.

Airborn Dr.

Bent Tree Plaza Pkwy.

Sunbelt Dr.

Westgrove Dr.

Dallas North Tollway/Dallas Parkway

N

ADDISON AIRPORT

Ledgemont Ln.

Liberty Plaza Dr.

Keller Springs Rd.

Keller Springs Rd.

Bent Tree Forest Dr.

Dooley Rd.

Carrollton

Addison Rd.

Airport CONFERENCE CENTER

Pkwy

Quorum Dr.

Mildred St.

Arapaho Rd.

Wiley Post Rd.

Billy Mitchell Dr.

Lindberg Dr.

Lindberg Dr.

Business Ave.

Commercial Dr.

Surveyor Blvd.

Realty Rd.

Runyon Rd.

Centurion Way

Arapaho Rd

Spectrum Dr.

Belt Line Rd.

Prestonwood Blvd.

Belt Line Rd.

TOWN HALL

Beltway Dr.

Beltway Dr.

Beltwood Pkwy.

Landmark Blvd.

Quorum Dr.

Sakowitz Dr.

Oaks North Dr.

Bellbrook Dr.

Winnwood Rd.

Dome Park

Proton Rd.

Quorum Dr.

Verde Valley Ln.

Celestial Rd.

Montfort Dr.

Sidney Dr.

Woodway Dr.

Inwood Rd.

Dallas North Tollway/Dallas Parkway

Spring Valley Rd.

Farmers Branch

Midway Rd.

Dallas

635

LBJ Freeway

635

growth is also aided by the Dallas North Tollway, which bisects the town providing a brief 15-minute trip (except in rush hour) to and from downtown Dallas. While the nearby Dallas/Fort Worth International Airport is the second busiest commercial aviation airport in the world, the Addison airport can boast that it is the third busiest general aviation airport in the United States.

The city of Addison was incorporated in 1953 under the mayor/alderman form of government. In 1982 that was changed to the mayor/city council form and the name changed from city to town. This was done to counter the effects of its impressive growth and encourage the small town feel that the residents desired. Retaining that small town atmosphere in the midst of the booming Metroplex is not just a name change. It's an ongoing policy. For example, the council members and city manager, like good small town officials, know most of the residents by name.

FREE VISITOR SERVICES

ADDISON TOWN HALL
5300 Belt Line Road (P.O. Box 144, 75001-0144), just east of Montfort Drive • 450-7000 • Monday–Friday 8–5 • W

Free brochures, maps, and theater schedules are among the items available here. Located in the antebellum style home at the rear of the small Prestonwood Place Shopping Center on the south side of Belt Line Road, across from the larger Prestonwood Mall. Even if you don't need assistance, the architecturally appealing town hall is worth a visit because it is unique among the city and town halls in the Metroplex. Built in 1939 to resemble a Southern plantation mansion, it features an imposing entrance, a graceful spiral staircase that winds up to the second floor, and elegant rooms with fireplaces, high ceilings, and large windows that even its conversion to office space cannot diminish. Brochures on restaurants and hotels are also available at the Addison Conference and Theatre Centre, 15650 Addison Road, Monday–Friday 8–5.

PUBLICATIONS

Current information about Addison events and restaurant reviews may be found in the Arts and Entertainment Guide published each Friday in *The Dallas Morning News*; the weekly *Dallas Observer,* which is available free at restaurants and tourist attractions throughout the Dallas area; and the monthly *D Magazine,* available on newsstands.

COMMERCIAL TOURS

CENTER LINE AVIATION TOURS
4545 Eddie Rickenbacker (P.O. Box 667, 75001), at Addison Airport • 490-7676 or 490-7045 • Seven days 9–6
Flying tours that originate at the Addison Airport and cover the major sights of Dallas and some of the mid-cities. Thirty-minute tour for $89 a person, 60 minutes $129, 90 minutes $199.

HISTORIC PLACES

Two structures that go back to Addison's earlier days are the **Cotton Gin** built in 1902 and the **Addison School Building** built in 1914. The gin stands on the west side of Addison Road, south of the Addison Airport. The school, at 5300 Belt Line, was closed in 1964 after fifty years of service. The building is now occupied by the Magic Time Machine Restaurant.

MUSEUMS AND ART GALLERIES

CAVANAUGH FLIGHT MUSEUM
4572 Claire Chennault (75228) on east side of Addison Airport (follow signs off Addison Road) • 380-8800 • Monday–Saturday 9–5, Sunday 11–5 Closed Thanksgiving, Christmas, New Year's Day • Adults $5.50, Children 6–12 $2.75, 5 and under free • W +
Four hangars hold this growing collection of fully restored military aircraft flown in wars from World War I to Vietnam. What

sets this museum apart from most other aviation museums is that nearly all the warbirds on display are air worthy and flown on a regular basis. To keep them flyable, one hangar is devoted to maintenance. Here you can look under the skin of these famous aircraft and talk to the mechanics about them. The more than 30 aircraft in the collection range from the World War I Sopwith Camel to U.S. and Russian jets like the F86E Sabre Jet and the MiG-21. A MiG-17 is set-up so you can sit in the restored cockpit. Want first-hand flying experience? Then take a flight in a World War II military trainer. A 30-minute flight in one of the two open-cockpit primary flight trainers costs $110 to $125. Flying in the AT-6 Texas, a closed cockpit advanced flight trainer, costs $200. (All plus sales tax.) Warbird passengers must be at least 18 years old and flights must be booked at least 48 hours in advance. Other facilities include a history of military aviation memorabilia gallery, gift shop, snack bar, and outdoor picnic area.

OUTDOORS

ADDISON PARKS
Parks and Recreation • 450-2851
Although small, Addison's parks provide a variety of facilities for recreational activities, including playgrounds and sports courts, as well as quiet areas for relaxing. Several of the parks have lighted walking and jogging trails with the longest being the 2.5-mile jogging and bike trail in Les Lacs Linear Park at 3901 Beltway Drive. Call for information.

MUSIC AND PERFORMING ARTS

WATERTOWER THEATRE
15650 Addison Road (75248), 3½ blocks north of Belt Line, under the Addison Water Tower • 450-6232 or 800-ADDISON (233-4766) • Tickets about $18 for most productions • W +
This award-winning state-of-the-art theater is designed so both the seating and performance area can be transformed for an elaborate stage presentation or a more intimate theater-in-the-round,

whichever best fits each production. Under this flexible arrangement, seating can be varied to hold an audience of 250 to 300. The
October-to-June season normally features five productions running the gamut from comedies and musicals to new plays and the
classics with most casts composed of professionals from the
Metroplex area. Each production is put on Thursday, Friday, and
Saturday at 8 p.m. over a three-week period. The theater is an
integral part of the Addison Conference and Theatre Center,
which is used for a wide variety of meetings as well as numerous
events to which the public is invited.

SPORTS

ICE SKATING

ICE CHALET
Prestonwood, 5301 Belt Line (75240), at Tollway
Metro 980-8575 • Monday–Saturday 10–9, Sunday noon–6
General skating activities including lessons, hockey, and
broomball. Public skating times and fees vary.

ICEOPLEX
15100 Midway Road (75244) • 991-7539 • Public hours vary
Adult skating $5.50, Children 12 and under $4.50
Two ice rinks open for public skating sessions at varying times,
days and evenings. Call for schedule. Skate rental $2.25. Lessons
available.

OTHER POINTS OF INTEREST

MARY KAY WORLD HEADQUARTERS AND MUSEUM
16251 Dallas Parkway (75241), on Dallas North Tollway at
Westgrove exit • 214/687-5889 • Free • W +
Mary Kay herself has said that, "With 13 floors and 13 main
elevators, this building is perfect for a company that was founded
on Friday, September 13th, 1963." The Mary Kay Museum,
which relates the Horatio Alger-type history of Mary Kay and her

world-wide cosmetics firm, is open for a self-directed tour Monday–Friday 9–5. Conducted tours, available Tuesday–Friday at 9 a.m. and 4:30 p.m., are by appointment only made at least 48 hours in advance by calling 972/687-5720. Tours of Mary Kay's manufacturing facility, located at 1330 Regal Row in Dallas, can also be arranged by calling the same number at least 48 hours in advance. Conducted plant tours are held Tuesday–Friday at 10:30 a.m. and 2 p.m. (See DALLAS/INDUSTRY TOURS.)

ANNUAL EVENTS

MAY

TASTE ADDISON
Third weekend (Saturday–Sunday) • Streetside at the Addison Conference and Theatre Centre, 15650 Addison Road 450-7000 or 800-ADDISON (233-4766) • Admission $1, Children 3 and under free • W
Sometimes known as the Addison Rhythm and Chews, the main features of this festival are tastings from 50 of the town's restaurants and continuous entertainment for both adults and children on two stages. Musical performers routinely include some of the better known groups of Texas and the Southwest playing in a variety of styles. Plus arts and crafts, carnival rides, midway games, and a car show. Free shuttle buses from Prestonwood mall on Belt Line east of the Dallas North Tollway, or park in the lots on Quorum Drive north of Belt Line Road.

AUGUST

SPIKEFEST
First weekend (Saturday–Sunday) • Greenhill School Sports Center, 14225 Midway Road at Spring Valley, south of Belt Line Road (P.O. Box 7444, 75209) • 214/526-8806 or 888-3VOLLEY (888-386-5539) • Free • W
Volleyball is the second most popular team sport in the United States, second only to basketball, and this is the largest amateur

grass court, three-on-three volleyball tournament in the country. Over 500 men, women, and coed teams compete at every level from beginners and those mainly out for the sun and fun to a hair below professional. Players and spectators can take part in technique clinics to improve their volleyball expertise, as well as other sub-events including a speed spike contest with the speed of the spikes measured with radar guns.

SEPTEMBER

ADDISON'S OKTOBERFEST
Third weekend (Thursday–Sunday) • Streetside at the Addison Conference and Theatre Centre, 15650 Addison Road 450-7000 or 800-ADDISON (233-4766) • Admission $1, Children 3 and under free • W

Oktoberfest in September? Yes, to coincide with the opening of the world's best known Oktoberfest in Munich, Germany. This four-day festival kicks off on Thursday evening with the tapping of the first keg of Oktoberfest beer. Considered an authentic recreation of the Munich celebration, it features German food, drink, and entertainment including folk dancing. Among the other activities are an arts and crafts show, carnival rides and midway games, sing-alongs, a petting zoo and other children's entertainment. Free shuttle buses from Prestonwood Mall on Belt Line Road east of the Dallas North Tollway, or try for the very limited parking on Quorum Drive north of Belt Line.

SHOPPING

ANTIQUES, ANTIQUES
5100 Belt Line Road (75240), in the Village on the Parkway Shopping Center • 239-6124 • W

This 6,000-ft^2 showroom houses more than 50 dealers selling antiques and collectibles including rare books and estate jewelry.

DISCOUNT MODEL TRAINS
4641 Ratliff Lane (75248) • 931-8135 • W

Whether you just like to watch model trains or they are your hobby, you'll enjoy seeing the trains here. And if it is your hobby, or you get the fever while there, this shop has everything you need to get started or expand your personal railroad. All at discount prices.

KITTRELL-RIFFKIND ART GLASS
5100 Belt Line Road #820 (75240) • 239-7957 • W

The only all-glass gallery in North Texas, it displays the works of more than 200 artists featuring items such as jewelry, goblets, delicate perfume bottles, vases, and unique sculptures.

PRESTONWOOD
5301 Belt Line Road (75240), at Dallas North Tollway
Metro 980-4275 • W +

Neiman Marcus, Dillard's, Penney's, Lord and Taylor, and Mervyns anchor about 130 specialty stores and restaurants in this mall. Also an ice rink (see SPORTS, above).

THE UNLIMITED LIMITED ANTIQUES MALL
15201 Midway Road (75244) • 490-4085 • W

More than 175 dealers are located under one roof in this 38,000-ft^2 building, selling antiques, classic furniture, collectibles, and artwork.

DINING OUT

$ = Under $12, $$ = $12–$30, $$$ = Over $30 for one person excluding drinks, tax, and tip

ADDISON CAFE
5290 Belt Line (75240) at Montfort #108, east of Tollway in Prestonwood Place Shopping Center • 991-8824 • Lunch Monday–Friday, dinner seven days • $$ • Cr. • W +

This cafe offers French cuisine in a romantic setting that seems out of place in the strip shopping center across from Prestonwood

Mall. Menu items are all in French with taste-tempting English explanations. Among the fish entrees available are sea bass, filet of sole, salmon, and, a house specialty, roasted lobster. Meat entrees include steaks and sauteed tournedos of beef, plus a variety of classic French versions of lamb, veal, chicken, and rabbit. Bar.

BLUE MESA GRILL
5100 Belt Line (75240), at Tollway in Village on the Parkway Shopping Center, • 934-0165 • Lunch and dinner seven days $-$$ • Cr. • W +

The Blue Mesa may be located at the southeast junction of the Tollway and Belt Line, but both the decor and the food are contemporary Southwestern. For a taste of this distinctive and innovative Santa Fe cuisine, try one of the samplers or the mixed grill entrees. The regular mixed grill consists of beef tenderloin stuffed with Mexican cheeses, blue crab and shrimp cake, and potato chile tart. The seafood mixed grill has chile basted shrimp, blue crab enchilada Veracruzano and grilled fish of the day. Vegetarian entrees available. Children's menu. Highly popular for Sunday brunch (10–3). Signature drink from the bar is the blue margarita.

CHAMBERLAIN'S STEAK & CHOP HOUSE
5330 Belt Line (75240), east of Tollway between Montfort and Prestonwood • 934-2467 • Dinner Monday–Saturday, seven days in December only • $$-$$$ • Cr. • W +

The decor of warm woods and original 1930s lithographs establish the classic chop house ambiance and the menu created by the chef-owner fulfills this image. Naturally, the list of entrees is heavy on beef. Steak options range from a petite filet mignon to a 24 oz. porterhouse, but they also serve pork, lamb and veal chops, chicken, and seafood, with occasional wild game specials. Bar. Valet parking available.

JASMINE CHINESE RESTAURANT
4002 Belt Line, #200 (75244), west of Tollway between Midway and Marsh • 991-6867 • Lunch and dinner seven days • $$ • Cr. W (elevator on east side of building)

Whatever your choice of Chinese cuisine, you'll probably find it on the menu in this upstairs restaurant with a decor that leans toward nightclub ambiance. Entrees go from delicate Cantonese and Mandarin specialties to hearty Hunan dishes to spicy hot Szechuan favorites. Bar/lounge. Entertainment.

LEFTY'S LOBSTER & CHOWDER HOUSE
**4021 Belt Line #101 (75244), west of the Tollway and Midway
774-9518 • Dinner seven days • $$ • Cr. • W**

As the name says, you can get lobster (whole or stuffed, baked, boiled, or broiled) and Boston clam chowder here. The menu also offers lobster bisque and steamed clams among the appetizers. The fish of the day is served either sauteed with a lemon, garlic, and white wine sauce or stuffed with cracker, shrimp and crab, and the lemon/garlic/wine sauce. Specialties include some Cajun dishes like Lefty's Pasta with jumbo shrimp, andouille sausage, and crawfish in a Cajun cream sauce. Children's menu. Bar. Valet parking available.

MAY DRAGON
**4848 Belt Line (75244), west of Tollway at Inwood • 392-9998
Lunch and dinner seven days • $$ • Cr. • W**

An upscale Chinese restaurant with the reputation of being one of the best in the Metroplex. The extensive menu offers entrees in a variety of cuisines from Cantonese to Szechuan, all presented in a tradition of fine dining. Specialties include Peking duck, crispy whole red snapper in Hunan sauce, and sesame chicken, which the chef-owner lists on the menu as "World Champion Chicken." If you want to participate, you can "roll your own" appetizer of Asian-style rolls made from lettuce, Asian pancakes, or rice paper. Bar. Piano music Friday–Saturday evenings.

MI PIACI RISTORANTE ITALIANO
**14854 Montfort (75240), east of Tollway, south of Belt Line
934-8424 • Lunch Monday–Friday, dinner seven days • $$
Cr. • W**

No shortcuts here. They make their own pasta and, because the emphasis is on Northern Italian cuisine, it's made according to the recipe used at home by the women of Bologna, a city known for its culinary skills. They also use imported pasta and risotto (rice) when either serves the entree better. The menu features authentic regional specialties such as *Risotto con Patate e Salsiccia,* Italian rice with roasted potatoes, homemade Italian sausage, and spinach; and *Costata di Vitello,* grilled center-cut veal T-bone with seared onions, roasted garlic, and sage potatoes. Bar. Valet parking available.

REMINGTON'S SEAFOOD GRILL
4580 Belt Line (75244), west of Tollway at Inwood • 386-0122
Lunch Monday–Friday, dinner seven days • $–$$ • Cr. • W +

Generous serving of consistently good food is the reputation this restaurant has built since it first opened in 1978. Specialties include scrod, snapper, and softshell crabs in season. Among the selection of fried entrees is the pecan-crusted catfish filet and fried shrimp or oysters. If you prefer your seafood broiled, one choice is the broiled seafood sampler with scrod, sea scallops, and Gulf shrimp. Children's menu. From 5 to 6:30 p.m. there are bargain specials for early-bird diners. Bar.

RUGGERI'S RISTORANTE
5348 Belt Line (75240), east of the Tollway • 726-9555
Lunch Monday–Friday, dinner seven days (reservations recommended) • $$ • Cr. • W

Among the more popular Northern Italian entrees on the menu of this highly regarded Italian restaurant are two veal dishes: *Vitello di Scampi,* veal and shrimp sauteed with garlic, shallots, white wine, and butter; and Ruggeri's special veal chop, a 16-oz chop grilled and topped with wild oyster mushrooms and Marsala wine. Other entrees offer a variety of both traditional and innovative pasta dishes, seafood, chicken, lamb, and beef. Piano music nightly. The level of service consistently earns high praise. Bar. Valet parking available. (Another location: 2911 Routh, Dallas 214/871-7377.)

CLUBS AND BARS

IMPROV
**4980 Belt Line (75240), west of the Tollway at Quorum Drive
404-8501 • Admission $10–$15 • AE, MC, V • W**
A comedy club featuring national comedians on the club circuit and live improvisation and sketch comedy. Shows Wednesday, Thursday, Sunday 8:30 p.m., Friday–Saturday 8:30 and 10:30. Restaurant and bar.

ROCK BOTTOM BREWERY
4050 Belt Line (75244), west of the Tollway between Midway and Marsh • 404-7456 • Cr. • W
This brewpub could just as easily be listed under DINING OUT because it serves lunch and dinner daily (ribs, pizza, pasta, Tex-Mex $$). But it's most popular on Tuesday, Friday, and Saturday evenings when you can enjoy the house brews while listening and dancing to jazz or rock. Lots of room with 14,000 ft^2 inside and 4 acres of parking outside. Bar. Valet parking available.

SAMBUCCA MEDITERRANEAN JAZZ CAFE
15207 Addison Road (75248), east of Tollway and north of Belt Line • 385-8455 • Cr. • W
As the name says, this is a cafe and a place to listen to live jazz. The cafe is open for lunch Monday–Friday, and dinner every night (pasta, chicken, and seafood $$). The swinging sounds come out at night, every night. On Monday nights there's a 16 piece Big Band. Bar. Valet parking available. (Second location: 2618 Elm, Dallas 214/744-0820.)

LODGINGS

*For a double room: $ = Under $80, $$ = $80–$120, $$$ = $121–$180, $$$$ = $181–$250, $$$$$ = Over $250; Room tax 13%
For detailed listings see Metroplex Lodgings Section, p. 360.*

COURTYARD BY MARRIOTT
4165 Proton Drive (75244), west of Tollway, off Midway south
of Belt Line • 490-7390 or 800-321-2211 • $$ • W + two rooms
No smoking rooms

DALLAS MARRIOTT QUORUM
14901 Dallas Parkway (75240), Dallas North Tollway at Belt
Line exit, on Tollway west access road south of Belt Line
661-2800 or 800-228-9290 • $$ • W + 11 rooms
No smoking rooms

THE GRAND KEMPINSKI DALLAS
15201 Dallas Parkway (75248), Dallas North Tollway at Belt
Line exit, on Tollway west access road north of Belt Line
386-6000 or 800-426-3135 • $$$$ • W + 10 rooms
No smoking rooms

HARVEY HOTEL—ADDISON
14315 Midway (75244), west of Tollway, south of Belt Line
near Proton Dr. • 980-8877 or 800-922-9222 (Reservations)
$$–$$$ • W + 5 rooms • No smoking rooms

HOLIDAY INN EXPRESS
4103 Belt Line (75244), west of Tollway and Midway
991-8888 or 800-HOLIDAY (465-4329)(Reservations) • $–$$
W + 2 rooms • No smoking rooms

HOMEWOOD SUITES HOTEL—ADDISON
4451 Belt Line (75244), west of Tollway between Addison Rd.
and Midway • 788-1342 or 800-225-5466 • $$–$$$ • W + 5
suites • No smoking suites

LA QUINTA INN AND SUITES DALLAS/ADDISON
14925 Landmark Blvd. (75240), west of Tollway and south of
Belt Line • 404-0004 or 800-531-5900 • $$ • W + 5 rooms
No smoking rooms

ARLINGTON

The first settlers in this area were the nine tribes of the Caddoan and Wichita Confederation, which included the Cherokee, Delaware, Biloxi, Caddo, and Waco. Over the centuries their agricultural settlements had been visited by several European explorers including Cabeza de Vaca in 1535 and LaSalle in 1687. But in 1841 they lost their lands in a battle to the Texas Rangers. Here in 1843 Sam Houston, President of The Republic of Texas, signed his new nation's first peace treaty with the Confederation, a treaty that moved them farther west and set up a boundary between the new white settlers and the Indians.

Trading posts soon sprung up along that boundary. One such post was established by Colonel Middleton Tate Johnson who arrived in 1846 to take command of the Texas Rangers at what became known as Johnson Station. He soon bought a large piece of land and built a plantation. His large home became a stage stop for three forks of the Overland Stage route that connected Dallas, Fort Worth, and Austin. Johnson founded the site for Fort Worth and donated the land for its court house, earning him the historical recognition as the Father of Tarrant County. Johnson County is also named after him.

By 1876 Dallas and Fort Worth were well enough established that the Texas and Pacific Railway decided to build a line con-

ARLINGTON

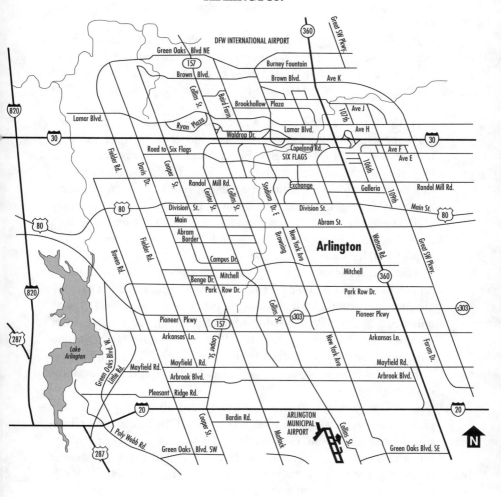

necting them. A mid-route depot site was selected on the prairie and soon residents of Johnson Station and other small settlements in the area moved to the new railroad and that depot grew into the frontier town named Arlington after Robert E. Lee's home town in Virginia.

Arlington was a typical frontier town with false front buildings, saloons, and gambling. In the 1890s a water well was drilled in the middle of the town, but instead of drinking water, it produced mineral water, which started a local mineral crystal industry that lasted into the 1930s.

Agriculture was the main industry until the early 1950s when GM opened an auto assembly plant and that brought in other industry. Then, in 1961, Six Flags Over Texas opened as the largest amusement park in the state. The choice of Arlington for this theme park was a natural because it had long been an entertainment center between Dallas and Fort Worth. In the early 1930s people rode the Interurban trains here to bet on the horses at Arlington Downs Race Track and gamble at places like the Top-O-Hill Terrace.

Those attractions have long since disappeared, but Arlington's reputation as the Midway of the Metroplex continued when the city became home of a major league baseball team in 1971. It was enhanced by the 1983 opening of Wet'N Wild, the largest water park in the U.S. (now called Six Flags Hurricane Harbor), and was most recently solidified by the opening of The Ballpark in Arlington, the new home of the Texas Rangers and an entertainment complex of itself.

If you stay at a participating hotel (and almost all the hotels participate) you can get a free pass to use **The Trolley—Arlington's Entertainment Connection.** That's not just THE trolley, but a fleet of air-conditioned trolley buses that run between the hotels and the major attractions in the entertainment district at 30-minute intervals so you don't have to drive (or pay parking fees). Check with your hotel front desk.

In 1902, when the population was about 900, alcohol prohibition went into effect. Arlington is still somewhat dry today. Beer can be sold in grocery stores, and restaurants and bars can serve liquor, but there are no package liquor stores in the city.

FREE VISITOR SERVICES

ARLINGTON VISITOR INFORMATION CENTER
1905 E. Randol Mill Road, 76011 • 461-3888 or 800-342-4305 • W +

Free brochures, maps and information on sightseeing, lodging, dining, and shopping in Arlington and the Metroplex can be obtained here in person or by a mail or phone request. Travel counselors available daily from 9–5.

PUBLICATIONS

Current information about Arlington events, activities, nightlife, theater, movies, and dining often are published in *Star Time,* published every Friday in the *Arlington Star-Telegram;* the Arts and Entertainment Guide published each Friday in *The Dallas Morning News;* the weekly *Dallas Observer,* which is available free at restaurants and tourist attractions throughout the Dallas area; and the monthly *D Magazine,* available on newsstands.

COMMERCIAL TOURS

THE BALLPARK IN ARLINGTON TOUR
1000 Ballpark Way • 273-5098 • Adults $5, Seniors $4, Children 13 and under $3 • Tour ticket booth on south side of The Ballpark on Randol Mill Road • W Variable

Depending on the Texas Rangers game operations, the 50-minute tour may include a visit to the clubhouse, the press box, owners suite, the dugout, and batting cages. On days when the Rangers are at home, tours are run on the hour from 9 to noon Monday–Friday and 10 to noon on Saturday. No tours on home game Sundays. When the team is away, tours are on the hour 9–4 Monday–Friday, 10–4 Saturday, and noon to 4 Sundays. A combination ticket for the tour and a visit to the Legends of the Game Baseball Museum (see MUSEUMS, p. 45) costs $10 for adults, $8 for seniors, and $6 for children 6–13.

BIRD'S-EYE VIEW

THE OIL DERRICK AT SIX FLAGS
(Admission. See Six Flags Over Texas in FAMILY FUN AND KID STUFF, p. 51.)

From the observation deck on the top of this 300-foot tower, you can orient yourself on the layout of both this park and its watery companion across the highway, as well as enjoy a bird's eye view of all of Arlington and much of the mid-cities and the skylines of Dallas and Fort Worth. If you look sharp, you may even be able to spot your car in the monster parking lot.

HISTORIC PLACES

HISTORIC HOMES

There are several well-preserved homes in the city that were built in the late 1800s and early 1900s. The following are a few examples. Many of the houses along West Abram Street, from the 700 to 1600 block, have been renovated to provide a relatively intact street scene from the early 1900s. The **McKinley-Woodard House** at 400 East 1st was built in 1890 and The **Ghormley-Arnold House** at 404 was built in 1906. The **Cooper House** at 211 Willis was built as a Classical Revival residence in 1878 and later moved to this location where it served as the city library until 1962 and is now the home of the Arlington Women's Club. Also built in the late 1800s was The **Hutchenson-Smith Home** at 312 Oak, which in 1886 was part of the original townsite and is listed in the National Register of Historic Places. Most of these homes are private residences not open to the public.

JOHNSON PLANTATION CEMETERY AND LOG CABINS
512 West Arkansas Lane • 460-4001 • Open by appointment
Adults $3, Children $2 • W

Several log structures from the pioneer communities that pre-date Arlington have been moved to this site, including two log cabins dating from 1854 and 1858, a one-room school house, and a barn. Two small way-stations for the Interurban Trolley, which ran between Dallas and Fort Worth from 1902 to 1936, and the well bowl from the mineral well that once stood in the center of the city are also here. Colonel Middleton Tate Johnson, the Father of Tarrant County, is buried in the small cemetery.

MUSEUMS AND ART GALLERIES

ANTIQUE SEWING MACHINE MUSEUM
804 West Abram • 275-0971 • Monday–Saturday 9:30–5
Adults $3, Seniors $2.50, Children $2 (Five and under free)
America's first sewing machine museum features more than 150 vintage machines dating back as far as 1853 and memorabilia depicting the history and development of this important invention. Among the collection are several models by Elias Howe, who patented the first practical sewing machine, and a 1950 Singer that originally belonged to the actress (Francis Bavier) who played "Aunt Bea" on the "Andy Griffith Show."

ARLINGTON MUSEUM OF ART
201 West Main at Pecan (76010) • 275-4600
Wednesday–Saturday 10–5 • Free • W
This is an old department store in downtown Arlington converted to a simple, spacious museum consisting of one large main gallery and a smaller gallery on the mezzanine. It emphasizes the works of both veteran and emerging Texas artists and also features regional, national and international contemporary art in ten changing exhibits yearly. Gift shop.

CENTER FOR RESEARCH AND CONTEMPORARY ART
University of Texas at Arlington, Fine Arts Building, Cooper at Border Street • 272-3143 • Monday–Friday 10–5, Thursday evening 5–8 p.m., Saturday 12–5. Closed Sunday • Free • W
This gallery features national artists in all mediums ranging from painting to sculpture to performance art. Gallery 171, a student-run gallery, is next door. It is also free, but hours vary. (See COLLEGES AND UNIVERSITIES, p. 48.)

FIELDER HOUSE MUSEUM
1616 West Abram Street at Fielder Road • 460-4001
Wednesday–Friday 10–2, Sunday 1:30–4:30, or by appointment
Non-resident Adults $5 ($1 discount with receipt from an
Arlington business), Students and children 6 and over $2,
Families $10 maximum • W ground floor only, ramp at side

When constructed in 1914, this two-story house overlooked James Park Fielder's 215-acre farm. One of the first brick homes in the area, it was the first with indoor plumbing. The permanent exhibits include a replica of a general store, an early 1900s barbershop, a period bedroom, and a basement with an old home laundry and a scale model of a locomotive that used to run between Dallas and Fort Worth. Other exhibits highlight area history and the museum frequently hosts traveling exhibits. Parking in rear. Picnic tables.

LEGENDS OF THE GAME BASEBALL MUSEUM AND CHILDREN'S LEARNING CENTER
The Ballpark in Arlington, 1000 Ballpark Way • 273-5600
March–October: Monday–Saturday 9 a.m–7:30 p.m. Sunday
noon–5; November–February: Tuesday–Saturday 9–5, Sunday
noon–5, Closed Monday • Adults $6, Seniors $5, Children 6–13
$4 • W Variable

The museum covers the history of baseball from an early 18th century version of the game to the present. Exhibits include items from the Texas League, the Negro Leagues, and the history of the Texas Rangers. Among the more than 130 artifacts on loan from the National Baseball Hall of Fame and Museum in Cooperstown, New York are jerseys worn by Ty Cobb and Babe Ruth, bats used by Lou Gehrig and Ted Williams, and Joe DiMaggio's glove. Fans can sit in a video booth and create a video of themselves doing a play-by-play for a Rangers game. Upstairs, on the third floor, the Children's Learning Center offers kids from kindergarten through sixth grade the opportunity to learn about communications, math, science, geography, and history through interactive activities related to the principles of baseball. This is the first such learning center offered by a major league baseball team. A combination ticket for the museum and the ballpark tour (see

COMMERCIAL TOURS, p. 43) costs $10 for adults, $8 for seniors, and $6 for children 6–13.

RIVER LEGACY LIVING SCIENCE CENTER
701 Northwest Green Oaks Blvd. (76006) at Cooper Street in River Legacy Parks • 860-6752 • Tuesday–Wednesday, Friday–Saturday 9–5, Thursday 9–8, Closed Sunday–Monday
Adults $3, Children 2–18 $2, under 2 free • W +

The center features ways for children and other visitors to interact with living exhibits of insects, fish, amphibians, reptiles, and other native wildlife. A ten-minute (TV) "ride" on a river raft takes visitors through the four seasons and covers the history of the Trinity River. Fitting in perfectly with the preservation of nature themes illustrated inside, the building itself is an attraction for the ecology minded. Designed to resemble the wingspan of a huge bird, it has been described as "a dazzling example of 'sustainable design'—the use of energy-efficient methods and minimal materials in construction." This means that recycling and recycled materials were used in every possible way, even the dark green tiles in the restrooms are made from crushed windshield and bottle glass, and the patio decking is of reclaimed plastic and wastewood. Gift shop.

SPORTS LEGACY—THE GALLERY OF SPORTS ART
The Ballpark in Arlington, 1000 Ballpark Way, Suite 122
461-1994 • Open seven days 10–6 and for one hour after Ranger games • Free • W +

Reputed to be the nations' largest art gallery devoted to sports, it features original art, limited edition lithographs, statues, and autograph memorabilia of all sports.

UNIVERSITY OF TEXAS AT ARLINGTON SPECIAL COLLECTIONS
Central Library, 702 College Street • 272-3393
Monday–Friday 8–5, Saturday 10–5 • Free • W +

With the exception of the collections at the state capital, this is the largest collection of manuscripts and documents on Texas. It includes a cartography library, Texas writers' manuscripts, and a

large collection of manuscripts, newspapers, books, and photographs on Mexican political history. The Texas Labor Archives are
also here; however, these archives and some of the other collections
are restricted to serious researchers. Tours can be arranged for a minimum of 10. (See COLLEGES AND UNIVERSITIES, below.)

OUTDOORS

LAKE ARLINGTON
6300 West Arkansas Lane • 451-6860 • W Variable
   This 2,250-acre city lake in the southwest corner of the city is
popular for boating, sailing, water skiing, and fishing. On its
shoreline are Richard Simpson Park, Bowman Springs Park, and
the Lake Arlington Golf Course.

ARLINGTON PARKS
Parks and Recreation Department
717 West Main (76010) • 459-5474
   The 46 city parks offer facilities for hiking, roller-skating, bik-
ing, boating, fishing, swimming, picnicking, golf, tennis, and a
variety of other sports and activities. Among the major parks are
River Legacy Parks (701 and 1650 Northwest Green Oaks
Blvd.), which combine to form 400 acres of natural landscape
winding along the Trinity River and are the home of the Living
Science Center; **Randol Mill Park** (1901 West Randol Mill
Road) with nature trails, tennis courts, and a fishing pond; and
Veterans Park (3600 West Arkansas Lane), which features a
bandshell, wildlife areas, playing fields, hiking and equestrian
trails, an 18-hole disc golf course, and the water conserving
Xeriscape Gardens.

COLLEGES AND UNIVERSITIES

UNIVERSITY OF TEXAS AT ARLINGTON (UTA)
703 West Nedderman Drive, 76019 • 272-2222 • W + But
not all areas
   With an enrollment of more than 26,000 students from 80
nations studying in 9 academic units, UTA is the second-largest

component in the mammoth University of Texas System. The more than 80-building campus traces its history back through a succession of military and vocational schools that occupied the site over the years to the one wood-frame building of Arlington College, which was founded in 1895 with 75 students.

Visitors are welcome at intercollegiate sports events at **Maverick Stadium** and other athletic facilities. In the fine arts complex at Cooper and 2nd are the music department's **Irons Recital Hall, Mainstage Theatre, Studio Theatre,** and the university's art galleries. The **Planetarium** in the physics department (272-2467) offers a show every first Friday of the month (Adults $2, Seniors and Children $1). Some of the special collections at the **UTA Library** are open to visitors (see MUSEUMS AND ART GALLERIES, p. 48). There is limited visitor parking near most buildings. Pick up a visitors pass at the UTA Police Department at 2nd and Davis. Campus tours lasting up to an hour are available with a week's notice. Tours of the UTA Engineering Lab are also available for a minimum of 10 visitors with a week's notice (272-2571).

MUSIC AND PERFORMING ARTS

ARLINGTON CHORAL SOCIETY
Various locations • 460-7464 or Arlington Visitor Information Center 461-3888

Approximately 60 members perform both classics of choral music and popular pieces at various locations including the Irons Recital Hall in UTA.

ARLINGTON PHILHARMONIC
P.O. Box 201229, 76006 • 275-8965 or Arlington Visitor Information Center 461-3888

This orchestra puts on about four classical and three pops concerts a year. Concerts are performed at a variety of locations. Call for schedule and prices.

JOHNNIE HIGH'S COUNTRY MUSIC REVUE
Arlington Music Hall, 224 North Center Street at Division
(P.O. Box 820007, Fort Worth 76182) • Metro 817-226-4400
or 800-540-5127 • Adults: $9 and $10, Children under 12 $5
W Variable

Johnnie High, who has been putting on this musical revue in various cities in North Texas for more than twenty years, has made Arlington his troupe's permanent home. The troupe of 25 singers, dancers, and entertainers perform country and gospel tunes with the country music shows Saturdays at 7:30 p.m. and a gospel show every first and third Friday at 7:30. Also special shows on holidays.

SUNDAY EVENING IN THE PARK CONCERTS
Veterans Park, 3600 West Arkansas Lane • 459-5474
Free • W Variable

Concerts and live performances are held at the bandshell in Veterans Park each Sunday in May and June. Programs include bands, orchestras, string ensembles, singers, and individual musicians. Call for schedule and show times.

THEATRE ARLINGTON
305 West Main • 275-7661 • Admission • W side door

This community theater with a professional director usually presents about six productions a year in the intimate 200-seat theater. Productions range from award-winning plays to musicals. Most shows run Thursday–Saturday for four to six weeks. Admission $5–$16.

UNIVERSITY OF TEXAS AT ARLINGTON CONCERTS AND THEATER
Fine Arts Building • W Variable

The Irons Recital Hall is the setting for concerts nearly every night during the fall and spring semesters (272-3471). These range from classical to jazz and instrumental to voice. Most concerts by UTA students or faculty are free. A minimum admission is charged for non-university group performances. Student and other theater groups put on a number of productions in the Mainstage and Stu-

dio Theatres (272-2650). Admission $2–$5 for most performances. Call for concert and show schedules and reservations.

FAMILY FUN AND KID STUFF

CREATIVE ARTS THEATRE AND SCHOOL (CATS)
**1100 West Randol Mill Road • 265-8512 • Adults $7,
Children $6 • W +**
   This after-school performing arts school for children and youth
(and adults, too) uses student casts for its six productions during
the school year and three more in its summer series. School-year
shows usually run for several weekends with both matinee and
evening performances. The summer series shows, aimed at smaller children, are usually presented for four days one week a month
with morning and early afternoon performances. Free theater
tours are available Monday–Friday 10:30–6. Reservations are
required for tours that include stops in the costume shop, dance
studios, and 400-seat theater where a demonstration of theater
lighting is given.

MODEL RAILROAD DISPLAY
**Forum Value Mall, Store 230 (Fort Worth and Mid-Cities Model
Railroad Club, P.O. Box 181281, Arlington 76096-1281)
Saturday 1–9, Sunday noon–6 • Free • W**
   Hundreds of HO scale model trains (⅛₇th real size) are on display and operating here most weekends. The trains are on a link-
up of several modules ranging from four to eight feet that belong
to individual members of the club, and which account for the
diversity of railroad names on the trains, sidings around the layout, scenery, and level of detail.

MOUNTASIA FAMILY FUN CENTER
1111 Wet'N Wild Way • 460-3600 • Pay as you play • W Variable
   Three 18-hole miniature golf courses take players through
caves, waterfalls, and a variety of other obstacles. Clubhouse
includes about 90 video and skill games and an ice cream parlor
and other concessions.

SIX FLAGS HURRICANE HARBOR
1800 East Lamar Blvd. (76006), directly across I-30 from Six Flags Over Texas • 265-3356 • Open seven days mid-May–mid-August, weekends only early-May–mid-September • Adults $22.96, Children 3–9 $18.32, Seniors (60 +) $13.68, all plus tax. Under 2 free • Parking $5 • Major credit cards accepted

Billed as "America's largest water park, this 47-acre park, now part of the Six Flags family of parks, offers a wide variety of water activities for everyone from the thrill-seeker to those who just want to float the day away. Among the slides for the daredevils are The Black Hole, which starts in a space station atop a tower and zips down through 500 feet of wet black tubes, and another that plunges down a 300-foot waterway from 6 stories up. The Wave Pool offers ocean-sized waves to body-surf, or if you want something gentler you can tube the quarter-mile Lazy River at 2 mph and Lagoona Beach offers a beach with shaded picnic areas (no glass containers or alcoholic beverages). Kids park. Live music shows and music videos, locker rooms, playground, gift shop, tube and raft rentals. Professional lifeguards. (Note: Admission usually changes every year.)

SIX FLAGS OVER TEXAS
I-30 at Hwy. 360 (P.O. Box 90191, 76010) • Metro 817/640-8900 Open seven days mid-May–late August, weekends March–early May and September–October, several weeks in October for Halloween Fright Fest and late November–December for Holiday in the Park (call for schedule) • Adults: $31.97, Children under 48″ tall and Seniors (55 and over) $25.99, all plus tax. Under 2 free. Discounted two-consecutive-day tickets available. Varying admissions Halloween and Holiday in the Park • Parking $6 • Major credit cards accepted • W Variable

Open since 1961, this 205-acre theme park now attracts more than 3 million visitors a year to its more than 100 rides and shows, making it the most popular tourist attraction in the state. It keeps them coming back by adding new rides and changing rides and shows every year. Everything is included in the admission price except food, souvenirs, video and concession games, and the special concerts in the Music Mill. The park is divided into sections depicting Texas under the flags of Spain, France, Mexico, the

ARLINGTON ENTERTAINMENT DISTRICT

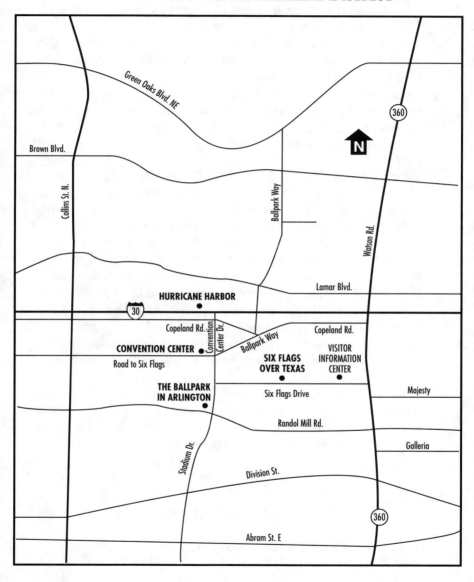

Republic of Texas, the Confederate States of America, and the United States, and much of the entertainment and food in each section is fitted to that section's national theme.

Perhaps the best known of the park's major thrill rides is The Texas Giant, the world's tallest wooden roller coaster that hits speeds over 60 mph and three times has been voted the top roller coaster in the world. Several other roller coasters in the park compete with it for the award for speed and heart-pounding, including an indoor coaster and The Flashback, which drops from a 125-foot tower, whips through three loops at speeds of 55 mph, and then does it all backward. Other thrill rides include a 17-story parachute drop, The G-Force Anti-Gravitational Test Facility, where gondolas drop like falling elevators, and the log flume ride that is guaranteed to cool you off on a hot day. For the less thrill-bent, there are (somewhat) tamer rides like The Right Stuff, a computerized multimedia system that creates the sensations of twisting, turning, and zooming in a supersonic aircraft. And those who want even softer thrills can ride the old-style narrow-gauge train that circles the park, view the world from the top of The Oil Derrick (see BIRD'S-EYE VIEW, p. 44), or attend one of the many shows ranging from stunts to music and animal acts. Concerts by well-known entertainers on selected nights in the 10,000-seat Music Mill Amphitheater. Admission $5–$10. Purchase tickets at the concert gate.

For children there's The Silver Star an old-fashioned carousel with 66 prancing wooden horse and Looney Tunes Land with a number of rides and play activities suited to thrill the littler ones.

(Note: Admission usually changes every year.)

SPORTS

BASEBALL

THE BALLPARK IN ARLINGTON
1000 Ballpark Way (Southwest of Six Flags Over Texas)
Game parking $5 • W + But not all areas

Seating 49,292 for a ballgame, this red brick and granite ballpark is the home of the Texas Rangers and an attraction in itself.

On the facade are 35 cast-stone steer heads and 21 cast-stone stars, and massive 4 × 19-foot architectural frieze sculptures depicting scenes from Texas history including a cattle drive, The Alamo, oil wells, Texas Rangers (the original ones) calling for volunteers, and baseball scenes. Located outside the 122 luxury bay suites are 67 sepia-toned murals depicting baseball's greatest players. Also in the building are the Legends of the Game Baseball Museum and Children's Learning Center and Sports Legacy—The Gallery of Sports Art (see MUSEUMS AND ART GALLERIES, p. 45). When all the development plans are finished, The Ballpark will be the centerpiece of a 270-acre entertainment complex open all year long that includes two man-made lakes stocked with catfish (fishing permitted), and will include shops and restaurants along the lakes, and a 20,000 seat amphitheatre for concerts.

THE TEXAS RANGERS BASEBALL CLUB
The Ballpark in Arlington (P.O. Box 90111, 76004-3111)
273-5100 • Tickets $4–$24
Perhaps it's the new ballpark, but whatever the reason, after years of poor showings, the Texas Rangers are now a potent force in the American League and contenders against the Dallas Cowboys for the heart of the local sports fans. They play about 80 home games in the season from April until October.

GOLF

PUBLIC COURSES

CHESTER W. DITTO GOLF COURSE
801 Brown Blvd. (76011) • Metro 817/275-5941 • 18-hole
course. Green fees: Weekdays $10, Weekends/Holidays $12.
Juniors/Seniors $6. Open to walk-ins.

LAKE ARLINGTON GOLF COURSE
1516 Green Oaks (76013) • 451-6101 • 18-hole course. Green
fees: Weekdays $10, Weekends/Holidays $12. Juniors/Seniors
$6. On north end of the lake.

MEADOWBROOK GOLF COURSE
1300 East Dugan (76010) • Metro 817/275-0221 • 9-hole course.
Green fees: Weekdays $7, Weekends and holidays $8.75.
Juniors/Seniors $4.75. Open to walk-ins.

PRIVATE COURSES

Call for green fees.

ROLLING HILLS COUNTRY CLUB
401 West Lamar (76011) • Metro 817/261-6221 • 18-hole course.

SHADY VALLEY GOLF CLUB
4001 West Park Row (76013) • 275-8771 or
Metro 817/261-4747 • 18-hole course.

TENNIS

ARLINGTON TENNIS CENTER
500 West Mayfield Road, From I-20, take Matlock exit then
north to Mayfield • 557-5683 • Twelve lighted courts
Fee $2.50 per person for 1½ hours

RANDOL MILL PARK
1901 West Randol Mill Road • Parks and Recreation
Department 459-5474
  The six lighted courts are available free on a first-come basis.
In city park with variety of facilities.

OTHER POINTS OF INTEREST

ARLINGTON CONVENTION CENTER
1200 Ballpark Way (76011) • 459-5000 • W+
  In the heart of Arlington's entertainment district, this center
hosts a wide variety of events and shows open to the public, such
as The International Doll Exposition, Texas Indian Market (see
ANNUAL EVENTS, below) and the Taste of Arlington. Admission depends on event. Parking for most events $4.

OFFBEAT

AIR COMBAT SCHOOL
921 Six Flags Drive, # 117, near entrance to Six Flags Over Texas • Metro 817/640-1886 • $37 + tax

Here's your chance to try to be a Top Gun. After a brief ground school orientation and vertigo training, you'll don a G-suit and crash helmet, get strapped into an actual fighter cockpit and spend about 30 minutes engaged in simulated high-speed air combat that challenges you with enemy targets and SAMS that lock on. Appointment recommended.

ANNUAL EVENTS

MARCH

TEXAS INDIAN MARKET
Friday–Sunday late in month • Arlington Convention Center, 1200 Ballpark Way • 459-5000 or Metro 817/265-2602 Admission $8 • Parking $4 • W +

Some 300 artists and craftsmen from 20 states and five foreign countries display their crafts. Live entertainment includes Indian and Spanish dancers, singers, and musicians. Demonstrations by artists.

JUNE

TEXAS SCOTTISH FESTIVAL AND HIGHLAND GAMES
Friday–Sunday early in month • Maverick Stadium, University of Texas at Arlington • 654-2293 • Adults $9, Children $3.50 W Variable

Lots of kilts and bagpipes provide the authentic Scottish atmosphere for a non-stop flow of events and contests that include Highland bagpipe and drumming competitions, dance contests, a parade, and USA vs. Canada athletic matches. Scottish food and drink.

RIVERFEST
Friday–Sunday mid-month • River Legacy Park, 703 Northwest Green Oaks • 277-9481 • Admission $4 • W Variable
This festival offers artisan booths, a children's area, sports area, and continuous entertainment on three stages.

OCTOBER

TEXAS GUITAR SHOW
Friday–Sunday mid-month • Arlington Convention Center, 1200 Ballpark Way • 459-5000 or Metro 817/265-2602 • Admission $10 • Parking $4 • W +
Guitar enthusiasts will find an assortment of rare and expensive guitars displayed side-by-side with the unusual and reasonably priced instruments and accessories.

SHOPPING

ANTIQUE SAMPLER MALL
1715 East Lamar • 861-4747 • W
More than 150 dealers display antiques ranging from crystal, jewelry, and quilts to European and American furniture. The tearoom is a popular lunch spot (under $10) and serves afternoon tea by reservation.

ASIAN DISTRICT SHOPS
Strip malls along Pioneer (Spur 303) and Arkansas west of Hwy. 360 • W Variable
For a cultural adventure as well as a culinary treat, try shopping the Asian shops and bakeries in this area that cater to the more than 10,000 mostly Chinese and Vietnamese residents who live in the city. Among the more interesting shops is the **Hong Kong Market** at Pioneer and New York. This supermarket is fully stocked with an extensive assortment of fresh and packaged imported oriental foods from the basics to the exotic, plus fresh fish and meats. And if you want to make the presentation of your oriental cuisine look more authentic, they sell everyday china and plastic dishes with

colorful patterns. Expect a little trouble getting English-speaking help. There are several restaurants in this market center including Arc-en-Ciel (see DINING OUT, below). Another Asian shop worth a visit is **Pho '95** at 2525 Arkansas Lane.

COOPER STREET CRAFTS MALL
1701 South Cooper • 261-3184

More than 350 artists and crafters exhibit their wares at this small, tightly-packed shop. Included in the hand-made items available are traditional and country handicrafts, folk art objects, jewelry, silk and dried floral arrangements, woodwork, holiday decorations and wearable art. Supervised children's play area. Open seven days, call for hours.

SIX FLAGS MALL
2911 East Division at Hwy. 360 • 640-1641 • W

Dillards', Foley's, Penney's, and Sears anchor about 115 shops and restaurants and a movie theater. Strollers for rent at Customer Service.

THE UPSTAIRS GALLERY
1038 West Abram • 277-6961

Arlington's oldest gallery features original art in a variety of media including oils, watercolors, prints, drawings, pottery, and sculpture. Open Tuesday–Saturday.

DINING OUT

$ = Under $12, $$ = $12–$30, $$$ = Over $30 for one person excluding drinks, tax, and tip

ARC-EN-CIEL
2208 New York Avenue at Pioneer • Metro 817/469-9999
Lunch and dinner seven days • $ • Cr. • W

Of the 225 entrees on the menu, about half are Americanized versions of classic dishes from Szechuan and Hunan cuisine and the rest are authentic Chinese dishes. Order off the menu or sit at your table and select from the large variety of appetizers, entrees, and desserts on the many carts the waitresses wheel around the room. Children's menu. Located in the shopping center with Hong Kong Market. Another location in Garland.

CACHAREL
2221 East Lamar, northwest of intersection of I-30 and Hwy. 360 • Metro 817/640-9981 • Lunch Monday–Friday, dinner Monday–Saturday. Closed Sunday and major holidays • $$$ Cr. • W +

Located in the penthouse of the nine-story Brookhollow Two, this entertainment district restaurant offers elegant dining on a Country French-American cuisine. The selections on the small but innovative menu change daily offering six or seven different appetizers, entrees, and desserts to choose from. For dinner, you may select a la carte or have a no-frills fixed price three-course dinner for $32.50 that on a typical evening may offer such selections as an appetizer of sauteed sea scallops with pesto ravioli and roasted bell pepper sauce, an entree of grilled veal loin steak served with sauteed shrimp and shiitake mushrooms in a tarragon cream sauce, and a dessert of almond tulip with assorted berries and coconut ice cream. Children's menu. Bar. Reservations suggested. Fixed price lunch $15.50. Rated one of the best restaurants in the Metroplex by readers of *Conde Nast Traveler's Magazine.*

FRIDAY'S FRONT ROW SPORTS GRILL
1000 Ballpark Way, in The Ballpark in Arlington • Metro 265-5192 • Lunch and dinner seven days • $–$$ • Cr. • W +

An in-the-ballpark restaurant that's definitely above the usual ballpark concession. Sure, many of the dishes have ballpark related names, like the "Time-Out Tostada Pizza" or "Home Run Slider," but those are also indications of the variety of the menu. Not just hamburgers, hot dogs, and sandwiches (in half dozen varieties), but also stone hearth baked pizza, *calzones,* and dinner entrees that range from grilled salmon to Kansas City strip steaks. Better than typical ballpark food; even the prices are reasonable. Children's menu. Beer. Located on the "Home Run Porch" in right field.

PICCOLO MONDO
829 East Lamar, in Parkway Central Center off North Collins Street • Metro 817/265-9174 • Lunch Monday–Friday, dinner seven days • $$ • Cr. • W +

This is mostly northern Italian cuisine, which means more cream and less tomato sauces. For example, a popular combination is an appetizer of shrimp with mushrooms and cream sauce followed by an entree of medallions of beef tenderloin sauteed with crushed peppercorns, cognac, and cream. The menu offers pasta, veal, beef, seafood, chicken, and vegetarian dishes. Bar. Piano music Saturday and Tuesday evenings.

PORTOFINO RESTAURANT
226 Lincoln Square, Copeland and Collins • 861-8300 • Lunch Monday–Friday, dinner Monday–Saturday. Closed Sunday • $$ Cr. • W

House specialties at this Italian restaurant include three versions of roasted duck (*anitra*), chicken topped with shrimp and mushrooms in light wine, lobster, and a dish of assorted fried seafood. The extensive menu includes classic dishes such as *prosiutto* and melon appetizer, *tortellini* soup, and popular pasta dishes like *Fettucinni Alfredo*. Also beef, veal, chicken, and seafood entrees.

CLUBS AND BARS

COWBOYS
2540 East Abram • Metro 817/265-1535 • W

Dancing to live C&W bands on a Texas-sized 3,500-ft^2 dance floor (claimed to be the largest in the state) every Wednesday–Sunday evenings starting at 7 p.m. Dance lessons Wednesday and Friday 7-8 and Sunday 4–8. Cover $5 and up depending on band.

HUMBERDINKS BAR AND GRILL
700 Six Flags Drive • 640-8553 • W

This is also the home of the Big Horn Brewery, Arlington's first brewery with the town's tallest bar. Live bands on Wednesday, DJ other nights. Also 30 TVs including 3 with big screens.

J. GILLIGAN'S BAR AND GRILL
400 East Abram • 274-8561 • W
Live entertainment Thursday–Saturday. Cover ($3–$4) on those nights. Serving lunch and dinner daily since 1979.

TRAIL DUST STEAK HOUSE
2300 East Lamar Blvd. • 640-6411 • W
Mesquite grilled steaks, ribs, and chicken dinners starting at 5 p.m. daily and noon on Sunday. But then, starting about 7, there's live C&W music for dancing every night.

LODGINGS

For a double room: $ = Under $80, $$ = $80–$120, $$$ = $121–$180, $$$$ = $181–$250, $$$$$ = Over $250); Room tax 13%.
For detailed listings see Metroplex Lodgings Section, p. 383.

ARLINGTON COURTYARD BY MARRIOTT
1500 Nolan Ryan Expressway (76011), south of I-30
277-2774 or 800-321-2211 • $$ (+13%) • W + 8 rooms
No smoking rooms

ARLINGTON HILTON
2401 East Lamar Blvd. (76006), north of I-30 • 640-3322 or 800-527-9332 • $$–$$$ (+13%) • W + 3 rooms
No smoking rooms

ARLINGTON HOLIDAY INN
1507 North Watson Road (76006), take Hwy 360 north to Avenue K/Brown Blvd., then west • $–$$ (+13%) • W + 2 rooms • No smoking rooms

ARLINGTON MARRIOTT
1500 Convention Center Drive (76011), south of I-30
261-8200 or 800-442-7275 • $$–$$$ (+13%) • W + 20 rooms
No smoking rooms

FAIRFIELD INN BY MARRIOTT
2500 East Lamar Blvd. (76006), north of I-30 • 649-5800 or
800-228-2800 • $ (+13%) • W+ 5 rooms • No smoking rooms

THE SANFORD HOUSE BED AND BREAKFAST
506 North Center (76011), at Sanford, downtown, south of I-30
861-2129 • $$$ (+13%) • W+ one room

RADISSON SUITE HOTEL
700 Avenue H East (76011), north east of intersection of I-30
and Hwy. 360 • 640-0440 or 800-333-3333 • $$-$$$ (+13%)
W+ 5 rooms • No smoking rooms

SIDE TRIPS

KOW BELL INDOOR RODEO
Mansfield. TX Hwy 157 and Mansfield Hwy., about 11 miles
south of Arlington (P.O. Box 292, Mansfield 76063)
Metro 817-477-3092 • Saturday–Sunday at 8 p.m.
Adults $4–$6, Children under 12 $2–$3 • W Variable

The cowboys compete in all the usual rodeo events at this
rodeo every weekend year-round. In fact, it's the only year-round
rodeo in the Metroplex. Plus on Monday and Friday nights they
have bull riding competitions.

DALLAS

DALLAS COUNTY SEAT • 1,024,000 • MOST AREA CODES 214 (SOME 972, THESE EXCEPTIONS NOTED IN LISTINGS)

The question the history of Dallas poses is not how it grew to be the seventh largest city in the United States, but why. How did what is now the nation's largest inland city overcome its lack of the traditional foundations for the growth of a great city such as a wealth of natural resources, or a port, or a navigable natural waterway? Dallasites have a ready answer to that question of why. They explain the city's growth as the inevitable result of the community's unrelenting can-do attitude, business sense, and an aggressive entrepreneurial spirit that overcame, and continues to overcome, all obstacles. And history seems to bear them out. The citizens have truly learned the fine art of creating advantages where none existed before.

Less imaginative interpreters explain it by the crossing of a north-south railroad and an east-west intercontinental railroad in 1873, which tied the city to the extensive rail networks of the Midwest and Northeast. This crucial crossing made Dallas a distribution crossroads that offered cheap rail transport and gave shippers a huge competitive edge over water transport.

But no matter which explanation you favor, Dallas has grown dynamically, and "dynamic" is the word for Dallas.

DOWNTOWN DALLAS

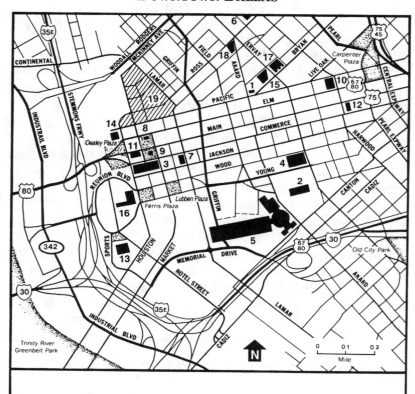

1. Chamber of Commerce
2. City Hall
3. County Courthouse
4. Dallas Central Public Library
5. Dallas Convention Center
6. Dallas Museum of Art
7. Bus Terminal
8. John Neely Bryan Log Cabin
9. John F. Kennedy Memorial
10. Majestic Theater
11. Old Red Courthouse
12. Police and Courts Building
13. Reunion Arena
14. The Sixth Floor: Kennedy Museum
15. Thanksgiving Square
16. Union Station
17. U.S. Post Office
18. Y.M.C.A.
19. West End Historic District

BRYAN'S TRADING POST

The city had its pioneer beginning in the early 1840s when the Republic of Texas built a military road from Austin across the Trinity River to the Red River. It was on this road in 1841, on the open prairie near the three forks of the Trinity, that John Neely Bryan, a bachelor and lawyer from Tennessee with a taste for adventure, set up a trading post to sell to the Indians.

When the Texans forced the Indians to move west, Bryan laid claim to 640 acres and sketched out a town. He soon learned his claim to the land was disputed by both the Peters Colony, which controlled 16,000 square miles of north Texas farmland, and John Grigsby, a hero of the Texas War for Independence. Bryan persisted however, and over the years was able to resolve both the claims in his favor.

Bryan's dream was to use the Trinity River to make his town an inland port with steamboats connecting it to the Gulf of Mexico, 400 miles away. But the river didn't cooperate. It remained contrarily unnavigable; sometimes a raging torrent and other times a dry dusty trickle. True, one steamboat did made the treacherous journey, but it took it many months to accomplish.

NAMED AFTER "MY FRIEND DALLAS"

Bryan named his new town after "my friend Dallas." To this day, no one is sure who that friend was. Some believe it was the Vice-President of the United States, George Mifflin Dallas, who was for the annexation of Texas. As it turned out, in 1846, after the annexation, the Texas Legislature did name the newly established county in honor of the vice-president. But there's no proof that was who Bryan meant when he named the city. It might as easily have been some longtime friend back in Tennessee.

With his town mapped out and named, Bryan set out to attract settlers. At first he wasn't too successful. In 1851, the reported population was only 163. But by 1856 that had almost doubled to about 300 residents, who then, perhaps with a sense of future grandeur already in hand, voted to incorporate it. The population just about doubled again a few years later with the arrival of some 350 French, Belgian, and Swiss settlers whose goal was to build a Utopian colony they called La Reunion. Many in this group were skilled artisans, writers, scientists, artists, musicians, and naturalists. The colony was a failure, but the nucleus of knowledge, education, and appreciation of art and music in its residents no doubt gave birth to what is today a thriving abundance of cultural activities and strong citizen support of them. Some say it was these new residents who provided the solid bedrock on which was built the modern city's image as one of the most cosmopolitan cities in the U.S.

THE CROSSING OF THE RAILROADS

Utopia didn't work, but the can-do attitude of the Dallasites obviously did. In 1872, when the population was about 1,200, the city fathers, by means legal and nefarious, lured the Houston and Texas Central Railroad to divert from its planned route and go through Dallas. Some reports say that Bryan was still living then and was among those who welcomed the first train. A year later, the Texas and Pacific line arrived. As their names stated, the Houston and Texas ran from Galveston and Houston north through the center of the state, while the Texas and Pacific started at Texarkana, on the state's eastern border, where it hooked up with other lines coming from the Midwest, and was heading to the Pacific. Dallas suddenly became a major trade center as merchants from Chicago and St. Louis rushed to set up warehouses at this crossing.

BOOMS AND BUSTS

The railroads provided the economic link that started the city's unabated surge of growth. Dallas became an important shipping point for items like leather and buffalo hides and the area's agricultural products to the Midwest and East and manufactured products from the Midwest and the East to Texas. The population zoomed to around 7,000.

The railroads spurred the first boom and soon that was linked with the agricultural boom that centered on cotton. Later booms included the oil business. The wells were not even near the city; in fact, attempts to drill for oil within the city all turned up dry holes, but the financial and technical support was in Dallas and the city became the region's business center for the drilling industry with more than 450 oil companies establishing headquarters in Dallas at one point. Dallas also became the home base for many insurance companies, which some people say was due in part to a 1908 Texas law requiring any insurance company doing business in the state to keep a substantial part of its reserves in the state. Banking, real estate, and high-tech industries all have brought booms to the city at various times. And for every boom there was usually at least one bust centered around the same business or industry that caused it.

DALLAS BECOMES A FASHION CENTER

In 1907, perhaps drawn by the cosmopolitan ambiance of the city, Neiman Marcus opened an "exclusive woman's ready-to-wear store" in downtown. This store put Dallas on the national fashion map and ultimately on the international fashion map. Building on that tradition, in 1957, two young developers, Trammell Crow and John Stemmons, opened a Home Furnishing Mart, inviting manufacturers and wholesalers to come display their products. Over the years this has grown into what is now the Dallas Market Center, the largest wholesale trade complex in the world. Although most of this center is only open to wholesalers, its very presence makes it easier for area shopkeepers to stay in the forefront of the newest trends, especially in fashion.

DALLAS BECOMES BRYAN'S DREAM

In 1965 Dallas and Fort Worth agreed to build an airport between them that would serve the entire region. This proved to be the link that would pull together all the disparate cities in the area and consolidate them into one gigantic Metroplex. And with the opening of the giant Dallas/Fort Worth International Airport in 1973, John Neely Bryan's dream of Dallas becoming a major inland port was truly realized.

NEIGHBORHOODS

Like any large city, Dallas is a conglomerate of neighborhoods. Most of these are residential with just a sprinkling of restaurants and shops. The neighborhoods with the greatest concentrations of places of special interest to visitors that are worth exploring are: the Arts District, Deep Ellum, Greenville Avenue, McKinney Avenue, and the West End.

THE ARTS DISTRICT
Northern edge of the downtown business district
(DART Light Rail PEARL Station)
In 1978, as part of its plan to revitalize downtown, the city council decided to concentrate new arts facilities in an eleven-block area just north of the central business district. In 1984 The **Dallas Museum of Art (DMA)** opened as the anchor and center-piece of this new district, which has since earned a reputation as a world-class arts and cultural center. Located just a few blocks west of I-75 (Central Expressway), it is bounded on the north by Woodall Rodgers Freeway (Hwy. 366), on the east by Routh Street, on the south by Ross Avenue, and on the west by St. Paul Street. In addition to the DMA, the arts facilities in this 60-acre district are the **Morton H. Meyerson Symphony Center, Arts District Theatre, Belo Mansion, Dallas Black Dance Theatre, Booker T. Washington High School for the Performing Arts,** and **Artist Square.** Built at the same time as the DMA, the privately-owned **Trammell Crow Center** fits in by showcasing art exhibitions in its lobby display area and its outdoor sculpture garden. Other non-art buildings include the **Cathedral Santuario de Guadalupe,** a survivor from the city's early years, and the city-owned 1,650-space Arts District Parking Garage.

DEEP ELLUM

East of downtown. South of the railroad, around Elm Street from Central Expressway (I-75) east to Fair Park

The name originated because locals referred to this area as the deep end of Elm Street—and pronounced it Deep Ellum. Just east of the 1873 crossing point of the city's first two railroad lines, it was an area of industry, warehouses, and Dallas' earliest black community. Before World War II this was the cultural center as well as the principal amusement and shopping district for the city's growing African-American population. During its heyday, Deep Ellum's jazz and blues clubs featured such legendary home-grown musicians as Huddie "Leadbelly" Ledbetter and Blind Lemon Jefferson before they became nationally known. After World War II, the people and businesses started moving out and the area declined. But now Deep Ellum has been revitalized by artists, musicians, actors, and business people opening night clubs, galleries, shops, theaters, and restaurants, and it is once again gaining a reputation as an entertainment and retail shopping district.

GREENVILLE AVENUE

Northeast of downtown. From Ross Avenue north to past LBJ Frwy. (I-635) (DART Light Rail MOCKINGBIRD and PARK LANE Stations)

The Greenville Avenue Strip offers visitors something for both day and night. All along the Strip there are restaurants and nightclubs catering to almost every taste and budget. Clustered mostly on the south end are small shops in old storefronts selling everything from antiques to used clothing and resale furniture, and specialty food stores with the emphasis on Mediterranean, Middle Eastern, and health foods. As you go farther north, especially past Mockingbird, you'll find more glitz and glamour in the stores and restaurants, which tend toward the nationally franchised variety.

MCKINNEY AVENUE

North of downtown, just past the Arts District.

In the late 1800s, the more successful Dallasites started to move their families out of downtown into the more rural areas on the road to the town of McKinney. Today most of the old homes along McKinney Avenue have been converted to restaurants, galleries, unique shops, and nightclubs, and the area has been made more popular by the reconstruction of the old McKinney Avenue Trolley. (See GETTING AROUND, below.) You can pick up the trolley near the DART Light Rail St. Paul Station.

THE WEST END HISTORIC DISTRICT
West end of downtown. Centered on west end of Market Street from Commerce to Woodall Rodgers Freeway (DART Light Rail WEST END Station)

Part of the original city set up by John Neely Bryan, this is where early Dallas had its start. Later, as the downtown moved farther east, this became known as the West End and developed into a factory and warehouse district. Now it is a 20-block historic district that has been transformed into a bustling neighborhood of restaurants, clubs, and shops set in and among the restored buildings. Attractions in this district include "**Old Red,**" the 1892 red sandstone courthouse, **West End Marketplace, Bryan Cabin, Kennedy Memorial, The Sixth Floor Museum** and its counterpoint, **The Conspiracy Museum.** In addition to the DART Light Rail, the Rail Runner routes include this area. (See GETTING AROUND, below.) **Reunion Arena,** home to the three Dallas' professional sports teams, and **Reunion Tower** are on the southwest corner of the district.

GETTING AROUND

DRIVING IN DALLAS

Aside from morning and evening rush hours during the business week, there's probably less traffic congestion in Dallas than in any city of comparable size. However, parking is a problem, especially downtown. There are plenty of commercial garages and parking lots, but they can be expensive. The problem with driving is not so much the traffic as the layout of the city. With a few exceptions, downtown is basically a grid of mostly one-way streets, but spreading out from there, many of the streets seem to run off in all directions like unregulated spokes of a wheel.

If you only plan to use the main highways and streets, a simple map, like the one in this book, will do. But if you plan any extensive discovery driving, we suggest you invest in a good street map, or a streetfinder-type map book, and plot your route before you set out.

DART BUSES

If you're staying downtown, you can eliminate the hassles of driving and the expense of parking in the downtown area during the day on weekdays by using the Dallas Area Rapid Transit (DART) shuttle bus system known as the **Rail Runner.** This system offers two routes that operate Monday–Friday from 6 a.m. to 7:30 p.m., and rides cost only 50 cents. The fare is valid for downtown bus and rail travel in any direction for up to 90 minutes—even a return trip on the same route. Route 570 runs every 10 minutes and loops around the Arts District, West End Historic District, and Dallas City Hall. It serves the DART Light Rail system passengers (see below) through direct connections with St. Paul Station and Akard Station. Route 517 circles Union Station, the City Hall and library, and the Farmers Market areas every 20 minutes. It connects with Union Station providing service to both light rail and commuter rail passengers. In addition to these visitor-oriented routes, DART operates more than 100 bus routes in and around the city. Correct change is required.

DART LIGHT RAIL

Another alternative to driving is the DART Light Rail system, which runs safe, clean, air-conditioned, electric trains that can whisk you in minutes from one place to another along a line that runs roughly north-south through the center of the city. (See DART Light Rail map.) Trains run frequently from early morning to late at night and fares are $1 each way—50 cents each way if both stations are in downtown—and day tickets are available

DALLAS DART LIGHT RAIL STATIONS

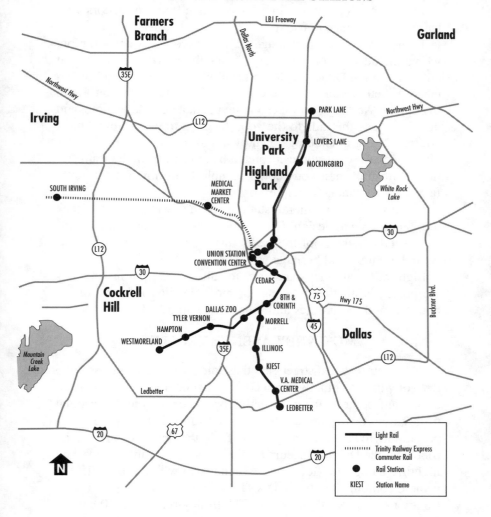

Farmers Branch

LBJ Freeway

Dallas North

Garland

Northwest Hwy

35E

Irving

L12

PARK LANE

Northwest Hwy

University Park

LOVERS LANE

MOCKINGBIRD

Highland Park

SOUTH IRVING

MEDICAL MARKET CENTER

White Rock Lake

30

L12

UNION STATION CONVENTION CENTER

30

Cockrell Hill

CEDARS

8TH & CORINTH

75

Hwy 175

Buckner Blvd.

DALLAS ZOO

TYLER VERNON

MORRELL

45

Dallas

HAMPTON

WESTMORELAND

35E

ILLINOIS

L12

Mountain Creek Lake

KIEST

V.A. MEDICAL CENTER

Ledbetter

LEDBETTER

20

67

20

N

	Light Rail
	Trinity Railway Express Commuter Rail
●	Rail Station
KIEST	Station Name

for $3. If there's a station near where you want to go, it's a bargain. Unlike the Rail Runner routes, which are designed primarily to help visitors get around the downtown area and only for limited days and times, the light rail is designed primarily for Dallas residents, so it operates every day and is a boon to visitors who learn the easy steps to use it.

To help you take advantage of this excellent transportation, we've included a note on every Dallas listing from here on that tells if there is a DART Light Rail station within easy walking distance. Whether you're at the Convention Center and want to zip over to the West End for lunch or staying at a downtown hotel and decide to take the kids to the zoo, there's a train for you. And if you're staying outside of downtown and not located near a station, check to see if you can catch a bus to and from the train station. With transfers, you should be able to do this for the same fare. Correct change is required.

When you're at a light rail station, take a few moments to check the station art and design. Each station has a unique visual identity that tells the story of the area's historic roots, cultural diversity, and architectural heritage.

Light rail route maps and easy-to-follow ticketing instructions are posted at all the stations. For more detailed information on both bus and train routes and schedules, call 979-1111.

MCKINNEY AVENUE TROLLEY

With four restored street cars that date back to as early as 1906 (two of which originally serviced passengers in Portugal and Australia), and some of the track dating back a century to the original trolley line, this is more a historic and fun ride than pure transportation. However, it can get you from the downtown Arts District, near the Dallas Museum of Art, to the restaurants, shops, and nightlife along the McKinney Avenue strip without a car. If you want to combine it with the DART Light Rail, you can pick up the trolley near the St. Paul station. The trolley runs from 10 a.m. to 10 p.m. Sunday–Thursday and until midnight on Friday and Saturday. Fare is $1.50 for a round trip, but there's a one-day unlimited use ticket available for $3. Correct change is required. Going the full 2.8-mile route takes about 30 minutes (855-0006).

FREE VISITOR SERVICES

DALLAS CONVENTION & VISITORS BUREAU
1201 Elm Street, Suite 2000 (75270) (DART Light Rail AKARD Station) • 746-2677 or 800-C-DALLAS (800-232-5527) for Information Packet • W +

The Dallas Convention & Visitors Bureau serves all the information needs of visitors to the city. Call or write for an information packet. Visitors guides include *Dallas Weekends, Dallas Walking Tours, Dallas Today,* and a quarterly calendar of events. Some publications are available in French, German, Japanese, Spanish, and Portuguese.

When in Dallas you can pick up these and other publications at one of the **Visitor Information Centers** listed below.

WEST END MARKETPLACE
603 Munger (DART Light Rail WEST END Station) • W • Open Monday–Friday 11–8, Saturday 12–8, Sunday 12–6

DOWNTOWN CENTER
1303 Commerce (DART Light Rail AKARD Station) • W • Open Monday–Friday 8–5, Saturday 9–5, Sunday 11–5

NORTHPARK CENTER
8950 North Central Expressway (DART Light Rail PARK LANE Station) • W + • Open Monday–Saturday 10–6, Sunday 12–6

THE DALLAS AMBASSADORS
The city of Dallas sponsors The Dallas Ambassadors, young men and women who stroll the downtown streets weekdays from 11:30 a.m. to 6 p.m. to provide assistance to visitors. Trained in the geography and landmarks of Dallas, they aid visitors with directions and other information. The Ambassadors carry maps and radios and are easily recognized by their red and blue uniforms. They are also trained in first aid and CPR.

DALLAS EVENTS HOTLINES
Convention & Visitors Bureau Dallas Events Hotline 746-6679
Dallas Morning News Arts and Entertainment Hotline 522-2659
Department of Parks and Recreation Hotline 670-7070

PUBLICATIONS

Current information about Dallas events, activities, nightlife, theater, movies, and dining is published every Friday in the "Arts and Entertainment Guide" in *The Dallas Morning News*; the weekly *Dallas Observer* and *The Met,* which are available free at restaurants and tourist attractions throughout the Dallas area; and the monthly *D Magazine,* available on newsstands. *Texas Monthly Magazine,* also available on newsstands, highlights reviews of a smaller number of Dallas restaurants and events in its city listings in the back of the book.

COMMERCIAL TOUR SERVICES

DALLAS SURREY SERVICES
211 East Colorado (75203)
(DART Light Rail WEST END Station) • 946-9911
Horse drawn surreys that can accommodate six to eight passengers operate nightly on Market Street in the West End beginning at about 6:30 p.m., weather permitting. Tours are available to several areas and prices range from $25–$35 for four passengers plus $5 for each additional. If you call ahead, arrangements can be made to pick up your party at most downtown hotels.

GRAY LINE TOURS
5125 Cash Lane (75247) • 630-1000
Gray Line offers several daily scheduled morning and afternoon sight-seeing tours with pick-ups at the major hotels. Dallas city tours are in the morning, JFK Historic District tours in the afternoon, and Southfork Ranch tours are offered several afternoons each week. Reservations required. Call for schedule and prices.

TOURS DALLAS
P.O. Box 227093, 75222-7093 • 948-8687

This tour line offers several scenic and historic two-hour minivan tours including an architectural tour conducted by a professional architect. Fare for all tours: Adults $20, children 6–12 $10. All tours originate at Dealey Plaza in the 400 block of Elm. Reservations are recommended.

WALKIN' AND TALKIN'
528-3453

Reservations are required for this two-hour walking tour of the downtown business and arts district that highlights art, architecture, and historical information including tales of the famous and infamous residents. All tours leave from the West Lobby of El Centro College at Market and Main streets. Adults $7.50, seniors and students $6.50.

INDUSTRY TOURS

MARY KAY COSMETICS MANUFACTURING FACILITY
1339 Regal Row (Mailing address: Mary Kay World Headquarters, 16251 Dallas Parkway, 75248)
972/687-5720 • Free • W

On Friday, September 13, 1963, Mary Kay opened a small storefront cosmetics store in Dallas. Now Mary Kay Cosmetics is an international company. Tours of this facility where a variety of Mary Kay products are prepared are conducted Tuesday–Friday at 10:30 a.m. and 2 p.m. by appointment only, made at least 48 hours in advance. Mary Kay Museum in the Mary Kay World Headquarters is also open for tours. (See ADDISON/OTHER POINTS OF INTEREST, p. 31.)

MRS BAIRD'S BAKERY TOUR
5230 Mockingbird (75205), at Central Expressway • 526-7201
Monday, Wednesday–Thursday 10–4, Friday 10–6 • Call for reservations • Free • W

See how bread and donuts are made while learning the history of this popular Texas bakery. All visitors are given a sample of hot buttered bread fresh from the oven. Parking and tour entrance at side of bakery facing Central Expressway. Tour lasts 45 minutes to an hour. Children must be at least six years old to take the tour.

SELF-GUIDED TOURS

SELF-GUIDED WALKING TOURS

The Convention & Visitors Bureau offers a free downtown walking tours map/brochure. The designated tours include a Central Tour, which takes about an hour, and four branch tours: Civic Tour (30 minutes), Farmers Market Tour (30 minutes), Arts District Tour (45 minutes), and West End Tour (30 minutes). Or you can use it to devise your own tour of just the places that interest you.

SELF-GUIDED WALKING/DRIVING TOURS

A *Dallas Sculpture Tour* map/brochure is also available from the Convention & Visitors Bureau. This includes a tour of sculptures in 32 locations in the downtown area, most of which can be viewed on a walking tour, and another 42 locations where you can drive to see outdoor sculpture throughout the city.

BIRD'S-EYE VIEW

The three places open to the public offering the best panoramic view of the city are the three levels in the 50-story **Reunion Tower** at the **Hyatt Regency Dallas Hotel** (300 Reunion Blvd.). The Reunion Tower's geodesic dome has been a landmark in the Dallas skyline since it opened in 1978. View elevators make the trip from ground to the observation levels in a little over a minute. The lowest level is The Lookout, an observation floor that offers visitors both a bird's-eye view of downtown Dallas and a scenic view for many miles in every direction from both indoor and outdoor viewing areas. (Sunday–Thursday 10–10, Friday–Saturday 9–midnight. Adults $2, seniors and children under 12 $1.) On the next level is the hotel's Antares Restaurant.

Named for the brightest star in the Scorpio constellation, the restaurant offers lunch, dinner, and Sunday brunch all with a view that changes as the restaurant rotates at the rate of one revolution every 55 minutes. (See DINING OUT, p. 146) And at the highest level is The Dome, the Hyatt's cocktail lounge, which also revolves once every 55 minutes. Parking at the hotel is expensive, but The Tower is within easy walking distance of the DART Light Rail UNION Station or you might try parking at Reunion Arena.

The view is not as spectacular, but you can get an enjoyable bird's-eye view of downtown from the Nana Grill on the 27th floor of the tower of the **Wyndham Anatole Hotel** (2201 Stemmons Frwy. I-35E) and from Laurel's restaurant on the 20th floor of the **Sheraton Park Central Hotel** (12720 Merit Drive).

FAIR PARK

East of downtown, bounded by Parry Avenue, Cullum Blvd., Fitzhugh Avenue, and Washington Avenue (P.O. Box 159090, 75315) • 670-8400 or 890-2911 (English and Spanish Information Line) • W Variable

For most world's fairs, the design and construction of buildings is based on a short life ending when the fair ends. Not so with the building put up for the Texas Centennial Exposition of 1936, a world's fair in which Texas celebrated its one hundredth anniversary of independence from Mexico. For that event, Fair Park was built on the site used for Texas' state fairs since 1886, and it was built solidly to remain after the Centennial as the heart of state fairs for many years. It was built so solidly, in fact, that the park, now more than 60 years old, has been designated a National Historic Landmark—the largest historical landmark in the state—in recognition of its significant collection of art deco buildings from the 1930s.

Fair Park still lives up to that primary mission, hosting the annual State Fair of Texas, one of the largest state fairs in the U.S., for approximately three weeks every fall (see ANNUAL EVENTS, p. 135). But the rest of the year, this 277-acre city park

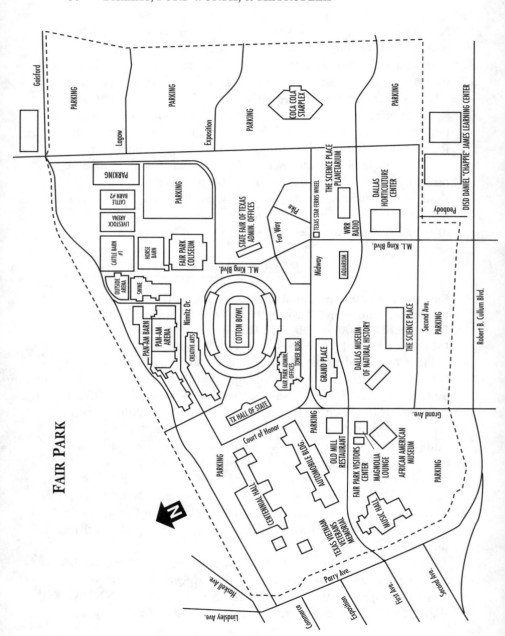

FAIR PARK

is an attraction itself as a site rich in museums, historic places, and entertainment and sports venues. Admission is free to the grounds, which are open daily except for the week before the state fair and during the fair itself. However, individual admissions are charged to most of the major attractions in the park. Parking is free except during the State Fair and some special events. Over six million people visit Fair Park annually.

Normal open hours are given for each of the attractions listed below, but most are open longer hours during the State Fair. Some are also closed on major holidays. Call to confirm.

HALL OF STATE

3939 Grand Avenue (Dallas Historical Society, P.O. Box 26038, 75226) • 421-4500 • Tuesday–Saturday 9–5, Sunday 1–5. Closed Monday • Free, except for special exhibits • W Variable

Built as a centerpiece of the 1936 Texas Centennial, this elegant building is an outstanding example of art deco architecture. The bronze entry doors, ornamented with symbols of the industrial and agricultural life of Texas, lead into the Hall of Heroes with its bronze, larger-than-life-sized statues of six heroes of the Republic of Texas: Stephen F. Austin, Sam Houston, Mirabeau B. Lamar, Thomas J. Rusk, James Walker Fannin, and William Barret Travis. Five rooms branch off this hall in the shape of a T. Immediately ahead is the four-story Great Hall with an immense gold seal, with symbols representing the six nations of which Texas was a part, and two huge murals depicting major events in the history of the state. To the left and right of the Hall of Heroes are four rooms designated to tell the story of each of the four regions of the state: east, west, north, and south. The Dallas Historical Society, which is the operator and caretaker of the building, sponsors frequent changing exhibits. Gift shop.

THE MUSEUMS OF FAIR PARK

AFRICAN AMERICAN MUSEUM
3536 Grand Avenue (P.O. Box 150153, 75315) • 565-9026
Tuesday–Thursday 12–5, Friday 12–9, Saturday 10–5,
Sunday 1–5. Closed Monday • Free except for occasional
special events • W

This museum is the only one in the Southwest devoted to the preservation and display of African-American artistic, cultural, and historical materials. It offers a treasury of art and culture that recognizes the vital presence of Black culture in the Metroplex and in the world. Among these treasures is the Billy R. Allen Folk Art Collection, one of the largest collections of African-American folk art in the nation. In addition to the folk art, the museum's permanent holdings include a small, but rich collection of traditional African art objects including masks, sculptures, gold, and textiles; and a collection of contemporary works of African-American fine art by local, national, and internationally recognized artists. It houses the Heritage Center, featuring exhibits from its historical collection and archives of materials pertaining to the African-American experience. The museum sponsors traveling exhibits as well as a number of lectures and conferences during the year. A popular monthly event is "Jazz Under the Dome" every third Friday night (admission fee). It also sponsors an annual jazz festival in September and the annual Texas Black Invitational Rodeo, which is held at Fair Park Coliseum in May. Gift shop.

AGE OF STEAM RAILROAD MUSEUM
1105 Washington Street (P.O. Box 153259, 75315), in northwest
corner behind the Centennial Building • 428-0101
Thursday–Friday 10–3, Saturday–Sunday 11–5. Closed
Monday–Wednesday • Adults $3, children 12 and under $1.50

This outdoor collection includes more than 28 historic pieces of railroad equipment on display including Dallas' oldest surviving depot, Pullman sleeping cars, lounge cars, and several of the largest and most powerful locomotives in the world. Most of the equipment is from the period 1900–1950. Some of the cars can be boarded. The museum is owned and operated by the Southwest Railroad Historical Society. Gift shop.

THE DALLAS AQUARIUM
First Street and Martin Luther King Blvd. (P.O. Box 150113, 75315) • 670-8443 • Seven days 9–4:30. Closed Thanksgiving and Christmas days • Adults $2, children 3–11 $1, Under 3 free • W+

Fish that live in the desert. Fish that wear disguises. Four-eyed fish, and fish that walk are among the weird and wonderful aquatic residents here. The aquarium is home to a varied collection of nearly 4,000 creatures of both freshwater and saltwater species from around the world. Special attractions include shark and piranha feeding on alternate afternoons every day but Monday; an Amazon Flooded Forest Exhibit that showcases approximately 20 species of fish found in the Amazon River of South America; and The World of Aquatic Diversity exhibit featuring 25 displays highlighting the bizarre adaptations of a variety of marine and freshwater species. The breeding lab has a viewing window to provide a behind-the-scenes look at the aquarium's ongoing conservation projects to preserve rare and endangered species.

DALLAS MUSEUM OF NATURAL HISTORY
3535 Grand Avenue (P.O. Box 150349, 75315), just inside the Grand Avenue entrance off Cullum Blvd. • 421-DINO (421-3466) • Seven days 10–5. Closed Thanksgiving and Christmas days • Adults $4, children 3 and older $2.50, under 3 free. Free admission Monday 10–1. • W+ But not all areas

"Natural History" in its title means this museum documents the diversity of past and present environments and the changing face of Texas over millions of years. To do this it offers extensive displays and dioramas of Texas wildlife, plants, and minerals. Among its features are The Hall of Prehistoric Texas, which includes a reconstructed dinosaur and the nation's largest prehistoric sea turtle; a working paleontology lab, and City Safari, a hands-on science discovery center for children. A program is underway to revitalize the permanent exhibits by making them more interactive for visitors. The museum also usually offers two major national or international traveling exhibits each year. Gift shop.

THE SCIENCE PLACE AND TI FOUNDERS IMAX® THEATER
1318 Second Avenue between Grand and Martin Luther King (P.O. Box 151469, 75315) • 428-5555 • Seven days 9:30–5:30. Closed Christmas Day • Adults $6, seniors and children 3–12 $3, under 3 free. Extra admission to IMAX Theater and Planetarium • W + But not all areas

Lift 1,000 pounds with one hand, learn the shocking truth about electricity in the Electric Theater, step inside the body shop to see a real beating heart, or get face-to-face with a (robotic) dinosaur that growls. You can do all this in the hundreds of hands-on exhibits in this popular museum that goes to the limit to let you touch and turn and press buttons to make science interactive and fun. And for a real moving movie experience, take in the show at the IMAX Theater, in which each of the 329 seats is scientifically designed to give the viewer such an optimum view of the 79-foot dome screen that it feels like you're in the film. Cafeteria and gift shop. In a separate building, on First Avenue, about a block away, are more examples of science and technology in action and **The Science Place Planetarium,** which features sky shows Monday–Saturday. Discounted combination tickets are available for the museum, the IMAX Theater, and the Planetarium.

FAIR PARK PERFORMANCE AND SPORTS VENUES

For schedules and ticket information, call 670-8400 or 890-2911 (English and Spanish Information Line)

BAND SHELL
Musical concerts and plays are performed in this 4,500-seat amphitheater.

COCA COLA STARPLEX AMPHITHEATER
(1818 First Avenue. 428-8365)

This 20,000-seat amphitheater is the site for about 40 live concerts each year featuring world-renowned entertainers.

COTTON BOWL STADIUM
(939-2222)

The 72,000-seat stadium is the site of many sports events including the Cotton Bowl Football Classic on New Year's Day, the annual football games pitting rivals Grambling and Prairie View A&M each September and University of Texas and University of Oklahoma during the State Fair, SMU and other college football games, and the home soccer matches of the Dallas Burn. It also hosts a variety of concerts and the spectacular Fourth of July fireworks display. (Wheelchair access at stadium sections 4–7.)

COLISEUM
(939-2222)

With 7,116 seats, it hosts rodeos, horse shows, and other sporting events including the indoor polo matches of the Dallas Dragoons.

CREATIVE ARTS THEATRE

This art deco building contains two performance stages, exhibition sites, and a music arena.

MUSIC HALL
(909 First Avenue. 565-2226)

The 3,420-seat hall is home for the Dallas Summer Musicals, the opera, ballet, and a variety of concerts. Restaurant.

OTHER POINTS OF INTEREST IN FAIR PARK

DALLAS HORTICULTURAL CENTER
3601 Martin Luther King Blvd. (P.O. Box 152537, 75315)
428-7476 • Tuesday–Saturday 10–5, Sunday 1–5. Closed
Monday. (Grounds open at all times, access through rear gate)
Free • W

There are a dozen separate gardens, a conservatory, and a greenhouse on the 7.5 acres of this center. Among these are an antique rose garden, a garden featuring plants used for medicinal and culinary purposes, a garden with over 300 varieties of iris, and a xeriscape garden of native and adapted plants that require minimal supplemental water and maintenance. Among the more popular gardens is the *Grand Alle du Meadows,* which is patterned after the classic French landscape garden with colorful plants outlining a broad promenade that culminates in a 50-foot geyser fountain in the midst of an expansive "Fan of Color." The conservatory houses the Plants of Africa Collection, while the native plants surrounding the greenhouse complex represent six vegetative regions of the state of Texas. Admission is charged only for occasional special exhibits held in the conservatory.

TEXAS STAR FERRIS WHEEL

At a little over 212 feet (about 20 stories high) this is the tallest ferris wheel in North America. It can carry 264 riders in 44 gondolas on a ride that lasts from 12–15 minutes. On a clear day, from the top, riders can see 40–45 miles. Tickets: $3.50. Operates only during the State Fair and for selected special events.

OTHER MAJOR BUILDINGS IN FAIR PARK

The **Automotive Building, Grand Place, Centennial Hall** and other major buildings in the park not only have important roles as exhibit areas during the State Fair, but are also used during the rest of the year for a variety of exhibits and events including antique and craft shows and flea markets.

HISTORIC PLACES

THE BELO MANSION
2101 Ross Avenue (75201) in the Arts District (DART Light Rail PEARL Station) • 969-7066 (Dallas Bar Association) for tours • Free

In the late 1890s, this Neoclassical mansion was constructed for Colonel Alfred H. Belo, founder of the *The Dallas Morning News,* on Ross Avenue, which was then a fashionable street lined with grand homes. Construction was completed in 1900, a year before his death. By 1926 Ross Avenue was no longer a fashionable address and the building became a funeral home, which had its time of fame in 1934 when thousands of people stood in line to view the body of Clyde Barrow, who lay in state after being killed in an ambush set by Texas Rangers. The Dallas Bar Foundation bought and meticulously restored the mansion in 1977. Today, it is the lone survivor of those early stately homes and is listed in the National Register of Historic Places. Now known as the Dallas Legal Education Center, it houses the offices of the Dallas Bar Association, which offers a monthly tour from September to May. Call for details.

DEALEY PLAZA NATIONAL HISTORIC LANDMARK DISTRICT/KENNEDY ASSASSINATION SITE
Downtown in the West End area around the triple underpass of Elm, Commerce, and Houston Streets (DART Light Rail WEST END Station)

Built over the original townsite, the plaza's art deco garden structures were completed in 1940 and named after George Bannerman Dealey, the publisher of *The Dallas Morning News* and a local civic leader. In November 1963, President John F. Kennedy was assassinated while riding in a motorcade passing through Dealey Plaza. In 1993, The National Park Service declared the plaza and surrounding area a National Historic Landmark District (see THE SIXTH FLOOR MUSEUM, p. 98). There are now fountains and a JFK memorial plaque in the plaza's park.

FREEDMAN'S CEMETERY
North of Downtown, between Hall, McKinney, and North Central Expressway

The first burials here were slaves prior to the Civil War. After that war, it became known as the "Old Colored Cemetery" and then as the Freedman's Cemetery. When it closed in 1927, there were approximately 18,000 graves in the four-acre plot. In 1989, after several intrusions had already been made by roadways and other private developments, Black Dallas Remembered, Inc. and other preservation groups protested a plan to widen a major freeway that would desecrate a large portion of the cemetery. After negotiations with the city, the remains of 1,500 of Dallas' earliest citizens, freed slaves who founded Freedman's Town after the Civil War, were reintered in property adjacent to the original site. This cemetery has been designated a Texas Archaeological Site, a Texas Historic Landmark, and a Dallas Historic Landmark. Plans are in progress to build a Freedman's Memorial here.

HALL OF STATE
See FAIR PARK, p. 79.

HISTORIC DOWNTOWN BUILDINGS

It wasn't until the mid-1890s that downtown Dallas construction took on any semblance of permanence. And, of course, as in any booming business district, older buildings come down to make way for new and bigger ones that make more efficient use of the precious real estate. As a result, with few exceptions, most downtown buildings of historic importance are not even a century old. The following highlight just a few of the buildings of historic interest to the development of downtown. For a complete list see the Convention & Visitors Bureau's free Downtown Walking Tours map/brochure (see SELF-GUIDED WALKING TOURS, p. 78).

THE ADOLPHUS HOTEL (1912)
1321 Commerce Street

The Adolphus is the sole survivor of the several grand downtown hotels of the early 20th century. St. Louis brewery magnate, Adolphus Busch was responsible for the Beaux Arts architecture of his namesake hotel. The high-quality detailing, executed in granite, terra cotta, and bronze is rare in Texas buildings of that period.

MAGNOLIA BUILDING (1922)
Commerce and Akard Streets

This Renaissance-Revival 29-story skyscraper was thought to be the tallest building south of Washington D.C. when it was built and retained that title for more than two decades. In 1934 it was topped with the 15-ton Pegasus or Flying Red Horse, the symbol for the Magnolia Petroleum Company (later Mobil Oil). Pegasus became the symbol for the Dallas skyline and the unofficial mascot of the city at that time, and today is seen as a beloved sentimental landmark.

MAJESTIC THEATRE (1922)
1925 Elm Street

The Majestic is the only example left on Dallas' once thriving Theater Row, a Great White Way several blocks long. Originally built as a vaudeville palace, it was the first to install air-conditioning and started showing talking pictures during the 1920s. Completely restored, the Renaissance Revival-style theater is now a performing arts theater. It is listed in the National Register of Historic Places.

MUNICIPAL BUILDING/OLD CITY HALL (1914)
2015 Main Street

The fifth floor of this building was once the city jail. It is still used by the Dallas Police Department and it was in the basement of this building that Lee Harvey Oswald, the alleged assassin of President John F. Kennedy, was shot by Jack Ruby.

OLD RED COURTHOUSE (1892)
Houston and Commerce Streets

The structure was designed in the Romanesque-Revival style and built of Pecos red sandstone with red granite from Texas and blue granite from Arkansas. This is the fifth permanent courthouse to occupy this site on land originally donated by John Neely Bryan in 1850 explicitly for a county courthouse. Plans are being developed to turn this historic building into a museum.

SANGER BROTHERS DEPARTMENT STORE/EL CENTRO COLLEGE (1919)
Main and Lamar Streets

The Sanger brothers made marketing history when they opened the first store in Dallas to offer merchandise in departments, a one-price system, retail charge accounts, home delivery, shopping by telephone, and fringe benefits for employees that included an employees' savings and loan association and a free night school at the store. It was also the first store to hire female sales persons and have free rides home for unmarried female employees, with one of the brothers acting as guardian. The Sanger Brothers store made downtown the place to shop. Most of the original buildings in the Sanger Brothers complex were torn down to make way for the Dallas Community College District's El Centro campus, and the remaining buildings have been completely renovated to house the school. Some of the old millinery items and display counters from the store are now in the Milliner Supply Company, across the street at 911 Elm. This company is also a part of downtown Dallas history because the building dates from the 1890s and the company is the oldest downtown retail store still owned and operated by its founder.

UNION STATION (1916)
400 South Houston

During the height of railroad travel, The Union Terminal Company was formed in 1912 to create this one central passenger facility to replace the five depots used by the nine railroads serving the city. At that time the depot handled as many as 85 trains a day. As train travel declined, so did Union Station. The building was restored in 1974, but the same cannot be said of train travel. At the time this guide went to press there were no passenger trains serving the city. The station is connected by a tunnel to the DART Light Rail UNION Station and to the Hyatt Regency Hotel, which uses the grand hall and other rooms on the second floor for banquets.

SWISS AVENUE HISTORIC DISTRICT
Northeast of downtown, Swiss Avenue between La Vista Drive and Fitzhugh Avenue

This neighborhood was among the most prestigious in Dallas in the early 1900s. About a mile of the avenue is listed in the National Register of Historic Places because of the restored grand homes. Of particular note are the 2800 and 2900 blocks, which are called **The Wilson Blocks** after Frederick P. Wilson who built some of the homes in the late 1890s. For information about tours call the Historic Preservation League, 821-3290.

MUSEUMS AND ART GALLERIES

AFRICAN AMERICAN MUSEUM
See FAIR PARK, p. 79.

AGE OF STEAM RAILROAD MUSEUM
See FAIR PARK, p. 79.

BIBLICAL ARTS CENTER
7500 Park Lane at Boedeker (P.O. Box 12727, 75225) • 691-4661
Monday–Saturday 10–5 (Thursday 10–9), Sunday 1–5 Closed
Thanksgiving, Christmas Eve & Day, and New Year's Day
Galleries Free. Miracle of Pentecost Presentation: Adults $3.75,
children 6–12 $2, under 6 free • W +

Nondenominational art that illustrates the Bible is the theme here, with several permanent exhibits in the galleries, including a life-size replica of the Garden Tomb of Christ, and exhibits that change every 8–12 weeks. The major attraction is the Miracle of Pentecost Presentation, a 30-minute light and sound show high-lighting the 124-ft wide by 20-ft high oil painting by Torger Thompson depicting the reception of the Holy Spirit by the Apos-tles. The mural, which took almost three years to create, contains over 200 Biblical characters, many of them life-size. A unique feature of the light and sound show is that it is totally audio nar-ration in darkness for the first eight minutes. Shows are once an hour starting on the half hour. Gift shop.

THE CONSPIRACY MUSEUM
See OFFBEAT, p. 132.

DALLAS FIREFIGHTERS MUSEUM
3801 Parry (75226) at Commerce, across from Fair Park
821-1500 • Monday–Friday 10–4 • Free. Donations accepted
W downstairs only
You have to ring the doorbell to get in this historic firehouse, which was a working station from 1907 until 1975. Inside, the museum is packed tight with fire trucks, fire fighting equipment, photographs, and other memorabilia illustrating the history of the Dallas Fire Department from 1873 to the present. Displays include the 1936 Texas Centennial Exposition Hook and Ladder Truck and the 1884 Ahrens horse-drawn steam pumper called "Old Tige" after the nickname of W. L. Cabell, mayor of Dallas at the time. Upstairs rooms show how the firemen lived at the sta-tion in quarters at the top of the brass sliding pole they used to make a quick descent to the truck. Tours are informal and can last a half hour to an hour depending on your interest and questions. Parking is a problem only during the State Fair.

DALLAS MEMORIAL CENTER FOR HOLOCAUST STUDIES
7900 Northaven Road (75230) Downstairs in the Jewish
Community Center • 750-4654 • Monday–Friday 9:30–4:30,
Thursday until 9, Sunday 12–4. Closed Jewish and most

national holidays • Recommended donation: Adults $2, children
$1 • W (elevator)

Visitors enter this small museum and research library through
a boxcar once used to transport people to the concentration
camps. Audio tapes are provided for a free self-guided tour that
lasts about 45 minutes as it traces in photos and other artifacts the
horrors of the Holocaust from the first days of the Nazi regime in
1933 through the liberation of the death camps. Films are shown
on request. Video documentaries and testimony tapes and other
audio-visual materials are available for loan. These are free for
teachers; for all others there is a $2 fee and $10 deposit. Bookstore.

DALLAS MUSEUM OF ART
**1717 North Harwood (75201), between Harwood and St. Paul
in the Arts District (DART Light Rail ST. PAUL Station)
922-1200 • Tuesday–Wednesday, Friday 11–4, Thursday 11–9,
Saturday–Sunday 11–5. Closed Monday, Thanksgiving,
Christmas, and New Year's Day • General Admission Free,
charge for special exhibitions • W +**

In 1984 the Arts District was born when this elegant museum
opened. The new facilities provided the Dallas Museum of Art
(DMA) with a large and impressive home for its significant collections of treasures from many cultures and disciplines it had
been gathering since 1903.

In the Art of the Americas collection, there are extensive examples from the lost civilizations of Aztec, Maya, Nasca, and
Anasazi, as well as noted 20th century artists such as Church, Sar-
gent, Happer, Benton, O'Keeffe, and Wyeth. Serving as the
anchor for the American collection is DMA's extensive holdings
in American gold objects, stone sculpture, ceramics, and textiles.
Art of Europe includes works by Monet, van Gogh, Gauguin,
Degas, Cézanne, and Vuillard. This collection also includes 20th
century works by Picasso, Giacometti, and Léger. The extensive
Arts of Africa collection includes Egyptian, Nubian, and sub-
Saharan sculpture and important masterworks by the Ibo, Luba,
Yoruba, and Senufo peoples. Arts of Asia and the Pacific features

beautiful examples from Southeast Asia, China, and decorative arts from the Japanese Meiji and Edo periods. This collection also contains Indonesian textiles and sculpture.

The pieces in the Contemporary Art collection trace the development from abstract expressionism through pop art to the present. One of the largest collections of post-1945 art in the Southwest, it includes masterpieces by Pollock, Johns, Rothko, Stella, and Warhol. One of the notable components of this collection is the range of works created by Texas artists.

Of special interest is The Reves collection, in the Decorative Arts wing, which is a unique showcase for important works by Renoir, Toulouse-Lutrec, Redon, and others, as well as English silver, Chinese porcelain, and original painting and correspondence from Sir Winston Churchill, all in a setting patterned after the French Riviera villa of the Reves, who donated the collection. A portion of the DMA's sculpture collection is on exhibit in the Sculpture Garden, which is divided into galleries by a series of waterfalls. The DMA also hosts some of the world's most significant and exclusive traveling exhibitions, usually three each year.

A number of tours and talks are given by both docents and staff. The most frequent free tours are given Tuesday–Friday at 1 p.m. and Saturday–Sunday at 2. Check for times of the others. Thursday evenings there is live music, art talks, and even the special exhibitions are free after 5 p.m. Free art activities for children on Saturdays. In the GTE Collections Information Center, visitors can use computer workstations to view images from the DMA, read short essays about artists and their works, and even print out a color image of a DMA masterpiece to take home. Museum store.

There are two restaurants in the DMA. Seventeen-Seventeen is an upstairs and upscale dining room open for lunch Tuesday–Sunday 11–2 and occasionally for dinner, even after the museum is closed. (Information and Reservations 922-1260.) The more casual Atrium Cafe is open for lunch every day the DMA is open and also for dinner on Thursday evening. Parking in the underground garage ($2). Access from either Harwood or St. Paul streets.

DALLAS MUSEUM OF NATURAL HISTORY
See FAIR PARK, p. 79.

DOLLHOUSE MUSEUM OF THE SOUTHWEST
2208 Routh Street (75201), three blocks east of McKinney 969-5502 • Tuesday–Saturday 10–4:30, Sunday 1–4. Closed Monday and major holidays • Adults $4, seniors and children under 12 $2

One of the dollhouses on display here is of a captain's coastal Victorian home, so it's appropriate that this museum is itself located in a Victorian style house from the 1920s. Included among the more than a dozen historically authentic miniature houses on display are a 1900s New York townhouse, a Texas farm, an English bakery, and a 16th century French armorer's shop. Miniature furnishings created by regional professional designers include clocks that can be wound and musical instruments that can be played. Also displays of antique toys and dolls. Gift shop.

FRONTIERS OF FLIGHT MUSEUM
Love Field at Terminal LB-18 (75235) Cedar Springs at Mockingbird Lane • 350-1651 • Monday–Saturday 10–5, Sunday 1–5 • Tours: Adults $2, children under 12 $1

The exhibits here take the visitor through the history of flight from Greek mythology through man's first balloon flights to the Space Shuttle. The collection includes photographs, models, uniforms, and vintage airplane parts. Memorabilia include a radioman's chair from the ill-fated dirigible *Hindenburg*. Parking tickets from the terminal garage can be validated for a discount.

INTERNATIONAL MUSEUM OF CULTURES
7500 West Camp Wisdom Road (75236), west of Clark Road, on campus of the International Linguistics Center • 972-709-2406 Tuesday–Friday 10–5, Saturday–Sunday 1:30–5. Closed Monday Tour: Adults $2, children $1 • W (Access on south side)

The goal of this museum is to increase understanding of cultural diversity. It does it through both life-size and miniature exhibits depicting the lives of culturally diverse people living today all around the world. For example, in one section progressive exhibits tell the life story of a Peruvian native boy from birth to retirement. Exhibits change about every six months.

The museum is affiliated with the **International Linguistics Center** next door. Less than half the world's 5,000-plus languages are in writing and this is the international headquarters of the Wycliffe Bible Society, which trains linguists to work with remote native populations to establish a written language and teach the people to read and write it. Wycliffe linguists have made more than 450 translations of the Bible. A one-hour guided tour is conducted Tuesday–Friday at 10 a.m. (Suggested donation adults $2, children $1.) A free ½ hour cassette tour is also available at other times. Call for details (709-2427).

MCKINNEY AVENUE CONTEMPORARY
3120 McKinney Avenue (75204) • 953-1212 • W +

This gallery provides exhibition space as part of its interdisciplinary program of art exhibitions, theater performances (in The MAC), concerts, and lectures to showcase the latest developments in all media.

OLD CITY PARK HISTORIC VILLAGE
1717 Gano Street (75215), between Harwood and Ervay Streets, just south of I-30 • 421-5141 • Tuesday–Saturday 10–4, Sunday 12–4. Buildings closed Monday, but grounds open • Adults $5, seniors $4, children 3–12 $2. Family maximum $12 • W Variable

Step into the past in Texas as you stroll the red brick streets and visit more than 35 historic structures that illustrate how people lived in North Texas between 1840 and 1910. All the structures have been moved to this 13-acre park from their original sites and meticulously restored. In addition to visiting places like the general store, the bank, a log cabin, a Southern colonial mansion, and the Victorian parlors of the George House and Hotel, you can watch the blacksmith, printer, and potter recreate their wares. The park is operated by the Dallas County Heritage Society, which sponsors several special events and festival during the year including Candlelight at Old City Park on several weekends during the

Christmas season. Gift shop. Brent Place, a restaurant in an 1876 farmhouse, offers lunch daily (Reservations 421-3057). Limited parking inside park. Ample free parking across Gano Street.

MEADOWS MUSEUM OF ART
Owens Fine Arts Center, SMU Campus, Bishop Blvd. and Binkley Avenue (75275) • 768-2516 • Monday–Tuesday, Friday–Saturday 10–5, Thursday 10–8, Sunday 1–5. Closed Wednesday and most holidays • Free ($3 donations suggested) W +

During business trips to Spain in the 1950s, Texas oil financier and philanthropist Algur H. Meadows was so impressed by the spectacular collection of Spanish masterpieces in Madrid's Prado Museum that he began his own collection of Spanish Art. In 1962, as part of a $35 million endowment, he donated his collection to SMU. As a result, this museum houses one of the finest and most comprehensive collections of Spanish art outside of Spain and the premier collection of Spanish art in the United States. The 670 objects in the permanent collection include major works dating from the Middle Ages to the present, including masterpieces by some of Europe's greatest painters: Velázquez, Rivera, Zurbarán, Murillo, Goya, Miro, and Picasso. Highlights of the collection include Renaissance altarpieces, monumental baroque canvases, exquisite rococo oil sketches, polychrome wood sculptures, impressionist landscapes, modernist abstractions, and a comprehensive collection of the graphic works of Goya. Free public tours are offered from September through May on Sundays at 2 p.m. and selected Sundays during the summer. Group tours at other times can be arranged (fee).

Throughout the year, the Meadows Museum presents a series of public lectures, symposia, and gallery talks featuring university professors, visiting scholars and artists. It also hosts film series and concerts by local and international musicians. Call for details. Limited free parking is available on the west side of the Meadows School of Arts at Hillcrest and Binkley avenues. Additional parking is available on the east side of the campus in the W-5 lot on

Airline Road north of Mockingbird Lane and in the parking garage at the corner of Airline Road and East Binkley.

The Elizabeth Meadows Sculpture Garden (6100 Bishop) displays a collection of major works by such modern masters as Auguste Rodin, Aristide Maillol, Jacques Lipchitz, Henry Moore, David Smith, Claes Oldenburg, and Isamu Noguchi. Open seven days 8:30–5. Closed campus holidays.

The Gallery, located in SMU's **Hughes-Trigg Student Center** (3140 Dyer Street at Ownby Drive), is a showcase for the works of students of the Meadows School of Arts. It also offers contemporary work by regional, national, and international artists; and historical work from all cultures in precisely focused, academically curated exhibitions. The Gallery is open Monday–Tuesday, Friday 10–5; Thursday 11–5, Saturday–Sunday 1–5. Closed Wednesday and most holidays. Admission is free. Parking is available in the lot north of Boaz Hall at Binkley Avenue and Ownby Drive.

THE SCIENCE PLACE AND TI FOUNDERS IMAX® THEATER
See FAIR PARK, p. 79.

THE SIXTH FLOOR MUSEUM
411 Elm Street (75202) at Houston in the West End District (DART Light Rail WEST END Station) • 653-6666 or 653-6659
Open seven days 9–6. Closed Christmas Day • Adults $5, seniors $4, students 12–18 $3, children 6-11 $2, under 6 free
W + Access on north side of building
The original corner window from which Oswald allegedly fired the shots that killed President John F. Kennedy is now encased in glass as one of the many exhibits that examine JFK's life, times, death, and legacy. The Kennedy family did not want this site memorialized, and the people of Dallas surely wanted to put this dark period in the city's history behind them. But every day people came to the assassination site to retrace the motorcade route, explore the grassy knoll, and point to the corner window of "the sixth floor." Finally, it was decided it was better to provide a clear

and evenhanded historical presentation than to continue to hope the memories of the assassination would fade. Today this museum hosts close to half a million visitors annually.

Operated by the Dallas County Historical Foundation, the museum is located on the sixth floor of the Dallas County Administration Building (formerly the Texas School Book Depository), the location of the so-called "sniper's perch." JFK's life and death are illustrated through the use of nearly 400 photographs, 45 minutes of documentary film, and other interpretive artifacts and material. Among the exhibits are a large scale model of Dealey Plaza prepared by the FBI for the Warren Commission in 1964, and an exhibit of over a dozen still and movie cameras that were used to record the events of November 22, 1963. These include the amateur movie camera used by Abraham Zapruder, the only camera to record the entire assassination. For additional insight on how people still recall this tragic event several decades later, read (and write in) the Memory Books.

Audio tour tapes are available in English and six foreign languages for a small additional fee. There is also a special audio tour tape for children 6-11. Museum store. Pay parking lots to the north and west of the building usually charge $2–$3.

(*Note:* For a differing view of the JFK assassination, see THE CONSPIRACY MUSEUM, in OFFBEAT, p. 132.)

TELEPHONE PIONEER MUSEUM OF TEXAS
One Bell Plaza, 208 South Akard Street (75202) at Commerce
464-4359 • Free • W (elevator)

Access to the upper floors of this building is restricted to employees; however, there is a special elevator that only goes to this second floor museum. Here you'll find the story of the past, present, and future of telephone technology told in a number of interactive audiovisual displays. A map brochure available at the entrance leads you through a self-paced tour. Exhibits include a life-size mannequin of Alexander Graham Bell and dioramas of the people behind the scenes who make your telephone work today. A theater presentation sums it all up. Little kids will enjoy the talking bear and the huge talking telephone. Usually open

Tuesday–Friday during business hours, but best to call for precise open times. Gift shop.

TRAMMELL CROW CENTER
2001 Ross (75201) at Harwood, in the Arts District (DART Light Rail PEARL Station) • 979-6348 • W + But not all areas
The gardens surrounding this 50-story office building feature more than 20 pieces of 19th and 20th century bronze sculptures by such artists as Rodin and Maillol. In addition, more than 10,000 square feet of exhibition space inside the building is used for art exhibitions.

SPECIAL GARDENS

DALLAS ARBORETUM AND BOTANICAL GARDENS
8525 Garland Road (75218), on eastern shore of White Rock Lake • 327-8263 • Open seven days March–October 10–6, November–February 10–5. Closed Thanksgiving, Christmas and New Year's Day • Adults $6, seniors $5, children 6–12 $3, five and under free. Parking $2 • W Variable (Transportation for the mobility impaired and wheelchairs available for loan free)
In the early 1930s Everette Lee DeGolyer, an active community leader, started a search for a site for Dallas's first arboretum. Fifty years later, his plans for a botanical preserve became a reality on the land he had willed to Southern Methodist University, which was purchased by the city expressly for the garden. DeGolyer's 44-acre gift combined with the neighboring 22-acre Camp Estate, purchased by the Dallas Arboretum and Botanical Society, now constitute this arboretum on the eastern shore of White Rock Lake.

Twenty-five acres are devoted to ornamental gardens and 41 acres to natural woodlands, creating an oasis in the heart of one of Dallas' oldest neighborhoods. The **Lay Ornamental Garden,** also known as Mimi's Garden, offers two acres of perennials in an English-style garden. It was designed to use native Texas plants and others adapted to local conditions. The **Jonsson Color Garden** offers an almost six-acre display of over 15,000 chrysanthemums each fall and one of the nation's largest azalea collections, more than 2,500 varieties, in bloom each spring. The **Palmer Fern Dell** features shade-loving ferns and rhododendrons that are kept cool with a periodic micro-mist fog. The **Hunt Paseo de Flores** is a quarter-mile linear garden. The **Woman's Garden,** the newest in the arboretum, is set on a site that features a series of terraced walkways and garden spaces aligned to enhance views of the lake.

A major attraction is the **DeGolyer House,** which is on the National Register of Historic Places and, along with the smaller **Camp House,** is one of the two historic homes on the grounds. Completed in 1940, the one-story house encompasses 13 rooms and 7 baths in 21,000 square feet. It was the first in Dallas to be built with central air-conditioning. The 4.5 acres of gardens surrounding the house boast a magnolia allee, a rose garden, fountains, and hundreds of annuals. Tours of the home are given on a regular schedule.

Special events are held every season with the major one being Dallas Blooms, held for about a month in the spring when more than 200,000 flowering bulbs color the gardens. In fall there is the colorful Autumn at the arboretum, and the holiday season, from late November through late December, brings Christmas at the arboretum. About 300,000 visitors tour the arboretum annually. Gift shop. Picnic area.

DALLAS HORTICULTURAL CENTER
See FAIR PARK, p. 79.

OUTDOORS

DALLAS NATURE CENTER
7171 Mountain Creek Parkway (75249), southwest near Joe Pool Lake. Take Mountain Creek exit off I-20 then south 972-296-1955 • Open seven days, 7 a.m. to sunset • Free • W Visitor Center

Part of this 360-acre wilderness preserve sits on the escarpment that runs from north of Dallas south almost to Austin making it the highest point in Dallas County and offering great views of Joe

Pool Lake. It is the habitat for a wide variety of native wildlife and wildflowers and other plants. Facilities include a butterfly garden, seven miles of hiking trails, picnic areas, and a visitor center. The center is a bird-of-prey rescue facility.

DALLAS PARKS

Park and Recreation Department, City Hall, 1500 Marilla (75201) (DART Light Rail CONVENTION CENTER Station) 670-4100, For activities in Dallas parks 670-7070

If you want to get away from it all, the Park and Recreation Department has just the places for you. This department maintains more than 20,000 park acres including 17 lakes with 4,400 surface acres of water, and more than 50 miles of jogging and bike trails at 25 locations. It provides leisure, recreational, and cultural activities at 406 neighborhood, community, and regional parks; 251 tennis courts, 227 play sets, 127 soccer fields, 127 multipurpose courts, 97 softball diamonds and 28 baseball diamonds, 78 neighborhood and 23 community swimming pools, 42 recreation centers, 41 football fields, 6 golf courses and 2 golf driving ranges, and 5 tennis centers. In addition, its facilities include the Dallas Aquarium, Dallas Arboretum, Dallas Horticulture Center, Dallas Zoo, Fair Park, and Samuell Farm.

The following are a few of its larger parks and the facilities in each. All are open from 6 a.m. to midnight and admission is free.

BACHMAN LAKE PARK
3500 Northwest Hwy. (75220), Take Northwest Hwy. (Loop 12) exit off I-35E (Stemmons Fwy.) and go east

Fishing is permitted in 205-acre Bachman Lake, which is ringed by a roller skating and jogging track. Other facilities include picnic tables with grills, multipurpose fields, a soccer field, and playground. A concession rents paddle boats. Free parking off Lakefield Dr. and Northwest Hwy. This is also the location of the **Bachman Recreation Center** (2750 Bachman Dr. 75220. 670-6266), which offers facilities and programs designed to meet the needs and interests of persons with disabilities aged 6 and up.

The 42,000-square-foot center is staffed by therapeutic recreation professionals. Facilities include a 25-meter pool, hot tub, full gymnasium, weight room, arts and crafts room, and a theater. A fishing pier is located on the lake adjacent to the building.

FAIR OAKS PARK
7600 Fair Oaks (75231), between Park Lane and Walnut Hill/Kingsley

This 234-acre park has a variety of courts, diamonds, and sports fields, 16 lighted tennis courts, a one-mile hard surfaced trail, and picnic areas. Its hike and bike trail is part of the 10-mile trail that starts at White Rock Lake, goes through Fair Oaks, and ends at Belt Line and Coit.

L. B. HOUSTON PARK AND NATURE TRAIL
California Crossing at Wildwood • Located along the Dallas side of the Elm Fork of the Trinity River, south of Northwest Hwy.

Most of this 476-acre wilderness preserve has remained undisturbed for hundreds of years. As a result, it is a jewel for nature lovers and bird watchers. Facilities include 4 miles of soft-surface and 4 miles of hard surface trails, and well over 100 picnic tables. It is also the site of the L. B. Houston Tennis Center, which has 12 lighted courts.

KIEST PARK
3080 South Hampton Road (75224)

Among the facilities in this 258-acre park are a neighborhood swimming pool, a number of varied sports courts and fields, more than two miles of hard surface trail, and picnic areas. Facilities at The Recreation Center (2324 W. Kiest Blvd.) include 16 tennis courts. Free parking in lots located off Hampton Road and Rugged Dr.

HARRY MOSS PARK
8000 Greenville (75243) at Royal, Take I-75 (Central Expressway) north to Royal Lane, then east to Greenville

Facilities in this 284-acre park include play areas, multipurpose fields, soccer fields, and a 1¼-mile hard surface trail.

WHITE ROCK LAKE PARK
8300 Garland Road (75218)

Its 1,873-acres surround the lake. Facilities include an 11-mile hike and bike trail that follows the water's edge most of the way, play areas, and a variety of sports fields, and more than 200 picnic tables. The **Bath House Cultural Center,** a meeting, exhibition, and performance space is located in the park on the east side. The Dallas Arboretum and Botanical Gardens adjoins the park on the east. Paddleboats can be rented on the west side of the lake. Canoes and sailboats are permitted on the lake. Free parking lots in the park.

COLLEGES AND UNIVERSITIES

DALLAS COUNTY COMMUNITY COLLEGE DISTRICT
Headquarters 701 Elm Street (75202) • 860-2135 • W

In 1966 the district's first college, El Centro, began operation in the downtown central business district with more than 4,000 students. Today it is a comprehensive two-year system comprising seven campuses throughout the county enrolling nearly 50,000 students in credit courses leading to associate degrees and a similar number of non-credit students each semester, making it the largest undergraduate institution in Texas and among the six largest community college systems in the nation. The district also operates a job training and business services center and a center for educational telecommunications. Most of the campuses offer visitors student theatre, dance, art, and photographic exhibitions.

Two of the seven campuses of this county community college district are in the city of Dallas.

EL CENTRO COLLEGE
Main & Lamar (75202) (DART Light Rail WEST END Station) • 860-2037

This college is housed in the downtown Dallas site of the completely renovated nine-story historic Sanger Brothers Department Store Building built in 1919 (see HISTORIC PLACES, above). Visitors are welcome at the Food and Hospitality Service Department's lunch on Wednesday and dinner on Thursday. The five-course meals are prepared by the students in the nationally acclaimed culinary arts program. The cost is $6 per person. Performances at the college theatre include occasional children's theatre productions (978-0110).

MOUNTAIN VIEW COLLEGE
4849 West Illinois Avenue (75211) • 860-8680
Started in 1970 as the second of the district's seven campuses, it is located on 200 acres in the southwestern section of the city. The college's long horizontal buildings gracefully blend in with the campus' attractive natural environment of rocky ravines, native plants and trees, and a central creek. Two glassed-in pedestrian bridges connect the east and west complexes and provide a spectacular view of the area. Among the college's programs is the two-year course at the Performing Arts Musical Theatre Conservatory. Students are admitted by audition only and put on live theater performances throughout the year. Call for performance information.

SOUTHERN METHODIST UNIVERSITY (SMU)
Hillcrest Avenue between Mockingbird Lane and Daniel Avenue (75275) • 768-2000 • W Variable
Dallas' oldest and most prestigious university, SMU was founded in 1911 and opened to students in 1915. When the University opened, it consisted of two buildings, a 35-member faculty and 706 students. Today its 163-acre campus of red brick buildings has grown up around the neoclassical style of one of those original buildings, Dallas Hall, named in appreciation of the city's support. SMU now has a full-time faculty of close to 500 and serves about 9,500 students with 68 undergraduate degree programs, 42 master's programs, 18 doctoral programs, 18 professional degrees, and 5 certificate programs. The divisions of the university are the Dedman College of Humanities and Sciences, Meadows School of the Arts, the School of Engineering and Applied Science, Edwin L. Cox School of Business, Perkins

School of Theology, and the SMU School of Law. The university is owned by the South Central Jurisdiction of the United Methodist Church; however, from its founding, SMU has been nonsectarian in its teaching.

Visitors may park in the W-5 lot south of Dedman Center, the parking garage at SMU Blvd. and Airline Road, the visitor parking area between the Cox School of Business and Boaz Hall, the visitors' area at Ownby Stadium, spaces west of the Hamon Arts Library and Greer Garson Theatre on Hillcrest, and the spaces on University Blvd. north of Perkins Administration Building. Occasionally some lots may be designated for special event parking. Call SMU Department of Public Safety for information, 768-3388.

SMU is a rich center of cultural activity for Dallas with museum offerings, visual and performing arts productions, and lecture series. Its intercollegiate sports programs are also highly popular.

The premier cultural center on campus is the **Meadows School of Arts/Owens Fine Art Center Complex** at Bishop Blvd. and Binkley Avenue on the west side of the campus (768-3510). The major attraction here is the **Meadows Museum of Art,** which houses one of the finest collections of Spanish art outside of Spain (see MUSEUMS AND ART GALLERIES, p. 91). In addition, approximately 400 public arts events are held in the school and fine arts complex each year including eight major theatre productions, two dance productions, six to eight special exhibitions; and opera, symphony, choral, wind ensemble and organ concerts. Performance facilities include the **Bob Hope Theatre, Greer Garson Theatre, Margo Jones Theatre, Caruth Auditorium, Charles S. Sharp Performing Arts Studio,** and **O'Donnell Lecture/ Recital Hall.** (See MUSIC AND PERFORMING ARTS, p. 109.)

More than 100 public lectures are given each year in **McFarlin Auditorium,** Hillcrest Avenue and McFarlin Blvd., as well as in several of the schools. These provide opportunities to hear outstanding speakers in diverse fields including national and international figures, some of SMU's leading faculty members, and outstanding academicians from all over the world. Some of these are free and some, like the Willis M. Tate Distinguished Lecture

SOUTHERN METHODIST UNIVERSITY

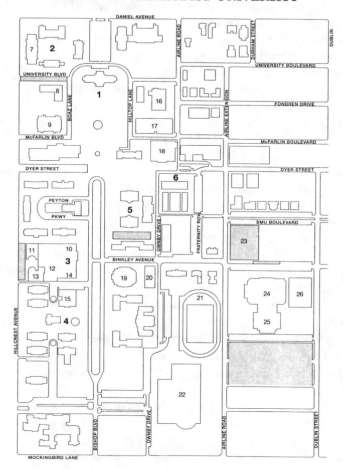

Schools
1. Dedman College
2. School of Law
3. Meadows School of the Arts
4. Perkins School of Theology
5. Edwin L. Cox School of Business
6. School of Engineering and Applied Science

Points of Interest
7. Underwood Law Library
8. Perkins Administration Building
9. McFarlin Memorial Auditorium
10. Meadows Museum
11. Greer Garson Theatre
12. Bob Hope Theatre
13. Jake and Nancy Hamon Arts Library
14. Caruth Auditorium
15. Bridwell Library
16. Science Information Center
17. Fondren Library
18. Hughes-Trigg Student Center
19. Joe Perkins Natatorium
20. A.R. Barr Pool
21. Morrison-Bell Track
22. Ownby Stadium
23. Parking Garage
24. Moody Coliseum
25. Dedman Center for Lifetime Sports
26. Haggar Tennis Stadium

Visitor Parking

Series, have an admission fee. For information call the SMU Lecture Programs Office (768-8283).

More than 2.9 million volumes are housed in the six general and special libraries on campus. All the libraries put on special exhibitions based on their holdings at various times and some have limited access arrangements for non-students.

SMU Mustang teams compete in most major intercollegiate sports in season. For information and schedules on all intercollegiate sports, call the SMU Sports and Information Office, 768-2883. For tickets call 768-GAME (768-4263).

The SMU Mustang football team is part of the 16-member Western Athletic Conference. Home football games are held at the **Cotton Bowl Stadium** in Fair Park. Pay parking is available on the Fair Park grounds.

With the exception of its golf teams, most of the other sports events are held on campus. Men's and women's basketball and women's volleyball are held at **Moody Coliseum,** 6024 Airline Road at Binkley Avenue. Men's and women's tennis matches are held in the **Haggar Tennis Stadium,** 3005 Binkley Avenue at Dublin Street. Men's and women's swimming & diving events are held at the **Joe Perkins Natatorium,** 6024 Bishop Blvd. at Binkley Avenue. Men's and women's track & field meets are held at the **Morrison-Bell Track,** 6001 Airline Road between Mockingbird Lane and Binkley Avenue. Men's and women's soccer matches are held at **Westcott Field,** 6001 Airline Road between Mockingbird Lane and Binkley Avenue.

All of these campus sports facilities are in the southeast corner of the campus and all have access for the disabled. Parking is available in the W-5 lot located along Airline Road north of Mockingbird Lane, and in the parking garage at the corner of Airline Road and Binkley Avenue. Parking fees vary by event.

MUSIC AND PERFORMING ARTS

The Dallas Morning News Arts and Entertainment Hotline 522-2659. Dallas Convention & Visitors Bureau Events Hotline 746-6679.

ARTTIX (871-ARTS, 871-2787), a centralized, non-profit ticketing service, handles ticket sales for a number of local arts and cultural organizations.

THEATERS AND OTHER PERFORMANCE SPACES

BOOKER T. WASHINGTON HIGH SCHOOL FOR THE PERFORMING AND VISUAL ARTS
2501 Flora Avenue (75201) (DART Light Rail PEARL Station) 720-7300 • W

The two performance theaters in this school across from the Dallas Theater Center are used for plays and concerts by the talented students who had to pass a screening to be selected for enrollment. In addition to emphasis on academic excellence, the school trains the students in dance, music, theatre, and the visual arts. Call for schedule.

BRONCO BOWL
2600 Fort Worth Avenue (75211) • 943-1777 W + (But not all areas)

The 3,000-seat arena with a state-of-the-art sound and lighting system hosts concerts by top entertainers and Broadway-style shows. (This eclectic entertainment complex also offers a nightclub with dancing, bowling, billiards, and a games arcade.)

COTTON BOWL STADIUM
See FAIR PARK, p. 79.

DALLAS CONVENTION CENTER
650 South Griffin (75202) (DART Light Rail CONVENTION CENTER Station) • 658-7000 • W + (But not all areas)

When it isn't being used for conventions—and Dallas ranks near the top of the convention cities in the nation—this center's arena and theater are used for live theater and concerts by visiting artists. This is the home of the Junior Black Academy (658-7144), which uses the center theaters for its theatrical and dance productions and the other facilities for its art exhibits.

DALLAS THEATER CENTER/ARTS DISTRICT THEATER
2401 Flora (75201) (DART Light Rail PEARL Station)
522-8499 • W Call ahead

Located across Artists Square from The Meyerson, this theater is designed to meet the needs of each production in relation to the interaction between the actors and the audience with one of the most flexible arrangements for seating and staging in the nation.

DALLAS THEATER CENTER/KALITA HUMPHREYS THEATER
3626 Turtle Creek Blvd. (75219) • 526-8210 • W (Call ahead)

This theater building was the only theater and one of the last buildings designed by Frank Lloyd Wright. Its square boxes and circular core are reminiscent of Wright's design of the Guggenheim Museum in New York City, which he did about the same time. The theater hosts a full season of professional theater productions ranging from the classics to musical comedies. Volunteer guides are frequently available to conduct tours, but you have to call ahead and make an appointment.

FAIR PARK MUSIC HALL
See FAIR PARK, p. 79.

MAJESTIC THEATRE
1925 Elm (75201) (DART Light Rail PEARL Station)
880-0137 • W +

This 1,648-seat theater frequently hosts touring concerts and a Broadway show series as well as dance productions by local groups. (See also HISTORIC PLACES, p. 87.)

MCFARLIN MEMORIAL AUDITORIUM
**SMU campus, McFarlin Blvd. and Hillcrest Avenue (75275)
768-3129 • W +**

SMU's largest performance facility hosts year-round activities including classical music concerts, the Willis M. Tate Distinguished Lecture Series, dance performances, screenings, and plays. Concerts and dance performances by internationally acclaimed artists and groups are also held here under the sponsorship of **The International Theatrical Arts Society (TITAS).** For information on TITAS performances call 528-5566. (For parking information, see COLLEGES AND UNIVERSITIES/ SMU, p. 104.)

MORTON H. MEYERSON SYMPHONY CENTER
2301 Flora Street (75201) at Pearl (DART Light Rail PEARL Station) • 629-0203 • W +

The musical centerpiece of the Dallas Arts District is home of the Dallas Symphony Orchestra, the Dallas Wind Symphony, and the Turtle Creek Chorale. Opened in 1989, the 2,062-seat center was named by its principal donor, H. Ross Perot, after one of his top assistants. This is the only symphony center designed by the internationally known architect I. M. Pei. It has won acclaim for both its architectural significance and its acoustics. One of the features of the center is the hand-built $2 million, 4,535-pipe Fisk Organ, one of the largest mechanical-action organs ever built for a concert hall. It is played on four manual keyboards, each with 61 notes, and a pedal keyboard with 32 notes. Call about tours.

MOUNTAIN VIEW COLLEGE PERFORMING ARTS MUSICAL THEATRE
(See COLLEGES AND UNIVERSITIES/Dallas County Community College District, p. 104.)

PEGASUS THEATER
3916 Main Street (75226) • 821-6005 • W +

This small professional theater located in Deep Ellum specializes in original and offbeat comedies with productions year-round. Tickets about $12–$15.

POCKET SANDWICH THEATER
5400 East Mockingbird (75206) • 821-1860
A neighborhood theater known locally for professional-quality productions of all types of plays, but with a leaning toward comedies and melodramas. Its Christmas season production of "Scrooge" has earned the status of being a city tradition. The sandwich in the name may have come from the sandwiches (and beer, wine, etc.) for sale that you can enjoy during the performance.

REUNION ARENA
777 Sport Street (75207)(DART Light Rail UNION Station)
939-2770 • W +
When it's not being used by the Dallas Mavericks, the Dallas Burn, or Dallas Stars, or for other sports events, this 15,520-seat arena is the frequent site of major pop and country concerts, theatrical events, and even the circus. And there isn't a bad seat in the house. Events Line 670-1395.

SAMMONS CENTER FOR THE ARTS
3630 Harry Hines (75219) • 520-7788 • W
The performance spaces here include a hall with performance seating for up to 260 and recital halls. One popular series given here is Sammons Jazz featuring local jazz artists in a relaxed setting for nominal prices. The facilities are also used for rehearsals and workshops by dozens of local music, arts, and cultural organizations. This multi-use facility is also known as a nonprofit arts incubator providing an office home for more than a dozen emerging and midsized nonprofit arts organizations. The building is the converted Turtle Creek Pump Station, which is the oldest public building in Dallas, completed in 1909 and the sole source of water for the City of Dallas until 1930.

SMU THEATERS AND PERFORMANCE SPACES
In addition to **McFarlin Memorial Auditorium** (see p. 111), the following are all located in the **Meadows School of the Arts** building, Bishop Blvd. at Binkley Avenue. SMU-ARTS (768-2787). Events include classical concerts, musicals, lectures, films,

plays, seminars and other school functions. Most productions are presented by SMU students and faculty during the academic year. (For parking information, see COLLEGES AND UNIVERSI-TIES/SMU, p. 104.)

Bob Hope Theatre: A 390-seat proscenium stage theatre that features an assortment of events including dance, opera, theatre productions, and film screenings.

Greer Garson Theatre: A 386-seat thrust stage theatre offering theatrical performances.

Margo Jones Theatre: A 125-seat black box theatre offering theatrical events.

Caruth Auditorium: A 490-seat concert hall housing the Fisk Opus 101 pipe organ. A variety of Meadows School of the Arts and other music-related performances are given here.

STARPLEX AMPHITHEATER
See FAIR PARK, p. 79.

TEATRO DALLAS
2204 Commerce (75201) • 741-1135 • W

The works presented here reflect Dallas' rich Hispanic heritage with plays by classical and contemporary Latin American and Hispanic American playwrights. Also dance performances.

THEATRE THREE
2800 Routh Street (75201), in the Quadrangle • 871-3300 • W +

Theater-in-the-Round presenting year-round productions of a wide variety of plays, musical revues, and occasional children's theater.

DANCE

ANITA N. MARTINEZ BALLET FOLKLORICO
4422 Live Oak (75204) • 828-0181

A professional Hispanic dance company that puts on several performances each year. Call for schedule.

DALLAS BLACK DANCE THEATRE
2627 Flora Street (75221) • 871-2376

The 12 members of the city's oldest continuously operating dance company perform modern dance by well known choreographers. Performances are given at the Meyerson Center, the Majestic Theatre, and at other performance spaces in the city. The company has also performed in Washington D.C., Great Britain, and other places around the country and the world.

FORT WORTH DALLAS BALLET
696-3932

This is not a merger of the Fort Worth and Dallas ballet companies, as the name may imply, but rather an expansion of the performances of the professional Fort Worth Ballet to Dallas to fill in the void left when the Dallas Ballet was dissolved in 1988. Dallas performances are usually held at the Music Hall in Fair Park.

MUSIC

DALLAS BACH SOCIETY
P.O. Box 140201, 75214-0201

Not just Bach, but the full range of baroque and classical period music is performed under the auspices of this society. Its season runs from September–April with at least one performance each month, usually on a Saturday or Sunday. Performances are given in the Morton H. Meyerson Symphony Center, in several Dallas neighborhood churches, and in facilities in nearby Metroplex cities, such as the Mesquite Arts Center.

DALLAS CHAMBER ORCHESTRA
Sammons Center for the Arts, 3630 Harry Hines Blvd. (75219) (Office) • 520-3121

This group performs classic works from the 17th and 18th centuries. Concerts are European style—without a conductor. It usually performs eight concerts in its September–May season. Friday evening performances are given at the Episcopal Church of the Transfiguration, Hillcrest and Spring Valley; Sunday matinee and evening performances are at the Caruth Auditorium at Hillcrest and Binkley on the SMU campus. Individual tickets: Adults $17, Seniors $12, Students $10

DALLAS CLASSIC GUITAR SOCIETY
P.O. Box 190823, 75219 • 528-3733
   The greatest classical guitarists in the world have appeared in concert with the society, including: Andres Segovia, John Williams, Julian Bream, and Christopher Parkening. The society's season runs from September through April with at least one concert each month in two series: the International Series, featuring the best in the world, is held at the Morton H. Meyerson Symphony Center; and the Master Series, which showcases outstanding but lesser known international guitarists, is held at SMU's Caruth Auditorium. It also sponsors a series of concerts by emerging artists at the Dallas Museum of Art.

DALLAS JAZZ ORCHESTRA
P.O. Box 743875, 75374 • 644-8833
   A 20-piece big band that plays original and traditional big band jazz. It gives a spring and fall concert at the Meyerson Symphony Center and other performances around the city including free summer concerts on Sunday afternoons in various city parks.

DALLAS OPERA
The Centrum, 3102 Oak Lawn, Suite 450 (75219) (Office)
443-1043 (Tickets 443-1000)
   Nationally known, the Dallas Opera company has been staging the classics for more than 40 years. Its November–February season usually features five operas performed at Fair Park Music Hall. Single tickets range from $25 to $104.

DALLAS SYMPHONY ORCHESTRA
Morton H. Meyerson Symphony Center, 2301 Flora Street
(75201) at Pearl (DART Light Rail PEARL Station) • 871-4000
(Box Office 692-0203)
   When the calendar turns over to the year 2000, the Dallas Symphony will celebrate its 100th anniversary. The symphony pre-

sents a full schedule of programs from late August through May in its Classical and SuperPops Series featuring a wide variety of guest artists and conductors. Classical performances are usually Thursday–Saturday with a Sunday matinee. Pops concerts are Friday–Saturday evenings and Sunday matinees. It also performs during the summer in the parks and at various events including the International Summer Music Festival.

DALLAS WIND SYMPHONY
528-5576
The 45-piece orchestra is known as "America's Premier Windband" because it is the only professional civilian wind band active in the nation. Local concerts are given at The Meyerson. Call for schedule.

DALLAS PUBLIC LIBRARY AFTERNOON CONCERTS
1515 Young Street (75201) • 670-1700 • W +
Outstanding local musicians and singers are featured in these free concerts put on in the Main Library auditorium or in the Plaza outside on most Sundays at 3 p.m. every month except November–January. Parking is available in the library's underground garage. Call for schedule.

GREATER DALLAS YOUTH ORCHESTRA
Sammons Center for the Arts, 3630 Harry Hines Blvd.
(75219)(Office) • 528-7747
The Greater Dallas Youth Orchestra (GDYO) offers a continuum of musical education for young musicians, aged 5 through high school, who have been selected by competitive auditions. Members of the Dallas Symphony and other qualified professionals coach the students on a regular basis. The GDYO puts on four concerts a year in The Meyerson Symphony Center, including the annual "Side-by-Side" Concert with the Dallas Symphony. In addition, depending on age and training, the students may participate in one or more of another half dozen or so concerts as members of the Young Performers Orchestra, the Philharmonic Orchestra, or the Dallas String Ensemble, all of which give con-

certs in various locations in the city. Most concerts are free. Call for schedule.

SAMMONS JAZZ
Sammons Center for the Arts, 3630 Harry Hines Blvd. (75219) (Office) • 520-7788

This is the only regular on-going jazz performance series in the Metroplex featuring local jazz artists playing all forms of jazz from Swing to Be-Bop, from Dixieland to Fusion. The jazz sessions are held in Meadows Hall at the Sammons Center the first Wednesday of each month from 7 p.m. to 10 p.m. from February–December. Tickets $12–$16.

TURTLE CREEK CHORALE
Morton H. Meyerson Symphony Center, 2301 Flora Street (75201) at Pearl (DART Light Rail PEARL Station) • 526-3214

Bach to Broadway is the range of programs in the concerts offered by this 200-member male chorus. Most performances are in The Meyerson. Call for information.

THEATRE

DALLAS SUMMER MUSICALS
6013 Berkshire Lane (75225) (Office) • 691-7200

Every June–August since 1941, this nonprofit organization has brought national touring companies of Broadway shows to the Fair Park Music Hall. Ignoring the seasonal limits of its name, the organization also presents the State Fair Musical and other shows, ranging from Las Vegas style revues to drama, in the fall and winter. Tickets 373-8000.

DEEP ELLUM OPERA COMPANY
501 Second Avenue (75226), at Hickory • 823-2907

This company offers alternative theater. Its August–May season usually includes about seven shows running weekends for four weeks each. The company is located and performs at the Hickory Street Annex Theatre.

THE GRYPHON PLAYERS
526-1158
Classical works from Euripides to Shaw and the absurdist theatre of Beckett and Ionesco and others are the forte of this company, which uses a variety of performance spaces. Call for information.

KITCHEN DOG THEATRE
McKinney Avenue Contemporary (The MAC), 312 McKinney Avenue (75204)• 953-1055
Originally formed by students in SMU's Graduate Actor Training Program, this small company has evolved to be the resident company at The MAC. The ensemble is committed to producing works that challenge our moral and social consciences, both classic and original works. In keeping with this mission, the critically acclaimed Kitchen Dog has produced two world premiers, two American premiers, and five Southwestern premiers. They drew their name from Samuel Beckett's *Waiting for Godot.* Tickets $8–$12.

SHAKESPEARE FESTIVAL OF DALLAS
Sammons Center for the Arts, 3630 Harry Hines Blvd. (75219)(Office) • 559-2778
With more than a quarter of a century of productions behind it, this is the oldest free Shakespeare festival in the Southwest and the second oldest in the nation, giving up the oldest title only to New York City's festival. Each summer it presents two of The Bard's plays outdoors in Samuell-Grand Park Amphitheatre, 6200 East Grand. Cast with mostly professional actors, the performances are given Tuesday–Sunday evenings at 8:15 (gates open at 7:30) with the two plays rotating and each play given for three days each week for six weeks. Audiences average more than 60,000 each season. Bring a blanket or lawn chair, and insect repellent. In addition, during the rest of the year the nonprofit sponsoring organization offers the Shakespeare Festival of Dallas Spotlight Series, which features highly acclaimed actors performing their unique interpretation of Shakespeare's greatest works, usually in the Majestic Theatre.

FAMILY FUN AND KID STUFF

Note: For a comprehensive list of family fun and kid stuff we suggest getting a copy of Exploring Dallas with Children: A Guide for Family Activities *by Kay McCasland Threadgill (Republic of Texas Press, 1996, $12.95).*

DALLAS AQUARIUM
See FAIR PARK, above.

DALLAS CHILDREN'S THEATER
Crescent Theater, 2215 Cedar Springs (75201) at Maple
978-0110 • W
Most of the productions put on by this professional company are family oriented, rather than strictly for children. While offering excitement, fun, and adventure for the whole family with about a dozen productions a year, they frequently deal with serious subjects with plays such as *To Kill a Mockingbird.* Performances are given both at the Crescent Theater and the El Centro College Theater at Main and Market, downtown. Tickets for most shows cost about $11 for adults and $9 for children 3–18. Crescent Theater parking is available across the street under The Crescent Shops. El Centro parking is on the street or in downtown parking lots.

DALLAS THEATER CENTER TEEN/CHILDREN'S THEATRE
Kalita Humphreys Theater, 3636 Turtle Creek (75219)
526-8210 • W (Call ahead)
Children's classics are the favorites among the several productions this company puts on each year. The teens and children in the productions are from the Dallas Theater Center's own theater school, which trains young people from ages ranging from about 4 to 19.

DALLAS PUPPET THEATRE
2266 Valley View Center (75240) • 972-716-0230 • W
This company of puppeteers puts on about a half dozen shows a year, mostly lighthearted adaptations of the classic children's

stories. Shows are aimed at the youngster so they are put on weekend afternoons and rarely last more than an hour. They also feature an adult series and an annual production of *A Christmas Carol.*

DALLAS WORLD AQUARIUM
1801 North Griffin (75202) in the West End District • 720-2224 Seven days 10–5. Closed Thanksgiving and Christmas • Adults $5, Seniors and children 3–12 $3 • W +

There are more than 80,000 gallons of seawater in the numerous large aquarium tanks here that include a 22,000 gallon walk-through tunnel tank. Each tank represents a different dive destination ranging from British Columbia to Fiji, and each teems with marine life indigenous to that part of the world. Exhibits in this privately-owned aquarium include bonnet head sharks, stingrays, cuttlefish, seadragons, jellyfish, giant groupers, and a vast assortment of colorful smaller fish that live in the reefs. Also featured are blackfooted penguins in an outdoor exhibit. There is a feeding at one of the exhibits every half-hour from 11 to 4:30. Educational films shown in banquet area upstairs unless closed for a scheduled event. Audio tape tours $2. Restaurant open for lunch. Gift shop.

DALLAS ZOO
650 South R.L. Thornton Frwy. (I-35E) (75203), about 3 miles south of downtown, from I-35E take Marsalis exit and follow Zoo signs. (DART Light Rail ZOO Station) • 670-8626 (Office), 670-5656 (Recording) • Seven days 9–5 (can stay until 6) Adults $5, seniors $4, children 3–11 $2.50, under 3 free Parking $3 • W + But not all areas

More than 2,000 mammals, reptiles, amphibians, and birds representing 377 species live in this 100-acre park with many roaming freely in areas designed to be as close to their natural habitat as possible. Founded in 1888, this zoo is still developing and growing with at least one major new exhibit to be opened each year for the next few years.

The zoo is divided into two major areas: Zoo North and the Wilds of Africa.

Follow the walkways of **Zoo North** to get a close-up view of rhinos, giraffes, lions, tigers, ocelots, cheetahs, elephants, chimpanzees, red pandas, camels, llamas, wallabies, kangaroos, and many of the more than 700 birds in the zoo's collection. This area also features the Bird and Reptile Building with its renowned collection of nearly 120 reptile and amphibian species including Chinese alligators, which are in extreme danger of extinction, and the Rainforest Aviary, where you can watch brightly colored exotic birds fly all around you. Another highlight of Zoo North is the Children's Zoo, where children can touch and pet smaller, domestic animals, as well as learn how to be responsible pet owners.

The 25-acre **Wilds of Africa,** one of the more popular exhibits, features the six major habitats of Africa. This is the first zoo exhibit in the world to include every major habitat of the entire continent and has been named as the best African zoo exhibit in the country. Within the exhibit, bush, desert, forest, woodland, river, and mountain environments allow some 86 species of birds and mammals to dwell in surroundings that accurately mimic their native habitats. Some of these are mandrill baboons, bongos, zebras, the rare okapi, storks, klipspringers, and lowland gorillas. Much of the exhibit can be seen from the walking trail, but to see it all take the Monorail Safari ($1.50 for age 3 and up). This specially designed monorail is the only one in the U.S. that is engineered to climb and turn. The cars are open on the side facing the exhibit so all have a good view. Live narration is given during the 20-minute ride, which covers one mile.

Restaurants, picnic areas, and gift shop. Strollers, including doubles, can be rented.

MALIBU FUN CENTER & MALIBU GRAND PRIX
**11130 and 11150 Malibu Drive (75229), take Walnut Hill Ln.
exit off Stemmons Frwy. (I-35E) and go west to Malibu Dr.
620-7576 (Fun Center), 247-5318 (Grand Prix) • Open seven
days, call for hours • Admission free, pay by the game**

This side-by-side entertainment complex includes four miniature golf courses, batting cages, video games, bumper boats, and scaled down racing cars sized for both adults and children 8 and up.

MODEL TRAIN EXHIBIT
**Dallas Children's Medical Center, 1935 Motor Street (75235), between Stemmons Frwy. (I-35E) and Harry Hines Blvd.
640-2000 • Open seven days 5:30 a.m.–10 p.m. • Free • W +**

The largest permanent model train exhibit in the U.S. is in the lobby of this children's medical center. As you enter, you see this $400,000 train exhibit in which eight trains run simultaneously over more than 1,000 feet of track that winds around models of some of America's most famous landmarks including Mount Rushmore, the Grand Canyon, and even the Dallas skyline. For a bird's-eye view go to the second floor observation area. The exhibit is free, but parking costs $1.50 for the first hour.

VIRTUAL WORLD
**9330 North Central Expressway (75231) at Park Ln. in UA
Theatre Plaza • 265-9664**

In this digital playworld you can be the pilot controlling a 30-foot-tall walking tank or fly a souped-up hovercraft in a space race. Prices for the right to be a virtual warrior go from $7–$9. This gives you about 20 minutes game time that includes a mission briefing, about 10 minutes of cockpit time, and a mission review. Call for reservations.

SPORTS

BASKETBALL

DALLAS MAVERICKS
Reunion Arena, 777 Sports Street (75207) (DART Light Rail
UNION Station) • 939-2800 or 988-9365
An NBA franchise since 1980, the Mavericks play in Reunion
Arena from November through April. Tickets $9–$27.

BICYCLING

The city of Dallas maintains more than 500 miles of bike trails
all over the city. Bike trail maps are for sale at City Hall for about
$2 or by mail for $3.25. (City of Dallas, Department of Transportation, Room 5C-S, 1500 Marilla, 75201.) Most bike shops
also have the maps. Bachman and White Rock Lake areas have
the longest trails, and bike shops in those areas have rentals.

COLLEGE SPORTS

See COLLEGES AND UNIVERSITIES/SMU, p. 104.

FENCING

LONE STAR FENCING CENTER
2636 Walnut Hill Ln. (75229) • 352-3733
Coaching by a three-time Olympian is available. Call for information.

GOLF

PUBLIC COURSES

CEDAR CREST PARK GOLF COURSE
1800 Southerland (75203) • 670-7615 • 18-hole course. Green
fees: Weekdays $11, Weekends/holidays $14.

L.B. HOUSTON MUNICIPAL GOLF COURSE
11223 Luna Road (75229) • 972-670-6322 • 18-hole course.
Green fees: Weekdays $13, Weekends/holidays $16.

GROVER KEETON PARK GOLF COURSE
2323 Jim Miller Road (P.O. Box 17458, 75217) • 670-8784
18-hole course. Green fees: Weekdays $11, Weekends/holidays $14

LONE STAR GOLF CENTER
2101 Walnut Hill (75229) • 972-247-4653 • 9-hole par 3 public
course. Call for fees.

STEVENS PARK GOLF COURSE
1005 North Montclair (75208) • 670-7506 • 18-hole course.
Green fees: Weekdays $13, Weekends $16.

TENISON PARK GOLF COURSE
3501 Samuell Blvd. (75223) • 670-1402 • 36-hole course. Green
fees: Weekdays $13, Weekends/holidays $16.

PRIVATE AND SEMI-PRIVATE COURSES

Call for green fees.

BENT TREE COUNTRY CLUB
5201 Westgrove (75248) • 972-931-7326 • 18-hole course.

BROOKHAVEN COUNTRY CLUB
3333 Golfing Green Dr. (75234) • 972-241-2761 • 54-hole course.

BROOK HOLLOW GOLF CLUB
8306 Harry Hines Blvd. (75235) • 637-1914 • 18-hole course.

DALLAS ATHLETIC CLUB
4111 LaPrada (75228) • 972-279-6517 • 36-hole course.

DALLAS COUNTRY CLUB
4100 Beverly Dr. (75205) • 521-2151 • 18-hole course.

LAKEWOOD COUNTRY CLUB
6430 Gaston Avenue (75214) • 821-7690 • 18-hole course.

NORTHWOOD CLUB
6524 Alpha Road (75240) • 972-934-0544 • 18-hole course.

OAK CLIFF COUNTRY CLUB
2200 West Redbird Lane (75232) • 333-3595 • 18-hole course.

PRESTON TRAIL GOLF CLUB
17201 Preston Trail Dr. (75248) • 972-248-8448 • 18-hole course.

PRESTONWOOD COUNTRY CLUB (THE CREEK COURSE)
P.O. Box 796607, 75240 • 972-233-6166 • 18-hole course.

ROYAL OAKS COUNTRY CLUB
7915 Greenville Avenue (75231) • 691-0339 • 18-hole course.

SLEEPY HOLLOW GOLF AND COUNTRY CLUB
4747 South Loop 12 (75217) • 371-3433 • Thirty-six-holes; one course private, one course semi-private.

HOCKEY

DALLAS STARS
Reunion Arena, 777 Sports Street (75207) (DART Light Rail UNION Station) • 467-8277

The Stars play NHL Hockey at the Reunion Arena from September through April. Tickets $14–$57.50.

ICE SKATING

All skating rinks are open seven days. Call for hours.

AMERICA'S ICE GARDEN
Plaza of the Americas, 600 North Pearl (75201) (DART Light Rail PEARL Station) • 922-9800 • Open seven days

This rink is located in the atrium of the Plaza of the Americas office tower and hotel complex. The $7 admission includes skate rental. Validated parking available across street from rink at Pearl and San Jacinto.

DALLAS ON ICE
700 Munger Avenue (75202), between Market and Record (DART Light Rail WEST END Station) • 969-RINK (969-7465) Open seven days from Friday after Thanksgiving to end of February

Dallas' first outdoor ice rink offers public skating, live ice shows, and is used as a practice rink for the Dallas Stars. Admission $6. Skate rental $3.

GALLERIA ICE SKATING CENTER
Galleria, 13350 Dallas North Tollway (75240), at LBJ Frwy. (I-635) • 972-392-3363 • Open seven days

The rink is located on the lower level of Galleria mall. Admission $5. Skate rental $2.50. Free beginner classes on Saturdays. Free mall parking.

ICE CAPADES CHALET
Prestonwood Town Center, 5301 Belt Line Road (75240), at Dallas North Tollway • 972-980-8988 • Open seven days

Admission to this mall rink is $5. Skate rental $2. Free mall parking.

INDOOR POLO

DALLAS DRAGOONS
Fair Park Coliseum • 520-7656 • Admission

This professional arena polo team usually plays its National Polo League matches on Saturdays year round. Tickets $15

SOCCER

DALLAS BURN
Cotton Bowl, Fair Park • 373-8000 • Admission

The Cotton Bowl is home field for Dallas' newest professional (outdoor) soccer team, which competes in the Western Conference. Season is from April–September.

DALLAS SIDEKICKS
Reunion Arena, 777 Sports Street (75207) (DART Light Rail UNION Station) •653-0200

This is Dallas' professional indoor soccer team playing in the Continental Indoor Soccer League. Season is from June-September with most games scheduled on weekends. Tickets $7–$22.

TENNIS

DALLAS PARKS TENNIS CENTERS
Park and Recreation Department, City Hall, 1500 Marilla (75201) • 670-4100.

There is a scattering of tennis courts in neighborhood parks all over the city; however, the following parks each have a tennis center which is city-owned but privately managed. Reservations may be made one day in advance with fees based on prime time (evenings, weekends, and holidays) and non-prime time (weekdays 9–5). Depending on the park, prime time fees are either $5 or $6 for 1½ hours court time; non-prime fees are $2–$4. There's a $1 reservation fee. The Tennis Centers also offer lessons, ball-machine rentals, and each has a tennis pro shop.

FAIR OAKS
7501 Merriman Pkwy. • 670-1495 • 16 lighted courts.

FRETZ
14700 Hillcrest • 972-670-6622 • 15 lighted courts.

KIEST
2324 West Kiest Blvd. • 670-7618 • 16 lighted courts.

SAMUELL-GRAND
6200 East Grand Avenue • 670-1374 • 20 lighted courts.

L. B. HOUSTON
11225 Luna Road • 670-6367 • 16 lighted courts.

OTHER POINTS OF INTEREST

ARTIST SQUARE
South of Woodall Rodgers Frwy. between Pearl and Leonard, just north of the Meyerson Symphony Center • W

Nestled in the midst of the Arts District, this plaza is the scene of a diverse selection of arts, music, and dance activities and festivals throughout the year.

BATH HOUSE CULTURAL CENTER
521 East Lawther Dr. (75218), at White Rock Lake
670-8749 • W +

At one time, back in the 1930s and '40s, it was a bath house for swimmers at White Rock Lake. Abandoned in the 1950s, it was rescued by the city in 1979 and turned into a neighborhood cultural center. Now it is well known for its wide range of activities that include concerts, children's theater, art and photography exhibitions, dance performances, and classes and workshops in the arts.

BRYAN CABIN
Dallas County Historical Plaza, Elm and Market Streets, West End Historic District (DART Light Rail WEST END Station) W

The tiny pioneer-style log cabin in this large plaza is a reconstruction of a cabin typical of the 1840s when John Neely Bryan settled in this area. Also on the square is a large tile map of early Dallas County.

DALLAS CITY HALL
1500 Marilla (75201), at Ervay (DART Light Rail CONVENTION CENTER Station) • 670-3011 • W +

Located near the Dallas Convention Center, this building has an inverted sloping front, which makes its ten levels seem to lean over the street. Famed architect I. M. Pei designed it to slope outward and upward at a 34° angle with the building held and balanced by a network of U-shaped cables in the floors and walls. Sculpture by Henry Moore and a reflecting pool adorn the ceremonial plaza in front, which is often used for public events and festivals.

DALLAS MARKET CENTER COMPLEX
2100 Stemmons Frwy (I-35E), just north of downtown
655-6100 • W + But not all areas

This is the world's largest wholesale trade complex with more than a million wholesale buyers attending markets here each year. Located on 175 acres, the Center's buildings occupy 9.2 million square feet in eight separate marketing facilities: The World Trade Center, Apparel Mart, Menswear Mart, Trade Mart, Decorative Center, Home Furnishing Mart, Market Hall, and the InfoMart.

Only two buildings within the Center are open to the public, and then only on a limited basis.

Market Hall, the largest privately owned exhibition hall in the U.S., is the scene of boat shows, car shows, crafts shows, and numerous other events open to the public but charging admission.

InfoMart (1950 Stemmons Frwy. • 746-3500 • W+ is the world's largest high-tech information center, housing offices and showrooms of more than 115 information technology companies. Most of the offices are only open to people in the business; however, the building itself and some of its facilities are open to the public. InfoMart hosts trade shows, seminars, and classes on computers and information technology. Most Saturdays there is some type of free event open to the public at which computer instruction is given. Also, monthly, more than a dozen user groups from the North Texas area hold a forum here to exchange information. (Call 746-5678 or 800-232-1022 for schedule of exhibits and events.) The InfoMart is housed in a unique building whose glass and lacework arch architecture is designed to resemble London's Crystal Palace, which was built in 1851 for the first World's Fair and International Technology Exhibition. Great Britain's Parliament has recognized the building as the official successor to the Crystal Palace, which was destroyed by fire in 1936. The Crystal Fountain in the atrium is made of 471 pieces of handmade crystal and is an exact replica of the Crystal Palace's original fountain. The 4,200 windows are 10 × 6 feet in size and the exterior arches are made of recycled aluminum. Free guided tours for individuals are given Monday–Friday at 11 a.m. Free parking. Restaurants. Bookstore.

DALLAS PUBLIC LIBRARY
Central Library, 1515 Young Street (75201), downtown (DART Light Rail CONVENTION CENTER Station) • 670-1400 • W + But not all areas

Its vast lending library is just one of the highlights of this eight-story library. It has an outstanding genealogy collection and the largest children's center in the country. It also offers performance space for dance, theater, music, children's shows, films, and lectures, has permanent exhibits of rare books and manuscripts including a copy of the Declaration of Independence printed by Benjamin Franklin, and the largest display of Navajo blankets in the country. In addition it offers frequent special exhibits. Call for schedule of events. Gift store.

JOHN F. KENNEDY MEMORIAL
Memorial Plaza, Main and Market Streets, West End Historic District (DART Light Rail WEST END Station) • W

This memorial to our 35th President, who was assassinated nearby, was designed by architect Phillip Johnson, a Kennedy family friend, as a place for meditation. Stark and simple, it consists of four walls, about 30-foot high, open to the sky, creating the effect of an open tomb enclosing a memorial plaque.

NEIMAN MARCUS' ORIGINAL DALLAS STORE
1618 Main (75201) at Ervay Street (DART Light Rail ST. PAUL Station) • 573-5800 • Monday–Saturday 10–5:30. Closed Sunday and major holidays • W

In Texas, and just about everywhere else in the world, the name Neiman Marcus stands for a long tradition of sophisticated service and good taste. It wasn't long after it opened in 1907 that Texans who could afford to shop anywhere in the world started to shop here instead of New York or Paris. Neiman Marcus helped put Dallas on the national and international fashion map. This store was built in 1914 and enlarged over the years. It is now the flagship store of a chain. Among Neiman Marcus' many claims to fame is its annual Christmas catalog, which always includes "His and Her" gifts that gently spoof its rich customers. Among past

His and Her gifts offered were a pair of airplanes, a two-seater submarine, matching hot-air balloons, and a pair of Chinese junks. (All of which sold.) Even if you feel it's too pricey for your budget, a permanent exhibit on the 5th floor that tells the history of "The Store" is worth a visit as is the 6th floor's legendary Zodiac room where Dallas socialites have been lunching for decades. "The Store" and another downtown tradition, The Adolphus Hotel, jointly sponsor the nation's only holiday parade just for kids. The free Neiman Marcus/Adolphus Children's Parade is held on a Saturday early in December. Called "The Miracle on Commerce Street," because it draws corporate sponsorship that benefits the Children's Medical Center of Dallas, it is broadcast on TV to more than 100 million households from Alaska to the Bahamas. (Parade Hotline 640-8383.)

OUTDOOR SCULPTURE

Art is everywhere in Dallas with more than 150 statues, murals, and pieces in corporate lobbies on public view in the downtown area alone. It is the outdoor sculpture, however, that seems to best capture the strong, dynamic spirit of the city. The Dallas Convention & Visitors Bureau offers a free map/brochure pointing out the location of 32 major pieces of sculpture you can see while strolling through the Arts District and downtown, and dozens more in outlying areas.

PIONEER PLAZA CATTLE DRIVE MONUMENT
Young and Griffin Streets, between Dallas Convention Center and City Hall • (DART Light Rail CONVENTION CENTER Station) • Free • W

Forty-seven larger-than-life-size bronze longhorns move down a rocky bluff through a flowing stream in this plaza park, driven by three cowboys on horseback; one leading, one watching from the bluff, and one chasing a stray. Sculpted by Robert Summers of Glen Rose, it's not a large herd, as old time herds went, but it still makes the world's largest bronze monument. It's wide open so you can walk through it, and as you do, you may get a feeling of the immense power and energy of the longhorns that the riders had to control on those legendary cattle drives when the herds numbered in the thousands. Plans are in the works to increase the size of the herd to seventy. The 4.2-acre park is actually located on a site of the historic "Shawnee Trail" that was used for drives like this starting in the mid-1850s. It adjoins Pioneer Cemetery, founded in 1848 and the resting place of some of Dallas' first citizens. Free but limited parking.

THANKS-GIVING SQUARE
Surrounded by Akard, Ervay, Bryan, and Pacific Streets, downtown (DART Light Rail AKARD Station) • Thanks-Giving Square Foundation, P.O. Box 1777, 75221 • 969-1977
Free • W Variable

Architect Phillip Johnson, who designed the John F. Kennedy Memorial (see above) designed this tiny triangular park in praise of the universal spirit of the Thanksgiving tradition found in all the world's religions. An island of serenity amidst the bustle of downtown, it includes a 50-foot bell tower with three large bronze bells, a water wall, a reflecting pool, and the spiraling white marble interfaith Chapel of Thanksgiving. Beneath the chapel, the Hall of Thanksgiving tells of the American Thanksgiving tradition. The Chapel is open weekdays 9–5, weekends and holidays 1–5. There is an entrance to the park from the underground pedestrianway (see OFFBEAT, below).

OFFBEAT

THE CONSPIRACY MUSEUM
110 South Market (75202) between Main and Commerce, downtown (DART Light Rail WEST END Station) • 741-3040
Monday–Friday 10–6, Saturday–Sunday 10–7 • Monday–Friday $5 person. Weekends: Adults $7, Seniors $6, children $3
W Variable

This small, privately funded museum came into existence because so many people rejected the Warren Commission Report that Oswald assassinated President Kennedy. The exhibits present a case for the theory that someone other than Oswald did it. But the displays aren't just confined to who killed JFK. They offer theories on the assassinations and cover-ups of Presidents Lincoln, Garfield, and McKinley, as well as of Bobby Kennedy and Martin Luther King. Some of the exhibits and videos are in the basement (elevator). The museum staff conducts complimentary 30–45-minute walking tours of the JFK assassination area for patrons most weekends at 11, 1, and 3. Gift shop just inside entrance is open without a ticket. Pay parking on nearby lots.

DALLAS UNDERGROUND PEDESTRIANWAYS AND SKYBRIDGES

Downtown • (Nearest entrance from DART Light Rail AKARD Station) • Open normal business hours weekdays • Free • W Variable (Elevators at some entrances) (See Map, p. 134.)

Forget the downtown traffic. During the day on weekdays, you can get around much of downtown without crossing a street by using the more than two miles of underground pedestrianway tunnels (and elevated skybridges). These aren't dark, dank, and spooky tunnels either. Most of them are bright and lined with shops and restaurants. A few exit on the street, but most exit to the lobbies of major office buildings and hotels. One even gets you right in the heart of Thanks-Giving Square. Unfortunately, this system is in three clusters that aren't interconnected, so depending on where you want to go, occasionally you may have to come up and actually cross a street or two to get to the next section.

MEDIEVAL TIMES DINNER AND TOURNAMENT

2021 North Stemmons Frwy. (I-35E) (75207), at Market Center Blvd. • 761-1800 or 800-229-9900 • Tuesday–Saturday evenings, Sunday afternoon. Closed Monday • Adults about $36, seniors about $32, children under 12 about $22 • Reservations recommended • W Variable

The year is 1093 and you are the guests in the (air-conditioned) castle of the royal family. As you dine on a four-course dinner in authentic Middle Ages style, without utensils, you'll witness medieval pageantry, horsemanship, swordplay, falconry, sorcery, and a jousting tournament. Call for showtimes.

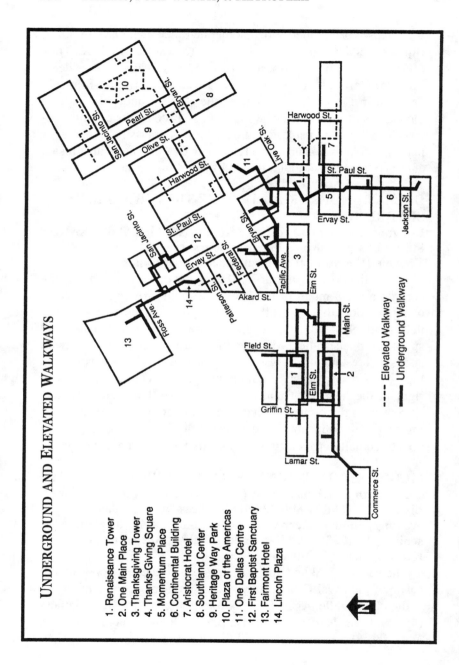

UNDERGROUND AND ELEVATED WALKWAYS

1. Renaissance Tower
2. One Main Place
3. Thanksgiving Tower
4. Thanks-Giving Square
5. Momentum Place
6. Continental Building
7. Aristocrat Hotel
8. Southland Center
9. Heritage Way Park
10. Plaza of the Americas
11. One Dallas Centre
12. First Baptist Sanctuary
13. Fairmont Hotel
14. Lincoln Plaza

- - - - Elevated Walkway
───── Underground Walkway

ANNUAL EVENTS

JANUARY

SOUTHWESTERN BELL COTTON BOWL CLASSIC
New Year's Day • Cotton Bowl Stadium, Fair Park (Cotton Bowl Classic Association Office, 1300 West Mockingbird Ln., 75356) 634-7525 • Game tickets $40–$50 • Parking $8 • W + But not all areas (Access at Stadium Sections 4–7)

After Dallas entrepreneur J. Curtis Sanford watched SMU battle Stanford in the 1936 Rose Bowl, he decided that Dallas should have a bowl game of its own. The result was this football classic which was started in 1937 and has been played in the same stadium and on the same field for more than 60 years. L.D. Meyer, the nephew of TCU coach Dutch Meyer, scored the Cotton Bowl's first points before 17,000 fans when he booted a 33-yard field goal in the opening quarter of the 1937 Classic. In fact, Meyer scored every TCU point in the Frogs' 16-6 triumph over Marquette that New Year's Day. The original Cotton Bowl had a capacity of 46,200. But thanks to an SMU player named Doak Walker and the tremendous crowds he attracted to see SMU play, in 1948 the stadium was expanded to a capacity of 67,431. Later, "The House that Doak Built" was expanded again to its present capacity of around 72,000.

The two football teams that tangle on the natural grass field in the present Classic are selected from the 38 universities that make up the Western Athletic Conference, The PAC 10 Conference, and the Big 12 Conference; conferences that are spread over 20 states stretching from the Mississippi River to Hawaii.

DALLAS VIDEO FESTIVAL
Thursday–Sunday early in month • Dallas Museum of Art, 1717 North Harwood (75201) (DART Light Rail ST. PAUL Station) (Office: 1950 Stemmons Frwy., Suite 2005, 75207) 651-8600 • Day passes $8–$10, Festival pass $25 • W +

For more than ten years, this festival has been offering a comprehensive view of the past, present, and future of video by presenting the work of video pioneers. Parking in the Dallas Museum of Art underground garage.

USA FILM FESTIVAL/KIDFILM FESTIVAL
Saturday and Sunday in mid-month • AMC Glen Lake Theater, 9450 North Central Expressway at Walnut Hill Ln. (Office 2917 Swiss Avenue 75204) • 972-395-9034 • Tickets $3 • W

This is the oldest and largest children film festival in the nation. It features a diverse lineup of film and videos that appeal primarily to children, but also to adults. Events include appearances by acclaimed TV and film makers. Free theater parking.

DALLAS MORNING NEWS SWIMMING AND DIVING CLASSIC
Two days in mid-month • SMU Natatorium, 6024 Bishop Blvd., at Binkley • 768-2883 • W

The six best NCAA college swimming teams in the country compete in this annual event. Frequently these teams include Olympic champions or contenders. Call for schedule and ticket prices. Parking in the W-5 lot on Airline Road north of Mockingbird Lane and in the parking garage at Airline Road and Binkley Avenue.

JANUARY–FEBRUARY

DALLAS WINTER BOAT SHOW
Late January–early February • Dallas Market Hall, 2200 Stemmons Frwy. (I-35E), take Market Center exit off I-35E, (Office: P.F. Smith Enterprises, 6220 North Belt Line Road, Suite 208, Irving 75063) • 972-550-1052 • Adults $6, children under 12 $3, under 3 free • W +

Hundreds of boats and boat accessories are on display in the more than 210,000 ft^2 of Market Hall display space. This show has been an annual event for more than 40 years and always features new models of all type boats from 40-foot cruisers to personal watercraft; most at special "Boat Show" prices. Look for discount admission coupons in the local papers. Free parking.

FEBRUARY

TRI DELTA CHARITY ANTIQUES SHOW

Thursday–Sunday late in month • Dallas Convention Center, 650 South Griffin at Young (DART Light Rail CONVENTION CENTER Station) (Office: P.O. Box 8070, 75205) • 691-9306 Tickets $8 • W+

Dealers from U.S. and abroad sell fine antiques and art at this popular charity show, which has been an annual event every February or early March for more than 20 years. It also features lectures and special exhibits on some aspects of antiques and fine art. Underground Convention Center parking $5.

MARCH

DALLAS BLOOMS

All month • Dallas Arboretum and Botanical Gardens, 8525 Garland Road (75218) • 327-8263 • Adults $6, Seniors $5, Children 6–12 $3, Five and under free. Parking $2 • W Variable

When spring comes to Dallas, then Dallas Blooms at the arboretum with a spectacular display of more than 200,000 flowering bulbs that color the gardens. (See SPECIAL GARDENS, p. 100.)

DALLAS NEW CAR AUTO SHOW

Five days in mid-month • Dallas Convention Center, 650 South Griffin at Young (DART Light Rail CONVENTION CENTER Station) • 939-2700 • W+

This is one of the largest new car shows in the country with almost all the new models, both domestic and foreign, on display. Call for ticket prices. Underground convention center parking $5

APRIL

USA FILM FESTIVAL

Eight days in mid-month • AMC Glen Lake Theater, 9450 North Central Expressway at Walnut Hill Ln. (Office: 2917 Swiss Avenue, 75204) • 821-6300 • W

In addition to showings of the best new American and foreign films, this eight-day event includes the National Short Film and

Video Competition, special award ceremonies and retrospectives of an ourstanding director and actor, and opening and closing night premiers of new works by artists in attendance. Created in 1971, it is now one of the oldest film festivals in the U.S. Over more than a quarter century it has presented the world, national, or regional premiers of thousands of feature films and short works and has brought to Dallas hundreds of leading directors, actors, producers, screenwriters, historians, and critics to discuss films with the audience. Call for ticket prices, which are kept low to ensure maximum accessibility.

MAY

ARTFEST
Friday–Sunday of Memorial Day weekend • Fair Park
(Artfest c/o The 500, Inc. 11300 North Central Expressway,
Suite 415, 75243) • 361-2011 • Admission $5 (children 4 and
under free) • W +
Typically over 800 artists from across the U.S. apply to participate in this three-day event, which draws about 80,000 patrons and is the largest art show and outdoor festival of its kind in the Southwest. Applicants' works are submitted to a jury composed of art critics, museum curators, artists, and other arts community representatives, and about 300, representing all media, are selected to be in this family festival of arts and entertainment. Activities include live and silent art auctions, continuous musical entertainment, demonstrations by artists, and 5K and 10K runs for adults as well as the "Kiddie Kilometer" race for kids. Kids also get to see and participate in free arts and crafts activities and special entertainment in an indoor air-conditioned area. All proceeds benefit the cultural arts of Dallas. Pay parking available in Fair Park and in commercial lots nearby.

JUNE

HOOP-IT-UP BONANZA
Saturday and Sunday in mid-month • Record at Ross in the Historic West End District (DART Light Rail WEST END Station)(Office: 4006 Belt Line Road, Suite 230, 75244) 972-991-1110 • Free for spectators • W

What started as a popular street basketball tournament in Dallas in 1986 went national in 1989, got an NBA/NBC relationship in 1992, and is now a huge charity event running from March through November with more than 50,000 3-man teams entering competitions on a 55-city tour in the U.S. and tours in Europe, Canada, and Mexico. Basketball players of all ages can participate in the amateur 3-on-3 games with players matched by age, skill, and height. Wheelchair teams are included. The winners advance to regional action, then can go on to the World Finals where the top team meets a team of NBA legends. In Dallas 300,000 spectators come to see the games played on 40 × 40-ft courts. First team to hit 16 wins. There's a 30-minute game time limit, but most don't last that long. While the highlight of the weekend is basketball, there's also music and entertainment and special events. Pay parking in commercial lots.

JULY

TASTE OF DALLAS
Friday–Sunday in mid-month • Market Street in Historic West End District (DART Light Rail WEST END Station) (Office: 1801 North Lamar, Suite 444, 75202) • 720-7107 • W

The attraction here is the samplings of the diverse cuisine from some of Dallas' finest restaurants. Continuous live entertainment on three stages and a special children's area. Admission and entertainment are free, but to do the tasting you have to buy coupons. Pay parking in commercial lots.

AUGUST–SEPTEMBER

DALLAS MORNING NEWS DANCE FESTIVAL
Labor Day weekend • Artist Square/Arts District
(DART Light Rail ST. PAUL Station) • 953-1977 • Free • W

This weekend extravaganza showcases the dance talent in the Metroplex. It usually includes performances by dance troupes including the Fort Worth Dallas Ballet, The Anita N. Martinez Ballet Folklorico, The Dallas Black Dance Theatre, and the dance students at Booker T. Washington High School. Call for schedule.

SEPTEMBER

MONTAGE
Saturday–Sunday in mid-month • Arts District
(DART Light Rail ST. PAUL Station) • 361-2011 • W

The streets of the Arts District are turned into a showcase for a wide variety of art forms including theatre, music, dance, painting, sculpture and photography for this outdoor family festival fundraiser. Call for schedule.

SEPTEMBER–OCTOBER

STATE FAIR OF TEXAS
Twenty-four days in late September and early October
Fair Park, east of downtown, bounded by Parry Avenue,
Cullum Blvd., Fitzhugh Avenue, and Washington Avenue
(Office: P.O. Box 150009, 75315 • 565-9931) • Adults $9,
Seniors and kids under 48″ tall $5, Under 3 free • W Variable

With annual attendance figures well over three million, this is the largest state fair in the U.S. It may also have the largest greeter of any state fair. Big Tex, a 52-foot giant cowboy wearing 7-foot

7-inch-high boots and a 5-foot-high, 75-gallon cowboy hat, greets all his visitors with a booming "Howdy folks!" The first state fair was held at this location in 1886. That fair opened with a downtown parade and each year that tradition is continued with an opening day parade along Main Street. As with all state fairs, the livestock competitions (with an average of 10,000 entries), agricultural exhibits, cooking contests, and the arts play a continuing role. But there's more: much, much more. In fact, each year they seem to cram in more exhibits, more musical entertainment, more shows, and more demonstrations.

Each fair's events are built around a theme, but almost always feature animal acts, circus acts, puppet shows, U.S. Marine Corps Drum and Bugle Corps and Silent Drill team performances, and free concerts by a variety of well-known entertainers on the Main-Stage. There's also always a major auto show in the Automobile Building and all the Fair Park museums (see FAIR PARK, p. 79) have extended hours and special exhibits. Plus there's a special musical in the Music Hall, major college football games in the Cotton Bowl, loads of events and activities for kids, and a carnival midway with the tallest ferris wheel in North America, an 80-year-old carousel, and about 60 other rides. And to end each day, there's a nightly parade and a fireworks spectacular.

In other words, there's something for everyone from 10 a.m. to 10 p.m. every day.

Fair grounds parking is available for approximately 8,000 vehicles ($5). For parking, enter Fair Park lots off Cullum Blvd. at Martin Luther King Jr. or Grand. DART Park and Ride buses are available weekends from various locations (749-3800 or 979-1111 for schedule). Buses cost $6 round trip.

Check the newspapers for admission discount offers.

NOVEMBER–DECEMBER

CHRISTMAS AT THE ARBORETUM

Late November to after Christmas • Dallas Arboretum and
Botanical Gardens, 8525 Garland Road (75218) • 327-8263
Adults $6, seniors $5, children 6–12 $3, five and under free.
Parking $2 • W Variable

The highlight of this month-long event is the tour of the historic
21,000-square-foot DeGolyer House, which is decorated from
floor to ceiling with displays of thousands of twinkling lights,
trees, and ornaments. The 66-acre gardens will also display holiday colored pansies, hollies, and evergreen.

SHOPPING

DALLAS FARMERS MARKET

1010 South Pearl (75201) • 939-2808 • Open seven days dawn
to dusk • W

One of the few remaining farmers markets in the country, it is
also one of the largest with many hundreds of farmers selling fresh
fruits, vegetables, herbs, plants, and flowers here every day. Sales
are held in open sheds spread over four city-owned blocks. During
the year, special holiday festivals and events are offered. Under the
auspices of the Dallas Chapter of the American Institute of Wine
and Food, cooking classes are offered by some of Dallas' finest
chefs in spring and fall in the Market Resource Kitchen.

GALLERIA

LBJ Frwy. (I-635) at Dallas Parkway North (75240)
702-7100 • W + But not all areas

There are more than 200 stores in this four-level mall including
the only Dallas locations of Macy's, Marshall Fields, Nordstrom,
Saks Fifth Avenue, and Tiffany & Co. Patterned after the barrel-
vaulted glass atrium style of the 19th century Galleria Vittorio
Emanuele in Milan, Italy, this bright mall also features more than

two dozen fast food and full service restaurants, an indoor ice rink, and the attached Westin Hotel. Some covered parking.

HENRY JACKALOPE
6731 Snider Plaza (75205), one block west of Hillcrest and Lovers Lane • 692-8928 • W

Not just "Western Wear," but "Dallas Chic" southwestern and western wear. Everything from handmade Rocketbuster boots to alligator belts. Features Double D Ranchwear and such contemporary designers as Christine Foley and Michael Simon. Closed Sunday.

HIGHLAND PARK VILLAGE
Preston Road at Mockingbird Lane (75205) • 559-2740 • W

One of the first shopping centers in the country when it was built in 1931, Highland Park Village has been continuously updated and is now the home of an eclectic collection of shops and restaurants that include the ordinary and some prestigious international shops and boutiques that could be equally at home on Los Angeles' Rodeo Drive.

INFOMART
1950 Stemmons Frwy. (I-35E) • 746-3500 • W+

See OTHER POINTS OF INTEREST/Dallas Market Center Complex, p. 128.

INWOOD TRADE CENTER
Inwood Road (75247) two blocks west of I-35E
689-4222 • W Variable

This center is an example of the many outlet centers in Dallas. Some excellent quality products can be found in the stores here at outlet prices. Among the stores are AtCost Warehouse, Accessory Mart, Bottoms Up, Clothes Out Closet, Crate & Barrel Outlet, Design Lighting and Accessories, Designers Group, Far East Menswear, The Real Outlet, Second Base, Shoe Fair, and The Sofa Source.

LOVE FIELD ANTIQUE MALL
6500 Cedar Springs (75235) at Mockingbird, across from the entrance to Love Field • W

The ads for this mall describe it as the largest antique and classic car mall in the United States. There are approximately 250 dealer booths and a section of classic cars under one roof in this air-conditioned 70,000-ft^2 building. The booth area overflows with antique furniture, art objects, china, silver, crystal, jewelry, and collectibles. Most booths are unattended. If you need assistance, pick up a phone and someone will come. Otherwise just carry your selection to the checkout. Whether you're a classic car buff or not, the collection here is worth a visit. A few of the cars are for sale, but most of the collection is only for display. Restaurant.

MAPSCO
5308 Maple Avenue (75235) • 521-2131 • W

If you want to get around Dallas, the Metroplex, or the world, this place has a street guide, map, atlas, globe, or whatever else you need to get from point A to point B. Other store locations at 13536 Preston Road in Dallas (960-1414) and 6118 Camp Bowie in Fort Worth (817-332-1111). Mapsco area maps and street guides are also available at bookstores and supermarkets and other retail locations in the Metroplex.

NORTHPARK CENTER
Northwest Hwy. (Loop 12) at North Central Expressway (US75) (75231) (DART Light Rail PARK LANE Station. Shuttle bus to mall) • 363-7441 • W + But not all areas

The most popular (and profitable) Neiman Marcus in the chain is located in this mall along with Abercrombie & Fitch, Lord & Taylor, Barneys New York, Foleys, Dillards, JC Penney, and more than 150 other specialty stores and restaurants. Opened as the most elegant mall in Dallas in 1965, it has continued to maintain its upscale ambiance for shoppers while at the same time attracting non-shoppers to its frequent art displays, activities, and festivities. It is especially known for its holiday events. Lots for kids of all ages here including the Dallas Cowboy Pro Shop, a mini-branch of the Dallas Museum of Natural History, The Disney Store, Warner Bros. Studio Store, and the inimitable FAO Schwarz. Also a Dallas Convention & Visitors Bureau booth. Valet and covered parking.

PARK CITIES ANTIQUE MALL
4908 West Lovers Lane (75209), three blocks west of Inwood
350-5983 • W

More than 70 dealers display a wide variety of antiques from France, England, and other countries including furniture, fine linens, and estate jewelry as well as a number of collectibles. Excellent friendly assistance available. Entrance on side.

RED BIRD MALL
3662 West Camp Wisdom Road (75237) at US 67
296-1491 • W +

While most of the other major malls are in central or north Dallas, this one serves south Dallas and the southern suburbs. Dillard's, Foley's, JC Penney, and Sears anchor over 140 specialty stores.

THE SHOPS AND GALLERIES OF THE CRESCENT
200 Cedar Springs (75201) at Maple • 871-8500 • W

The Crescent, named for its fanlike shape, is a complex of a hotel, an office center, and a small outdoor shopping village that offers a truly distinctive collection of specialty and antique shops, art galleries, and restaurants. Underground parking. Closed Sunday.

VANTAGE SHOE WAREHOUSE
2200 block of Vantage Street (75207) • 631-4812 • W

There are Vantage men's and women's outlet shoe stores on this street offering name brand designer shoes at a fraction of regular cost. In addition, they often have sales that cut prices even more. There are six other Vantage locations throughout the city, most of which are highly advertised on billboards and other outdoor signs.

WEST END MARKETPLACE
603 Munger Avenue (75202) at Market Street (DART Light Rail WEST END Station) • 748-4801 • W (Elevator entrance on Munger near Planet Hollywood entrance)

Located in the heart of the West End Historic District, this is a combination shopping and entertainment center with four floors in three adjoining buildings filled with unique shops, fast food eateries, restaurants, and a multi-nightclub complex. You can buy everything from t-shirts and souvenirs to fine Texas wines and art in various media created by local artists and artisans. Pay parking in nearby lots ($2–$5 day) or metered parking on street.

WHOLE FOODS MARKET
2218 Greenville • 824-1744 • W

There are several stores in the Metroplex that carry natural foods, but this one is one of two in Dallas and four in the Metroplex that are part of the country's largest chain of natural foods supermarkets. It carries what is probably the largest selection in the area of organically grown vegetables and fruits, plus seafood and meats without growth hormones or other additives. Deli/restaurant in the store. Other locations: 7205 Skillman at Kingsley (341-5445); Coit at Belt Line, Richardson (972-699-8075); and 2201 Preston at Park, Plano (972-612-6729).

DINING OUT

$ = Under $12, $$ = $12–$30, $$$ = Over $30 for one person excluding drinks, tax, and tip.

ADELMO'S RISTORANTE
4537 Cole Avenue (75205), at Knox • 559-0325 • Lunch and dinner Monday–Friday, dinner only Saturday. Closed Sunday and major holidays • $$ • Cr. • W

A quick scan of the dinner menu will show that this warm little bistro is not your everyday Italian restaurant. Adelmo's creative cuisine is inspired by the eastern Mediterranean region from France to the Middle East. Choices for starters, for example, include escargot, lobster ravioli, lamb sausage, and an hors d'oeu-

vres serving of calamata olives, anchovies, and onions. The most
popular specialties of the house include a 20 oz. veal chop and
grilled rack of lamb. The owner-operated restaurant is in a charming two-story house with close but cozy seating at tables set with
white tablecloths, fresh flowers, and candles. Early-bird prices
6–6:30 p.m. Bar.

ALESSIO'S
4117 Lomo Alto (75219), just north of Lemmon Avenue
521-3585 • Lunch Monday–Friday, dinner seven days • $$–$$$
Cr. • W

The northern Italian specialties here include grilled double veal
chops steeped in five herbs, *fettucine Genovese,* and *gnocchi*
made with gorgonzola. The decor includes original paintings.
Pianist and vocalist on Friday–Saturday. The owner-operator
emphasizes personal service. Semi-formal dress requested. Bar.
Valet parking.

ANTARES
**300 Reunion Blvd. (75207) in Reunion Tower (DART Light Rail
UNION Station) • 712-7145 • Lunch Monday–Saturday, Brunch
Sunday, dinner seven days • $$ • Cr. • W**

At 50-stories above the street, the menu runs second to the
view, but a close second. As the restaurant gently revolves, to give
you an enchanting 360° panorama of the city in a little less than
an hour, you can order from a menu featuring New American cui-
sine. Offerings include a wide choice of beef dishes, but is
weighted toward seafood entrées that range from seared sea scal-
lops with chili-peanut dressing as an appetizer to the Antares Plat-
ter, which includes portions of rock lobster tail, red snapper,
clams, scallops, mussels, and blackened chicken. Children's por-
tions at half price. Bar. Semi-formal in evening. Complimentary
valet parking next door at the Hyatt Regency Hotel.

ANZU
4620 McKinney Avenue (75205)(DART Light Rail ST. PAUL Station to connect with McKinney Avenue Trolley) • 526-7398 Lunch Monday–Friday, dinner Monday–Saturday. Closed Sunday, Thanksgiving, Christmas, New Year's Day • $$-$$$ Cr. • W +

Pacific Rim and nouvelle Japanese fare are still dominant on the menu with Japanese-influenced staples like *udon* noodles, sushi, sake, and a variety of stir-fry, tempura, and teriyaki dishes. A popular entree is sake-marinated grilled cod. In a melding of East meets West, the menu also includes more eclectic choices, like roast pork tenderloin with five spices, that loosely fall under the heading of New American cuisine. Sleek setting includes intimate booths with a flight of bright-colored origami birds fluttering across the ceiling. Bar. Valet parking.

ARTHUR'S
8350 North Central Expressway (US 75) (75206) at 1000 Campbell Centre, take Caruth-Haven Exit #13 • 361-8833 Lunch Monday–Friday, dinner Monday–Saturday. Closed Sunday and major holidays • $$ • Cr. • W

As it approaches its 50th anniversary, Arthur's retains its sedate and classy old-styled dining room with crystal chandeliers, white linens, and candlelight. And the menu remains much the same as it has to attract Dallasites for close to half a century with offerings of steaks, seafood, lamb, veal, fowl, and pasta entrées. The chef caters to special requests not on the menu, especially for elaborate desserts such as Bananas Foster and Cherries Jubilee. Bar. Live music and dancing nightly in lounge area. Valet parking.

BEAU NASH
2215 Cedar Springs (75201) at McKinney, in Hotel Crescent Court (DART Light Rail ST. PAUL Station to connect with McKinney Avenue Trolley) • 871-3240 • Breakfast, lunch, and dinner seven days. Closed major holidays • $$-$$$ • Cr. • W +

This hotel dining room offers casual dining in an elegant setting overlooking the serene gardens. The chefs working in the open kitchen prepare appetizers and entrées that creatively fuse

New American cuisine with a touch of Northern Italian, such as steak pizza, lobster sandwiches, and angel hair pasta with lump crab meat. Frequent menu changes offer a variety of seafood and steak entrées. High level of unintrusive service. Music Thursday–Saturday evenings. Lounge. Valet parking.

CAFÉ ATHENEE
5365 Spring Valley (75240) at Monfort • 239-8060 • Lunch and dinner Monday–Saturday. Closed Sunday, Thanksgiving, Christmas • $$ • Cr. • W +

Romanian (Transylvanian), Greek, and European cuisine in a cozy English library setting may seem incongruous, but this popular restaurant carries it off with appetizers like Gypsy Snack (Romanian ham and eggplant salad) or White Caviar Salad, and entrées like Veal Athenee (sauteed in light marinara sauce with fresh mushrooms, brandy, topped with provolone cheese) or rack of lamb prepared in the old world Romanian style. Other entrées include veal, chicken, pork, seafood, duck, and quail. They make their own breads, pasta, desserts, and Romanian sausage.

CAFÉ PACIFIC
24 Highland Park Village (75205), Mockingbird Lane at Preston Road • 526-1170 • Lunch and dinner Monday–Saturday. Closed Sunday, Thanksgiving, Christmas, New Year's day $$–$$$ • Cr. • W +

To get you off to a pleasant start while you look at the menu, there's a complimentary dish of strips of crisp sweet-potato fries. But from then on seafood is king. There are some meat items on the menu, but the house is most famous for its seafood specialties. Among the starters is ceviche stocked with chunks of lobster, shrimp, and scallops. Entrées range from shrimp and crab cakes to the catch of the day special, which may be a culinary delight such as Chilean sea bass or Gulf red snapper. All served in an intimate, sophisticated club-like glass and brass setting. Bar. Street and valet parking.

CELEBRATION
**4503 West Lovers Lane (75209) between Inwood and Lemmon
351-5681 • Lunch and dinner seven days. Closed Thanksgiving,
Christmas Eve and Christmas • $ • Cr. • W +**

From the outside it looks like home (a rustic house) and inside
it's as close as you'll get to down-home cooking in a restaurant.
Meat loaf, pot roast, southern fried or baked chicken, and other
homestead mainstays are all on the menu. The unpretentious,
hearty meals are served family style, with serve-yourself bowls of
salads and loads of vegetables; naturally including choices like
southern style black-eyed peas and okra. And just like at home,
most meals even include seconds. The setting and service are just
as unpretentious as the food, and just as comfortable, too. Special
menus for children, seniors, and the health-conscious. Bar.

CHEZ GERARD
**4444 McKinney (75205), at Armstrong (DART Light Rail ST.
PAUL Station to connect with McKinney Avenue Trolley)
522-6865 • Lunch Monday–Friday, dinner Monday–Saturday.
Closed Sunday and major holidays • $$–$$$ • Cr. W +**

This is the type of small, cozy restaurant you'd expect to find
in the French countryside, right down to the flowery print wall
covering and lace curtains. And the menu promotes the same feeling of authenticity with classics like escargot, onion soup laced
with melted cheese, and crawfish souffle. Substantial, time-honored Gallic recipes are reinterpreted here with a respect for tradition combined with a spark of creativity to produce specialties
like grilled snapper with rosemary mignonnette and pine nuts.
Other entrées of seafood, veal, lamb, and beef are both elegantly
presented and pleasing to the palate. Children's menu. Outdoor
dining area. Bar.

CITY CAFÉ
**5757 West Lovers Lane (75209), just west of North Dallas
Tollway • 351-2233 • Lunch and dinner seven days. Closed
major holidays • $$–$$$ • Cr. • W +**

It started out as a casual neighborhood restaurant that offered
variety to its local customers by changing the menu every two

weeks. Except for a few customer favorites, like its famed fresh tomato soup, they still change the hand-painted menu every two weeks rotating dishes of seafood, veal, game, beef, pasta, fowl, pork, and lamb. But the biggest change is that the little neighborhood bistro's reputation for culinary creativity has broadened its following way out of the local area. The menu offers both simple and sophisticated choices of regional and New American fare that ranges from California through the Southwest to the Cajun country with a typical menu including entrées like trout stuffed with crawfish, braised lamb shank, and Louisiana crab cakes. Bar.

DAKOTA'S
600 North Akard Street (75201), at San Jacinto (DART Light Rail AKARD Station) • 740-4001 • Lunch Monday–Friday, dinner seven days • $$–$$$ • Cr. • W + (elevator)

This elegant downtown and downstairs restaurant offers courtyard dining by a cascading waterfall or inside dining in a grill room setting of rich wood paneling and marble. Entrées grilled over native Texas woods highlight the menu of classic American cuisine with a touch of the Southwest offering choices that include beef, seafood (a local favorite is the grilled swordfish), lamb, and fowl. They also make their own pasta (and breads) and the menu is sprinkled with items marked as "lighter fare." A bargain is the three-course *prix fixe* "twilight menu" offered until 6 p.m. for about $16. Bar. Pianist Friday–Saturday evenings. Valet parking.

DEL FRISCO'S DOUBLE EAGLE STEAKHOUSE
5251 Spring Valley Road (75240) • 972-490-9000 • Dinner Monday–Saturday. Closed Sunday, Thanksgiving, Christmas Day $$–$$$ • Cr. • W +

It's not often you'll hear "oohs" and "ahhs" from jaded expense account diners, but those sounds almost become a chorus here as the meat-eaters dig into the thick prime, aged beef that is the hallmark of this chain. The menu reflects the restaurant name with the major items being all steak, steak, steak—with the ribeye and the strip getting most of the play. They also have a few other items on the menu, including lobster, but all seem almost an afterthought.

Warm, classy Texas saloon atmosphere with carved bas-relief longhorns on the dark-wood paneling. Often crowded so you may have to wait even with reservations. Bar. Valet parking.

8.0 RESTAURANT AND BAR
2800 Routh Street (75201), in The Quadrangle between McKinney and Laclede • 969-9321 • Lunch and dinner seven days. Closed Thanksgiving and Christmas Day • $ • Cr. • W

The eclectic menu plays both sides of the cholesterol street with a variety of burgers served with fries on one side and on the other imaginative vegetarian dishes like a plate of grilled portobello mushrooms with brown rice and a fresh vegetable. Daily blue and green plate specials often sell out early. Also soups and salads and "Fried Purple Worms," all in generous portions. Children's menu. Several local artists contributed to the funky wall murals. Patio. Bar. Trendy entertainment Thursday–Saturday nights bring in wall-to-wall people.

THE FRENCH ROOM
**1321 Commerce Street (75202) at Akard Street in The Adolphus Hotel (DART Light Rail AKARD Station) • 742-8200 or 800-221-9083 (Reservations required) • Dinner Monday–Saturday. Closed Sunday and major holidays • $$$
Cr. • W + (Special elevator)**

Opulent. Posh. Sumptuous. Plush. Beautiful. Those are just a few of the words used to describe The French Room's setting. With its baroque painted ceiling, layered tablecloths, drapes, and hand-blown crystal chandeliers of 17th century design, the room evokes the sensation of entering a realm in which King Louis XV would feel at home. The service is suave and unobtrusive. The cuisine is Neoclassic, that is classic French cooking creatively adapted to contemporary American taste. Appetizers, for example, may include organically grown Texas escargot sauteed in truffle oil with wild mushrooms, tomatoes, and garlic; or jumbo lump crab cake with a whole grain mustard demi and tomato confit. A Neoclassical entrée might be a pan-seared filet of beef tenderloin served *au poivre* with a baked portobello mushroom and shallot tart with basil cabernet sauce; or peppered loin of New Zealand venison on caramelized Bermuda onions and rosemary spätzle with cranberry port wine sauce. A *prix fixe* chef's menu with several choices for each course is available for $56 ($82.50 with wine). Semi-formal dress. Bar. Music Friday-Saturday. Validated valet parking. All no smoking. Rated five diamonds by AAA and four stars by Mobil.

GOOD EATS CAFE
3888 Oak Lawn Avenue (75219), at Blackburn Street
522-3287 • Lunch and dinner seven days • $ • Cr. • W

The motto here is "Good food that's good for you," and the emphasis is on generous portions of home-style cooking of entrées like mesquite grilled chicken, barbecued brisket, seafood, and steaks. Children's menu. Bar. Other Dallas locations at 6950 Greenville Avenue at Park Lane (691-3287) and 702 Ross Avenue in the West End Historic District (744-3287). Other locations throughout the Metroplex.

INDIA PALACE
12817 Preston Road (75230), take Preston Road exit 21 off
I-35E • 972-392-0190 • Lunch and dinner seven days • $$
Cr. • W

The extensive menu of Northern Indian dishes here gives you a wide choice of exotic tastes to try. The intense dry heat of the traditional tandoor ovens generates the flavor while retaining the moistness of many of the dishes, such as the low-fat Tandoori chicken. There are also many grilled items using beef, chicken, and lamb, and numerous vegetarian dishes all imbued with delicate spices. And, of course, there are curries and curried dishes that you can call the shots on as far as how spicy hot you want yours. Children's menu. Bountiful all-you-can-eat lunch buffet. Consistently rated one of best Indian restaurants in the city. Semi-formal dress suggested in evening. Bar.

JAVIER'S
4912 Cole Avenue (75205), between Monticello and Harvard
521-4211 • Dinner seven days • $$ • Cr. • W

They've been serving authentic Mexican food here for around 20 years. The decor is cozy old colonial Mexico studded with antiques, but the cuisine leans more to modern, sophisticated Mexico City style. No Tex-Mex here. Instead there are traditional dishes like *Barra de Navidad* in which shrimp is sauteed in a sauce of orange juice, coffee, and tomato; or steak prepared with mushrooms and brandy. A little hard to find. Call for directions. Bar. Valet parking.

JENNIVINE
3605 McKinney Avenue (75204) between Blackburn Street and Lemmon Avenue (DART Light Rail ST. PAUL Station to connect with McKinney Avenue Trolley) • 528-6010 • Lunch and dinner Monday–Saturday. Closed Sunday and Christmas Day $$ • Cr. • W

The menu at this charming European-style bistro delightfully wanders through British, French, Asian, and Southwestern U.S. dishes, and often ingenious combinations of those cuisines. Perhaps to give each of these culinary influences a fair chance, the menu changes daily. Specialties include rack of lamb, duck, beef tenderloin, seafood, and pâté platters. Outdoor dining available. Early bird menu. All no smoking. Bar.

LANDMARK CAFE
3015 Oak Lawn Avenue (75219)at Cedar Springs Road in Melrose Hotel • 521-5151 • Breakfast seven days, lunch Monday–Friday and Sunday brunch, dinner Monday–Saturday. Closed Saturday lunch, Sunday dinner. • $$$ • Cr. • W +

The attractive, bright, and airy dining room done in mirrors and marble is the setting for an eclectic menu featuring what the chef calls New World cuisine—an innovative and creative blending of influences from Mexican, Italian, Cajun, Asian, and Southwestern cuisines. Specialties include pasta-crusted salmon, beef tenderloin, grilled veal medallions, and sizzling shrimp. Especially popular for business breakfasts and Sunday brunch. Semi-formal dress at dinner. Bar. Valet parking.

LA TRATTORIA LOMBARDI
2916 North Hall Street (75204) near McKinney Avenue
954-0803 • Lunch Monday–Friday, dinner seven days.
Closed major holidays • $$–$$$ • Cr. • W

For about two decades, old style Italian offerings have been the heart of the menu at this comfortable neighborhood trattoria-style restaurant where the service is also polished old style. Pasta dishes include *Fettucine del Pescatore* (fettucine pasta served with shrimp, scallops, green lip mussels in garlic olive oil and herb sauce) and *Cannelloni Verdi Tricolore* (green cannelloni stuffed with meat and spinach and served with a red and white sauce). Among the meat choices is a veal chop marinated with special herbs, grilled and served with Marsala wine sauce; and fish specialties include Crab *Cannelloni.* Outdoor dining available. Bar. Valet parking.

LAUREL'S
12720 Merit Drive (75251), in Sheraton Park Central Hotel
851-2021 • Dinner Monday–Saturday. Closed Sunday • $$$
Cr. • W +

The view of downtown through the floor-to-ceiling windows of this 20th floor North Dallas hotel is just the icing on the cake of the quiet and elegant setting and impeccable service that enhance the menu featuring a cuisine that melds North and South American recipes. Among the appetizers, the *enchilada* packed with shrimp and lobster is a local favorite. Entrées include steaks, rack of lamb, seafood, veal, and a mixed grill with antelope, lamb and quail. *Prix fixe* menu, including wine, for about $50. Health-conscious menu marks calories and fat content. Bar. Pianist or harpist nightly. Valet parking.

THE MANSION ON TURTLE CREEK
2821 Turtle Creek Blvd. (75219) at Gillespie Street in The
Mansion on Turtle Creek Hotel • 559-2100 or 800-527-5432
Lunch and dinner seven days • $$$ • Cr. • W

This is the only restaurant in Texas—not just the Metroplex, but all of Texas—to consistently earn a rating of five diamonds from AAA and five stars from Mobil. The restaurant is in a wing of a

1920s-era cattle baron's Italian Renaissance style mansion converted to the award-winning hotel. While opulent, the restaurant's rooms easily create a warm, residential ambiance because they occupy what was originally the living room, with an intricately carved ceiling and fireplace at each end; the library, which retains its original oak paneling; and the glass-walled veranda with a view of the landscaped courtyard. The cuisine is basically Southwestern with a Texas flair, created by the long-time award-winning executive chef Dean Fearing. It is also delightfully varied and creative, making superlative use of seasonal regional ingredients, including Hill Country game, to present offerings going from what are now classic Mansion starters, like *tortilla* soup and warm lobster taco, to sugarcane glazed salmon and pan-seared ostrich filet. *Prix fixe* dinner about $80. Bar. Music nightly. Semi-formal dress for dinner and Sunday brunch. Valet parking.

MEDITERRANEO
18111 Preston Road (75252) at Frankford Road, take Preston Road exit 21 off LBJ Frwy. (I-635) • 972-447-0066 • Lunch Monday–Friday, dinner Monday–Saturday. Closed Sunday and major holidays • $$–$$$ • Cr. • W +

In keeping with its name, the menu features innovative cuisine based on that of Northern Italy and Southern France served in a casual setting of Roman arches and soft colors creating a Mediterranean villa ambiance. Among the interesting appetizers is a serving of marinated and grilled portobello mushrooms with herb goat cheese *crostini,* oven-dried yellow tomatoes, and honey mustard. This culinary creativity continues in the pasta dishes like *linguini* with smoked scallops, summer vegetables, mushrooms, extra virgin olive oil, and tomato-basil broth. Entrées include grilled double cut lamb chops, with tomato glaze, herb goat cheese and whipped potatoes; and cherry glazed roasted duck breast with pecan wild rice and orange-*grappa* sauce. Bar. Classical guitarist Monday–Thursday dinner. All no smoking. Valet parking.

MIA'S
4322 Lemmon Avenue (75219) • 526-1020 • Lunch and dinner Monday–Saturday. Closed Sunday, Christmas and New Year's Day • $$ • MC, V • W +

This small, family-owned, no-frills neighborhood restaurant takes Tex-Mex to new heights. All the classics are here: *chimichangas, chiles rellenos, fajitas, flautas, enchiladas, chalupas;* and all of the high quality that Mama would serve to her own family. Children's menu. Beer and wine only. Large portions— some of the appetizers could make a meal—and family friendly service. Expect to wait at peak hours.

MORTON'S OF CHICAGO
501 Elm Street (75202) in West End Historic District (DART Light Rail WEST END station) • 741-2277 • Dinner only seven days. Closed major holidays • $$$ • Cr. • W (Call ahead)

What could be more appropriate than to have a Chicago steakhouse in a former speakeasy? But the dark woods and etched glass decor of this basement restaurant is more like that of a posh Edwardian men's club than a Prohibition booze joint. No written menu, so you order after your server has—usually flawlessly and sometimes passionately—proclaimed the whole list, complete with samples of the offerings of various types and sizes of prime steaks, with some lamb, chicken, lobster (the most popular order after steaks) and other seafood choices stuck in. The steaks, which can border on the gargantuan, are prime meat mindfully cooked on an open grill. Rounding off a meal with a cigar and brandy seems almost *de rigueur* here. Semi-formal dress. Bar. Valet parking. Another location at 14831 Midway in Addison (972-233-5858).

THE OLD WARSAW
2610 Maple Avenue (75201) • 528-0032 • Dinner only seven days • $$$ • Cr. • W

The "old" in the name has a double meaning because this is one of the oldest Continental restaurants in Dallas. Sticking to the tried and true, they serve traditional French and other European fare like lobster crepes, steak *au proivre, chateaubriand,* braised pheasant, duckling, and rack of lamb. The darkly rich atmosphere of the mirrored room serves as a romantic background for strolling violinists who serenade you while you dine. Semi-formal dress. Bar. Valet parking.

THE PALM
701 Ross Avenue (75202), at Market in the West End Historic District (DART Light Rail WEST END Station) • 698-0474 Lunch and dinner Monday–Friday, dinner only Saturday–Sunday. Closed Thanksgiving and Christmas Day $$$ • Cr. • W +

It's best known for its huge steaks, but if you want a BIG lobster, they can satisfy that hunger, too. They claim that some of the ones they jet in from Maine are big enough to pilot the plane. The decor at this bustling chain steakhouse is simple with sawdust on the floor and colorful cartoon caricatures of local and other celebs on the wall. Besides beef and lobster, the menu also offers veal, seafood, and poultry as well as bountiful pasta dishes. Semi-formal dress. Bar. Valet parking.

PATRIZIO
25 Highland Park Village (75205) at Mockingbird Lane and Preston Road • 522-7878 • Lunch and dinner seven days. Closed Thanksgiving, Christmas, and New Year's Day • $$ • Cr. • W

Oil paintings and oriental rugs set the mood in this Italian *trattoria* which serves traditional pizza and pasta of all kinds that are a cut above most of its competitors. Outdoor dining available. Bar. Valet parking. Another location (Patrizio North) at 1900 Preston Park Blvd. in Plano (972-964-2200).

PEGGY SUE BBQ

6600 Snider Plaza (75205), at Hillcrest and Daniels across from SMU • 987-9188 • Lunch and dinner seven days. Closed major holidays • $ • MC, V • W

As with any famed barbecue place, the oak-smoked meat is the reason customers come to Peggy Sue's. What's a little unusual here is that you get an extra reward in that the steamed vegetable sides are just as tasty and almost as famous. It also has a claim to fame in its homemade fried pies, which customers say are the best in town. Children's menu. Beer and wine only. In business for 45 years and the decor pleasantly harks back to its start in the '50s. All no smoking.

THE PYRAMID ROOM

1717 North Akard (75201) in Fairmont Hotel (DART Light Rail AKARD Station) • 720-2020 • Lunch Monday–Friday, dinner Monday–Saturday, Sunday brunch • $$$ • W +

If one item could sum up and embody the refined cosmopolitan ambiance of this restaurant it would be the between-course champagne sorbet served in lighted ice-sculpted cygnets. From the comfortable armchairs set at tables covered with brilliant linens to the glistening silver, the whole setting speaks of opulence and elegance. The Continental menu features an intriguing variety of well-prepared and presented choices in beef, veal, lamb, fowl, and seafood entrées. *Prix fixe* dinner about $36 ($58 with wines) is an excellent value. Music nightly. Semi-formal dress. Bar. Valet parking.

THE RIVIERA

7709 Inwood Road (75209), just south of Lovers Lane 351-0094 • Dinner seven days. Closed major holidays $$$ • Cr. • W

Both Southern France and Northern Italy share the real Riviera on the Mediterranean, and the innovative cuisine at this petite restaurant is inspired by the classic dishes of both those sunny regions and the bounty of the sea. The setting is simple but elegant Country French, enhanced with a scattering of paintings and a few antiques. While some of the offerings are pure French or pure Italian in origin, most are a joyful blending of the two; like lobster with herbed potato *gnocchi,* marinated tomatoes, grilled red onions, and Dijon sauce. Other seafood entrées include sauteed rainbow trout with cape scallops, argula, and a champagne chive sauce; and red snapper with lump crab meat. Meat dishes include grilled veal chops with *prosciutto risotto;* and medallions of beef tenderloin. It is consistently cited as one of the top restaurants in Dallas for food, service, and unhurried dining, so expect a wait most evenings. Semi-formal dress. Bar. Valet parking. All no smoking.

RUTH'S CHRIS STEAK HOUSE
5922 Cedar Springs Road (75235) between Inwood Road and Mockingbird Lane, two blocks south of the entrance to Love Field • 902-8080 or 800-544-0808 Ext 07 • Dinner seven days (Lunch available for about two weeks prior to Christmas) Closed Thanksgiving and Christmas Day • $$$ • Cr. • W +

When Ruth Fertel took over the Chris Restaurant in New Orleans more than 30 years ago, she added her name in front and started a nationwide chain of upscale steak houses that now has two locations in Dallas. The steaks are all aged, never-frozen, corn-fed prime beef. Except for the petite filet, steak portions are large. All are cooked in specially built broilers at 1,700–1,800 degrees, to lock in the juices, and served sizzling in melted butter. In addition to beef, the menu offers seafood, including lobster and King crab, lamb and veal chops, and chicken. *A la carte* side dishes include eight types of potatoes. Cigar-friendly bar. Valet parking. Second location at 17840 North Dallas Parkway between Trinity Mills and Frankford (972-250-2244 or 800-544-0808 Ext 50).

S & D OYSTER COMPANY
**2701 McKinney Avenue (75204), at Boll (DART Light Rail ST.
PAUL Station to connect to McKinney Avenue Trolley)
880-0111 • Lunch and dinner Monday–Saturday.
Closed Sunday and major holidays • $$ • MC, V • W**

The building is more than 100 years old and S&D has been serving New Orleans style seafood in this neighborhood store setting for more than 20 of those years. Gumbo, raw oysters on the half shell, oyster loaf, shrimp, and a variety of other fresh Gulf seafood dishes are on the menu. All are simply prepared and you can have most of them broiled, boiled, or fried to your liking. Children's menu. Beer and wine only.

SONNY BRYAN'S SMOKEHOUSE
**2202 Inwood Road (75235) near Harry Hines Blvd. • 357-7120
Lunch only seven days. Closed major holidays • $ • No Cr. • W**

With walls tinted by years of pit smoke and an all-pervading aroma of meat and spicy barbecue sauce, this shack is considered by many as a piece of Dallas history. First opened in 1958, it still offers seating in one-armed school desks or outside on picnic tables. More important, it still serves up tender brisket, ribs, and sausage that have pleased customers all these years. The onion rings are touted as the best in the city. Always crowded, but service is fast. Beer only. Other locations at: 302 North Market in the West End Historic District (744-1610); 325 North St. Paul, in the underground pedestrian tunnel (979-0103); Macy's third level in Galleria (851-5131), 4701 Frankford at North Dallas Parkway (972-447-0102), and in Las Colinas at 4030 North MacArthur Blvd. (972-650-9564).

STAR CANYON
**3102 Oak Lawn (75219), in The Centrum at Cedar Springs
520-STAR (520-7827) • Lunch Monday–Friday, dinner seven
days. Closed major holidays • $$$ • Cr. • W +**

The Lone Star setting and Lone Star cuisine at this restaurant have made it so popular reservations are hard to come by. (If you're from out-of-town, try six weeks in advance.) Among the signature dishes is bone-in cowboy ribeye with red chile onion rings. Other New Texan dishes include roasted chicken with garlic whipped potatoes, grilled quail, grilled coriander-cured venison, and shark steak. All include a palate-pleasing twist, like black-bean roast banana mash side for the pan-seared salmon, and grits laced with bits of littleneck clams along with the pork chops. The vegetarian platter features wild mushrooms, jicama-corn-slaw taco, and wood-roasted vegetables. Bar. Valet parking. All no smoking.

CLUBS AND BARS

Clubs and bars change almost as often as the phases of the moon. For current information about Dallas nightlife see the Arts and Entertainment Guide in Friday edition of The Dallas Morning News; *and the weekly* Dallas Observer *and* The Met, *which are available free at restaurants, clubs, and tourist attractions throughout the Dallas area. Following is a sampling of the variety of clubs and bars in the city that were up-and-running and popular at the time this book was published. They are broken down by the type music.*

BLUES

BLUE CAT BLUES
2617 Commerce Street in Deep Ellum • 744-CATS (744-2287)

THE BONE
2724 Elm Street in Deep Ellum • 744-BONE (744-2663)

MUDDY WATERS
1518 Greenville Avenue • 823-1518

CARIBBEAN

DREAD-N-IRIE
2807 Commerce in Deep Ellum • 742-IRIE (742-4743)

ROYAL RACK REGGAE CLUB
1906 Greenville Avenue • 824-9733

TROPICAL COVE
1820 West Mockingbird Lane • 630-5822

COUNTRY

COUNTRY 2000
10580 Stemmons Frwy. • 654-9595

RED RIVER
10310 Technology West • 972-263-0404

SONS OF HERMAN HALL
3414 Elm Street at Exposition • 747-4422

STAMPEDE
5818 LBJ Frwy. at Preston • 972-701-8081

DANCE

BLIND LEMON
2805 Main Street in Deep Ellum • 939-0202

CLUB BLUE PLANET
8796 North Central Expressway at Park Lane • 369-7009

EDEN 2000
5500 Greenville Avenue • 361-9517

LAKESIDE
3100 West Northwest Hwy. • 904-1770

RED JACKET
3606 Greenville Avenue • 823-8333

ECLECTIC

BLUE MULE
1701 North Market #105 in West End • 761-0101

CLUB CLEARVIEW
2806 Elm Street in Deep Ellum • 283-5358

CLUB DADA
2720 Elm Street in Deep Ellum • 744-DADA (744-3232)

DALLAS ALLEY
Market at Munger in West End Marketplace • 972-988-WEST
(972-988-9378)

LIZARD LOUNGE
2424 Swiss Avenue • 826-4768

POOR RICHARD'S PUB
1924 Greenville Avenue • 821-9891

TREES
2709 Elm Street in Deep Ellum • 748-5009

VELVET E
1906 McKinney at St. Paul • 969-5568

LATINO, TEJANO

CHANCES
9840 North Central Expressway at Walnut Hill • 691-0300

CLUB BABALU
2912 McKinney Avenue • 953-0300

TEJANO RODEO
7331 Gaston Avenue • 321-5540

JAZZ

DREAMS CLUB
7035 Greenville Avenue • 368-4981

STRICTLY TABU
4111 Lomo Alto • 528-5200

SAMBUCCA
2618 Elm Street • 744-0820

TERILLI'S
2815 Greenville Avenue • 827-3993

LODGING

For a double room: $ = Under $80, $$ = $80–$120, $$$ = $121–$180, $$$$ = $181–$250, $$$$$ = Over $250; Room tax 13%.
For detailed listings see Metroplex Lodgings Section, p. 364.

THE ADOLPHUS
1321 Commerce Street (75202) downtown between Field and Akard (DART Light Rail AKARD Station) • 742-8200 or 800-221-9083 • $$$$–$$$$$ (+13%) • W + 6 rooms
No smoking rooms

ARISTOCRAT HOTEL OF DALLAS
1933 Main Street (75201) at Harwood, downtown (DART Light Rail ST. PAUL Station) • 741-7700 or 800-231-4235
$$$ (+13%) • W+ 4 rooms • No smoking rooms

BEST WESTERN MARKET CENTER
2023 Market Center Blvd. (75207), at I-35E (Stemmons Freeway) • $–$$$ (+13%) • 741-9000 or 800-275-7419
W + 2 rooms • No smoking rooms

BRISTOL SUITES HOTEL (DALLAS)
7800 Alpha Road (75240), take Coit Road Exit off I-635 (LBJ Freeway), go north to Alpha Road • 972-233-7600 or 800-922-9222 • $$$–$$$$ (+13%) • W+ 3 suites No smoking suites

COMFORT INN
8901 R.L. Thornton Freeway (75228), take Exit 52B from I-30 East • 324-4475 • $$$ (+13%) • W+ 2 rooms • No smoking rooms

COURTYARD BY MARRIOTT—LBJ AT JOSEY
2930 Forest Lane (75234), take Josey Lane exit off I-635, then south to Forest Lane • 620-8000 or 800-321-2211 • $–$$ (+13%) • W+ 2 rooms

DALLAS NORTHPARK COURTYARD
10325 North Central Expressway (US75) (75231) at Meadow Road • 739-2500 or 800-321-2211 • $$ (+13%) No smoking rooms

DALLAS NORTHPARK RESIDENCE INN
10333 North Central Expressway (US75) (75231) at Meadow Road • 450-8220 or 800-331-3131 • $$ (+13%)

DOUBLETREE HOTEL AT CAMPBELL CENTRE
8250 North Central Expressway (US75) (75206) at Northwest Highway • 691-8700 or 800-222-TREE (800-222-8733) • $$ (+13%) • W+ 8 rooms • No smoking rooms

DOUBLETREE HOTEL AT LINCOLN CENTRE
5410 LBJ Freeway (I-635) (75075), at North Dallas Tollway 972-934-8400 • $$$ (+13%) • W+ 5 rooms No smoking rooms

EMBASSY SUITES LOVE FIELD
3880 West Northwest Highway (75220), near Lemmon
357-4500 • $$$ (+ 13%) • W + 8 rooms • No smoking rooms

EMBASSY SUITES HOTEL—DALLAS MARKET CENTER
2727 Stemmons Freeway (I-35E)(75207), take Inwood Road exit
then West side access road • 630-5332 or 800-EMBASSY
(800-362-2779) • $$$ (+ 13%) • W + 4 rooms
No smoking rooms

THE FAIRMONT HOTEL
1717 North Akard Street (75201), at Ross in the Arts District
(DART Light Rail AKARD Station) • 720-2020 or 800-527-4727
$$$$ (+ 13%) • W + 8 rooms • No smoking rooms

HOLIDAY INN SELECT—LBJ NE
11350 LBJ Freeway (I-635) (75238), at Exit 13
(Jupiter/Kingsley) • 341-5400 or 800-346-0660
$–$$ (+ 13%) • W + 2 rooms

HOLIDAY INN SELECT—MOCKINGBIRD LANE
1241 West Mockingbird Lane (75247), at I-35E • 630-7000 or
800-442-7547 • $$–$$$ (+ 13%) • W + 2 rooms. No smoking
rooms

HOTEL ST. GERMAIN
2516 Maple Street (75201), near Cedar Springs Road
871-2516 • $$$$$ (+ 13%)

HYATT REGENCY DALLAS
300 Reunion Blvd. (75207), downtown (DART Light Rail
UNION Station) • 561-1234 or 800-233-1234 • $$–$$$$
(+ 13%) • W + 27 rooms • No smoking rooms

LE MERIDIEN DALLAS
650 North Pearl Street (75201), in Arts District (DART Light
Rail PEARL Station) • 979-9000 • $$–$$$ (+ 13%) • W + 5
rooms • No smoking rooms

MANSION ON TURTLE CREEK (DALLAS)
2821 Turtle Creek Blvd. (75219) • 559-2100 or 800-527-5432
$$$$$ (+13%) • W+ one room • No smoking rooms

MELROSE HOTEL
3015 Oak Lawn Avenue (75219), at Cedar Springs Road
521-5151 or 800-635-7673 (Reservations) • $$$–$$$$ (+13%)
W+ 6 rooms • No smoking rooms

RADISSON HOTEL AND SUITES
2330 West Northwest Highway (75220), at I-35E • 351-4477 or
800-254-8744 • $$–$$$ (+13%) • W+ 2 rooms
No smoking rooms

RESIDENCE INN—NORTH CENTRAL
13636 Goldmark Drive (75240), US75 at Midpark Road
669-0478 or 800-331-3131 • $$–$$$ (+13%) • No smoking
suites

RENAISSANCE DALLAS HOTEL
2222 Stemmons Freeway (I-35E) (75207), near Market Center
631-2222 or 800-892-2233 (in Texas), 800-468-3571 (Outside
Texas) • $$$–$$$$ (+13%) • W+ 6 rooms • No smoking rooms

STEMMONS TRAIL COURTYARD
2883 Stemmons Trail (75220), two blocks east of I-35
352-7676 or 800-231-2211 • $$ (+13%) • W+ 2 rooms
No smoking rooms

STONELEIGH HOTEL
2927 Maple Avenue (75201), take Oaklawn exit off I-35 to
Maple, then right about a mile • 871-7111 • $$$–$$$$$(+13%)
W+ 3 rooms • No smoking rooms

WESTIN HOTEL
13340 Dallas Parkway (75240), just north of I-635 in the
Galleria Mall • 934-9494 or 800-228-3000 • $$$$ (+13%)
W + 8 rooms • No smoking rooms

WYNDHAM ANATOLE HOTEL
2201 Stemmons Freeway (I-35E) (75207), across I-35E from
Dallas Market Center • 748-1200 or 800-WYNDHAM
(800-996-3426) • $$$–$$$$ (+13%) • W + 5% of rooms
No smoking rooms

FARMERS BRANCH

DALLAS COUNTY • 25,000 • AREA CODE 972

This city traces its origin to 1841 when it was part of Peters colony, a large land grant awarded by the Republic of Texas to the Texas Land and Emigration Company in exchange for bringing in settlers to this vast unoccupied territory. Thomas and Sarah Keenan were the first to claim the head of family rights to 640 acres in this new tract. They built a house on a creek known as Mustang Branch, most likely named for the mustang horses that frequented the area and the mustang grapes that grew there. When other settlers moved in they called the area after the creek. But after Keenan and the other settlers started farming the rich black soil of the area, the creek became known as Farmers Branch and the settlement took on that name. Baby John Keenan, the first child born in the new colony, who only lived two months, is buried in the cemetery that was originally set apart by the Keenans from their 640-acre claim. Located in the 2500 block of Valley View Lane, it is one of the oldest cemeteries in Dallas County.

Farmers Branch has been credited with the first organized school as one of its many "firsts" in Dallas County. In 1846 it made another first by growing cotton, and the first cotton gin in the county was built here in 1849. The first tanning yard was set up around 1845. There was such a demand for leather at the time

170

FARMERS BRANCH

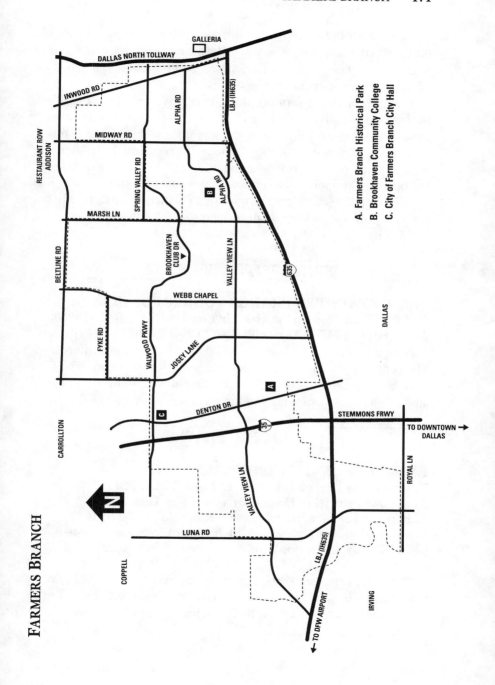

A. Farmers Branch Historical Park
B. Brookhaven Community College
C. City of Farmers Branch City Hall

that the owner didn't allow the hides to cure long enough so they became extremely hard when dry. Because of this, the stream on which the tanning yard was located soon became known as Rawhide Creek, a name that is still used.

There's not much farming done here anymore. In the city's twelve and a half square miles are more than 3,000 businesses including at least 60 Fortune 500 companies and two dozen foreign-owned firms. As a business center, it's residential population of 25,000 jumps to a workday population of 85,000. As a result of the business support of its tax base, the city is unique in that it offers free after-school care to qualified Farmers Branch families and free garbage pick-up to all residents.

The city is dry under the local options laws.

FREE VISITOR SERVICES

CITY OF FARMERS BRANCH TOURISM OFFICE
13000 William Dodson Parkway, in City Hall (P.O. Box 819010, 75381-9010) • 247-3131 or 800-BRANCH-9 (800-272-6249) • W

Note that this is an administrative office, not a visitor information center. You can pick up brochures and such here during business hours Monday–Friday, but it's best if you write or call in advance and let them send you the information you want.

HISTORIC PLACES

FARMERS BRANCH HISTORICAL PARK
2540 Farmers Branch Lane at Ford Road (75234-6214), from I-635 exit either Denton Drive or Josey Lane and go north to Farmers Branch Lane • 406-0183 or 406-0184
Summer: Monday–Thursday 9:30–8, Saturday–Sunday noon–8. Closed Friday and major holidays. Close at 6 in winter
Free • W Variable

In this 22-acre tree-shaded park on Farmers Branch Creek are a number of historic buildings that have been restored. Several of these were moved here from their original locations.

The Gilbert House, the oldest rock structure in Northeast Texas, is listed in the National Register of Historic Places. Completed in 1857, it has two-foot-thick limestone walls and chestnut plank floors.

The **Depot** was built around 1877 by the Dallas and Wichita Railroad, which was later sold to Jay Gould and the Missouri-Kansas-Texas Railroad. In 1924 it became a stop on the newly electrified Interurban Railway (see PLANO).

The **Queen Anne Victorian Cottage** was originally built in Gainesville in 1885 during the Victorian period when the architecture tended to be ornate with crossed gables, turrets and cupolas, wrap around porches, and porticos.

The **Church** was built in the 1890s in Renner, Texas. It's the type of church built during the end of the nineteenth century when the churches were commonly referred to as meeting houses because of their multiple use for church services, town meetings, and school and social events.

The **Log Structures** represent a pioneer homestead in the 1840s. Living history interpreters can often be seen here performing such tasks as blacksmithing, open hearth cooking, and quilting. Other original buildings include the **School,** built around 1900, and the **Dodson House** built in 1937.

Tours can be arranged by calling at least two weeks in advance. They are generally scheduled on Tuesdays and Thursdays.

The park is the site of several major events during the year including arts and crafts shows, antique car shows, and concerts. One Saturday in December the park is transformed into 19th Century England for the free annual Dickens in the Park celebration, which features costumed carolers, strolling minstrels, bell and voice choir concerts, horse-drawn carriage rides, readings of Dickens classics and scenes from his famous *A Christmas Carol* (information 919-2631). Also on Saturday afternoons in December, authentic English Teas are held in the Dodson House (reservations 406-0184).

OUTDOORS

FARMERS BRANCH PARKS
Parks and Recreation Department • 919-2620

The facilities in the city's more than two dozen parks include fields for most team sports, tennis courts, jogging trails, playgrounds, and picnic areas. Call for information.

COLLEGES AND UNIVERSITIES

BROOKHAVEN COLLEGE
3939 Valley View Lane (75244-4997), between Marsh and Midway • 860-4827 • W + But not all areas

One of the seven colleges in the Dallas Community College District, Brookhaven offers two-year academic and technical/occupational programs for approximately 8,000 students. The college's Center for the Arts offers a variety of cultural and entertainment events that are open to the public. These include art exhibits in the school's galleries and concerts, dance, and theatrical performances by students as well as nationally known talent in the 750-seat Performance Hall and the smaller Arena Theatre. Many of these events are free. If tickets are sold, general admission prices usually run from $3 to $15 (Box Office 860-4118). There is also a two-mile walking/jogging trail on the 200-acre campus.

MUSIC AND PERFORMING ARTS

See BROOKHAVEN COLLEGE, above.

FAMILY FUN AND KID STUFF

SANDY LAKE AMUSEMENT PARK
1800 Sandy Lake Road at I-35E (P.O. Box 810536, Dallas 75381) • 242-7449 • June–August seven days 10–6, April–May and September Wednesday–Sunday 10–6 • Admission $2, all amusements extra • W

This 60-acre park offers amusement rides, miniature golf, paddle boats, an arcade, pony rides, and picnic grounds with shade trees and a lake.

SPORTS

GOLF

PRIVATE COURSE

BROOKHAVEN COUNTRY CLUB
3333 Golfing Green Drive (75234) • 243-6151 • 54 holes. Green fees: Monday–Thursday $35, Friday–Sunday $55.

DINING OUT

NUEVO LEON
12895 Josey, Suite 100, at Valley View • 488-1984 • Lunch and dinner Monday–Friday, all meals Saturday, breakfast and brunch only Sunday • $ • Cr. • W

This is not your typical shopping center Tex-Mex restaurant. Sure, they serve some Tex-Mex here, but they don't call themselves a Mex-Mex restaurant for nothing. The main attractions on the menu are the dishes like *puerco en pasilla,* tender chunks of pork and slices of mushrooms in a *pasilla* sauce, which the menu describes as "one of the most authentic and traditional dishes of Mexico." Guitar music adds to the atmosphere at dinner and a harpist plays for Sunday brunch. Children's menu. Vegetarian dishes. Bar.

LODGINGS

For a double room: $ = Under $80, $$ = $80–$120, $$$ = $121–$180, $$$$ = $181–$250, $$$$$ = Over $250; Room tax 12%.
For detailed listings see Metroplex Lodgings Section, p. 377.

DALLAS MEDALLION
4099 Valley View Lane (Dallas 75244) • 385-9000 or
800-808-1011 (Reservations) • $$$–$$$$ (+12%) • W+ 7
rooms • No smoking rooms

DALLAS PARKWAY HILTON
4801 LBJ Freeway (Dallas 75244-6002) • 661-3600 • $$–$$$
(+12%) • W+ 5 rooms • No smoking rooms

HOLIDAY INN SELECT NORTH DALLAS
2645 LBJ Freeway (Dallas 75234) • 243-3363 or 800-HOLIDAY
(800-465-4329) • $$ (+12%) • W+ 4 rooms • No smoking
rooms

OMNI DALLAS AT PARK WEST
1590 LBJ Freeway (Dallas 75234) • 869-4300 or 800-460-8732
$–$$$ (+12%) • W+ 4 rooms • No smoking rooms

FORT WORTH

TARRANT COUNTY SEAT • 475,000 • AREA CODE 817

The war between the United States and Mexico over the border of the new state of Texas was not long over when, in June 1849, Company F, 2nd Dragoons established a frontier outpost on the bluffs overlooking the Trinity River to protect the settlements to the east, like Dallas, from Indian raids. The post was named in honor of Major General William Jenkins Worth, a hero in the conquest of Mexico City and now head of the U.S. Army in Texas and New Mexico. Worth never got to see the post named after him, dying of cholera in San Antonio about the time the post was being set up. (Worth's heroism was recognized in his home of New York City, too, with a 50-foot-tall monument at Broadway and Fifth.)

By 1853 the frontier had moved farther west and the soldiers went with it. Immediately the settlers moved in and took over the post buildings, which were better than the ramshackle cabins they were living in.

FORT WORTH "STEALS" THE COUNTY SEAT

The population had reached about 100 by 1856. Among its citizens were several town boosters who would make a present-day chamber of commerce proud. Dissatisfied that the town of Birdville was the county seat, they promoted an election to move

177

FORT WORTH

it to Fort Worth. They won, but the people of Birdville cried "foul" saying Fort Worth had stolen the election by bringing in men from outside the county to vote. True or not, another election was ordered, but by the time it could be scheduled, it was 1860, and the county government was well entrenched in Fort Worth and nobody wanted to move it again.

CHISHOLM TRAIL MAKES IT A BOOM TOWN

Soon after the Civil War, Texas cattlemen found out that long-horns selling for $5 a head in Texas would fetch $30 or more in northern markets. Thus started the long drives that saw some 10 million head of Texas cattle driven north—and into the history books and legends—between 1866 and the mid-1880s.

Among the many trails used for the drives was one set-up by Jesse Chisholm to the railhead at Abilene, Kansas. The Chisholm Trail ran right through Fort Worth, often right down the main street, causing the town to boom. This was the last stop before crossing into the Oklahoma Indian Territory, so the cowboys stocked up on beans and bacon and other supplies here and whooped it up a bit before setting out to push the huge herds through the last 300 miles of dust and mud.

On the return trip, with the herd sold and their pay burning in their pockets, this was the first Texas town they hit. And they usually hit it hard. The favorite place to let off steam was known as Hell's Half-Acre—located where the modern Fort Worth/Tarrant County Convention Center now stands spanning an area of 14 city blocks. This wide open section of town, made up almost entirely of saloons, gambling houses, and bordellos, was filled with lowlifes who did everything they could to separate the cowboys from their hard-earned dollars.

The townspeople saw solid prosperity just over the horizon when the Texas and Pacific Railroad headed their way in 1873. This would make Fort Worth the railhead instead of Abilene. They even incorporated and set up a bank; the population quickly doubled from about 2,000 to 4,000. But their high hopes were dashed when the Panic of 1873 struck, the railroad went bankrupt, and construction stopped 26 miles short of the town. Overnight the population dropped to about 1,000 as many people gave up their dream and moved to Dallas.

It was during this time that a Dallas newspaper, feeding the feud that was growing between the two towns, reported that Fort Worth was so dead a panther had been seen sleeping unmolested in the streets. This insult goaded the people of Fort Worth to action. At first it was a simple thumbing of the nose at Dallas: The fire department adopted a panther for a mascot and many clubs in town added Panther to their names. Then they turned serious. They needed a railroad to survive, and if the railroad wouldn't come to them, they'd go out and drag it in.

DRAGGING IN THE RAILROAD

They formed a construction company, reached an agreement with the railroad, and started to lay track. Every business operated with a minimum of help and sent its employees out to work on the right-of-way. The women worked in shifts to feed the men and take care of the mules. As if this wasn't enough of a challenge, they worked under the threat that if the railroad didn't reach Fort Worth before the Texas Legislature adjourned they would lose the land grant the state would pay the railroad. It's said that when it got down to the last days the crews just threw down track on ungraded ground, weighing them down with stones while, at the same time, the ailing representative from Fort Worth had himself carried into the Legislature each day to cast a vote against adjournment, and the city council moved the city limits out to meet the tracks.

Their tenacity and Fort Worth spirit paid off. On July 19, 1876, the railroad reached Fort Worth. As they had dreamed, this was the start of something big. Fort Worth became the end of the trail drives instead of the start. The ranchers made it their main shipping point and the city soon became known as "Cowtown." In time, several railroads had terminals here. Stockyards were built and in 1902 the big Chicago meat packers, Swift and Armour, built plants here.

BUTCH AND SUNDANCE IN HELL'S HALF ACRE

With the cowboys still driving herds to town, Hell's Half Acre continued to be a magnet for them. It was also a hangout for famous outlaws like Butch Cassidy and the Sundance Kid. Butch and Sundance, whose real names were George Leroy Parker and

Harry Longbaugh, often hid out from the police and the Pinkertons here. And it was here that Sundance met Etta Place, who later went with them on their ill-fated journey to South America. In 1900, while in town celebrating a bank robbery they did in Nevada, Butch, Sundance, and the rest of the Hole in the Wall Gang had their picture taken. According to the legend, Butch sent a copy of the picture to the Nevada bank's president with a note of thanks.

Hells' Half Acre was pretty well demolished around the time of World War I. It was also around this time that oil was discovered in nearby counties. Hundreds of oil companies set up in the city and it soon became an oil center. And during and after World War II the defense industry came to town to stay and several major corporations followed. Such events took up the economic slack of the declining stockyards' business as trucks replaced railroads, and as shippers and local feedlots and cattle auctions made large centralized stockyards obsolete. The Fort Worth Stockyards are still an important part of the city's economy, but now almost as much as a unique attraction as for the cattle business.

CULTURE COMES TO COWTOWN

Culture came to Cowtown starting in the 1930s with a big push from city boosters like millionaires Amon Carter, founder of *The Fort Worth Star-Telegram,* and industrialist Kay Kimbell. Following the example of these philanthropists, other wealthy citizens were equally generous in their support of the arts. Today, in addition to "Cowtown," Fort Worth calls itself "The Museum Capital of the Southwest." Among its numerous museums giving support to that title are such gems as the Amon Carter Museum and the Kimbell Art Museum. The arts also abound with theaters, a symphony, opera, and a botanical garden, and the city is the home of the Van Cliburn International Piano Competition, one of the most prestigious musical competitions in the world. Not exactly art, but fun, it is also the home of a zoo that has been acclaimed as one of America's "Top Five."

All this will be reinforced when the $60 million Nancy Lee & Perry R. Bass Performance Hall, in Sundance Square, is completed in 1998. When fully developed it will be the new home of the symphony, opera, ballet, as well as local and touring theater companies.

As a result, although the city still calls itself Cowtown and the town "Where the West Begins," and continually projects that image to pay tribute to its Old West heritage (businessmen in suits wearing 10-gallon hats and cowboy boots are a common sight), it now might more appropriately be thought of as the home of the sophisticated cowboy.

The Fort Worth city bus service, called The T, offers a Free Zone downtown bounded by Henderson, Jones, Belknap, and Lancaster streets. When boarding, just grab a Free Zone pass.

NEIGHBORHOODS

The three neighborhoods of special interest to visitors are: the Cultural/Museum District including nearby parks, gardens, and the zoo; the Stockyards National Historic District, and the Sundance Square Downtown Entertainment District.

CULTURAL/MUSEUM DISTRICT
**West of downtown. Museums: South of Camp Bowie Blvd.
between University and Montgomery. Parks and Gardens: off
University, north and south of I-30**

The Cultural District lives up to its name. Within easy walking distance of each other are the **Amon Carter Museum, Kimbell Art Museum, Modern Art Museum of Fort Worth,** the **Scott Theatre,** and the **Fort Worth Museum of Science and History** with its Omni Theater and Noble Planetarium. And if you like to walk, you don't have to go far to take in the **Will Rogers Memorial Center,** the home of the Southwestern Exposition and Livestock Show and Rodeo, which has been held annually for more than 100 years; and the **Casa Manana Theatre.** Immediately to the south of this cluster of culture is the **Fort Worth Botanic Garden, Trinity Park,** and **Forest Park** with its **Log Cabin Village** and the **Fort Worth Zoo.**

CULTURAL DISTRICT AND MUSEUMS

N

Bailey Ave.

7th St.

Arch Adams St.

1.75 miles to
Downtown
Fort Worth

Univ. of North
Texas Health
Science Center

Camp Bowie Blvd.

(P)

Amon
Carter
Museum

Kimbell Art
Museum

Lancaster Ave.

Modern Art
Museum

(P)

Scott
Theatre

Pioneer Tower

Will Rogers
Memorial
Complex

Casa
Mañana

University Dr.

(P)

Farrington
Field

(P)

Museum of
Science & History
Omni/Planetarium

Exhibit Hall

Equestrian
Center

Montgomery St.

(P)

Crestline Rd.

Livestock
Barns

Trinity Park

Harley Ave.

Botanic
Garden

THE STOCKYARDS NATIONAL HISTORIC DISTRICT
North of downtown. North Main from 23rd to 28th streets

The Stockyards, once the second largest in the country, played
a major role in the growth of Fort Worth. By 1873 the many rail
lines that extended like tarantula legs from downtown Fort Worth
included the Fort Worth Stockyards Belt Railway, which special-
ized in moving livestock. Cattle pens extended for nearly a mile
when the big meat packers established plants. In 1911 the area
was incorporated as Niles City, a community composed almost
entirely of the Stockyards, set up as a defense by the meat packers to keep their tax haven from being annexed by Fort Worth.
With a population of only 650 and property values of $25 mil-

The Stockyards Historic District

NE 28th St.   SH 183

2.25 miles to I-35W ⟶

Marine Creek

N. Main St.

P

Texas Gold Statue

N

Stockyards Blvd.

Rodeo Plaza

Billy Bob's
Texas

P

Turntable

Shops
Saloons
Restaurants

Cowtown
Coliseum

Livestock
Exchange
Bldg.

Hotel

P   B & B

White
Elephant
Saloon

Exchange Ave.

Visitors
Information
Center

Stockyards
Station

Tarantula Railroad

23rd St.

2.5 miles to
Downtown
Fort Worth

Horseback
Riding

lion, its per capita wealth led to it being called the "Richest Little Town in the World." But the meat packers lost in courts and in 1922, Niles City was annexed and became part of Fort Worth. In its time, more than 160 million head of livestock were processed through here.

The whole district is in the National Register of Historic Places and it looks a lot like it did a hundred years ago with many of the buildings closing in on being a century old. But today those old timers exist side-by-side with a thriving entertainment complex that plays up their age to keep alive the spirit of the Old West. The **Livestock Exchange Building,** for example, built in 1904, is now the appropriate location for The Stockyards Collection and Museum. This building still lives up to its name as the site of livestock auctions in which entire herds of cattle are bought and sold. The cattle aren't here, however, because the whole deal is done by satellite communications. The **Thannisch Building,** built in 1907, is now the Stockyards Hotel. And the **Cowtown Coliseum,** built in 1907, which made the history books as the home of the first indoor rodeo, still has wild west shows and professional rodeo competitions most weekends. Parking lots are at the eastern end of East Exchange. ($2 parking fee on weekends.)

SUNDANCE SQUARE DOWNTOWN ENTERTAINMENT DISTRICT
Downtown, Throckmorton to Calhoun and 2nd to 5th Streets

Surrounded by modern skyscrapers, this 14-block historic entertainment district has red-brick paved streets and courtyards that add to the early 1900s architecture that has been restored or replicated and now houses a collection of restaurants, live theaters and movie theaters, nightclubs, art galleries, and specialty shops. The square is named after the Sundance Kid, who, with his partner Butch Cassidy, hid-out in high fashion in the nearby Hell's Half Acre and became part of the legends of the Old West. One of the more fascinating aspects of Sundance Square is the extensive *trompe l'oeil* (fool the eye) paintings of Richard Haas, especially the three-story Chisholm Trail Mural on the south side of the building at 400 Main, which appears to have depth although it is a flat picture.

When it is fully operational, the center of the many attractions in Sundance will be the new Nancy Lee and Perry R. Bass Performance Hall, which occupies most of the block at Commerce and Fourth. This will be the capstone of the successful master plan launched by Bass Brothers Enterprises in 1982 to revitalize what was then the decaying downtown and create a vibrant marketplace for living, working, shopping, and entertainment.

The Convention and Visitors Bureau has a free downtown walking tour map that gives details on many of the buildings in this area (see SELF-GUIDED TOURS, pg. 189). While popular in the day, the area livens up even more in the evenings. The side-

HISTORIC DOWNTOWN

walks and street corners of Sundance are filled with strolling musicians, mimes, caricature artists, and other entertainers each Friday and Saturday evening throughout the year. One of the nicest, and most unusual, things about this entertainment district is that after 5 p.m. on weekdays and all day weekends and holidays, all the Sundance parking lots are free (look for the Sundance logo on the lot). On a bustling Saturday night, you may have trouble finding a space in a lot real close to where you want to go, but once you get parked, you won't have to pay.

FREE VISITOR SERVICES

FORT WORTH CONVENTION AND VISITORS BUREAU
415 Throckmorton (76102) at 4th • 336-8791 or 800-433-5747
Monday–Friday 8:30–5, Saturday 10–4 • W

Everything you want to know about Fort Worth, and then some, you can find out from the counselors here. Brochures, maps, and good advice and suggestions are freely available. There's parking on the street and in the visitor spaces in the lot at Throckmorton between 4th and 5th.

STOCKYARDS VISITOR CENTER
130 East Exchange Avenue, near the Stockyards Station
624-4741 • Monday–Friday 10–6, Saturday 10–7,
Sunday noon–6 • W +

A good place to drop in to pick up loads of free information before you start exploring the Stockyards. Note the mural on the wall. You can also sign up for a Stockyards Trails Walking Tour here (see COMMERCIAL TOURS, below). Information isn't restricted to the Stockyards. You can find out about attractions, lodging, and dining throughout the city.

PUBLICATIONS

Current information about events, activities, nightlife, theater, movies, and dining in Fort Worth and other Metroplex cities may be found in *The Star Time: Weekly Entertainment Guide* section published each Friday in *The Fort Worth Star-Telegram.* Events and activities in the Stockyards are also highlighted in the monthly *Fort Worth Stockyards Gazette,* which is available free at restaurants and tourist attractions throughout the city. A Convention and Visitors Bureau calendar of activities for each month is also available at hotels, restaurants, and many shops downtown and in the Cultural District and Stockyards. Some coverage of Fort Worth is also included in the *Dallas Observer,* available free throughout the Fort Worth/Dallas area.

COMMERCIAL TOURS

CLASSIC CARRIAGES
336-0400 (Recorded message) • Wednesday–Saturday after 7:30 p.m. (Weather permitting)

Horse-drawn carriage rides through Sundance Square and the downtown area begin at The Worthington Hotel, 200 Main. Up to four people can ride for $20, each additional is $5. Pick-ups at other hotels can be arranged.

HELL'S HALF ACRE AND SUNDANCE SQUARE WALKING TOUR
327-1178 • Friday–Saturday mornings at 9:30

A guided walking tour of downtown Fort Worth covering its history from its founding to the present day revitalization. The 2½-hour tour leaves from the Radisson Plaza Hotel lobby (100 East 8th Street at Main). $10 per person. Special tour arrangements available.

STOCKYARDS TRAILS WALKING TOUR
130 East Exchange Avenue • 625-9715 or Metro 817-988-6877
Monday–Saturday 10–4, Sunday noon–4

These tours take you on a guided walk through the historic Stockyards district. They leave from the Stockyards Visitor Center and last a little over an hour. Cost is $7 with special rates for seniors and children.

OTHER TOURS

Although there are no regularly scheduled daily driving tours of Fort Worth, the following reportedly are among those that provide escorted tours for individuals: Quentin McGown 531-4444, Silver West Limousine Service 870-1333, Texas Red Tours 740-0747, and Tours & More 923-4553. Contact the individual agency to determine prices, tour itineraries, services provided, and reservation policies. Contact the Convention and Visitors Bureau for information on other escorted tours or step-on guides for groups.

INDUSTRY TOURS

MRS BAIRD'S BAKERY TOUR
7301 South Freeway (76134), at I-35W South Freeway and
Sycamore School Road • 615-3050 • Monday & Wednesday
10–4, Friday 10–4 • Call for reservations three weeks in
advance • Free • W

See how bread is made while learning the history of this popular Texas bakery. All visitors are given a sample of hot buttered bread fresh from the oven. Parking at the front of the plant and the tour starts from the front door. Tour lasts 45 minutes to an hour. Children must be at least six years old to take the tour.

SELF-GUIDED TOURS

GET-ACQUAINTED DRIVING TOUR

Because Fort Worth is relatively easy to get around by car, it's possible to take a quick self-guided tour to get acquainted with the main streets, traffic, and the general location of major sights and attractions before you venture out to find a specific place. This drive can't cover everything of interest, but it will hit the highlights. With few exceptions, all the places mentioned in this tour that are marked in **bold-faced type** have listings in the various categories of this Fort Worth section.

Even though we've tried to make sure our driving instructions are clear and precise, it's probably a good idea to have a city map with you to check out the route as you follow the directions. You might also find it helpful, and safer, if you can record the directions into a portable tape recorder and play them back in your car in increments as you go.

It's also designed so you can stop to visit at any point and go on when you're ready.

Start at the Stockyards

You can start your tour from any place along the route, but we'll start at the entrance to the Stockyards with your car heading north at North Main and Exchange. (If coming from downtown, take Commerce Street north. It becomes North Main after you pass behind the County Courthouse and cross the Trinity River bridge.)

From Main, turn right (east) onto Exchange and go under the Stockyards sign, which has been welcoming visitors since 1910. On your right almost immediately will be the **White Elephant Saloon.** Further down the block, at 130 Exchange, is the **Stockyards Visitor Center.** If you haven't already stocked up on maps and brochures, stop and do that here. Farther down on the right is Stockyards Station, where the Tarantula Train stops. On the small rise at the east end of Exchange is what remains of the old Armour and Swift packing houses. Turn around at the end of the street.

Coming back west, now again on your right, are the **Tarantula Train** turntable, the Livestock Exchange Building, which also houses the **Stockyards Collection and Museum,** and the **Cowtown Coliseum.** On the lawn in front of the Coliseum is a statue of **Bill Pickett,** the first black inducted into the Cowboy Hall of Fame. Just past this, if you look up Rodeo Plaza, the street to your right, you should be able to see **Billy Bob's Texas** nightclub. Continue on Exchange. At the corner is the **Stockyards Hotel.** A block north on your right at 26th Street/Stockyards Blvd. is the **Texas Gold** statue, but you can see that when you have time to walk around the area. For now, turn left (south) on Main toward downtown.

Downtown and Sundance Square

After you cross the Trinity River and climb the hill, passing **Heritage Park** on your right and the **Tarrant County Courthouse** on your left, you'll be on Houston Street. Right about here is the site of the original Camp Worth. Get in the left lane. Just past this you'll go under the skywalk that connects the **Wor-ton Hotel,** on your left, with the **Fort Worth Outlet** which houses the **Tandy Ice Rink** and the **Tandy Subway Center** buildings on your right.

You're going to turn left on 2nd Street, but before you do, look ahead on the right side of the street in the 300 block of Houston where you should be able to see the **Caravan of Dreams Performing Arts Center.** Turn left on 2nd, go one block in front of The Worthington Hotel to Main and turn right putting you into the heart of **Sundance Square.**

Stay to your right. On your left, at 309, in the middle of the block is the **Sid Richardson Collection,** and past this is the Haltom Jeweler's 2½-ton cast-iron clock in front of 313 Main. This was the site of the first Knights of Pythias Castle erected in the world, in 1881. That castle burned down and was replaced by the present building in 1903, a castle still guarded by a 7-foot knight in armor in a niche on the front of the building.

As you cross 3rd Street, note the *trompe l'oeil* (fool the eye) artwork on the building on your right on the southeast corner. The best example of this style, the **Chisholm Trail Mural,** is on the south side of the building. You are going to turn right at the next street, so you may be able to get a glimpse of it then, or wait until you have a chance to walk around Sundance Square.

Turn right at 4th Street and go west. Houston is the first intersection. On the northwest corner, on your right, is the storefront **Modern at Sundance Square,** an annex of the Museum of Modern Art. Just past it, on 4th, is the entrance to the downstairs **Circle Theater,** and on the next corner, at Throckmorton, the **Fort Worth Convention and Visitors Bureau.** (If you want to stop at the Convention and Visitors Bureau, there *may* be some free reserved Convention and Visitors Bureau visitor parking spaces in the parking lot on the south side of 4th Street.) To your left, the winged sculpture in front of the skyscraper on the southwest corner of 4th and Throckmorton is called "The Eagle." The **Reata Restaurant,** on the 35th floor of the Bank One Building offers an excellent panoramic view of downtown.

Continue going west on 4th until it curves and runs into 7th, then turn right (west).

The Cultural District

The **Cattleman's Museum** will be on your left at 1301 West 7th just east of Summit. A few blocks farther, on your left, you'll pass one of the entrances to **Trinity Park.** The Botanic Garden is on the south end of this park, but we'll get to it later. Trinity Park is also the location of the annual productions of **Shakespeare in the Park.** Continue on 7th to the major intersection with University Drive and Camp Bowie Blvd. Turn left on University. Get in the right hand lane and turn right (west) at Lancaster. You are now in the **Cultural District,** once called the Acropolis of the Southwest. On your left is the **Will Rogers Memorial** complex, site of the annual **Southwestern Exposition and Livestock Show and Rodeo.** On your right is the **Kimbell Art Museum** and past that the **Amon Carter Museum.** On your left, near the corner, is the **Modern Art Museum of Fort Worth** and the **Scott Theatre.** Turn left onto Montgomery. Before the next corner, on your left is the **Fort Worth Museum of Science and History** with the Omni Theatre and Noble Planetarium. Turn left just past this onto Crestline Road and go east, passing behind the Will Rogers Memorial, back to University Drive. If you look to your left at the corner of University and Lancaster, you should be able to see the **Casa Manana Theatre** sign up the block on the left. If you continued straight on Crestline, it'd take you into Trinity Park and the **Van Zandt Cottage.** But don't go straight or left now, turn right (south) on University.

The Parks, Zoo, and TCU

A short way down University, on your right just before you reach I-30, is the entrance to the **Botanic Garden.** Continue past I-30 and after you cross the Trinity River again, on your left is the entrance to **Forest Park** and the **Fort Worth Zoo.** A little farther on, **Log Cabin Village** is on your right.

Continue south on University until you come to the school that gave the street its name, **Texas Christian University.** Get in the left lane and turn left (east) on Berry. Stay to the left. Several blocks farther, turn left on Forest Park Blvd. Stay on this, passing

PARKS AND ZOO DISTRICT

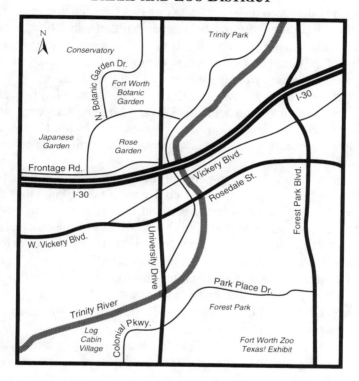

Forest Park your left, go under I-30, and then Trinity Park on the left, to 7th Street. Turn right on 7th and head back downtown.

The South End of Downtown

On your right at 7th and Lamar is Burnett Park, which contains the Henry Matisse sculpture "Backs." Across from this, on your left at 500 West 7th, is "The Texas Sculpture" in the plaza in front of the bank building. In the next block, on your left at 400 West 7th is the *Fort Worth Star-Telegram* Building, built in 1921. Get in the right lane and turn right (south) on Houston and then get in the left lane. Two blocks down, at 9th, on your left, is the **Fort Worth/Tar-**

rant County Convention Center. On your right, the wedge-shaped building on the southwest corner of Houston and 9th is the Flatiron Building. Inspired by similar buildings in Chicago and New York, when it was completed in 1907, its seven stories made it one of the tallest buildings in the Southwest. Panther heads adorning the facade are symbolic of the city's unofficial mascot.

At the end of the Convention Center complex, turn left between the Convention Center and the **Water Garden.** This area was once the rip-roaring section of town known as Hell's Half Acre. Follow the street around as it curves, turns north and becomes Commerce.

Continue on Commerce going north. At 8th Street, on your left is the Radisson Plaza Hotel. When it was formerly known as the Hotel Texas, this was where President and Mrs. Kennedy spent the night before going to Dallas where he was assassinated. Between 5th and 4th street, on your right, is the **Bass Performance Hall** which, when fully developed will be the city's premier center for the performing arts. City Center Tower II is in the next block, on your right, and just past this, on the corner of Commerce and 2nd is **Fire Station No. 1,** the city museum featuring 150 years of Fort Worth history.

This is the end of the self-guided tour to get you acquainted with the highlights of the city. If you started at any point other than the Stockyards, all you have to do is continue north on Commerce, which runs into Main and you're on your way to where this tour started.

SELF-GUIDED WALKING TOURS

The Convention and Visitors Bureau offers a free downtown walking tour map, which includes 59 sites. If you follow it all, it covers about three miles and takes about three hours to complete. However, it has sub-tours for art, architecture, and historic sites that cover one to two miles and take one to two hours to complete. Or you can use it to devise your own tour of just the places that most interest you.

BIRD'S-EYE VIEW

The only panoramic view open to the public in a downtown skyscraper is from the **Reata Restaurant** on 35th floor of the Bank One Building diagonally across from the Convention and Visitors Bureau on Throckmorton between 4th and 5th streets. Through the huge windows here you can see all of downtown and in every direction for several miles. Not exactly bird's eye, but a good low-level view (bird flying close to the ground) of downtown can be seen from the grounds of the **Amon Carter Museum. Heritage Park,** next to the Tarrant County Courthouse, offers a panoramic view of the Trinity Valley and the Stockyards area north of downtown.

HISTORIC PLACES

EDDLEMAN MCFARLAND HOUSE
1110 Penn Street (76102), south off West 7th • 332-5875
Monday–Friday tours on the hour 10–1 • Adults $2.50.
Children free

Built in 1899 on a bluff overlooking the Trinity River, in an area once called "Quality Hill," this is one of the last of Fort Worth's elegant Victorian homes of the cattle barons. The home was occupied by only two families in its history and its finely crafted woodwork and other architectural details remain largely unaltered from its original state. It's listed in the National Register of Historic Places. Another Victorian home in the National Register is the **Pollock-Capps House,** at 1120. Built in 1898, it was recently converted to offices. Street parking only.

ELIZABETH BOULEVARD HISTORICAL DISTRICT
Elizabeth between 8th Avenue and College Avenue, south of I-30, west of I-35

Elizabeth Boulevard is the central street in a neighborhood of grand homes of cattlemen and oilmen built between 1910 and 1930. At that time it was known as "Silver Slipper Row." The construction of the mansions ended with The Depression and smaller bungalows were built among the larger homes. The area is listed in the National Register of Historic Places and many of the houses have individual markers. All are private homes, not open to the public.

LOG CABIN VILLAGE
2100 Log Cabin Village Lane (76109), take Colonial Parkway off South University Dr. • 926-5881 • Tuesday–Friday 9–5, Saturday 10–5, Sunday 1–5. Closed Monday • Adults $1.50, Seniors and children (4–17) $1.25. Under 4 years old free W Variable
This is a living history museum containing seven pioneer cabins from the early and mid-1800s that were moved to the site, restored, and furnished with period tools and furnishings. Interpreters dressed in pioneer costumes demonstrate old crafts such as spinning and candle making. Milling equipment was installed into one of the cabins to convert it to a grist mill. There is also a staffed reproduction of a blacksmith shop from the period. One of the cabins was the home of Isaac Parker, the uncle of Cynthia Ann Parker who was captured by the Comanches as a young girl. She married Chief Nocona and was the mother of Quanah Parker, the last great Comanche war chief who helped bring about peace between the settlers and the Indian tribes of North Texas. Free parking adjacent.

PIONEER REST CEMETERY
626 Samuels, northeast of downtown
Open seven days 9 to dusk • W
This cemetery was started in 1850 to bury two children of Major Ripley Arnold, the officer who established Camp Worth. Arnold, reputedly a strict disciplinarian of his troops, was killed by one of his men at Fort Graham, near Hillsboro, Texas, in 1853. His body was brought back here to be buried with his children. Also buried here are General Edward H. Tarrant, after whom the county is named, and Ephraim M. Daggett, who was sometimes called the Father of Fort Worth in recognition of his importance in the city's early days. Daggett was so influential that his like-

ness was engraved on the city seal for the first 50 years of its existence. The graves of the pioneers are in the rear of the cemetery.
After this small cemetery was filled, the latter-day Fort Worth
giants and sinners were buried in **Oakwood Cemetery,** on Grand
Avenue between downtown and the Stockyards. These included
prominent cattle barons, like the little-known Fountain Goodlet
Oxsheer who once owned more than a million acres and 30,000
head of cattle, and oilman/rancher W.T. Waggoner who, in the
early 1900s, gave each of his three children 90,000 acres of oil-
rich land and 10,000 head of cattle.

TARRANT COUNTY COURTHOUSE
100 West Weatherford at north end of Main • 884-1726
Open to the public Monday–Friday during business hours • W
    Built between 1893 and 1895 of Texas pink granite and marble,
its Renaissance Revival style was designed to resemble the Texas
Capitol building. It cost over $400,000 and this extravagance so
incensed the taxpayers that in 1894, before the building was completed, they voted out the county commissioners who had voted
for it. Displays in the hallways show photographs from the original construction, historical prints of the county, and the $12 mil-
lion renovation in the 1980s that restored it to its original appear-
ance. Free tours are available. Listed in the National Register of
Historic Places. Street parking only.

ST. PATRICK'S CATHEDRAL COMPLEX
1206 and 1208 Throckmorton Street • 332-4915 • W
    Built of white Texas stone, the Gothic Revival cathedral was
completed in 1892. The oldest church in the city, it contains the
original hand-painted stain glass windows from Germany and a
bell cast in Troy, New York, that has been in use since 1889. The
church and St. Ignatius Academy next door, built in 1889, are in
the National Register of Historic Places. The late William J.
Marsh, organist at the cathedral for many years, was composer of
the state song, "Texas Our Texas."

STOCKYARDS NATIONAL HISTORIC DISTRICT
See NEIGHBORHOODS, p. 182.

THISTLE HILL
1509 Pennsylvania Avenue (76104), at south end of Summit Avenue • 336-1212 • Monday–Friday 10–3, Sunday 1–4. Closed Saturday. Tours begin on the hour • Adults $4, Seniors and children (7-12) $2 • W downstairs only

This mansion was built in 1903 as a wedding present from cattle baron W. T. Waggoner to his daughter Electra. In addition to being rich, Electra was considered a little eccentric. She set a record by being the first customer of Neiman Marcus to spend more than $20,000 in that store in one day, she never wore the same dress twice, came back from Europe with a butterfly tattoo, and spent three hours a day in a milk bath. The house, which Electra sold in 1910, contains 18 rooms, a 14-foot-wide oak grand stairway with Tiffany-style windows on the landing, and oak paneled halls. The new owner, Winfield Scott made several changes, the most prominent of which are the limestone columns on the front porch, which he had brought in from Indiana on special railcars. Later the house was used as a girls' school and finally fell into disrepair until it was saved and restored by a group of concerned Fort Worth citizens. Tours last about 45 minutes to an hour. Parking and the entrance are in the rear on Pruitt Street.

THE VAN ZANDT COTTAGE
2900 Crestline Road, in Trinity Park

Major Khleber Miller Van Zandt, a captain in the Texas Seventh Regiment, Confederate Army, settled in Fort Worth following the Civil War. A member of the Texas Legislature, a banker, merchant, and cattleman, he acquired 600 acres in the early 1870s, including this cottage, which had been used as collateral for a loan. The cottage is the only one in Fort Worth still standing in its original location. Although it is not open, the kitchen foundation is still visible behind it.

OTHER HISTORIC BUILDINGS

The following downtown buildings are among those in the city that are also listed in the National Register of Historic Places: **Hotel Texas** (1921) (now the Radisson Plaza Hotel); **Blackstone Hotel** (1929), 601 Main; **Burk Burnett Building** (1914), 500 Main; **Knights of Pythis Hall** (1903), 313 Main; **First Christian Church** (1914), 612 Throckmorton; **Fort Worth Club Building** (1925), 306 West 7th; **Neil P. Anderson Building** (1921), 411 West 7th; **Bryce Building** (1910), 909 Throckmorton; **W. T. Waggoner Building** (1919), 810 Houston; **Flatiron Building** (1907), 1000 Houston; **U.S. Post Office Building** (1933), Lancaster and Jennings; **Texas and Pacific Terminal Complex** (1928), West Lancaster; and **The Union Passenger Station** (1899), 1601 Jones Street. The histories of all these are included in the Downtown Fort Worth Walking Tour map available from the Convention and Visitors Bureau.

MUSEUMS AND ART GALLERIES

AMERICAN AIRLINES C. R. SMITH MUSEUM
4601 Hwy. 360 (76155) at FAA Road, south of Hwy. 183. Southwest of D/FW Airport • 967-1560 • Tuesday 10–7, Wednesday–Saturday 10–6, Sunday 12–5. Closed Monday and major holidays • Free • W +

Through large-screen films viewed from first-class airliner seats, interactive displays, hands-on exhibits, and videos, visitors can follow the history and world-wide operations of American Airlines from the 1930s to the present. Exhibits include a close-up look at a jet engine, airplane cockpit, a wind tunnel exhibit of the principles of aerodynamics, and how an airliner is flown and maintained. Gift shop.

AMON CARTER MUSEUM
3501 Camp Bowie Blvd. (P.O. Box 2365, 76113) at Montgomery and West Lancaster, in the Cultural District • 738-1933 Tuesday–Saturday 10–5, Sunday 12–5. Closed Monday and major holidays • Free • W + Use side entrance on Camp Bowie Blvd.

The story of Amon G. Carter is one of rags to riches. He came from an impoverished family to become a millionaire and the founder of *The Fort Worth Star-Telegram.* Carter definitely was not into the arts—in an interview with *Time* he said that in all his life he had only read about a dozen books. But he knew that a great city needed art and he wanted Fort Worth to be a great city. He started his art collection with the paintings and sculptures of Frederic Remington, Charles M. Russell, and other artists of the American West. When he died, he left his collection and a foundation to establish this museum. His early collection has been expanded to include all American art and, appropriately, the building that houses it was designed to resemble an American Indian lodge. Among the artists represented are Winslow Homer, William Michael Harnett, Grant Wood, Martin Johnson Heade, and Georgia O'Keefe. The museum also has a photography collection of more than 250,000 prints. These range from the earliest daguerreotypes to contemporary photographs including Southwest landscapes by Ansel Adams and the works of Dorothea Lange, Laura Gilpin, and Eliot Porter.

Videos on the collections are available for viewing in the museum theater. Free public tours are offered daily at 2 p.m. For group tours, call 737-5913 at least two weeks in advance. Bookstore. Free parking adjacent to museum off Camp Bowie Blvd. Additional free parking nearby in Will Rogers Memorial lots off Lancaster Street.

THE CATTLEMAN'S MUSEUM
1301 West 7th Street (76102) • 332-7064 • Monday–Friday 8:30–4:30. Closed weekends and major holidays • Free • W use rear parking lot entrance

The fascinating story of the development of Texas ranching and the cattle industry is told here on a self-guided tour through multi-media visuals and life-sized dioramas with talking mannequins, including a "talking longhorn." Added to this are displays of cowboy memorabilia and historic photos of legendary early Texas cattlemen like Charles Goodnight, who set up the Goodnight Trail, and Richard King, founder of the King Ranch.

Because this museum is in the headquarters of the Texas and Southwestern Cattle Raisers Foundation, it's appropriate that emphasis is given to the brand inspectors, the lawmen charged with tracking down cattle thieves. This starts with the statue of "The Brand Inspector" at the entrance to the building and is carried on inside with several displays.

FIRE STATION NO. 1—150 YEARS OF FORT WORTH
203 Commerce (76102) at 2nd Street, downtown • 732-1631 (History Department, Fort Worth Museum of Science and History) • Seven days 9–7 • Free • W

The building that houses this history of Fort Worth itself played a part in that history. On this site the city's first fire station was built in 1876. It was also the site of Fort Worth's original city hall with the city offices on the second floor and the volunteer firefighters on the first. Local legend has it that the firemen kept two panthers as mascots to tweak the nose of Dallas for saying Fort Worth was so quiet a panther could sleep downtown without being disturbed. The present structure, which replaced the original building in 1907, now is filled with graphics, photographs, documents, and other historical artifacts from the city's history. A self-guided walk-through will acquaint you with Fort Worth's growth and development from its birth as a military outpost on the frontier through its rowdy youth period as a cowtown to its present maturity as a modern city. Street parking or pay parking in adjacent garage.

FORT WORTH MUSEUM OF SCIENCE AND HISTORY
1501 Montgomery Street (76107) at Crestline, in the Cultural District • 732-1631 or Metro 817/654-1356 • Monday 9–5, Tuesday–Thursday 9–8, Friday–Saturday 9–9, Sunday 12–8. Closed Thanksgiving and December 24–25 • General admission: adults $5, seniors $4, children (3–12) $3, Under 3 free • W +

The largest museum of its type in the Southwest, it attracts more than a million visitors a year. Nine permanent galleries have exhibitions ranging from dinosaurs to computers, Texas history to the history of medicine. Interactive exhibits for all ages, but special hands-on areas for kids include Kidspace® and the DinoDig® where they dig for dinosaur bones in an outdoor area.

Admission also to the two major permanent attractions: The Noble Planetarium ($3) and the Omni Theater (Adults $6, seniors and children 12 and under $4). The Planetarium shows range from explorations of the heavens and beyond to Laser Magic. The Omni is an IMAX® theater with advanced super 70mm projections and sound system that present films on a tilted dome screen 80 feet in diameter so the film envelops the audience entirely in sight and sound. Shows are usually presented every hour on the half hour. Shows can be sold out at times, but advance tickets may be purchased at the museum box office or Ticketmaster locations throughout the Metroplex. Cafe and museum store. Free parking.

KIMBELL ART MUSEUM
3333 Camp Bowie Blvd. (76107) at Arch Adams, in the Cultural District • 332-8451 or Metro 817-654-1034 • Tuesday–Thursday and Saturday 10–5, Friday 12–8, Sunday 12–5. Closed Mondays, Thanksgiving, Christmas, New Year's Day • Free except for special exhibits • W +

Kay Kimbell, industrialist and entrepreneur, and his wife Velma started collecting art in the 1930s and shortly after, joined by his sister and her husband, Dr. and Mrs. Coleman Carter, formed the Kimbell Art Foundation. From then on the Kimbells continued to add to their collection and at Mr. Kimbell's death in 1964 he bequeathed this art collection and his entire personal fortune to the Foundation to establish and maintain a public art museum of the first rank in Fort Worth. His wishes have been well carried out by the Foundation which today owns and operates this museum, which has been called "America's Best Small Museum."

The permanent collection includes representative paintings by artists such as Gainsborough, Holbein, El Greco, Velazquez, Rembrandt, Cézanne, Picasso, Rubens, Van Dyck, and Monet. Its strongest area of holdings is in European paintings and sculpture from the Renaissance to the mid-20th century, but it also has a substantial collection of Asian arts, Meso-American and African pieces, and Mediterranean antiquities. Even the building housing this museum is widely regarded as one of the most outstanding public art gallery facilities in the world, especially acclaimed for its use of natural light.

A tour featuring highlights of the permanent collection is offered Sundays at 3 p.m. A tour for children aged five to nine years old is offered at the same time. A survey tour of selected loan exhibitions is available Tuesday through Friday and Sunday at 2 p.m. Interpreted tours for the hearing impaired are available by request. Admission is charged for some special touring exhibitions with tickets ranging from about $6 for adults to $2 for children 6–11. Public programs include lectures, classic films, theatre and music presentations. **The Buffet Restaurant** is open for lunch (see DINING OUT, below). Friday evenings a light dinner buffet is served with live music from 5:30–7:30 (reservations recommended). Bookstore. Free parking nearby.

MODERN ART MUSEUM OF FORT WORTH
1309 Montgomery Street (76107) at Camp Bowie Blvd., in the Cultural District • 738-9215 • Tuesday–Friday 10–5, Saturday 11–5, Sunday 12–5, Closed Mondays and holidays • Free • W +

Chartered in 1892 as the Fort Worth Public Library and Art Gallery, the Modern is the oldest art museum in Texas. The focus here is on modern and contemporary American and European art including paintings, sculpture, and works on paper. Represented in the permanent collection are works by Picasso, Pollock, Rothko, Stella, Warhol, and Motherwell. Contemporary sculpture is on view outdoors on the museum grounds, including *Chance Meeting* by George Segal—three life-size bronze figures standing on a street corner—which greets visitors at the entrance. In addition to its permanent collection, it has an active program of traveling special exhibitions. Tours can be arranged for groups by calling at least two weeks in advance. The Modern offers a series of free lectures and performances on Tuesday evenings at 7 p.m. September–November and February–April. Free parking. Museum store. Long-range plans are in the early development stage to build a new Modern on 11 acres to the east of the Kimbell at University and Camp Bowie.

THE MODERN AT SUNDANCE SQUARE
410 Houston at the corner of 4th Street • 335-9215
Monday–Wednesday 11–6, Thursday–Saturday 11–8,
Sunday 1–5 • Free • W +

This branch of The Modern features both exhibits from the permanent collection and temporary traveling exhibits. It is located in a spacious downstairs store in the historic Sanger Building, which was built in 1929 and is listed in the National Register of Historic Places. The museum store here appears to be more extensive than the one in the main museum. Street parking and Sundance parking lots nearby which are free after 5 p.m weekdays and all weekend.

SID RICHARDSON COLLECTION OF WESTERN ART
309 Main Street (76102) in Sundance Square • 332-6554
Tuesday–Wednesday 10–5, Thursday–Friday 10–8, Saturday
11–8, Sunday 1–5. Closed Monday and major holidays
Free • W +

On permanent display in this large one room gallery are 60 paintings and bronzes by premier Western artists Frederic Remington and Charles M. Russell. Reflecting the American West, the works are the legacy of late oilman and philanthropist Sid W. Richardson who collected them during the period 1942 to his death in 1959. These include Remington's *Buffalo Runners, Big Horn Basin* (1909) and *The Puncher* (1895) and Russell's *The Bucker* (1904) and *Buffalo Bill's Duel with Yellowhand* (1917). Self-tour with a free gallery guidebook. Gift shop. Street or commercial lot parking during weekdays. Free parking in Sundance lots after 5 p.m. weekdays and all weekend.

STOCKYARDS COLLECTION AND MUSEUM
131 East Exchange Avenue, in the Stockyard's Livestock
Exchange Building, Suites 111–114 • 625-5087 • Monday–
Saturday 10–5. Closed Sunday • Free (Donations accepted) • W

More a collection for browsing than a tidy museum, the rooms contain a widely diverse assortment of memorabilia and artifacts, most of which are related in some way to the history of the Stockyards, the railroads that served it, and the meat packing industry. These include saddles, antiques, and photographs. Also on display is a collection of gifts from every community visited by the 1986 Texas Sesquicentennial Wagon Train and a Native American exhibit featuring artifacts from many tribes with special emphasis on the last Comanche War Chief Quanah Parker. Gift shop.

TANDY ARCHAEOLOGICAL MUSEUM
2001 West Seminary Dr. in the library of the Southwestern Baptist Theological Seminary • 923-1921 • Open library hours, call for times • Free • W

The items in the permanent collection date from about 1500 B.C. to the seventh century A.D. and consist of artifacts uncovered at digs in Biblical sites in Israel. Visitor parking at the Memorial Building.

VINTAGE FLYING MUSEUM
505 NW 38th Street (76106), Hangar 33-S, adjacent to Meacham Airport • 624-1935 • Saturday 10–5, Sunday 12–5 • $3 donation

This is an antique aircraft restoration facility that literally builds "museums that fly." Tours cover displays of vintage aircraft, land vehicles, and support equipment in various stages of preservation. Prominent among these is "Chuckie," the last known B-17G *Pathfinder.* As the name states, this plane was one of those World War II B-17s especially equipped with secret target acquisition radar to lead waves of other B-17 Flying Fortresses to targets when clouds hid the targets from the bombardier's sights.

SPECIAL GARDENS

FORT WORTH BOTANIC GARDEN
3220 Botanic Garden Dr. (76107) at University Drive, in the Cultural District just north of I-30 • Information 871-7689 Seven days 8 a.m.–Sundown. • General admission free. Admission fees for Conservatory and Japanese Garden • W Variable

An 18-foot floral clock graces the entrance to this Botanic Garden, the oldest botanic garden in Texas. It displays more than 150,000 plants representing more than 2,500 native and exotic species in 110 acres of special gardens and natural settings. Seasonal plantings provide color throughout the year. In late April and October, visitors can enjoy more than 3,400 roses reaching peaks of bloom in the Rose Gardens. The Fragrance Garden is designed for the visually impaired, but all can enjoy the fragrant leaves to touch and smell.

The two areas that have admission fees are the Japanese Garden and the Conservatory. The seven-and-a-half-acre Japanese Garden features waterfalls and pools with Koi (imperial carp) fish, a Teahouse and Meditation Garden surrounded by evergreen shrubs, trees, spring flowers, and colorful fall foliage. Open daily April–October and every day but Monday, November–March. Hours vary. Adults $2 weekdays, $2.50 weekends and holidays; seniors $.50 discount, children (4–12) $1. (Ticket office 871-7685.) The Conservatory, which displays tropical plants, is open seven days all year. Adult admission is $1, seniors and children (4–12) $.50. Hours vary. Information on tours and programs 871-7682. Visitors number more than 600,000 annually. The headquarters of all affiliated state garden clubs, the Texas Garden Club, Inc. is located here. Free parking.

OUTDOORS

FORT WORTH NATURE CENTER AND REFUGE
9601 Fossil Ridge Road (76135), off Hwy. 199 (Jacksboro Hwy.), four miles west of Loop I-820, on Lake Worth • 237-1111 Tuesday–Saturday 9–5, Sunday 12–5. Closed Monday and major holidays • Free • W Call ahead

There are buffalo here, and if you're sharp-eyed, you may also see white-tailed deer, armadillos, wild turkeys, egrets, and herons roaming the prairies, forest, and marshes amid an abundance of wildflowers on this 3,500-acre sanctuary that remains much as it was 150 years ago. Nature programs, maps, and interpretive exhibits are available at the Hardwicke Interpretive Center. Hike the 25-mile trail system or canoe the Trinity river. Birdwatchers say it's a crossroads for both eastern and western species. Call for tour information and sign interpretive services.

FORT WORTH PARKS
Parks and Recreation Department • 871-8700

The crown jewels of the Fort Worth parks are the two major ones along the Trinity River southwest of downtown: **Trinity Park,** which adjoins the Cultural District north of I-30, and **Forest Park,** which is south of I-30. Trinity Park stretches for nearly two miles along the west bank of the Trinity River's Clear Fork. Built during The Depression, as part of the unemployment relief program, its present facilities include eight miles of jogging and cycling trails, an outdoor fitness course, the Fort Worth Botanic Garden, and a miniature train ride. Entrances are off West Lancaster Dr. and University Dr. Forest Park, farther to the south on the opposite bank of the Clear Fork, is most noted for two of its attractions: the Fort Worth Zoo and Log Cabin Village. Entrances are off Forest Park Blvd. and University Dr. The Parks and Recreation Department also maintains several small parks scattered throughout the city that offer a wide variety of facilities providing all sorts of recreational opportunities as well as quiet oases where one can get away from the hubbub of the city.

HERITAGE PARK
Bluff and Main Streets, north of Tarrant County Courthouse
871-8700 (Parks and Recreation Dept.) • Open at all times
Free • W Variable

This restful park is located on the bluffs above the Trinity River at the approximate site of the original Camp Worth. You can walk among water walls and waterfalls, and follow paths down to get a bird's-eye view of the Trinity River Valley to the north. Most of the 112-acre park is down the bluff. Hiking and biking trails. Boat and Recreation Center (293-4355), in the Tandy Parking Lot down on the river, rents canoes, kayaks, pedal boats, bicycles, and in-line skates. Open noon–dusk weekdays, 9 a.m. to dusk weekends March–October. Shorter hours rest of year. Although patrolled, the park is not the safest place to be after dark.

LAKE WORTH
Off Hwy. 199 (Jacksboro Hwy.) or Loop I-820 at northwest end of city • 871-8700 (Parks and Recreation Dept.) • Open at all times • Free • W Variable

A 3,560-acre city-owned lake with city parks and commercial facilities for fishing, boating, and other water sports and picnicking on the shoreline. Meandering Drive wanders almost all around it offering many scenic vistas. Location of Fort Worth Nature Center (see p. 206).

TRINITY RIVER TRAILS
These scenic trails currently extend more than 35 miles along the Trinity River and several feeding creeks. In addition to hiking, segments are available for biking, and horseback trail riding and some parts are paved for in-line skating. Future plans call for connecting the Fort Worth trails with the Arlington trail system.

COLLEGES AND UNIVERSITIES

TARRANT COUNTY JUNIOR COLLEGE
1500 Houston Street (76102) District Office • 515-7851

The four campuses in this county junior college system include two in Fort Worth: South Campus at 5301 Campus Drive, 76119 (515-4861), north of I-20 and west of I-35W; and the Northwest Campus at 4801 Marine Creek Drive, 76179 (515-2900), north of Loop 820. There are about 8,000 students at the South Campus and almost 4,000 at Northwest Campus enrolled in both academic and technical programs. TCJC ranks first in Texas and 21st in the nation in the number of associate degrees awarded annually. Visitors are welcome at the campus art galleries, which are open Monday–Friday 8–5 during the academic year. Additionally, the performing arts departments at both campuses offer a spring and fall schedule of widely ranging entertainment including stage productions and musical concerts. General admission for most theatre productions is $3 while many other events are free. Call for schedule.

TEXAS CHRISTIAN UNIVERSITY

2800 South University Dr. (TCU Box 297050, 76129) between Cantey and West Berry • 921-7800 or 921-7810 (Campus events information) • W Variable

In 1869 some Fort Worth citizens tried to get Addison and Randolph Clark to start a college in their city. Plans went forward, but when the notorious Hell's Half Acre grew up next to the planned building site, the Clark's went to Thorp Springs, 40 miles away, and started AddRan Christian College in 1873. From there, in 1895, the college moved to Waco, where its name was changed to Texas Christian University, and finally, in 1910, completed the circle back to Fort Worth. The name AddRan is still used in the title of TCU's College of Arts and Sciences.

Today the university has an enrollment of 7,000 students studying 79 undergraduate majors in 35 areas and 6 fields of doctoral study in the schools of business and education and the colleges of arts and sciences, nursing, and fine arts and communication. TCU is an independent, self-governing university affiliated with the Christian Church (Disciples of Christ), a mainstream, Protestant denomination that emphasizes understanding among the world's religions.

Among the many interesting buildings on the 237-acre campus is the **Robert Carr Chapel** (east side of University Dr.), which incorporates elements of several historic buildings in its delicate Williamsburg style and has a distinctive pulpit in the shape of a wine chalice. **Jarvis Hall** (west side of University Dr., just south of Cantey) built in 1911 is the only original campus structure whose neo-Georgian exterior is largely preserved.

The **Mills Glass Collection,** with its more than 2,500 examples of early American pressed glass, art glass, blown glass, cut glass, and porcelain, some pieces dating as far back as 1608, is open to visitors. It is located in the Faculty Center in Reed Hall (west side of University Dr., 921-7808). Another collection open to visitors is the **Oscar Monnig Meteorite Collection,** one of the finest private meteorite collections in the Southwest containing more than 400 different meteorites. About 30 of the main types of meteorites, some at least two feet in diameter, are on display in a small gallery in the front lobby of the Sid Richardson Physical Sciences Building (east side of University at Bowie). Private showing of the entire collection may be arranged by calling the TCU geology department at 921-7270.

Student, faculty, and traveling art exhibitions are held in the **J.M. Moudy Exhibition Hall** (east side of University Dr. at Cantey, 921-7601). A number of music, theater, and dance productions are put on here during the school year, including plays by the drama department and concerts by the TCU Orchestra and TCU Jazz Band. Public lectures and eminent guest speakers are also featured. Admission to most of these is either free or low-cost. The new **F. Howard and Mary D. Walsh Center for the Performing Arts** is under development on the west side of University at Cantey. When completed, this 50,000 square foot facility will wrap around the back of the adjacent 1,200-seat **Ed Landreth Auditorium,** providing a new recital hall, rehearsal halls, and a studio theater. The intimate recital hall in the Walsh Center will complement the Ed Landreth Auditorium, one of the finest acoustical halls in the area, which contains a world-class concert pipe organ and serves as the host site for dozens of guest performances including the Van Cliburn International Piano Competition (see ANNUAL EVENTS, p. 228).

Visitors are also welcome at intercollegiate sports events on campus. The TCU Horned Frogs compete in the Western Athletic Conference, the largest conference in NCAA Division 1A athletics. Sports fans can enjoy family-oriented fun outside Amon Carter Stadium (Stadium Dr. and Cantey) prior to every home football game. The carnival-like setting features live bands, street performers, and special activities for children and adults. Men's and women's basketball games are held in the 7,200-seat **Daniel-Meyer Coliseum** (Stadium Dr.) and baseball, volleyball, and most other sports are held at various locations on campus throughout the year. For sports schedules and ticket information call 922-FROG (922-3764). Tennis players are welcome to use the facilities of the **Mary Potishman Lard Tennis Center** (see SPORTS—TENNIS, p. 225).

Limited visitor parking is available near the Student Center (west side of University Dr.) and the Coliseum (Stadium Dr.). Off-campus parking is also available until midnight in the lots east and west of the University Christian Church. Visitors may pick up a campus map and view and extensive photographic history of the University in the **Dee J. Kelly Alumni and Visitors Center** (Stadium Dr. near the athletic complex). Campus tours may be arranged through the Admissions Office (921-7490).

TEXAS WESLEYAN UNIVERSITY
1201 Wesleyan (76105), between East Vickery and East Rosedale • 531-4444 (Metro 817-429-7010. Outside Texas 800-580-8980) • W + But not all areas

Founded in 1890 by the Methodist Episcopal Church, South, it was originally named Polytechnic College, which has the literal meaning "many arts and sciences." This concept has remained central to the mission of the university, which now has close to 3,000 students enrolled in programs leading to undergraduate degrees in the arts, humanities, science, business, and education, and graduate degrees in business, education, law, dentistry, and nurse anesthesia.

The campus is located on approximately 75 acres just four miles southeast of downtown Fort Worth on Polytechnic Heights, one of the highest points in the city. Although most of the buildings are relatively new, the school's heritage is reflected in some of its historic structures, such as the **Boyd House** (1895) in the Arts Complex, which is the oldest building on campus. Other buildings from the early days of the university include the **Oneal-Sells Administration Building** (1902), the **Ann Waggoner Fine Arts Building** (1908), **Mulkey Hall** (1909), the **Dillow House** (1912), and the **Firestation Theatre** (1914). However, most of these have gone through extensive remodeling over the years.

Visitors are welcome at many events, most of which are free. Exhibits of art by students, faculty, and area artists are held in the gallery in the **Law Sone Fine Arts Center,** 1201 Wesleyan. Hillard Hall, also in The Fine Arts Center, is the location for performances of the Wesleyan Singers, the Jazz Ensemble, Wind

Ensemble, the annual spring musical, and other voice and instrumental recitals. The location of theater performances varies but does include the intimate 57-seat Firestation studio theater housed in the former firestation and city hall of Polytechnic Heights. Call for details (531-4990). University varsity sports events open to visitors include men's soccer, basketball, baseball, and tennis, and women's volleyball, basketball, softball, and tennis. Most games are free to spectators. Game locations vary. Call 531-4210. Visitor parking is available at several locations on the campus.

MUSIC AND PERFORMING ARTS

ALIVE AT FIVE SUMMER CONCERTS
Sundance Square • 339-7777 • W

The "five" is 5 o'clock, the starting time of these free summer concerts usually held on Thursday evenings from 5 to 10 in the parking lot facing the Chisholm Trail Mural, between 3rd and 4th streets and Houston and Main. Entry by ticket, but free tickets are available in Sundance Square and through sponsors. Free parking in Sundance Square parking lots after 5 p.m.

CARAVAN OF DREAMS PERFORMING ARTS CENTER
312 Houston Street (76102) in Sundance Square • 877-3000 or Metro 817-429-4000 • Admission varies • W + But not all areas

This four-level entertainment complex includes a nightclub, live theater, dance facilities, and an open-air rooftop grotto bar featuring a 32-foot neon-lit geodesic "Desert Dome" and waterfalls. The nightclub, located on ground level, is a premier live performance venue, attracting national music acts in blues, rock, and jazz. The nightclub's wall murals depict the history of jazz and dance. Free evening/weekend parking in Sundance Square parking lots.

CASA MANANA THEATRE
3101 West Lancaster (76107), at University Dr., at east end of Cultural District • 332-2272 • Admission varies • W +

It was originally started in the early 1930s as an outdoor summer theater. Amon Carter reportedly hired famed showman Billy

Rose at $100 a day (a tidy sum during The Depression) to put on the first show. Rose shocked some citizens, and pleased others, by bringing in celebrated fan dancer Sally Rand as one of the headliners. In 1958 the old theater was replaced by the present geodesic dome, one of the first commercial uses of Buckminster Fuller's architectural creation. The 1,800-seat dome theater gained fame as the home of the world's first permanent musical theater-in-the round. For years the Casa Manana concentrated on summer musicals. Musicals still make up most productions, however, now the theater also puts on an occasional dramatic work, celebrity concerts, touring companies and children's theater (see FAMILY FUN AND KID STUFF, p. 217) on a year-round schedule. Free parking at the theater with overflow parking available across University Drive.

CASA'S THEATRE ON THE SQUARE
109 East 3rd Street (76102), in Sundance Square
332-3509 • W (elevator)

An intimate, 130-seat theater upstairs in the Knights of Pythias Building that mostly features touring shows on weekends. Shows usually Thursday–Friday at 8, Saturday at 5 and 9, and Sunday matinee. Tickets average $16–$20. Free evening/weekend parking in Sundance Square area parking lots.

CIRCLE THEATRE
230 West 4th Street (P.O. Box 470456, 76102) • 921-3040
Admission varies

The professional troupe performing in this intimate, downstairs theater usually presents six productions a year with the emphasis on Broadway and Off-Broadway shows. Tickets average $12–$16. Free evening/weekend parking in Sundance Square parking lots.

CLIBURN CONCERTS
Van Cliburn Foundation, 2525 Ridgmar Blvd. Suite 307, 76116
738-6536 (Tickets 335-9000) • Admission

Begun in 1976, this annual concert series presents some of the world's finest artists in recital. This is one of the activities of the Van Cliburn Foundation, which also sponsors concerts by past winners of the Van Cliburn International Piano Competition, which it holds every four years. (See ANNUAL EVENTS, p. 228.) The concerts in Fort Worth are usually given one evening a month in the Ed Landreth Auditorium at Texas Christian University.

FORT WORTH DALLAS BALLET
**6845 Green Oaks Road (76116) • 763-0207 (Fort Worth)
or 214-696-3932 (Dallas) • Admission varies**

This is not a merger of the Fort Worth and Dallas ballet companies, as the name may imply, but rather an expansion of the performances of the professional Fort Worth Ballet to Dallas to fill in the void left when the Dallas Ballet was dissolved in 1988. Fort Worth performances are held in the Fort Worth/Tarrant County Convention Center Theatre and will move to the new Bass Performance Hall when that facility is fully developed. Dallas performances are at the Music Hall in Fair Park. In addition to full production seasons locally, the company performs regularly throughout Texas and tours both nationally and internationally.

FORT WORTH/TARRANT COUNTY CONVENTION CENTER
**1111 Houston Street (76102), just north of I-30
884-2222 • Admission varies • W +**

Sure, there are lots of conventions and trade shows here (some of which are open to the public), but there's a lot more going on ranging from major concerts to ice hockey and ice shows. The 3,000-seat theater is presently home of the Fort Worth Opera and the Fort Worth Symphony, which will move to the Bass Performance Hall when that facility is ready for them.

FORT WORTH OPERA ASSOCIATION
3505 West Lancaster (76107) (Office) • 731-0833

This association sponsors the oldest continuing opera company in Texas, presenting three or four productions in its fall and winter season. Most company members are local professionals, but the association frequently brings in well-known artists for lead roles. Until the Bass Performance Hall facilities are ready, performances are usually given in the Convention Center's JFK Theatre or the Scott Theatre. Ticket prices range from about $10 to $45.

FORT WORTH SYMPHONY ORCHESTRA
4401 Trail Lake Drive (76109) (Administrative Office)
921-2676 (Office) 926-8831 (Box Office)
   This professional symphony orchestra, founded in 1925, puts on seven master concerts a year interspersed with several pops concerts in its September–May Fort Worth season. It also gives six children's concerts. Until the Bass Performance Hall facilities are ready, performances are usually given in the Fort Worth/Tarrant County Convention Center's JFK Theatre. Ticket prices range from $6 to $34. The core of the Symphony Orchestra is the **Fort Worth Chamber Orchestra,** composed of 36 full-time professional musicians recruited from across the U.S. In addition to the symphony season, the chamber orchestra puts on concerts throughout the year at The Ed Landreth Auditorium on the campus of Texas Christian University. It was the first chamber orchestra to tour the People's Republic of China after the cultural revolution (1983). Both orchestras also travel extensively giving as many as 180 performances before more than a quarter of a million people in the typical year.

FORT WORTH THEATER
3505 West Lancaster (76107) • 738-7491 • Admission varies
   The city's oldest theatre company offers both a Main Stage and The Studio series seasons. The Main Stage is entertainment served family style. The Studio series productions are designed to showcase a variety of playwrights and directors.

HIP POCKET THEATRE
1627 Fairmont Avenue (76104) • 927-2833
   Known for its innovative and original works, this theater group performs a wide range of productions from musicals to science fiction to comedy and spoofs in a variety of locations including its summer theater under the stars in the Oak Acres Amphitheater. Tickets $8–$14. Call for performance location and details.

JUBILEE THEATRE
506 Main (76102), in Sundance Square • 338-4411 • Admission varies • W +

One of only two theaters in Texas that showcases black performers, this 14-year-old troupe is the only African-American theater in the Metroplex that offers a full season of shows that range across drama, comedy, and musicals. Tickets average $8–$16. Free evening/weekend parking in Sundance Square parking lots.

ED LANDRETH AUDITORIUM
**Texas Christian University, University and West Cantey
921-7810 (Campus events information) • W +**

The 1200-seat Ed Landreth Auditorium, considered one of the finest acoustical halls in the area, contains a world-class concert pipe organ and serves as the host site for dozens of guest performances including the Van Cliburn Foundation Concerts and the Van Cliburn International Piano Competition (see COLLEGES AND UNIVERSITIES—TEXAS CHRISTIAN UNIVERSITY, p. 208, and ANNUAL EVENTS, p. 228).

STAGE WEST
3055 South University Dr. (76109) at Berry, next to TCU campus • 784-9378 (STG-WEST) • W +

This 200-seat professional regional theater puts on nine plays in two subscription series that run through the entire year. The Center Stage Series offers six plays which are well-known and basically mainstream ranging from classics to Broadway shows. These productions usually run about four weekends. The three plays in the Adventure Series, which are interspersed, are more on the cutting edge of theater and run two to three weekends. Single tickets run about $13–$16. Performances are normally Thursday–Sunday evenings with a matinee on Saturday.

TEXAS BOYS CHOIR
2925 Riverglen (76109) • 924-1482 or Metro 817-429-0066

Founded in 1946, this choir has built an international reputation, made 35 records and won 2 Grammys. Boys from 8 years to "change of voice" are eligible to participate. The two main groups in the choir are the professional touring choir, which has performed all over the U.S. and in several foreign countries, and the resident performing choir, which performs at many area festivals and usually gives at least one concert a year. Their repertoire includes show tunes, hymns, and contemporary songs. The choir now has branches in Dallas and Arlington, as well as the fully accredited school in Fort Worth, which is the home base of the three dozen or so boys in the elite touring choir. Tickets $5–$8. Call for information on local performances.

TEXAS GIRLS CHOIR
4449 Camp Bowie Blvd. (76107) • 732-8161

Not to be outdone by the boys, this choir also makes national and overseas tours. There are about 200 girls ranging in age from 8 to 15 divided into six choirs, with the top two being the concert choirs that put on about 100 performances annually. Some of these are free concerts at churches, malls, and hospitals, while other local concerts are held in performance halls with admission. Call for information on local performances.

WILL ROGERS AUDITORIUM
Will Rogers Memorial Center, 3401 West Lancaster (76107), in the Cultural District • 332-2272 • Admission varies • W +

The auditorium has 2,856 seats and hosts touring Broadway productions, celebrity shows, and classical concerts.

FAMILY FUN AND KID STUFF

BURGER LAKE
1200 Meandering Road (76114), off Hwy. 183 (River Oaks Blvd.) southeast of Lake Worth • 737-3414 • Admission • W

This one-acre spring-fed swimming pool with a sand bottom and two sand beaches is in a 17-acre park. Open early May

through Labor Day, 9 a.m. to dark. Picnic tables and grills. Lifeguards. Admission $5, children 5 and under free.

CASA MAÑANA PLAYHOUSE
**3101 West Lancaster (76107), at University Dr., at east end of
Cultural District • 332-2272 • Admission varies • W +**

The Playhouse is a professional children's theater troupe that
puts on children's plays in the domed Casa Mañana Theater. The
group usually puts on a play a month from October through May
with each performance running two or three weekends. Single
tickets $6.25. The troupe also has a theatrical training school for
kids from preschool to youths.

FORT WORTH ZOO
**1989 Colonial Parkway (76110), off University Dr. one mile
south of I-30 • 871-7050 (24-hour Info Line) • Open 365 days,
most days 10–5; weekend and holiday hours changed seasonally
(call) • Adults $7, seniors $3, children (3–12) $4.50, Under 3
free. Half-price admission on Wednesdays • W + But not all areas**

One of the "Top Five Zoos in America," this zoo is the home
of one of the largest animal collections in the Western Hemi-
sphere with nearly 5,000 exotic animals including lowland gorillas, cheetahs, bears, Komodo dragons, colorful bird exhibits, an
exciting birds of prey display, a world-famous reptile collection,
an on-site aquarium, and an insect exhibit. The oldest continuous
zoo site in Texas, it draws more than a million visitors a year.
Premier exhibits include the "World of Primates," a climate-con-
trolled tropical rain forest where you can literally come face-to-
face with intriguing gorillas, orangutans, and chimpanzees
through large viewing windows; "Asian Falls" with its vast array
of Asian wildlife including tigers, sun bears, elephants, and rhinos; "Raptor Canyon," where these majestic birds of prey can fly
above and around you; and TEXAS!, a recreated 19th century
pioneer town complete with both wild and domestic animals
indigenous to the state.

The zoo is renown for creating natural habitats for the animals
as if they were in the wild. One of the newer exhibits, features

South African black-footed penguins in the aquarium where visitors can see them both on land and through underwater viewing areas. In late spring, the annual "Zoo Babies" event highlights all the newborn at the zoo, including baby cheetahs, giraffes, and lions. What is reportedly the world's longest miniature train ride connects the Zoo with Trinity Park (see p. 220).

PAWNEE BILL'S WILD WEST SHOW
Cowtown Coliseum, 121 East Exchange, in the Stockyards
625-1025 • Admission • W Variable
Every Saturday from late April through September this family show turns the coliseum back in time to the days of Buffalo Bill with more than 70 animals, expert ropers and riders, trick shooters, a bull-whip artist, authentic prairie wagons, and even a stagecoach holdup. Parking at Stockyards Station or on the street.

PONY RIDES
Cowtown Corrals, 500 Northeast 23rd Street (76106), south end of The Stockyards • 740-0582 or Metro 817/429-9993
Rides available in the arena for children less than 7 years old at $10 hour.

THE STOCKYARDS
East Exchange Avenue
Items in The Stockyards of special interest to families are the Tarantula Train (see p. 220), in Stockyards Station at the east end of Exchange; the small amusement park near the visitor center; and the Rodeo and Pawnee Bill's Wild West Show in the Cowtown Coliseum. The Tarantula runs all year long while the others are seasonal with the amusement park open from March through October, and the coliseum shows mostly on weekends and during the summer season. Check with the Stockyards Visitor Center for schedules and prices.

TRAIN RIDE IN THE PARKS
2100 Colonial Parkway in Forest Park (76110) • 475-1233 or 336-3328 • Tuesday–Sunday late May–Labor Day, Closed Monday • Children 12 and under $1.62, Adults and youths $2.16

Billed as one of the world's longest miniature train rides, the two ornate scaled-down trains carry passengers on a five-mile round trip from the Forest Park Depot to Trinity Park Duck Pond and back. Weekdays the train runs on the hour, Saturday, Sunday, and holidays it runs every 45 minutes. Tuesday–Friday 11–5, Saturday–Sunday 11–6. Off-season it operates 11–5 on Saturday–Sunday and holidays only.

TARANTULA STEAM TRAIN EXCURSIONS
Depot locations: 140 East Exchange Avenue, in the Stockyards, and 2319 8th Avenue • 625-Rail (625-7245), Metro 817-654-0898 or 800-952-5717 • Adults $10, children (3–12) $5.50 • Call for schedule • W Call ahead

Tarantula's locomotive and restored vintage coaches make round trips along the nine-mile route between the two depots daily, with the steam locomotive doing the hauling Wednesday–Sunday. Passenger cars are equipped with ceiling fans, but are not air-conditioned. The touring coaches are open sided (with railings for passenger safety). Seating is on a first-come basis. Snacks, soft drinks, wine, and beer are available on board. The Tarantula Railroad also offers a daily round trip from Grapevine to the Stockyards and back to Grapevine. (See GRAPEVINE—FAMILY FUN AND KID STUFF.)

Why "Tarantula"? The name goes back to a map published in 1870 that depicted a vision of Fort Worth newspaper editor B. B. Paddock who saw Fort Worth at the center of nine radially extending rail lines. Some laughed at the map saying the map lines resembled a hairy-legged tarantula and the railroad center just a dream. But by the 1890s the railroads had laid the nine legs centered on Fort Worth. So, when Fort Worth businessman William Davis came up with his vision of an excursion steam train, he named it after Paddock's vision.

SPORTS

AUTO RACING

TEXAS MOTOR SPEEDWAY
North of Fort Worth at intersection of I-35W and Hwy. 114
(P.O. Box 500, 76101-2500) • 215-8500 • Admission varies
W + But not all areas

Texas' newest and largest auto race track, this 1.5-mile speedway is the site of both major NASCAR and Indy Racing League events including several 300- and 500-mile races. The track also plays hosts to major country and western and other celebrity concerts.

COLLEGE SPORTS

See COLLEGES AND UNIVERSITIES, p. 208.

EQUESTRIAN

COWTOWN CORRALS
500 Northeast 23rd Street (76106), south end of the Stockyards
740-0582 or Metro 817/429-9993

Horseback rides for both beginners and experienced riders along the Old Chisholm Trail. Adults: one hour $20. Each additional hour $15. Children 7–12 $15 hour. Trail rides by reservation leave six times daily. Night Chisholm Trail Camp Friday–Saturday nights. Pony rides for children less than 7 years old, $10 hour.

WILL ROGERS EQUESTRIAN CENTER
One Amon Carter Square (76107), in Will Rogers
Memorial Center in the Cultural District • 871-8150
Admission varies • W +

This is one of the nation's premier equestrian centers and the site of more than two dozen horse shows each year, ranging from the annual Miniature Horse Show (there are 200 breeders and 4,000 miniature horses registered in Texas) to the National Cutting Horse Association Super Stakes. The Center consists of two buildings: the 215,000-ft^2 Richardson/Bass Building and the 197,000-ft^2 Burnett Building. A 761-car garage is attached.

GOLF

PUBLIC COURSES

CARSWELL GOLF COURSE
6520 White Settlement Road (76114) • 738-8402 • 18-hole course. Call for green fees.

CASINO BEACH ACADEMY
7464 Jacksboro Hwy. (76135) • 237-3695 • 9-hole course. Call for green fees.

MEADOWBROOK MUNICIPAL GOLF COURSE
1815 Jensen Road (76112) • 457-4616 • 18-hole course. Green fees: Weekdays $10, Weekend/Holiday $12.

PECAN VALLEY MUNICIPAL GOLF COURSE
6400 Pecan Valley Dr. (P.O. Box 26632, 76126) • 249-1845 36-hole course. Green fees (18 holes): Weekdays $10, Weekend/Holidays $12.

ROCKWOOD GOLF COURSE
1851 Jacksboro Hwy. (76114) • 624-1771 • 27-hole course. Green fees (18 holes): Weekdays $10, Weekend/Holiday $12.

ROCKWOOD PAR 3 GOLF COURSE
1524 Rockwood Park (76114) • 824-8311 • 9-hole par 3 course. Call for fees.

SYCAMORE CREEK GOLF COURSE
100 North University Dr. (76107) • 871-8748 • 9-hole course. Call for green fees.

TIMBER-VIEW GOLF CLUB
4508 East Enon (76140) • 478-3601 • 18-hole course. Call for green fees.

Z. BOAZ GOLF COURSE
3240 Lackland Road (76116) • 738-6287 • 18-hole course. Green fees: Weekdays $10, Weekend/Holiday $12.

PRIVATE AND SEMI-PRIVATE COURSES

Call for green fees.

COLONIAL COUNTRY CLUB
3735 Country Club Dr. (76109) • 927-4243 • 18-hole course.

DIAMOND OAKS COUNTRY CLUB
5821 Diamond Oaks Dr. (76117) • 834-6261 • 18-hole course.

GLEN GARDEN GOLF AND COUNTRY CLUB
2916 Glen Garden Dr. (76119) • 535-7582 • 18-hole semi-private course.

GOLF CLUB AT FOSSIL CREEK
3401 Clubgate Dr. (76137) • 847-1900 • 18-hole semi-private course.

LAKE COUNTRY COUNTRY CLUB
7200 Golf Club Dr. (76179) • 236-3400 • 18-hole semi-private course.

MIRA VISTA COUNTRY CLUB
6600 Mira Vista Blvd. (76132) • 294-6600 • 18-hole course.

RIDGLEA COUNTRY CLUB
3700 Bernie Anderson Dr. (76116) • 732-8111 • 18-hole course.

RIVER CREST COUNTRY CLUB
1501 Western (76107) • 738-9221 • 18-hole course.

SHADY OAKS COUNTRY CLUB
320 Roaring Springs Road (76114) • 732-3333 • 18-hole par 3 course.

WOODHAVEN COUNTRY CLUB
913 Country Club Lane (76112) • 457-2143 • 18-hole course.

ICE SKATING

THE ICE AT TANDY CENTER
Fort Worth Outlet Square, One Tandy Center, Houston Street between 2nd and 3rd • 878-4800

A popular downtown rink for both skaters and watchers. Usually two public skating sessions Monday–Friday at 11–5 and 7:30–10 p.m., and Saturday–Sunday session 1–5. Admission $3.75. Skate rental $1.25. Free evening/weekend parking in Sundance Square area lots or park in the Tandy lots along the river and take the subway right into the rink.

RODEO

COWTOWN COLISEUM
121 East Exchange Avenue (76106), in the Stockyards
625-1025 or Metro 654-1148 • Admission • W

Constructed in 1907 to house the Fort Worth Stock Show, it was home of the first indoor rodeo in 1918 and now features professional cowboy and cowgirl rodeo events every weekend from April–September and occasionally during other months. Shows at 8 p.m. Tickets $8–$10.

SOUTHWESTERN EXPOSITION AND LIVESTOCK SHOW AND RODEO
See ANNUAL EVENTS, p. 228.

TENNIS

DON MCLELAND TENNIS CENTER
1600 West Seminary (76115) • 921-5134

Fourteen lighted outdoor courts and two covered courts. The two indoor courts are available for $20 for 1½ hours. Other courts are $2.50 per person before 5 p.m. and $3 per person after 5 p.m.

MARY POTISHMAN LARD TENNIS CENTER
3609 Bellaire North (76109), on Texas Christian University campus • 921-7960

All 22 lighted outdoor courts are recessed into the ground for better wind protection. Five-court indoor tennis complex. Covered courts $20 for 1½ hours anytime. Outdoor courts $2.50 per person for 1½ hours until 5 p.m. weekdays, $3 per person after 5 p.m. and on weekends. Additional charge of $1 for reservations on outdoor courts only.

OTHER POINTS OF INTEREST

FORT WORTH WATER GARDENS
Between Houston and Commerce Streets, downtown south of the Convention Center • 871-8700 (Parks and Recreation Dept.) Free • W

This $6 million 4.3-acre park of terraced concrete and cascading water is spread over 4.5 blocks of downtown. Completed in 1974, it was designed by Phillip Johnson, who also designed the Amon Carter Museum. The Gardens depict a miniature mountain scene enhanced with rivers, waterfalls, and pools, except the mountains only rise a little above street level while the pools go down to forty feet. Each minute, 19,000 gallons of water flow, fall, sparkle, gurgle, spray, and then are recirculated through the five major water features to do it all again. The biggest feature is the Active Water Pool in which 10,500 gallons of water per minute cascade from the upper edge, down multiple tiers and into a pool surrounded by stepping stones. If you're a little adventurous, you can walk the table-sized stepping stones down into the center. And these are not barren mountains; they are set among 500 species of plants and trees and the textured ground cover blends 32,000 plants of azaleas, junipers, Indian hawthorne, and English ivy. At night, the Water Gardens is illuminated with special lighting that simulates moonlight. On street parking.

LORD'S SUPPER DISPLAY
2500 Ridgmar Plaza (76150), in the Radio and Television Commission Building of the Southern Baptist Convention 737-6251 • Monday–Saturday 12–5, Sunday 1–5 • Free • W +

This is a life-size interpretation in wax of Leonardo da Vinci's famous painting of "The Last Supper." The work of a mother and daughter team, both named Katerine Stubergh, it took approximately 18 months to complete. A taped narration is given in English and Spanish.

OUTDOOR WESTERN ART
A tribute to Fort Worth's Western heritage can be found in several pieces of outdoor art around the city. These include:

Texas Gold, sculpture at North Main and Stockyards Blvd., depicting a herd of seven longhorn steers. Each steer represents one of the Texas families that began trying to preserve the longhorn breed in the early 1900s.

The Bulldogger, sculpture in front of the Cowtown Coliseum on East Exchange Avenue in the Stockyards, depicting Bill Pickett, the rodeo cowboy who originated the bulldogging event and was the first black cowboy inducted into the Cowboy Hall of Fame. The star attraction at the first indoor rodeo, Pickett's technique for downing the steer included sinking his teeth into its upper lip.

Midnight, sculpture outside the Amon G. Carter, Jr. Exhibits Hall in the Will Rogers Memorial Complex depicts the black stallion "Midnight" tossing a bronc rider, in keeping with the legend that no one ever rode this rodeo bronc.

The Brand Inspector, sculpture outside the Cattleman's Museum, 1301 West 7th Street. This life-size statue of a mounted brand inspector, brand book in hand as he checks out a longhorn, is dedicated to the men hired to track down cattle thieves.

Sweet Will Rogers Riding into the Sunset, statue in front of Will Rogers Coliseum, 3301 West Lancaster, depicts the famed Western humorist after whom the Coliseum is named. Rogers considered Fort Worth his second home. He's shown on his favorite horse, "Soapsuds."

Chisholm Trail Mural, a three-story painting on the rear of the building in the 400 block of Main Street that depicts a trail drive in the *trompe l'oeil* technique that fools the eye into thinking the flat painting has depth. This is one of the most photographed sights in Fort Worth.

THE CLIBURN ORGAN
Broadway Baptist Church, 305 West Broadway (76104)
334-8211 • W

The largest organ in Texas, it has a tone referred to as "French aesthetic," a quality perfected by the French organ builders of the 19th and 20th centuries in conjunction with great French organ virtuoso composers. It is an organ designed for both church and concert use, which means it can produce a variety of sounds to fulfill a symphonic breath of color and form. The $2.5 million organ is officially named the Rildia Bee O'Bryan Cliburn Organ, in memory of the mother and principal teacher of famed pianist Van Cliburn, who is a member of the church. It has 10,615 pipes, the largest being 37 feet long with a diameter of 17⅛ inches and the smallest pipe is eight inches long with a "speaking length" of ⁵⁄₁₆ inch. If the pipes were stretched end to end they would extend approximately five miles. In addition to its use in church services, it is occasionally played in concerts, some of which are free and others require admission. There is no set schedule for these performances. Call for information.

OFFBEAT

TANDY SUBWAY
Downtown • Free • W

The only privately owned subway in the world, it was originally intended to carry Tandy employees between the stations in the nearby riverside parking lots and their work in the headquarters buildings. But, thanks to the Tandy Corporation, you don't have to be a Tandy employee to take advantage of the free ride to avoid the hassle of downtown parking. The one-car trains run at frequent intervals between the 3,000 free parking spaces in the Tandy lots along the Trinity River (entrance at north end of Henderson) to the downstairs of the Fort Worth Outlet Square in the Tandy Building. Most of the route is outdoors, but the building end is a subway tunnel. The run takes about seven minutes. Trains operate Monday–Friday 5:30 a.m.–10:30 p.m., Saturday 8 a.m.–10:30 p.m., and Sunday 11:30 a.m.–7 p.m. Parking in the Tandy lots is also free, just make sure to remember near which station you parked your car.

ANNUAL EVENTS

Fort Worth Convention and Visitors Bureau Events Hotline 332-2000. For Sundance Square events information 339-7777.

JANUARY–FEBRUARY

SOUTHWESTERN EXPOSITION AND LIVESTOCK SHOW AND RODEO
Mid-January–Early February • Will Rogers Memorial Center, 3301 West Lancaster (76107), in the Cultural District 877-2400 • General Admission: Adults $5, Children (6–16) $2 W + But not all areas

The nation's oldest livestock show is now more than a century old. Usually scheduled for about 17 days starting mid-January and ending the first week in February, it is the biggest annual event in the city drawing approximately 800,000 visitors. Highlights include an all-western parade downtown, days and days of judging of around 19,000 head of livestock that range from pigeons and rabbits to bulls and horses, livestock auctions, commercial exhibits, a carnival midway, plus the nation's top cowboys and cowgirls competing and name entertainers performing at the rodeo. Rodeo performances nightly at 8 with matinees on weekends. (Rodeo Tickets $14–$16.) Parking lots on west side of complex ($3). Shuttle buses run weekends from noon to midnight from Billy Bob's Texas lot in the Stockyards, $1 one way.

APRIL

MAIN STREET ART FESTIVAL
Thursday–Sunday in mid-month • Main Street, downtown
336-ARTS (336-2787) • Free • W Variable

The brick-paved Main Street is blocked off extending from the courthouse south nine blocks, almost to the Convention Center, to become the site of the Southwest's largest art festival. The area is filled with outdoor arts and crafts shows with more than 200 participating artists. Also loads of food, and live entertainment with more than 400 entertainers performing almost continuously on three stages. Thursday–Saturday it goes on from late morning to midnight, Sunday to 8 p.m. Free evening/weekend parking in Sundance Square area commercial lots or try the Tandy lot and the subway. (See OFFBEAT, p. 228.)

MAY

MAYFEST
Thursday–Sunday closest to May 1st • Trinity Park • 332-1055
Admission • W Variable

Fort Worth's own rite of spring started out as a loosely organized community-wide picnic on the banks of the Trinity River in the early 1970s. The community still comes—or about 350,000 of them—but it's now definitely more organized with areas featuring sports, arts, and a variety of entertainment, and fireworks. There's also a children's area and activities. Nearby parking is free, but if you want to avoid the parking hassle, especially on the weekend, shuttle buses run from TCU Stadium and the Tandy Riverfront lot (50¢).

MASTERCARD COLONIAL GOLF TOURNAMENT
Usually third week in month • Colonial Country Club, 3735 Country Club Cir. (76109) • 927-4280 or 927-4281 • Admission W Call ahead

The nation's top golfers on the PGA tour compete for over a million dollars in prizes in this nationally televised tournament. The invitation-only tournament is more than 50 years old. Fort Worth's native son, Ben Hogan, won the first one in 1946 and went on to win four more Colonial titles, so the course—rated one of the ten toughest on the tour—is called "Hogan's Alley." Admission is free Monday and Tuesday for the practice rounds. Passes sell for $85 for the entire tournament, $35 per day for Wednesday (Pro-Am), Saturday or Sunday; and $25 a day for Thursday and Friday. Attendance averages about 140,000.

MAY–JUNE (EVERY FOUR YEARS)

VAN CLIBURN INTERNATIONAL PIANO COMPETITION
Van Cliburn Foundation, 2525 Ridgmar Blvd. Suite 307, 76116 • 738-6536

Technically, because it only occurs every four years, this is not an annual event; however, it earns a listing here because it is considered one of the most important music competitions in the world. In 1958, the young Texas pianist Van Cliburn won one of the most prestigious piano competitions in the world, the Tchaikovsky International Piano Competition in Moscow. His victory led to the organization of this competition to seek out other world-class concert pianists. First held in 1962, the competition has been repeated every four years since then with the tenth competition held in May–June, 1997. The next competition, the eleventh, will be held in 2001.

JUNE

CHISHOLM TRAIL ROUND-UP AND CHIEF QUANAH PARKER COMANCHE POW WOW
Friday–Sunday in mid-month • Stockyards National Historic District, North Main and Exchange • 625-7005 Admission • W Variable

The Old West lives again in this three-day celebration of the famous cattle drives that put Fort Worth on the map. A tradition that started in 1977, the festival now draws about 150,000 visitors. The festivities start Friday at 5 p.m. and go to 1 a.m., Saturday it's 9 a.m. to 11 p.m., and Sunday 11 a.m. to 6 p.m. Activities include a trail ride, street fair, authentic Native American exhibitions and dances, continuous live country and western entertainment on four stages, barbecue and chili cook-offs, a parade on Saturday, live gunfights and whip artistry demonstrations; armadillo, pig, and chuckwagon races; and street dances Friday and Saturday. A children's area features entertainment, a petting zoo, rides, and games. Charge for parking.

JUNE–JULY

SHAKESPEARE IN THE PARK
Two or three weeks late in June and early July • Trinity Park Playhouse, Trinity Blvd. and 7th Street, off Camp Bowie Blvd. 923-6698 • Admission • W Variable

A tradition for more than two decades is Fort Worth's outdoor presentation of The Bard's best. One of the Shakespeare's plays is performed every night but Monday over a two- or three-week period in late June and early July in this open air theater. Tickets $6–$12. Children 12 and under free. Also available, by reservation, is the Elizabethan Feast offering a menu of dinner packages. Go early, bring a blanket or a chair to sit on, and enjoy.

AUGUST

PIONEER DAYS
Friday–Sunday weekend before Labor Day • Stockyards National Historic District, North Main and Exchange 626-7921 • Admission • W Variable

Fort Worth salutes its pioneer heritage and the early days of the cattle industry with this Western wingding. Festivities start Friday evening at 6 and go to 1 a.m. Saturday 10 a.m. to 1 a.m., and Sunday noon to 11 p.m. Old West doings include demonstrations of pioneer skills, staged gunfights and a gunfight competition, a stunt show, rodeos, including a ranch rodeo for real ranch cowboys; wild west shows in the coliseum, a Western melodrama (extra charge), and continuous music on four stages. Children's area includes a Root Beer Garden. Admission $5. Parking $6.

OCTOBER

OKTOBERFEST
First Saturday–Sunday in month • Fort Worth/Tarrant County Convention Center, 1111 Houston Street, just north of I-30 924-5881 • Adults $6, seniors and children 7–16 $4, Children 6 and under free • W +

If you can't go to Munich for Oktoberfest, try this miniature version of the famed beer festival. There's plenty of oompah music to dance to as well as German and international food, also performing and visual arts make this an annual family festival in the true German spirit. And if you prefer other types of music you'll probably be able to hear it on one of the five stages. This is a fund-raiser for the symphony, so many groups representing both the local music scene and performing arts help out with their entertainment talents.

FORT WORTH INTERNATIONAL AIR SHOW
Saturday–Sunday in early or mid-month • Alliance Airport, north of city at I-35W and Hwy 170 (International Air Show, P.O. Box 821, 76101) • 870-1515 • Admission • W Variable

Fort Worth's place in aviation history is celebrated with heart-stopping displays of aerobatics, stunt flying, wing-walking, and parachute team drops. On the ground there are displays of all types of military and civilian aircraft as well as exhibits recounting the history of aviation. Adults $10, children 6 and older $5, under 6 free.

RED STEAGALL COWBOY GATHERING & WESTERN SWING FESTIVAL
Friday–Sunday late in month • Stockyards National Historic District, North Main and Exchange • 884-1945 • Admission W Variable

This annual gathering usually attracts about 35,000 to the three-day festival celebrating the cowboy way of life in both its reality and myth. The activities include ranch rodeos in which real cowboys compete in everyday cowboy skills such as branding, bronc riding, sorting, and team roping, and some definitely not everyday skills like wild cow milking. Also chuck wagon cooking, recitations of cowboy poetry, and musical entertainment that emphasizes Western Swing at five locations throughout the Stockyards. Parking in Stockyards' lots.

SHOPPING

ANTIQUE SHOPS

Two collections of antique and collectible dealers are at **Stockyards Antiques** and **The Antique Colony.** Stockyards Antiques is in a converted 1890s hotel at 1332 North Main, at Northside (624-2311) where the 30,000-ft^2 building houses 125 shops. There are 100 shops in The Antique Colony at 7200 Camp Bowie Blvd. at the intersection with Hwy. 183/Southwest Blvd. (731-7252).

DOUBLE EXPOSURE
6205 Sunset (76107) behind Ridglea Presbyterian Church
737-8038 • Monday–Saturday 10–5 • W

There are consignment shops (WOW!) and there are consignment shops (Ugh!). This is one of the WOW! variety, perhaps because it's run by Fort Worth's Junior League to support that organization's charities. Men's and women's almost new clothing is usually at 50% off. Also home furnishings.

FORT WORTH OUTLET SQUARE
Throckmorton and 3rd, just west of Sundance Square
390-3716 • W Variable (Elevator)

The name "Square" is loosely used here, because it's actually the indoor mall retail space between the two towers of the Tandy Center building. But the "Outlet" part of the title is appropriate because it has about three dozen upscale retail stores featuring outlet savings on brand name products. Anchor stores are Computer City (naturally, it's a Tandy Corporation chain) and Spiegel. Other stores cover the gamut of products from clothing for men, women, and children, to jewelry, to luggage, to vitamins. Sundance Square area parking tickets are validated after the stores open, or you can park at the Tandy lot and take the subway right into the "Square." (See OFFBEAT, p. 228.) Food court.

HULEN MALL
4800 South Hulen (76132), at Loop 820 (I-20) • 294-1200 • W Variable

Dillard's, Foley's, and Montgomery Ward anchor more than 125 specialty shops, mostly national chain stores, in this two-level mall. Outside parking for more than 3,500 cars and garage parking for another 1,000. Luby's cafeteria and a food court.

RIDGMAR MALL
2060 Green Oaks Road (76116), on I-30 and Hwy. 183
731-0856 • W Variable

The major stores in this two-level mall are Dillards, Neiman Marcus, Penney's, and Sears. They anchor more than 130 other specialty stores, mostly representatives of national chains, a cafeteria and fast food outlets. Outside parking.

WESTERN WEAR

This is "Where the West Begins," and to be in the West you have to wear Western, or at least something that pays tribute to both the cowboy heritage and the cowboy's fine sense of utilitarian wear, such as hats that keep off the sun and rain, long wearing jeans, or boots that help the rider keep his seat. Among the better known Western wear stores in the city are the collection of shops on East and West Exchange in the Stockyards, Luskey's Western Wear, 101 Houston at Weatherford, downtown (335-5833); Justin Boot Company Factory Outlet, 717 W. Vickery Blvd. (654-3103); and Ryon's Saddle and Ranch, 2601 North Main, just north of the Stockyards (625-2391).

DINING OUT

ANGELO'S BAR-B-QUE
2533 White Settlement Road (76107) at Vecek • 332-0357
Lunch and dinner Monday–Saturday. Closed Sunday and major holidays • $ • No Cr. • W +

Angelo's started serving hickory smoked brisket of beef and pork ribs in 1958 and since then has earned a reputation that not only keeps bringing in customers, but has virtually turned it into a shrine for barbecue lovers. Everything served with the traditional sauce, beans, potato salad, cole slaw, pickle, onion, and bread. If you can't decide among the choices on the simple list of plate dinners, try a combo plate of any two meats. Beer and wine.

THE BALCONY OF RIDGLEA
6100 Camp Bowie Blvd. (76116) at Winthrop, in Ridglea Village Shopping Center • 731-3719 • Lunch Monday–Friday, dinner Monday–Saturday. Closed Sunday and major holidays $$ • Cr. W (elevator)

This elegant upstairs restaurant offers seating in its mirrored dining room or on the glassed-in balcony that gives it its name.

The chef owner offers a continental menu that features specialties such as *Chateaubriand* for two, rack of lamb, and a variety of seafood. Children's menu. Jackets suggested for dinner. Pianist Friday and Saturday evenings. Bar.

THE BUFFET AT THE KIMBELL
3333 Camp Bowie Blvd., Kimbell Art Museum in the Cultural District • 332-8451 • Lunch Tuesday–Sunday, light dinner Friday 5:30–7:30. Closed Monday • $ • Cr. • W +

The cafeteria style restaurant setting itself is nothing special, but you are just steps away from the most elegant surroundings of the art treasures in this museum. And the food, although light lunch fare, offers a variety of non-standard choices of sandwiches, soups, salads, and simple, but sweet desserts. Beer and wine.

CAFÉ ASPEN RESTAURANT AND BAR
6103 Camp Bowie Blvd. (76116) • 738-0838 • Lunch and dinner Monday–Saturday. Closed Sunday • $$ • Cr. • W +

The creative menu here is a major draw with offerings that include imaginative salads, homemade soups, a club sandwich made with smoked salmon, and dinner selections like herb-crusted rack of lamb, veal chop *portobello,* and rainbow trout *amandine.* Irresistible homemade desserts buffet. Occasional poetry readings and live music. Bar.

CARSHON'S DELICATESSEN
3133 Cleburne Road (76110) near West Berry • 923-1907 Breakfast and lunch Tuesday–Sunday 9–3. Closed Monday and major holidays • $ • No Cr.

Almost three-quarters of a century after it was started as a kosher meat market in another location in 1928, Carshon's is now famed as a kosher-style deli that offers everything you'd expect in a deli from chicken soup to a huge selection of old-fashioned two-handed sandwiches and plate lunches. Beer and wine.

CATTLEMEN'S STEAKHOUSE
2458 North Main (76106), in the Stockyards, just north of Exchange Avenue • 624-3945 • Lunch and dinner seven days $–$$ • Cr. • W Call ahead

Founded in 1947, this restaurant has earned a place among the traditions of the Stockyards. As the name says, the big draw is the steaks, which are charcoal broiled and come in all sizes from an 8-oz filet to an 18-oz sirloin. Other choices include seafood and barbecued ribs. Bar.

CELEBRATION
4600 Dexter Avenue (76107), at Camp Bowie and Hulen 731-6272 • Lunch and dinner seven days • $–$$ • Cr. • W

In most restaurants that tout "home cooking" the "home" was probably an orphanage, but here it is like Mom used to make, especially if Mom had been to a distinguished cooking school. Fried chicken, pot roast, seafood; all simply prepared and served in large portions with salad and fresh vegetables family style—which means seconds on most entrees if you want them—and homemade desserts. Children's menu. Bar.

EDELWEISS RESTAURANT
3801-A Southwest Blvd. (76116) on the Old Weatherford traffic circle • 738-5934 • Dinner Tuesday–Saturday. Closed Sunday–Monday • $$ • Cr. • W

The decor in this 350-seat restaurant is that of a German beer hall and the atmosphere varies so you can choose between cozy corners with candlelight to being just a step or two short of an Oktoberfest party. An owner/chef from Germany means true German food with traditional dishes like *sauerbraten,* sausages, *rouladan,* and a variety of *schnitzels.* Also steaks and seafood on the menu. Band plays everything from polkas to waltzes for dancing nightly. Children's menu. Bar. Same location more than 30 years.

8.0 RESTAURANT
111 East 3rd (76102), in Sundance Square • 336-0880 Lunch and dinner seven days • $–$$ • Cr. • W

Steaks, seafood, pasta, and Tex-Mex items are all on the menu, but in addition to the routine choices, each category has its own unique specialties. The Tex-Mex choices, for example, include an appetizer of *ocho quesadillas* made with fresh spinach and sauteed mushrooms, and entrees of the 8.0 *potato enchiladas* with *ancho ranchero* sauce, or a fish taco platter with *tortillas, pico de gallo,* honey *jalapeño* tarter and black beans and rice. Then there's the appetizer called Fried Purple Worms (don't ask, just order). Another plus is that there are no preservatives, hormones, antibiotics, or "any other bad junk" in the meat products served here and everything else is made as pure and healthy as possible. Even the water and ice are filtered. The bar is a popular meeting place at night, so it can be noisy. Check out the wall murals by local artists. Free evening/weekend parking in Sundance Square area parking lots.

JOE T. GARCIA'S MEXICAN DISHES
2201 North Commerce (76106), near the Stockyards • 626-4356
Lunch and dinner seven days. Closed some major holidays
$–$$ • No Cr. • W (Through patio)
In 1935, Joe T. Garcia opened part of his home as a Mexican restaurant. Customers walked through the kitchen to get to the dining room and got beer from the family refrigerator. Now, the family still operates the restaurant, but over more than 60 years they've expanded the house until it fills about half a city block of what is probably the best-known Tex-Mex restaurant in the city. If the weather's nice, the garden patio is the best place to be. *Enchiladas, tacos, fajitas, chiles rellenos;* all the standard Tex-Mex dishes are on the menu. Actually, they're not on the menu, at least not on a printed one because there is none; the waiters spout it off for you. Dinners served family style with the usual accompaniments of rice, beans, chips, and hot sauce. Strolling *mariachis* enhance the atmosphere on weekends. Bar. (For what locals tout as the best place to get a Tex-Mex breakfast, there's Joe T. Garcia's Mexican Bakery with two locations, one around the corner from the restaurant at 2140 North Main and the other at 1109 Hemphill.)

HEDARY'S LEBANESE RESTAURANT
3308 Fairfield (76116), in the 6323 Shopping Center of Camp Bowie Blvd. • Lunch Tuesday–Friday, dinner Tuesday–Sunday. Closed Mondays. • $$ • Cr. • W

You've heard of *tabbuli* and *falafil* and *hummus,* but you're not sure exactly what they are, no less traditional Lebanese dishes called *sujak* or *shish tawuk.* Not to worry, Hedary's menu explains every dish in detail so you can order *shish tawuk* with competence, knowing it's lightly seasoned grilled chicken on skewers with bell peppers, tomatoes, and onions served with rice, and an order of *sujak* will be "a generous portion of Antoine's own hot beef sausage brought to you with hot, fresh baked bread, lemon juice, and tomato slices." Beer and wine. Lebanese music.

JUANITA'S RESTAURANT
115 West 2nd (76102), in Sundance Square across from The Worthington Hotel • 335-1777 • Lunch and dinner seven days. Closed major holidays • $ • Cr. • W

It looks like a classy Victorian restaurant you'd find in New York back in the early 1900s, but the menu is Tex-Mex , or maybe *nouvelle* Tex-Mex, with a touch of Cajun blended in. The standards are here—*enchiladas, tacos, fajitas*—however specialties also include chile butter chicken and quail braised in tequila. Latin/Mexican background music. Free evening/weekend parking in Sundance Square area parking lots. Valet parking.

LE CHARDONNAY
2443 Forest Park Blvd. (76110), near TCU campus • 926-5622 Lunch and dinner seven days. Closed major holidays. $$–$$$ • Cr. • W +

Take a chef-owner schooled in French cooking and expose him to Southwestern ingredients and you have the core of the menu in this restaurant that resembles a cozy Paris bistro with an outdoor terrace. *Escargot, pates,* steak Parisienne, duck, potato-crusted red snapper, and zesty lamb are just a few of the appetizers and entrees that result from this combination. Children's menu. Bar.

MICHAEL'S
3413 West 7th (76107) • 877-3413 • $$–$$$ • Cr. • W

The chef-partner titles his menu as "Contemporary Ranch Cuisine." That includes steaks, of course, from chicken fried to N.Y. Strip, but it also translates into entrees like Ranch Roasted Pork Tenderloin with roasted corn and red *chile salsa* cream sauce; Ranch Lamb Chops topped with goat cheese and raspberry *chipotle* sauce; Coal Roasted Salmon with *pico* relish butter sauce, and Michael's Ranch Baked Crab Cakes with lite-*ancho chile* cream sauce. Bar.

ON BROADWAY RISTORANTE
6306 Hulen Bend Blvd. (76132), in Hulen Point Shopping Center • 346-8841 • Lunch Monday–Friday, dinner seven days $–$$ • Cr. • W +

Thin crusted pizza with shrimp or grilled chicken are just a couple of the items on the predominantly Northern Italian menu that set this *ristorante* a cut above the normal strip-center Italian restaurant. Pastas, steaks, and seafood entrees include out-of-the-ordinary specialties like trout with a shrimp garnish in a tomato-wine-butter sauce, or peppered filet in a brandy cream sauce. Bar.

REFLECTIONS
The Worthington Hotel, 200 Main Street (76102), north end of Sundance Square • 882-1765 • Dinner Monday–Saturday. Closed Sunday • $$$ • Cr. • W +

The name comes from the reflecting pools that are the centerpiece of this dining room located on the mezzanine level. The atmosphere of subdued elegance, a chef who is creative and consistent, artistic presentation of palate-pleasing dishes, and unobtrusively efficient service combine to make the fine dining here a culinary occasion to reflect on. The menu offers American and regional dishes with a French influence. A fixed price menu ($28.95 including tax and tip) features a three-course meal. A typical fixed price dinner might start with an appetizer such as chilled peppered lamb loin or wild mushroom with pheasant sausage; a choice of Black Angus strip loin or sauteed Dover sole filets for the entrée, and a chocolate-pistachio *pate* or Jack

Daniels pecan pie for dessert. Semi-formal attire. Bar. Reservations suggested. Complimentary validated valet parking in hotel. Free evening/weekend parking in Sundance Square area commercial lots. Rated four diamonds by AAA.

REATA
500 Throckmorton Street (76102) Bank One Tower Building
336-1009 • Lunch and dinner Monday–Saturday. Closed Sunday
$–$$ • Cr. • W +

Go for the panoramic view—it's on the 35th floor—but stay for the food, which is upscale cowboy cuisine. Named for the ranch in the movie *Giant,* the menu appropriately features steaks. But these steaks aren't steer-tough and burned to a crisp, as was the custom in the old ranch days; these—the pan-seared pepper-crusted tenderloin, for example—are tender and cooked to your liking. Also a selection of Tex-Mex and seafood entrees. Bar. Valet parking and free evening/weekend parking in Sundance Square area parking lots.

RUFFINO'S ITALIAN RESTAURANT
2455 Forest Park Blvd. (76110), near TCU campus
923-0522 • Lunch and dinner Monday–Saturday.
Closed Sunday • $$–$$$ • Cr. • W +

Classic Italian fare is served in this cozy *trattoria*-style restaurant. Veal, chicken, beef, and seafood entrees all with tasty sauces. If you're really hungry try the family-style dinner for two, which runs from antipasto through pasta and entrée to dessert. Beer and wine.

SAINT-EMILION
3617 West 7th (76107), near the Cultural District • 737-2781
Dinner seven days • $$–$$$ • Cr. • W +

The decor of this brick home restaurant in so country French it could have been transplanted directly from a French village. And the menu follows through with well-crafted entrées that includes such culinary delights as seafood in a puff pastry, veal medallions, duck, lamb, and fresh fish flown in daily from the northeast. Wind it all up sumptuously with a dessert like a rum-laced *creme brulee.* Fixed priced dinner available (about $29). Bar.

CLUBS AND BARS

BILLY BOB'S TEXAS
2520 Rodeo Plaza (76106), in the Stockyards
624-7117 or Metro 817/589-1711 • Admission • W +

Known as the world's largest honky-tonk, Billy Bob's has room for 6,000, two dance floors, 40 bar stations, and is the only nightclub in the nation with an indoor arena where, every weekend, professional rodeo cowboys try to ride bulls that don't want to be ridden. Live country music is played every night with major country artists performing in concert most weekends. The Academy of Country Music and the Country Music Association have both awarded it the title of "Club of the Year" several times. Sunday–Thursday, general admission $1 before 6 p.m., $3 after; Friday–Saturday $1 before 5 p.m., $5.50–$8.50 after. Live music begins at 8 p.m. every night. Friday and Saturday: bull-riding at 9 and 10 and name entertainment begins at 10:30. Shops, arcade games, restaurant. Free parking during the day, pay parking at night.

CARAVAN OF DREAMS PERFORMING ARTS CENTER
312 Houston Street (76102) in Sundance Square • 877-3000 or Metro 817/429-4000 • Admission varies • W + But not all areas

This downstairs club is the Fort Worth Mecca for jazz and blues fans. That's not all they book, but it's the main program most of the time. The club is small so when a top name is booked, you'd best get your tickets early. Call for schedule. Or you can just enjoy the ambiance and view from the rooftop grotto bar. Free evening/weekend parking in Sundance Square area parking lots.

WHITE ELEPHANT SALOON
106 East Exchange Avenue (76106), in the Stockyards
624-1887 • Cover on weekends

The 1887 in the phone number isn't just a coincidence. A permanent place in Fort Worth's history was ensured for the saloon, then located downtown, when its owner, gambler Luke Short, outdrew and killed former marshal "Long Hair" Jim Courtright in

1887. There have been changes since 1887, of course, but today's saloon still recalls the Old West with its long, wooden stand-up bar with brass footrail. The saloon has been listed in *Esquire* magazine's 100 best bars in America. Upstairs is a cabaret theater where the Cowtown Opry performs every Saturday (admission), and next door is the White Elephant Beer Garden open April through October with live music and dancing on weekend nights.

LODGING

For a double room: $ = Under $80, $$ = $80–$120, $$$ = $121–$180, $$$$ = $181–$250, $$$$$ = Over $250; Room tax 13%.

For detailed listings see Metroplex Lodgings Section, p. 395.

AZALEA PLANTATION
1400 Robinwood Drive (76111) • 838-5882 or 800-68-RELAX (800-687-3529) • $$

ETTA'S PLACE
200 West Third at Houston in Sundance Square (76102)
Metro 817/654-0267 • $$$ • W + elevator and some rooms
All no smoking except for outside terraces

GREEN OAKS PARK HOTEL
6901 West Freeway (76116), off I-30 at Green Oaks exit
738-7311 or 800-772-2341 (In Texas), 800-433-2174
(Outside Texas) • $$ • W + 4 rooms • No smoking rooms

HOLIDAY INN FORT WORTH CENTRAL
2000 Beach Street (76103), off I-30 at Beach Street exit
534-4801 • $$ • W + 2 rooms • No smoking rooms

HOLIDAY INN NORTH
2540 Meacham Blvd. (76106) • 625-9911 or 800-465-4329
$$ • W + 3 rooms • No smoking rooms

LAQUINTA WEST
7888 I-30 West (76108) off Cherry Lane exit • 246-5511 or
800-531-5900 • $ • W+ 2 rooms • No smoking rooms

MISS MOLLY'S HOTEL
109½ West Exchange Avenue (76106), in Stockyards Historic
District, just west of Main • 626-1522 or 800-99MOLLY
(800-996-6559) • $$–$$$ • No smoking

RESIDENCE INN BY MARRIOTT
1701 South University Drive (76107), take University exit
off I-30, go south ½ mile • 870-1011 • $$–$$$ • W+ 2 suites
No smoking suites

STOCKYARDS HOTEL
109 East Exchange Avenue at Main (76106) in Stockyards
Historic District • 625-6427 • $$$ • No smoking rooms

THE TEXAS WHITE HOUSE
1417 Eighth Avenue (76104) • 923-3597 or 800-279-6491
$$ • No smoking in house

THE WORTHINGTON
200 Main Street (76102), downtown at Sundance Square
870-1000 or 800-477-8274 • $$$–$$$$ • W+ 15 rooms
No smoking rooms

GARLAND

DALLAS COUNTY • 195,000 • AREA CODE 972

According to the local stories, the city was originally founded to settle a feud between the two rival towns.

It started in 1886 when the Santa Fe Railroad laid its tracks about a mile to the east of the town of Duck Creek. Most, but not all, of the townspeople moved to the new area, called Embree, taking their post office with them. That same year, the MK&T Railroad came through, but declined to join the Santa Fe in a union station. Instead, the MK&T built its own depot a little farther north and called it Duck Creek, also.

A feud developed between Embree and the new Duck Creek, which were barely a mile apart, over the location of the post office. Each town tried to lure the citizens from the old Duck Creek to their community to reinforce their claim. It's said that the feelings ran so high that a man from one town dared not go "courting" in the other without courting trouble.

Finally, in 1887, a local judge came to a Solomon-like decision and persuaded Congress to move the post office between the towns and order both railroads to deliver the mail there. The post office was named in honor of the then Attorney General A. H. Garland. Surprisingly, the decision pleased everyone and the citizens of the new and old Duck Creek and Embree soon dissolved their towns and combined to form the new city of Garland.

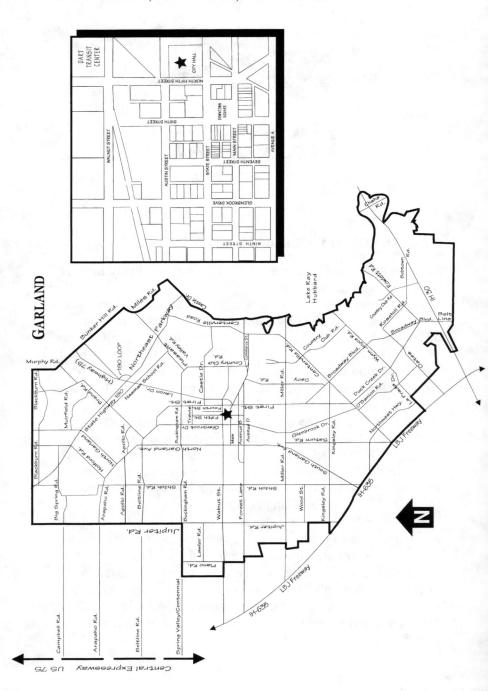

For many years, cotton was king here. But in the 1930s, during The Depression, farmers found the soil ideal for onions and onion farming became a major factor in the local economy. By the time World War II began, Garland had already started to change from an agricultural-based economy to an industrial community, and the onion business yielded to the defense industry. After the war, the industrial base stayed and grew and the city grew with it. And grew, and grew! As a result, Garland's 57 square miles tucked into the northeast corner of Dallas County is now a highly diversified industrial, high-tech center and the 9th largest city in Texas.

Garland is dry under the local options. Most restaurants and hotels/motels have private clubs that require you pay a small membership fee to buy alcoholic beverages by the drink.

FREE VISITOR SERVICES

GARLAND CONVENTION AND VISITORS BUREAU
200 Museum Plaza (4th and State) 75040 • 205-2749
Monday–Friday 8:30–4:30 • W

You can pick up free brochures, maps, and specific information about Garland and the surrounding area, and get help with hotel/motel accommodations. Located in the Landmark Museum. (See HISTORIC PLACES, below.)

HISTORIC PLACES

HERITAGE PARK
4th and State, east of City Hall

The area east of city hall is informally referred to as Garland's Heritage Park because it contains the old Santa Fe Railroad Depot with a railroad passenger car, and an historic home. The depot is now the home of the **Landmark Museum,** which features a small collection of memorabilia from Garland's early days. The Pullman car, which dates from the early 1900s, is being restored. Next door is the **Pace House,** a one-story frame house that is considered an excellent example of a Texas Victorian style farmhouse. Only the museum is open to the public (Monday–Friday 8:30–4:30. Free).

OUTDOORS

GARLAND PARKS
Parks and Recreation Department,
634 Apollo Road (75040) • 205-2750
The dozens of large and small parks scattered around the city offer a variety of outdoor facilities including jogging and bike trails, tennis courts, swimming pools, fishing piers, and picnicking. Although not the biggest in size, the John J. Audubon Park (342 Oates) is packed with outstanding facilities including the city's Surf and Swim Wave-Action Pool, the Carter Softball Complex, the Duck Creek/Audubon Park Hike and Bike Trail, a recreation center with gym, 10 soccer fields, playgrounds, and picnic areas. Call for details.

LAKE RAY HUBBARD
Take I-30 east to the lake • 214-670-0936
Open at all times • Fee and non-fee areas • W
This 22,745-acre lake on the East Fork of the Trinity River is located between Garland and Rockwall. Owned by the City of Dallas, it is used for water supply and recreation. There are facilities for boating, fishing, waterskiing, picnicking, and camping (fee). Several marinas on the lake rent boats. Garland's John Paul Jones Park stretches along almost all of the city's shoreline providing picnic areas and three fishing piers. *The Texas Queen* excursion boat operates from Elgin B. Robinson Park on the lake. This double decked paddlewheeler offers both daytime tours and dinner cruises. Call 722-0039 for schedule and fares.

WOODLAND BASIN NATURE AREA
2332 East Miller Road at Lake Ray Hubbard • Free
205-2750 (Garland Parks and Recreation) • W
A quarter-mile wooden boardwalk jutting into the marshy area of Lake Ray Hubbard provides an ideal platform for observing the

marsh inhabitants from armadillos to waterfowl. Best viewing in early morning or late afternoon. A half-mile nature trail extends north and south of Miller Road. Canoe launch and bank fishing.

MUSIC AND PERFORMING ARTS

GARLAND CENTER FOR THE PERFORMING ARTS
300 North 5th at Austin (P.O. Box 469002, 75046) • 205-2790 (information and tickets) • W +

This center houses two complete theaters that can stage everything from touring Broadway shows to symphony concerts. The main theater, which seats 720, features a proscenium stage, hydraulic orchestra lift, and state-of-the-art sound and lighting systems. The smaller theater has a booth-controlled sound and lighting system and seats 200.

The following organizations call this center their performance home. Phone numbers in parentheses are direct numbers for information.

Garland Civic Theatre (P.O. Box 461252, 75046 • 349-1331). Founded in 1968, this is the oldest community theater group in Dallas County. The Civic Theatre usually puts on six productions in its September to May season. The Mainstage offerings include comedies, mysteries, drama, and classics. Performances are usually Thursday–Saturday at 8 p.m. with matinees Saturday–Sunday at 2. Ticket prices range from about $9 to $14 depending on the production. The group also produces the Children on Stage Program, which has its own season each year (See FAMILY FUN AND KID STUFF, p. 250).

Garland Summer Musicals (205-2780). As its name says, this group, which was founded in 1983, presents one musical in June and one in July. Adult tickets $19, Seniors $17.

Garland Symphony Orchestra (553-1223). Founded in 1978, this 93-member professional orchestra offers six subscription concerts in its October through May season. Most concerts feature guest artists. Tickets range from $12–$27.

GARLAND COUNTRY MUSIC ASSOCIATION
605 West State Street (75040) • 494-3835 • W

This group sponsors what's known locally as the "Big G Jamboree," an every Saturday night performance of local and visiting western, gospel, and bluegrass groups. Performances are in their own theater. Adult tickets $6, children under 12 $4.

FAMILY FUN AND KID STUFF

GARLAND CIVIC THEATRE/CHILDREN ON STAGE
Garland Center for the Performing Arts, 300 North 5th at Austin • 349-1331 • W +

This is theater for children by children. The actors and technicians who work the shows are primarily students aged 8 through 18. Most of the productions are "school shows" held during the day for children bused from schools as field trips. However, there are also several weekend productions during the summer as well as one spring and one fall production, all with both matinee and evening performances. All seats are $4.

SURF AND SWIM
Audubon Park, 440 Oates Road (Exit Oates Road off I-635, go east to park) • 686-1237 or 205-2757 • Open daily June through September • W

The "surf" here is a wave-action pool that produces four-foot waves. This municipal pool has grass beaches, pecan groves, shaded picnic tables, bath houses, and a snack bar. You can rent tubes and rafts. Professional lifeguards are on duty at all times. Adults $4.50, youth 5–17 $3.25, seniors $2.75, children 4 and under free.

SPORTS

GOLF

PUBLIC COURSES

FIREWHEEL GOLF PARK
600 Blackburn Road (75040) • 205-2795 • Two 18-hole courses. Green fees: Weekdays $17, weekends $24.

The original course, now called the Old Course, has been ranked number one among public courses in Texas and the newer Lakes Course is ranked 12th.

UP TO PAR DRIVING RANGE AND GOLF COURSE
3015 North Shiloh Road (75045) • 530-0585 • 9-hole par 3 course. Call for fees.

PRIVATE COURSES

EASTERN HILLS COUNTRY CLUB
3000 Country Club Dr. (75043) • 278-3051 • 18-hole course. Green fees: $40–$50

OAKRIDGE COUNTRY CLUB
2800 Diamond Oaks Dr. (75044) • 530-8004 • 18-hole course. Green fees: Weekdays $46.50, Weekends $56.50.

SOFTBALL

JERRY CARTER SOFTBALL COMPLEX
Audubon Park, 550 Oates Road (75043), Exit Oates Road off I-635, go east to park • 613-7729 • W

This is not your ordinary softball park. It's a dream set-up for softball tournaments. The five softball fields are arranged in a "wagon wheel" configuration, all identical and all fenced at 300 feet. Players can warm up in either of two large fenced areas and there are eight batting cages. Other facilities include high-pressure sodium lighting, shaded bleachers, and electric scoreboards and time clocks. Recognized as one of the best in the state, this complex hosts state and national tournaments.

WINTERS SOFTBALL COMPLEX
Winter Park, 1330 Spring Creek Drive (75040) • 276-5483 • W

Another softball tournament facility with three identical back-to-back fields with 300-foot fences, glare-reducing lighting for night games, and an electric scoreboard. Adjacent to the softball complex is the 11-field Winters Soccer Complex.

TENNIS

GARLAND TENNIS CENTER
1010 West Miller Road (75047) • 205-2778

The fee for using any of the 14 lighted courts is $1.50 per person for 1½ hours.

ANNUAL EVENTS

JULY

STAR SPANGLED 4TH
**Three days including July 4th • Historic Downtown Square:
State, Main, and 5th Streets • (P.O. Box 469002, 75046)
205-2632 • Admission free • W**

Just about every community in the country has a Fourth of July celebration, but Garland celebrates this historic event for three days from 10 to 10 with a line-up of shows and concerts featuring national talent, other continuous entertainment, choreographed fireworks nightly, a midway, a children's area, arts and crafts booths, and a wide variety of special exhibits and demonstrations. Free shuttle service is available from the DART Transit Center at Walnut and 5th and the adjacent Williams Stadium. About 50,000 people attend over the three days.

OCTOBER

AUTUMNFEST
Saturday–Sunday of third weekend in month • Audubon Park,
550 Oates Drive • (P.O. Box 469002, 75046) • 205-2879
Admission free • W

The main ingredients of this Autumnfest weekend are an arts
and crafts show featuring about 300 artisans from all over the state,
the "It's a Gas" classic car show, and a Saturday evening concert.
Parking within the park is limited, but free shuttle service is available from the DART Transit Center, 6151 Duck Creek Drive.

SHOPPING

ANTIQUE SHOPS

There are several antique shops clustered around North 6th
Street and West Main.

GRAND PRAIRIE

**DALLAS AND TARRANT COUNTIES • 105,000
AREA CODE 972**

In 1863, during the Civil War, A.M. Dechman, a trader who was in charge of the commissary at Fort Belknap, had his wagon break down near a prairie home. Ever the trader, Dechman swapped his disabled wagon, the team of oxen, and $200 in Confederate money to the settler for about 240 acres of land. After the war a town grew up here that was named after him. In the 1870s, still the trader, he traded land in Dechman to get the Texas and Pacific Railroad to come to his town. The railroad did, but in the process the town was renamed Grand Prairie because the town sits on a vast expanse of grassland between two large bands of timber known as the Cross Timbers.

Dechman was not the first trader in the area. For years the Indians tribes from the north would meet with the southern tribes here to trade horses, cloth, grain, skins, and other items.

When Grand Prairie was incorporated in 1909, it only had an area of three square blocks and about fifty families.

The town grew slowly until the opening of several large defense plants in World War II spurred population growth. Today it is mostly a residential city with some light industry.

The city borders two lakes. Its newest attraction is Lone Star Park, which offers thoroughbred and quarter horse racing.

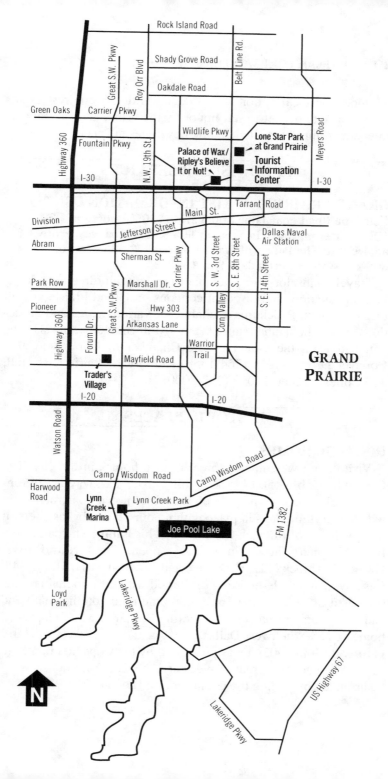

Under the local option laws the city is dry. Some restaurants have a special permit to sell liquor by the drink, and special permits are required to sell alcoholic beverages at special events.

FREE VISITOR SERVICES

GRAND PRAIRIE TOURIST INFORMATION CENTER
Belt Line Road near Lone Star Park, (75050) north of I-30 (Old Center may still be open at 605 Safari Parkway, Suite A-6, adjacent to The Palace of Wax) • Metro 972-263-9588 or 800-288-8386 • Seven days 9–5 • W +

Travel counselors are available to assist with directions, lodging, information, and discount coupons on Grand Prairie and all the Metroplex. Brochures available for various cities and attractions throughout the state. Visitor information can also be obtained from the Grand Prairie Chamber of Commerce, 900 Conover Drive, 75051 (264-1558) and Grand Prairie City Hall, 317 College Street, 75050 (237-8000).

HISTORIC PLACES

HISTORIC HOMES
Visitors are welcome to three historic homes in the city. The **Goodwin Cabin** (500 block South Carrier Parkway at Cottonwood Park) was built in 1846 of Tennessee notch-construction, in which everything lays in place with no pins, bolts, or fasteners. It was the home of Micajah Goodwin and his family who came here from Alabama. This cabin is always open. The **Jordan/Bowles Home** (700 block N.E. 28th Street and Bowles) was built in 1845. It is a typical double-house of the period with the two main rooms separated by an open hall, a room on the porch on the south end and side rooms in pairs on the north. The large white clapboard home at 125 Southwest Dallas Street is known as the **Copeland Home.** Built in 1902, it was purchased by the Copeland family in 1908. Visits to the Jordan/Bowles and the Copeland houses may be arranged by calling the Grand Prairie Library (264-9523).

THE PENN FARM AGRICULTURAL HISTORY CENTER
See JOE POOL LAKE, below.

OUTDOORS

GRAND PRAIRIE PARKS AND RECREATION DEPARTMENT, 326 WEST MAIN, 75050 • 237-8100

Among the facilities in 40 parks in the system are several miles of hike and bike trails, including a 1.8-mile National Recreation Trail in Fish Creek Linear Park, a forest preserve, an equestrian arena, swimming pools, tennis and other sports courts and fields, fishing ponds, creative playgrounds, and two golf courses.

JOE POOL LAKE
Trinity River Authority • 817-467-2104 • From I-20 take Great Southwest exit south; this becomes Lake Ridge Parkway and leads to Lynn Creek Park and Loyd Park • W Variable

Straddling the Dallas-Tarrant county line, the shoreline of this 7,470-acre lake is still being developed. It already has two Trinity River Authority (TRA) parks and one state park with facilities for boating, fishing, swimming, hiking, picnicking, and camping. The marina at the TRA day-use **Lynn Creek Park** (5700 Lake Ridge Parkway, 75052, Metro 817-640-4200) offers rentals for fishing, pontoon, and ski boats as well as water bikes, skis, and tubes. There is also an all-weather fishing pier (fee). **Loyd Park** (3401 Ragland Road, 75052, Metro 817-467-2104) includes a 3-mile hiking and an off-road bike trail and RV and tent camping area.

The largest park on the lake is **Cedar Hill State Park** (P.O. Box 2649, Cedar Hill 75106. 291-3900). From I-20 take FM 1382 exit, go south four miles to state park on the lake. Day use admission is $3. Among the facilities at this 1,850-acre park are a marina with boats and jet skis for rent, 2 lighted fishing jetties, a fishing barge, 5 miles of hiking trails and 12 miles of mountain bike trails, a swim beach, playgrounds, and campsites ($12–$15). The **Penn Farm Agricultural History Center** is also located inside this park. The farm is architecturally significant as a set of rural farm buildings used by a single family for over 100 years. It shows the evolution of structures constructed or adapted by the Penn family as needs changed and modern conveniences were added. The building complex is only the core of what at one time was a farm of over 1,100 acres. The farm is now frequently used as a setting for demonstrations and special events. For information call 291-3900. Admission.

MOUNTAIN CREEK LAKE
Grand Prairie Parks and Recreation Department • 237-8100
From Hwy. 303 (Pioneer Parkway) take FM 1382
(Belt Line Road) to Marshall Drive then east to lake • W

This 2,710-acre lake is primarily for power generating use, however boating and fishing are allowed. Horsepower limits on boats.

MUSIC AND PERFORMING ARTS

GRAND PRAIRIE ARTS COUNCIL
P.O. Box 531613, 75053-1613 • 642-2787

This council brings a variety of musical/theatrical events to the city throughout the year. Call for schedule. It also sponsors the annual Grand Prairie Summer Musical Event the last weekend in June. This features an orchestra and local talent and is held at the Grand Prairie High School.

FAMILY FUN AND KID STUFF

THE PALACE OF WAX
AND RIPLEY'S BELIEVE IT OR NOT!
601 East Safari Parkway (75050). From I-30 exit north at Belt Line Road; the museums can be seen from the highway
Metro 972/263-2391 • Open seven days at 10. Closed Thanksgiving, Christmas, and New Year's Day
Single or combined admission • W

These two unusual museums share a large onion-domed building that looks like something from an Arabian fantasy. The Palace of Wax exhibits life-size figures from real and reel Hollywood, history, fantasy, and religion. There are also displays showing how the wax artist has created the figures and you can be the judge of how life-like he has made them. The eight galleries in Ripley's Believe It or Not! display some of the bizarre oddities and fascinating facts that Robert Ripley collected on his travels to 198 countries during the 1930s. There are several hands-on exhibits and others that let visitors experience an earthquake and a Texas tornado. Some of these more active exhibits may be frightening to small children. Tickets to one museum cost $9.95 for adults and $6.95 for children 4–12. A combination ticket for both costs $12.95 for adults and $9.95 for children. Seniors get $1 off the one museum tickets, but not off the combo. Tax is added to all prices. Gift shop and game area.

SPORTS

BOATING AND FISHING

See Joe Pool Lake and Mountain Creek Lake, in OUTDOORS, p. 257.

GOLF

PUBLIC COURSES

FUN CITY
I-20 and FM 1382 (3990 Westcliff, 75052) • 262-0022 • 9-hole par 3 course that's being expanded to 18 holes. 9 holes $5, seniors $3.50. Also batting cages.

GRAND PRAIRIE MUNICIPAL GOLF COURSE
3202 Southeast 14th Street (75052) • Metro 972/263-0661 Three 9-hole courses. Green fees: $13.50 weekdays, $15.50 weekends.

I CARE FITNESS CENTER AND GOLF COURSE
242 Idle Wild (75051) • 264-2510 • 9-hole course.
Call for green fees.

RIVERSIDE GOLF CLUB
3000 Riverside Drive (75050) at Hwy. 360
Metro 817-640-7800 • 18-hole course. Green fees
(includes cart): $48 weekdays, $58 weekends.

SUNSET GOLF CENTER
4906 East Main (75050) • 331-8057 • 9-hole course. Green fees:
$11 weekdays, $14 weekends.

TANGLE RIDGE GOLF CLUB
818 Tangle Ridge Drive (75052), south of Joe Pool Lake
972-299-6837 • Green fees: $35 weekdays, $45 weekends. Club
house with dining room.

Although this 18-hole championship course is owned and operated by the city, it resembles a country club course.

PRIVATE COURSES

Call for green fees.

GREAT SOUTHWEST GOLF CLUB
612 Avenue J East (75050) • 647-0116 • 18-hole course.

WOODCREST COUNTRY CLUB
3502 Country Club Dr. (75051) • 299-6837 • 18-hole course.

HORSE RACING

LONE STAR PARK AT GRAND PRAIRIE
2200 North Belt Line (75050), take Belt Line exit off I-30 then
½ mile north • 263-RACE (263-7223) • Admission • W

Texas' newest Class 1 racecourse, Lone Star Park offers thoroughbred racing April–July and thoroughbred and Quarter Horse
racing October–November. Race days usually Wednesday–Sun-

day. Seven-story enclosed grandstand seats 8,000. On race days general admission $2, club house admission $5, self-parking $2, preferred parking $4, valet parking $5. Reserved seating available. Restaurants. Barns can accommodate up to 1,248 horses. Simulcasting from tracks around the country Wednesday through Monday in the Post Time Pavilion, which seats 1,800. On non-racing days, admission to the Post Time Pavilion is $1, self-parking $1, valet parking $5. Development plans include a family fun park with pony rides and a petting zoo adjacent to the Post Time Pavilion.

TENNIS

The Parks Department offers free tennis at more than two dozen courts in several parks and at the Grand Prairie High School. Most are lighted. For information call 237-8100.

ANNUAL EVENTS

APRIL

PRAIRIE DOG CHILI COOKOFF AND WORLD CHAMPIONSHIP OF PICKLED QUAIL EGG EATING
Saturday–Sunday early in month • Traders Village, 2602 Mayfield Road • Metro 972-647-2331 • Free (Parking $2) • W
If nothing else, the title ranks right up there with the longest titles of any Texas event. Fortunately, that's not all there is to this tongue-in-cheek tribute to "Texas Red," and some of the activities are as colorful as its title. The chili cookoff, which draws cooks from as far away as New York, is so popular they've had to limit it to 150 teams that compete making such variations as Horny Toad Chili and Cow Pasture Disaster Chili. Other non-cooking contests include the Original Anvil Toss and the Cuzin Homer Page Invitational Eat-and-Run Stewed Prune Pit Spitting Contest. And, of course, there's the pickled quail egg eating contest in which the winner eats the most in 60 seconds. On the more ordinary side, there's free, continuous entertainment both days and a

free dance Saturday night. About 80,000–85,000 people usually attend over the two days.

JUNE

ANTIQUE AUTO SWAP MEET
Saturday–Sunday early in month • Trader's Village, 2602 Mayfield Road • Metro 972-647-2331 • Free (Parking $2) • W

If it's on wheels, or ever was, there's a good chance you'll find it at this swap meet for car buffs. Usually about 600 collectors and vendors from across the country show off, horse trade, and sell cars, parts, accessories, and auto memorabilia.

AUGUST

WESTERN DAYS
Wednesday–Saturday early in month • Various locations Metro 972-263-9588 or 800-288-8386 (Grand Prairie Tourist Information Center) • Free (Admission to Rodeo)

The activities start mid-week but the big ones are on the weekend starting with a Professional Rodeo Cowboys Association (PRCA) rodeo on Friday night. Saturday features a free pancake breakfast, a parade, and another rodeo that night. Other events include country and western dancing.

SEPTEMBER

NATIONAL CHAMPIONSHIP INDIAN POW WOW
Saturday–Sunday weekend after Labor Day Trader's Village, 2602 Mayfield Road Metro 972-647-2331 • Free (Parking $2) • W

Representatives from dozens of Native American tribes from across the U.S. take part in this colorful celebration of culture and heritage that's open to the public. Tribal dance contests, arts and crafts, cultural heritage demonstrations, and Native American food are among the features of this Pow Wow. Original Indian arts and crafts are exhibited and sold. Sponsorship by the Dallas/Fort

Worth Inter-Tribal Association ensures authenticity of all aspects of the celebration.

OCTOBER

OKTOBERFEST
Saturday–Sunday mid-month • Trader's Village, 2602 Mayfield Road • Metro 972-647-2331 • Free (Parking $2) • W

Gigantic Bavarian-style tent biergardens with oompah band music are the mainstay of this Old World festival. And all the other trimmings are here to put the visitor in the mood of this traditional European festival with German, Czech, Norwegian, and Polish inspired decor and atmosphere. In addition to the continuous band music you can sing and dance to, there are folk dance exhibitions by dancers in colorful heritage costumes and authentic German food.

SHOPPING

SAMPLER ANTIQUE MALL
2985 South Hwy. 360 (75052), at Mayfield Road exit • Metro 972-647-4338 • W (Downstairs only)

A spacious two-floor building with uncluttered and well-displayed antiques and collectibles including some excellent furniture reproductions. Also a branch in Arlington at 1715 East Lamar (76006). Willow Tearoom, upstairs (Metro 972-602-3602) offers a menu of mostly salads and sandwiches for lunch daily (under $10).

TRADERS VILLAGE
2602 Mayfield Road (75052), take Mayfield exit of Hwy. 360, go east • Metro 972-647-2331 • Saturday–Sunday 8 to dusk • Free (Parking $2) • W

A Texas-size flea market occupies this 106-acre complex. First opened in 1973, it now attracts more than 1,600 dealers who set up in open lots, covered sheds, and enclosed buildings. Crowds of 45,000 to 60,000 bargain hunters come here each weekend to buy everything from antiques to garage sale items, imports to farm-fresh produce, and car parts and tires to jewelry. Some cheap flea market junk but also some great buys if you know what you're looking for and have comparison-shopped the discount stores before coming here. There are children's rides, including an antique carousel, and an arcade area, food vendors, stroller and wheelchair rentals. Some vendors take credit cards, but best to bring cash, too. Over two dozen free special events are scheduled throughout the year (see ANNUAL EVENTS, pg. 261). The RV park is the largest in the Metroplex.

DINING OUT

$ = Under $12, $$ = $12–$30, $$$ = Over $30 for one person excluding drinks, tax, and tip.

EATUMUP CAFÉ
1610 Polo Road (75052), from I-20 Carrier Parkway exit go south to Polo Road, then west • 602-3456 • Breakfast, lunch, and dinner seven days • $ • Cr. • W

It's a little off the beaten path, but this country café emphasizes home cooking and generous portions with a not-quite-standard café menu that includes Italian, Mexican, and American selections running from burgers to chicken fried steak to vegetarian entrees. But this is up-to-date country because the chef owner has set it up so you can also surf the Internet here. Children's menu.

MARSALA RESTAURANT
1618 North Hwy. 360 (75050), at Avenue K •988-1101 or Metro 972-988-3101 • Lunch Monday-Friday, dinner seven days $$ • Cr. • W

The French and Italian menu features a number of tableside dishes such as steak *au poivre,* a pepper crusted N.Y. strip flamed in a green peppercorn and brandy glaze; and strawberry chambord dessert. Other entrées include seafood, poultry, pasta, veal, beef, and fresh game. Also vegetarian and dietary entrees. Classical guitarist enhances the romantic atmosphere during dinner Wednesday-Saturday. Bar.

THE OASIS AT JOE POOL LAKE
5700 Lake Ridge Parkway (75052), near the Lynn Creek Marina
Metro 817-640-7676 • Lunch and dinner seven days
$ • Cr. • W

A major attraction here is that the restaurant floats on Joe Pool Lake with outside deck seating available. The menu includes seafood, steaks, pasta, and burgers. Among the specialties is a combo plate of pork ribs and a half chicken. Children's menu. Entertainment on Friday and Saturday evenings in the upstairs bar.

LODGINGS

For a double room: $ = Under $80, $$ = $80–$120, $$$ = $121–$180, $$$$ = $181–$250, $$$$$ = Over $250; Room tax 13%.
For detailed listings see Metroplex Lodgings Section, p. 386.

HAMPTON INN DFW AIRPORT
2050 North Hwy. 360 (75050), exit east at Carrier Parkway
988-8989 or 800-HAMPTON (800-426-7866) • $
W + 2 rooms • No smoking rooms

LA QUINTA INN
1410 Northwest 19th Street (75050), at I-30 • 641-3021 or
800-531-5900 • $ • W + 2 rooms • No smoking rooms

HOMEGATE STUDIOS & SUITES
1108 North Hwy. 360 (75050), at Avenue J • 975-0000
$ • W + 7rooms • No smoking rooms (Extended stays only.
Three night minimum.)

GRAPEVINE

TARRANT COUNTY • 33,000 • AREA CODE 817

More than 150 years ago, wagon trains brought the first settlers to the Grape Vine Prairie from Missouri, Tennessee, Alabama, Kentucky, and Ohio. Today, more than 50 million people a year come to Grape Vine Prairie. But most don't know it because they don't know that when they land at the huge Dallas-Fort Worth International Airport, they are really landing in Grapevine. That airport, the second busiest in the world, lies almost entirely within the city limits of this historic town.

And it is historic, one of the oldest settlements in North Texas, settled under the Lone Star Flag of the Republic of Texas in 1844, a year before Texas entered the Union. It was September of that year that General Sam Houston and other representatives of the Republic signed a treaty of "peace, friendship, and commerce" with leaders of the Comanche, Keechi, Waco, Delaware, and other tribes at Grape Vine Springs. Both the springs and Grape Vine Prairie were named after the wild mustang grapes that grew profusely in the area, names which originated with the nomadic Cherokee and other tribes that passed through the area and were carried on by the settlers.

By 1854 the community leaders felt there were enough settlers to justify a town. Several names were suggested, mostly honoring the first settlers, but it was finally agreed to carry on the name of Grapevine.

GRAPEVINE

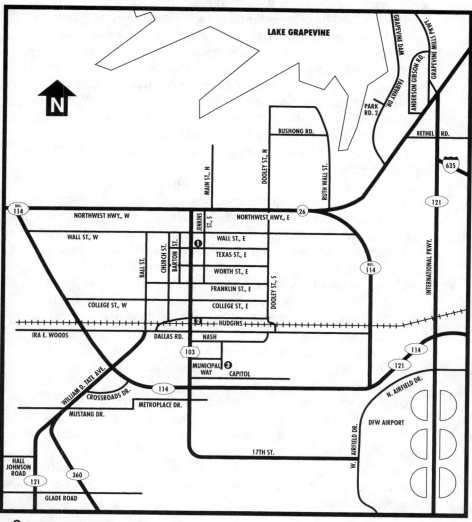

① CONVENTION & VISITORS BUREAU
② VISITORS INFORMATION CENTER
③ CONVENTION CENTER

Today much of outward signs of that history is preserved. The Main Street, for example, with its famed "Opry House," historical museum, and 38 other restored historic sites, has earned a listing in the National Register of Historic Places. This preservation is primarily due to the efforts of the community members who initially worked together in 1973 to save the landmark 1901 Cotton Belt Railroad Depot, which was slated for destruction. That successful effort lead to others and eventually to the formation of the present Grapevine Heritage Foundation and the Grapevine Historical Society. Working jointly, these two organizations have been able to hold onto Grapevine's past while the city moves rapidly into the future.

In keeping with the city's name, part of that future is the growing number of wineries that are settling here. There are already several wineries and tasting rooms in the city, and more on the way. If you're surprised that Texas produces wines, you may be more surprised to learn that Texas was making wine before California. Spanish missionaries established the first North American vineyards in what is now Texas in 1662. And about half of the more that two dozen species of grapes in the world are native to Texas. So it's not surprising that Texas wines frequently win gold medals at many of the major international wine competitions. Because Grapevine is in a "wet" area, you can do a tasting of the local wines, and buy a bottle and drink it on the winery patio.

Another recent addition, one which may bring in so many visitors as to change the face of the city, is the new Grapevine Mills Mall, a value mall expected to draw up to 16 million bargain shoppers annually.

For relaxation, just a mile north of downtown is the 7,380-acre Lake Grapevine with an extensive park system offering a variety of recreational facilities.

211 West Franklin, off Main. Most of these are private residences, not open to the public.

MUSEUMS AND ART GALLERIES

GRAPEVINE HERITAGE CENTER COMPLEX
701-707 South Main, 76051 • 424-0516 (Grapevine Heritage Foundation: Metro 817-481-0454 or 800-457-6338)
Depot Museum: Sunday–Friday 1–5, Saturday 10–5 • W

On this three-acre site are several restored buildings including the **1901 Cotton Belt Depot,** The 1888 **Cotton Belt Railroad Grapevine Section Foreman's House,** the reconstructed **Millican Blacksmith's Shop,** where the town smithy worked from 1909 to 1959; and the **Bragg House,** a tenant farmer's house built in 1907. The depot museum features exhibits and artifacts on city history that go back as far as dinosaur footprints. The depot now also serves as The Grapevine Visitor Information Center and, as a throw-back to its original status, the depot for the daily excursions of the **Tarantula Steam Train** (See FAMILY FUN AND KID STUFF, p. 273). A more up-to-date addition to the complex is the **Heritage Artisan's Center.** At this center skilled artisans demonstrate craftsmanship techniques used over 150 years ago to make boots, weave and hook rugs, sew quilts and other hand-crafted products. Many of the items made here are for sale and some of the artisans teach daily classes on their pioneer techniques. Outdoors are the **Heritage Gardens** and a small **Farmers Market** is usually set up here Wednesday afternoons and Saturday mornings from mid-May to mid-December.

OUTDOORS

GRAPEVINE LAKE
About one mile north of downtown Grapevine (From Main Street, go northeast on Hwys. 121/26 to Visitor Area)
Grapevine Lake Project, 110 Fairway Drive, 76051 • 481-4541
Most areas open at all times • Fee and non-fee areas • W

This 7,380-acre U.S. Army Corps of Engineer's lake is 19 miles long, stretching up into Denton County. Along its 146 miles of tree-lined shoreline are 7 developed parks and 5 undeveloped ones. The headquarters and visitor area is off Hwys. 121/26 near the dam and Silver Lake Park at the southeast end of the lake. Now the fourth busiest lake in Texas, facilities are available for power and sail boating (three marinas and boat rentals), fishing, swimming, water-skiing, wind surfing, hiking, trail bike riding, picnicking, and camping (fee and non-fee).

GRAPEVINE PARKS
Parks and Recreation Department • Community Activities Center, 1175 South Main (P.O. Box 95104, 76099) • 481-0351

The over three dozen parks in the system include facilities for a variety of team sports, tennis courts, swimming pools, picnic areas, trails, and a nature center. There are also playgrounds and plans in the works for a 100% wheelchair accessible playground.

MUSIC AND PERFORMING ARTS

GRAPEVINE CONCERT SERIES
Palace Theatre (308 South Main) and other locations
Ticket prices vary • W

More than a dozen concerts and storytelling fests are presented during the year with the productions moving outdoors in spring and early summer and into the Palace in winter. The mix is eclectic ranging from Bluegrass to Opera, folk to the big band sounds, and harps to accordions. Ticket prices vary by event, but are generally inexpensive.

THE GRAPEVINE OPRY
Palace Theatre (308 South Main) • 481-8733
Adults $8.25-$9.25, children $5.25-$6.25.
Senior discounts available except for special shows • W

There's a foot-stompin'-hand-clappin' country and western music show here every Saturday night at 7:30. In the early years, The Opry featured rising stars like Willie Nelson, Ernest Tubb, and the Judds. There still are occasional specials with nationally known artists, but most of the family entertainment is a variety showcase for local and regional musicians and other performers. A gospel country music showcase is held the fourth Friday of each month.

THE PALACE THEATRE
308 South Main, 76051 • 481-0454 • W

Built in 1940 as a movie theater, The Palace fell into disrepair after World War II and for a time was used as a hay barn. In 1975 it was rehabilitated enough to open as the home of the Grapevine Opry. The Opry remains its major tenant since the building was acquired by the Grapevine Heritage Foundation in 1991. The Foundation is going ahead with plans to expand the variety of performing groups using the theater with the goal of turning it into a true "Theater for the Performing Arts."

THE RUNWAY THEATRE
217 North Dooley Street, 76051 (just north of Northwest Hwy.)
488-4842 • Adults $9, seniors and children $7,
Matinees $6 • W

This community theater has been the home of the End of the Runway Players since 1983. The Players put on about eight productions a year, mainly comedies and musicals, in the September through July season. Curtain times are at 8 on Friday and Saturday nights and 3 for the Sunday matinee. Each production runs two to four weekends.

FAMILY FUN AND KID STUFF

ACT ONE CHILDREN'S THEATRE
3100 Timberline Drive, 76051 (Southwest of the D/FW
runways) • 488-7572 • Adults $7, children $6 ($1 less for
advance purchase) • W

Children's plays are put on here on Friday and Saturday evenings with each production running about three weekends. Then a couple of weeks off while they rehearse for the next show. Many of the cast and crew members are children and teens.

OLD-FASHIONED SODA FOUNTAIN
City Drug Store • 309 South Main, 76051 • 481-1561 • W

Ice cream sodas, malts, shakes, and banana splits are served to your order in old fashioned fountain glassware and the lemonade comes from real lemons, not from cans. Old-time favorites available include phosphates, egg creams, and cherry, vanilla, or chocolate Cokes. Fountain seating and booths.

TARANTULA STEAM TRAIN EXCURSIONS
Cotton Belt Depot (707 South Main) • 625-Rail (625-7245), Metro 817-654-0898 or 800-952-5717 • Adults: about $20, children (3 to 12) about $10 • W Call ahead

Based in Grapevine, the Tarantula Steam Train runs daily round-trip excursions to the Fort Worth Stockyards. Weekdays the train departs Grapevine at 10 a.m. riding the 21 miles of track to arrive at the Stockyards at 11:15. There are a couple of hours for riders to explore the Stockyard attractions (See STOCKYARDS listings in Fort Worth, p. 183) before the return trip leaves at 2 p.m. arriving at its home base in Grapevine at 3:15. Sundays the excursions run from 1 to 5:30 p.m.

Tarantula's primary steam locomotive, No. 2248, operates Wednesday through Sunday. Originally built in 1896 and fully restored, it pulls passenger cars and touring coaches dating from the 1920s. The passenger and touring cars have been restored with decor resembling day coaches from the early 1900s. Passenger cars are equipped with ceiling fans, but are not air-conditioned. The touring coaches are open sided (with railings for passenger safety). Seating is on a first come basis. Snacks, soft drinks, wine, and beer are available on board.

Why "Tarantula"? The name goes back to a map published in 1870 that depicted a vision of Fort Worth newspaper editor B. B. Paddock who saw Fort Worth at the center of nine radially extending rail lines. Some laughed at the map saying the map lines resembled a hairy-legged tarantula and the railroad center just a dream. But by the 1890s the railroads had laid the nine legs centered on Fort Worth. So, when Fort Worth businessman William Davis came up with his vision of an excursion steam train, he named it after Paddock's vision.

Visitors Bureau) • **Adults and teenagers $5, Seniors and Children 6-12 $1, Weekend pass $7 • W**

Grapevine's celebration of its prairie heritage is geared to living history. There are demonstrations of heritage arts and crafts, plus re-enactors and storytellers to make the past come to life. Even the competitors in the Winn Dixie Beef Stew Contest must wear costumes approximating 1850s settlers, and their campsites must either be pre-1850s Pioneer or post-1850s Chuck Wagon. A little more modern, but still in keeping with the theme, is the Antique Tractor and Farm Implement Show. The roster of entertainment includes extra performances of the Grapevine Opry, continuous music ranging from C&W to Rock on three stages, plus special entertainment Friday and Saturday nights and a street dance Saturday night. Sports events range from 5K and 10K runs to the sublime (a croquet tournament) and the ridiculous (The International Belt Sander Drag Race). There's also a small Children's Midway. All for a good cause—funding the projects of the Grapevine Heritage Foundation.

SEPTEMBER

GRAPEFEST
Second full weekend (Friday–Sunday) • Main Street Historic District • 481-0454 or 800-457-6338 (Grapevine Convention and Visitors Bureau) • General Admission: Adults $5, Weekend Pass $7, Seniors and Children (6–12) $1 • W

One of the largest wine festivals in the Southwest, GrapeFest's premier event is a black-tie Texas Wine Tribute Gala held on Saturday night featuring a gourmet dinner paired with award-winning Texas wines ($75 per person). But at the same time, on Main Street the festivities start that evening with entertainment by local and regional musicians on three stages and include a wine tasting and wine auction. On Saturday and Sunday, $10 will buy you a souvenir wine glass you can use during one of several wine-tasting sessions each day. Each session lasts an hour and a half and at the end you're asked to vote for the People's Choice awards for the best wines. Once again there's non-stop entertainment on the stages, plus wine seminars, storytelling, tennis and croquet tournaments, a vintage and classic car display, vineyard tours, a carnival, arts and crafts show, and a 5K Run. Among the other events are a bare feet Grape Stomp contest for the "Purple Foot" trophy, and a Champagne Brunch (Texas champagne, of course) on Sunday. This is another fund-raiser for the Grapevine Heritage Foundation.

SHOPPING

AIR NOSTALGIA
420 South Main, 76051 • 481-9005 • W

Art and other memorabilia relating to the history of aviation are featured here. But rail and auto transport aren't neglected in the extensive stock of prints, models, books, toys, and artifacts.

GRAPEVINE MILLS VALUE MALL
Hwy. 121 and International Parkway (FM2499), two miles north of D/FW Airport • W +

See OTHER POINTS OF INTEREST, p. 276.

JULIA'S ANTIQUES AND TEAROOM
210 North Main, 76051 • 329-0622 • W

More than 100 booths filled with antiques and collectibles are here. The shops are open Monday–Saturday 10–6 and Sunday 12–5. In addition, Tuesday through Saturday, you can lunch at Julia's Tearoom on soups, salads, sandwiches, and desserts that include the house specialty of buttermilk pie. Wednesday through Saturday, from 3 to 5 you can have afternoon tea, but this is by reservation only.

OFF THE VINE
324 South Main, 76051 • 421-1091 • W

This wine shop offers a selection of over 175 wines, including all the wines presented at the annual Texas New Vintage Wine and Food Festival, plus wine-related gift items ranging from a book on Scottish toasts to fudge sauce made with a Texas wine.

THE BRITISH EMPORIUM
130 North Main, 76051 • 421-2311 • W

A large selection of teas in tins and bulk are among the many imported foods found here. Although most items are from Britain, foods from other countries that were in the old British Empire, like India and South Africa, are also available.

DINING OUT

$ = Under $12, $$ = $12–$30, $$$ = Over $30 for one person excluding drinks, tax, and tip.

CHARLIE'S CAFÉ
120 South Main, 76051 • 421-6256 • Lunch and dinner Monday–Saturday. Closed Sunday • $ • MC, V • W

Home-style cooking with fresh ingredients is the rule here. Standards and local favorites include meatloaf, chicken fried steak, chicken dumplings, and coconut pie. Daily plate specials. Senior discount 3–6 p.m. Vegetarian entrées available. Children's menu.

DORRIS HOUSE CAFÉ
224 East College Street, 76051, one block east of Main • 421-1181 • Lunch Tuesday–Friday, Dinner Tuesday–Saturday. Closed Sunday–Monday. Reservations suggested Friday–Saturday dinner • $$ • Cr. • W

Think ahead and save room so you can top off one of the house specialties of roasted smoked duck or rack of lamb with the homemade strawberry cheesecake ice cream. Other entrées include a selection of fresh seafood dishes, chicken, and steak. A *prix fixe* three-course dinner is offered for about $25. Bar drinks served at the table. The setting is a restored home with a hand-carved staircase and six fireplaces. Built in 1896, it is considered one of the finest examples of Queen Anne architecture remaining in Grapevine.

JULIA'S TEAROOM
See Julia's Antiques and Tearoom, in SHOPPING, p. 280.

RAVIOLI RISTORANTE
120 East Worth, 76051, east of Main • 488-1181
Lunch Monday–Friday, Dinner every evening • $$ • Cr.
W Ramp on west side of building

Most entrees here are Northern Italian, a cuisine which tends more toward cream sauces than the tomato sauces favored in Southern Italy. The extensive menu includes a wide selection of pasta entrees plus chicken, veal, and seafood. If you just want pasta, you have a choice of six types and six sauces for less than $9. More imaginative entrees include Chicken Oceana (grilled chicken breast topped with shrimp, mushrooms, green onions, and a sherry cream sauce) and Veal Artichoke (sauteed veal in a sherry cream sauce with artichoke hearts and mushrooms). Bar.

SONNY BRYAN'S SMOKEHOUSE
322 South Park Blvd. 76051 (Hwy. 114 at Wall in Park West Shopping Plaza) • 424-5978 or 800-5-SONNYS (576-6697)
Lunch and dinner seven days • $ • Cr. • W

One of a Metroplex barbecue chain that's consistently rated high by area residents. Texas-style barbecue items include brisket, ribs, and smoked turkey. Also Tennessee-style pork barbecue. Children's menu. Surprisingly, vegetarian plates are available. Beer and wine.

LODGINGS

For a double room: $ = Under $80, $$ = $80–$120, $$$ = $121–$180, $$$$ = $181–$250, $$$$$ = Over $250; Room tax 12%.
For detailed listings see Metroplex Lodgings Section, p. 387.

DFW LAKES HILTON
1800 Hwy. 26E, 76051, 2.5 miles north of D/FW Airport
481-8444 or 800-445-8667 or 800-645-1019 (Reservations)
$–$$$ • W + 8 rooms • No smoking rooms

HYATT REGENCY DFW
International Parkway on D/FW Airport (P.O. Box 619014, D/FW Airport 75261-9014) • 972-453-1234 or 800-233-1234
$$$–$$$$ • W + 17 rooms • No smoking rooms

THE 1934 BED AND BREAKFAST
322 East College, 76051 (two blocks east of Main) • 251-1934
$$ •All no smoking

SIDE TRIPS

TOUR 18 GOLF COURSE
8718 Amen Corner, Flower Mound 75028 (From Grapevine, take Hwy. 121 North to FM 2499 to FM 1171, then west 6 miles) • 430-2000 or 800-946-5310

It's probably every golfer's dream to play such celebrated courses as Augusta, Cherry Hill, Doral, Sawgrass, and Firestone. This public course may be a way to make that dream come true. Or at least part of it. Tour 18 is promoted as the only golf course in the world where each of the 18 holes is a careful simulation of one of the greatest holes from a celebrated golf course; all those listed above and a dozen more. Green fees, which include golf cart and driving range balls are: Monday–Thursday $65 + tax, Friday–Sunday and holidays $75 + tax.

IRVING

DALLAS COUNTY • 160,000 • AREA CODE 972

One of the ways that the Republic of Texas used to settle its massive territory was through agreements offering huge tracts of land to entrepreneurs if they would bring in homesteaders. So much land for so many settlers. In 1841 such an agreement was signed with a group including William S. Peters, a musician and music publisher in Louisville, Kentucky. This group was given an enormous land grant covering several counties, including all of Tarrant County and all but a narrow band of eastern Dallas County—much of what is now the Metroplex. Because his name headed the list of group members, the area eventually became known as the Peters Colony. All of present-day Irving's more than 67 square miles lies entirely within Peters Colony.

But the city itself owes its origin to two young men, Julius O. Schulze, a railroad surveyor, and his survey team rod man Otis Brown. Recognizing the opportunity that railroads brought to communities, in 1902, while surveying a ten-mile route west of the Dallas County line for Chicago, Rock Island & Gulf Railway, they paid $2,169.30 for approximately 74 acres on which they planned to build a town. A year later, after they finished their stint with the Rock Island, cleared the land, and both got married within a week of each other, they drew their proposed townsite on a tablecloth. With the help of a special excursion train out of Dal-

IRVING

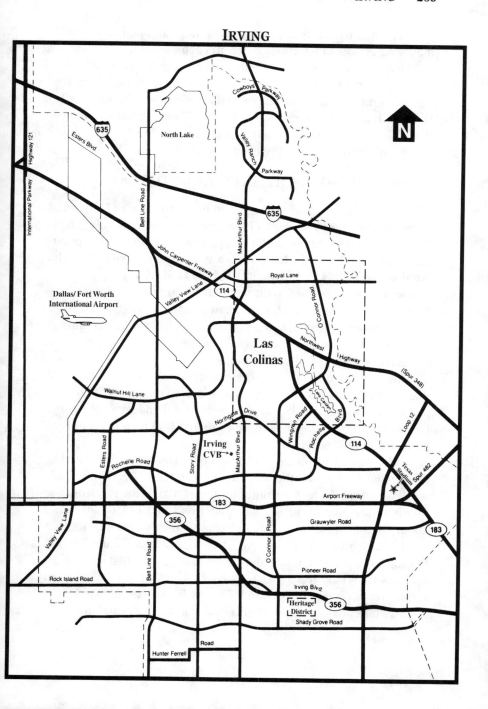

las, provided by the Rock Island, they held an auction at which they sold 20 lots at an average of $50 each.

They wanted a name to set the town apart, so they named it after one of the most popular writers of the time, Washington Irving. It's said the name was suggested by Netta Brown, Otis' wife, because Irving was her favorite author. Coincidentally, while at the University of Iowa, Schulze had been a member of a literary/debating society which was named after Irving.

LIVING IN THE SHADOW OF DALLAS

During the early years, Irving lived in the shadow of Dallas and grew slowly. The 1950 census listed the population as only 2,621. But, in the 1970s things started happening that jumped the population to over 100,000. In 1971 Texas Stadium was built as the home of the Dallas Cowboys, in 1974 the Dallas/Fort Worth International Airport opened with its eastern border in Irving's city limits and the major highways between the airport and Dallas passing through the city, and that same decade saw the beginnings of what would become the 12,000-acre planned residential/commercial community called Las Colinas.

Although the city is a corporate center and the home of more than 400 multi-national companies, it's convenient location next to D/FW Airport has led to the hotel/motel industry being the largest private employer with more than 7,000 people employed in the 52 hotels/motels.

If you stay in Irving and want to go to Dallas for the day, but don't want to drive all the way in, you can take The Trinity Railway Express, a diesel commuter train that makes the run from the South Irving Station at Rock Island Road and O'Connor Road about fifteen times a day on weekdays, mostly during morning and evening rush hours. It makes it to the Medical Center/Market Station in about 9 minutes and to the Dallas Union station in 16 minutes for $1 each way with transfers to either the Dallas Area Rapid Transit buses or the DART Light Rail System (See DALLAS). Plans are now in the works to expand the service times and a 14-mile leg from South Irving to Fort Worth is set to open in 1999. For information call DART at 214-979-1111.

While it continues to move forward at a rapid pace, Irving has not neglected its past, putting emphasis on the preservation and revitalization of its historic downtown area.

Under the local option laws, Irving is dry, however, you can buy alcoholic beverages with food in restaurants and in hotels/motels.

FREE VISITOR SERVICES

IRVING CONVENTION AND VISITORS BUREAU
3333 North MacArthur Blvd., Suite 200 (75062), in the Irving Arts Center. One mile north of Hwy. 183 or three miles south of Hwy. 114 • 252-7476 or 800-2-IRVING (247-8464) Monday–Friday 8–5 • W +

In addition to an array of maps, brochures, hotel and restaurant listings, and a calendar of events for visitors, this office sometimes has special discount coupons for area attractions.

COMMERCIAL TOUR SERVICES

LAS COLINAS WATER TAXI CRUISES
Smith Landing on the Mandalay Canal • 869-4321
Adults $3.25, Seniors $2.75, Children (3 to 13) $1.75

Scenic tours of the Mandalay Canal in Las Colinas in an authentic Venetian water taxi (power boat, not a gondola). Cruises throughout the Urban Center then goes across the 125-acre Lake Carolyn. Summer schedule: Monday–Friday 9–4, Saturday noon–10, Sunday noon–5. Closed major holidays and during severe weather and Saturdays from 6 to 7 p.m. Call for winter schedule. Also see the **Movie Studios at Las Colinas Tour** and **Texas Stadium Tour** under FAMILY FUN AND KID STUFF, p. 292.

SELF-GUIDED TOURS

HISTORIC TEXAS TRAILS

If you really want to get into the history of this part of Texas in general and Irving in particular, the Convention and Visitors Bureau provides a *Historic Trails Guide* brochure with maps and detailed directions for following three early Texas Trails that went through the area. These are The California Trail, favored by the forty-niners; The Bird's Fort Trail, established in 1841 and used by Sam Houston in 1843, when he was president of the Republic of Texas, to meet with the Indians and sign a friendship treaty at Bird's Fort; and The Eagle Ford Trail, which connected early settlements south of the Trinity River to communities further west.

LAS COLINAS MANDALAY CANAL WALK
Take steps down from Las Colinas Blvd. at O'Connor Road

An Old World style tree-lined cobbled walkway follows the canal a short distance past shops and restaurants one level below the street. A nice, gentle stroll if the weather is pleasant.

HISTORIC PLACES

HERITAGE DISTRICT
Downtown. Bounded by Rock Island RR on north, 6th Street on south, O'Connor Street on east, and South Brian on west • W

This downtown area is built on the original townsite drawn up by Schulze and Brown in 1903. The heart of this old area is **Heritage Park** at Main and Second Streets. This park is the site for one of Irving's oldest buildings, the Caster Cabin built in 1887; Irving's original water tower, an old windmill, the Rock Island Depot built in 1903, and the city's first library building, opened in 1941. Now the downtown area is mostly older homes and shops including antique shops and a corner drugstore with a soda fountain at Main and Irving Blvd. The Irving station for The Trinity Express is here at the South Irving Station at Rock Island Raod and O'Connor Road. This Railtrans commuter rail system links

Irving and Dallas. Long-range plans call for this system to link with Fort Worth by 1999 and eventually with D/FW airport.

OUTDOORS

IRVING PARKS
Parks and Recreation Department, 825 West Irving Blvd. (75060) • 721-2501

The almost 50 parks in the Irving system range in size from the one-acre Heritage Park (see above) in downtown to the 415-acre North Lake Park at the northern end of the city north of I-635. These offer the opportunity for a variety outdoor activities with facilities that include swimming pools, recreation centers, walking and jogging trails, sports fields and courts, playgrounds, racquetball and tennis courts, a golf course, picnic areas, and even a petting farm. For a map and details on each park contact the Parks Department.

COLLEGES AND UNIVERSITIES

NORTH LAKE COMMUNITY COLLEGE
5001 North MacArthur Blvd. (75038)
273-3000 or 273-3184• W

North Lake is a two-year college that's one of seven campuses of the Dallas County Community College District. Located on 276 wooded acres in the Las Colinas area, its architecturally interesting campus includes a nine-acre lake. The college offers both technical/vocational and academic programs to approximately 10,000 students. Daytime visitor parking is on Liberty Circle. Visitors are welcome to student drama and music productions. Most performances are at the college's 450-seat Performance Hall (Theater information 273-3569).

UNIVERSITY OF DALLAS
1845 East Northgate Dr. (75062) at Tom Braniff Dr.
721-5000 • W

Founded in 1956, this Catholic University is located on an 800-acre campus just northwest of Texas Stadium on hills that overlook the Dallas skyline. It has an enrollment of about 3,000 undergraduate students in its College of Liberal Arts. Sophomore students are offered a semester at the school's campus in Rome, Italy. Daytime visitors should park in designated visitor parking areas. The university offers an on-going series of free lectures by speakers of national repute in a variety of fields. Visitors are also welcome at student athletic events, drama and music performances. (Theater information 721-5061)

MUSIC AND PERFORMING ARTS

Arts Hotline and Arts Center Box Office: 252-ARTS (252-2787)

IRVING ARTS CENTER
3333 MacArthur Blvd. (75062), One mile north of Hwy. 183 or
three miles south of Hwy. 114 • 252-7558 or Metro
972-256-4270 • Office open Monday–Friday 8–5 • W +

Home of more than 20 Irving-based arts and cultural organizations. this arts complex includes two art galleries, the Main Gallery and the New Talent Gallery, featuring contemporary and traditional works by established and emerging artists. The galleries are open Monday–Friday 8–5, Saturday 10–5, Sunday 1–5. Closed holidays. It also is the site for theater and concert programs in its two state-of-the-art performance theaters, the 712-seat Carpenter Performance Hall and the 253-seat Dupree Theater. The galleries and some of the performances are free.

Following are some of the music and performing arts organizations which use this center. Each one's direct phone number for information is in parenthesis.

Irving Ballet (252-7558). The two-production season includes the *Nutcracker* in December and another ballet in the spring.

Irving Chorale (484-8580). A 70-plus mixed voice choir whose repertoire extends from classics to stage hits. Hosts four concerts annually, including one free concert in its October to June season.

Irving Community Concert Association (255-7161). For more than four decades, this association has brought top music and dance entertainers to perform in Irving during its October to April season.

Irving Community Concert Band (438-6259). The band offers afternoon and evening concerts year round that feature a varied program of marches, movie and show tunes, and traditional classical selections for band arrangement.

Irving Community Theater (594-6104). North Texas talent is cast in the five-production season of comedies, dramas, mysteries, and musical productions. Afternoon and evening performances in the November to July season.

Irving Symphony Orchestra (831-8818). The 70-member professional orchestra has been performing each season for more than three decades. Concerts include an annual Christmas concert, free family and youth concerts, as well as a 4th of July concert complete with fireworks at Williams Square in Las Colinas. Its season runs from July through April.

Las Colinas Symphony Orchestra (580-1566). This 93-member professional orchestra presents a six-concert subscription series with afternoon and evening performances during its October to May season.

Lyric Stage (554-8534). This locally produced professional musical theater company is dedicated to the development and preservation of the American musical. It offers afternoon and evening performances of this uniquely American art form in its October through March season.

Metro Players (255-8747). More than 1,600 professional and non-professional actors, singers, and dancers have been cast in the Metro Players productions of Broadway musicals and classical children's performances. Afternoon and evening performances in its January through September season.

New Philharmonic Orchestra of Irving (780-1079). This 65-member community orchestra presents a five-concert season of evening performances from October through May. Besides the full symphony, the members break down for concerts as the New Philharmonic Chamber Group, the Brass Quintet, and the Woodwind Quintet.

JAYCEE PARK CENTER FOR THE ARTS
2000 West Airport Freeway (75062), Hwy. 183 between Story and MacArthur Blvd. • 252-7558 ext. 249 or Metro 972-256-4270 ext. 249 • W

The art gallery here features about 25 exhibits each year. The center is also the home of the Irving Art Association, which offers art courses, professional artist demonstrations, and host the annual five-state "Texas and Neighbors Art Competition" in April.

FAMILY FUN AND KID STUFF

FRITZ PARK PETTING FARM
Fritz Park, 312 East Vilbig • 721-2501 (Parks and Recreation Department) or 721-2640 in June and July only • Open June and July, Tuesday–Saturday 10–6, Sunday 2–8 • W

Kids (and adults, too) can have as close an encounter as they want with all types of domestic farm animals and birds here. Free parking.

THE MOVIE STUDIOS AT LAS COLINAS TOUR
North O'Connor Road at Royal Lane (Building One in Dallas Communications Complex. Follow signs to Tour) • 869-FILM (869-3456) • Adults $11.95, Seniors (over 65)$9.95, Children (4–12) $6.95

Get a glimpse of TV and movie production techniques and how filmmakers create illusions as well as actual film props and memorabilia in this tour that takes about an hour. The state-of-the-art studios here in the vast Dallas Communications Complex have been used for films ranging from *Silkwood* to *Robocop*. The tour has several audience-participation stops, which seem designed more to delight the kids than the adults. This may be the reason why it whizzes through the National Museum of Communications exhibits, which range from a fifteenth-century printing press to vintage radios and TV to satellite communications. Open daily year round. Summer tours (mid-June–mid-August) are scheduled every hour beginning at noon. Call for other tour times. Gift shop.

TEXAS STADIUM TOUR
2401 East Airport Freeway (75062), at junction of Hwys. 183 and 114 and Loop 12) • 579-1414 • Adults $5, Seniors and Children (under 12) $3 • W

The tour leaves from the Official Dallas Cowboys Pro Shop just outside Gate 8 every hour on the hour Monday–Saturday 10–3 and Sunday 11–3. The tour, which lasts about an hour, includes a narration about the stadium, a view from the stands that seat 64,000 and a brief walk on the field, a view of the Dallas Cowboys' locker room, a walk-through of the Stadium Club, and a view of a private suite. All locations, of course, subject to what's going on in the stadium at the time and the tour may be canceled for special events. Private tours are also available for groups on the half hour every day but Sunday ($3 each with a minimum of $75 for under 25 persons.) Although best known as the home of the Dallas Cowboys, Texas Stadium is also frequently the site of concerts, festivals, and other major events. Gift shop.

MODEL AIRPLANE FIELD
North Lake Park, Belt Line Road north of I-635 (LBJ Freeway) • 721-2501 (Parks and Recreation Department) • W

Whether you fly model planes or just enjoy watching them, you'll find an ideal flying field here. The park's runway is 650 × 75 feet and there's a 75 × 75 feet pylon course.

SPORTS

BOATING

LAKE CAROLYN BOAT RENTALS
Mandalay Canal in Las Colinas • 869-4342

Want your own little sunset cruise or picnic on the water? You can rent an electric-powered boat that holds up five adults for $25 an hour or one that holds up to eight adults for $35 an hour and cruise the waters of the 125-acre Lake Carolyn on your own. Open Monday–Friday 4–8 p.m., Saturday noon to 10, Sunday noon to 5. Closed during severe weather and on major holidays. Reservations suggested.

EQUESTRIAN

5 BAR K STABLES
Off Tom Braniff Dr. west of Texas Stadium • 579-1140
Seven days 9 a.m to ½ hour before sundown

Located on the Elm Fork Ranch, the stables feature a full equestrian center with horses for adult riders, ponies for children, and more than 100 acres of scenic riding trails. Rentals are $20 an hour. Reservations are suggested, but not required.

LAS COLINAS EQUESTRIAN CENTER
600 West Royal Lane (75039), across from the Dallas Communications Complex • 869-0600 • W

English riding and jumping are the equestrian sports at this 42-acre center that's often called a country club for horses. Facilities include 104 permanent stalls for boarding, indoor arena, viewing lounge, and tack shop. Site of numerous horse shows including the prestigious annual National Equestrian Grand Prix. Visitors welcome to watch training. Riding lessons available. Call for information and fees.

FOOTBALL

DALLAS COWBOYS
1 Cowboys Parkway (75063) (Headquarters)
579-5000 (Tickets)

The name says Dallas, but Irving's Texas Stadium is the home field for the Cowboys (2401 East Airport Freeway at the junction of Hwys. 183 and 114 and Loop 12). And when they play there, the stadium is usually packed solid with fans because the Cowboys have brought home such a long string of play-off and Super Bowl Championships that they've become a national phenomenon. They've truly earned the title "America's Team." As evidence of that is the fact that while there are 30 teams in the NFL, almost a quarter of all the NFL team shirts, caps, and other souvenirs sold bear the Cowboys logo.

GOLF

PUBLIC COURSE

TWIN WELLS GOLF COURSE
2000 East Shady Grove (75060) • 438-4340 • 18-hole course. Green fees: Weekdays $16.50, Weekends $22. Junior and senior golfers discount weekdays.

PRIVATE OR SEMI-PRIVATE COURSES

FOUR SEASONS RESORT AND CLUB
4150 North MacArthur Blvd. (75038) • 717-0700 • 36 holes. Includes Cottonwood Valley Golf Club and the Tournament Players Course. Call for green fees.

HACKBERRY CREEK COUNTRY CLUB
1901 Royal Lane (75063) • 445-6546 • 18-hole course. Call for green fees.

LAS COLINAS COUNTRY CLUB
4900 North O'Connor Road (75062) • 541-1141 • 18-hole course. Green fees: Weekdays $50, Weekends $75.

ICE HOCKEY

DALLAS STARS
211 Cowboys Parkway (75063)(Headquarters) • 214/GO-STARS (214-467-8277)

Texas only National Hockey League team, the Stars play in league's Central division. Their home games are played in the Reunion Arena in Dallas, but they practice on the rink at their headquarters in the Dr. Pepper StarCenter Ice Arena.

ICE SKATING

DR PEPPER STARCENTER ICE ARENA
211 Cowboy Parkway (75063), in Valley Ranch off MacArthur Blvd. approximately 3.5 miles north of I-635/LBJ Freeway 214-GO-SKATE (214-467-5283)

This facility has two full-sized ice rinks. In addition to being the practice rink for the Dallas Stars, it also is home for the Dallas Junior Hockey Association, a senior hockey league, a figure skating club, and a speed skating club. Skating lessons are given here most days and public skating is also available when the rink is not otherwise booked. The Arena is next door to the headquarters of the Dallas Cowboys.

TENNIS

Lighted public courts are at Keeler Park, 520 S. Rogers; Nichols Park, 2310 East Newton; Northwest Park, 2800 Cheyenne; Senter Park, 901 South Senter; Sunrise Park, 1809 East Union Bower, and Cimarron Park, 210 Red River Trail. For information call Parks and Recreation 721-2501. Also after 5 p.m. on schools days and during the summer, the lighted courts at the following high schools are open: Irving (9 courts), 900 O'Connor;

MacArthur (9 courts)3700 North MacArthur, and Nimitz (6 courts)100 West Oakdale.

WATER SKIING

MUSTANG CANYON WATER SKI TEAM
650-0043

The Mustang Canyon in this team's name is a mile-long section of Hackberry Creek off O'Connor Blvd. north of Northwest Highway. This is the home base of the area's only professional water ski team. The ski area is certified by the American Water Ski Association as a world-record capable facility. Each year it attracts some of the top water skiing events in the country.

OTHER POINTS OF INTEREST

DALLAS-FORT WORTH INTERNATIONAL AIRPORT

Part of the D/FW Airport lies within the western boundary of Irving. You can watch airport activity, take-offs, and landings from the observation deck set-up just off the airport grounds at 30th and Carbon in Founder's Plaza. For details on how to do a self-guided tour of the airport, see GRAPEVINE/OTHER POINTS OF INTEREST, p. 276.

LAS COLINAS URBAN CENTER

One of the world's best known urban developments, Las Colinas (Spanish for "the hills") is a 12,000 acre master-planned community in the northeast corner of Irving. In addition to a business center with office towers housing corporate office of hundreds of multinational companies employing 70,000 workday residents, there are large single family and apartment villages for 25,000 full-time residents. Almost half of the development is devoted to a greenbelt, parks, and public recreational space. The development is noted for its Mandalay Canal with Venetian style water taxis, the world's largest equestrian statue, an equestrian center, a TV and motion picture production complex, four golf courses, and a resort and a number of hotels, restaurants, and shops.

Following is a listing of the major places of visitor interest in Las Colinas.

Dallas Communications Complex (869-0700). 6301 North O'Connor Road. This 125-acre development is a center for media, advertising, and communications and is the premiere film facility in the Southwest. The complex houses more than 120 communications-related companies servicing film, television, and other commercial projects. Except for the Las Colinas Movie Studio Tour, the buildings are not open to visitors.

Las Colinas Flower Clock. Hwy 114 and O'Connor Road. A huge, working clock with the hands set against the clockface of live flowers. New flowers are planted at least eight times a year to make sure there are fresh colors year-round.

Las Colinas Equestrian Center. (See SPORTS, p. 294)

Mandalay Canal. A gently winding canal leading to the 125-acre Lake Carolyn, it was designed to resemble an Old World waterway with cobblestone walkways, a few dozen shops and restaurants, and Venetian style motorboats serving as water taxis. One access to the canal is at O'Connor Road and Las Colinas Blvd. The canal, and the original hotel which is now the Omni Mandalay, were named by Ben Carpenter, one of the developers of Las Colinas, who recalled his World War II service in the Mandalay section of Burma.

Marble Cows. The stampeding Mustangs of Las Colinas have gathered all the fame, but on Bluebonnet Hill, at Hwy. 114 and Rochelle Road, are another group of Las Colinas' animals. Five marble cows, sculpted by Harold Clayton as a tribute to the ranches that once dominated the area, they add a touch of serenity to the landscape.

Mustangs of Las Colinas (869-9047). 5205 North O'Connor Blvd. in Williams Square. The world's largest equestrian sculpture, this is a bronze of nine wildly galloping mustangs rushing through a flowing stream. Created by African wildlife artist Robert Glen as a memorial to the heritage of Texas, it was seven years in the making. Each horse is one and half times life-size and weighs 2,000–3,000 pounds. Because the rose-colored granite Williams Square Plaza is the size of three football fields, even though the mustangs are boxed in on three sides by gleaming granite office towers they appear to run free. In the lobby of West Tower of Williams Square is the Mustang Sculpture Exhibit, which includes a short film about the creation of this impressive work. The exhibit is open Tuesday-Saturday 10-6. Closed major holidays. Admission is free.

Water Taxis (869-4321) Want to go someplace on the Mandalay Canal? Catch or call a water taxi. These Venetian style mahogany motorboats provide one-way transportation to more than a dozen locations in the Urban Center for a fare of less than a dollar.

OFFBEAT

ASHLEY'S WINE CELLAR
Sheraton Grand Hotel, 4440 West Carpenter Freeway (Hwy. 114) • 929-8400 ext. 237 (Reservations)

A wine cellar offbeat? Yes, this one is because it is a unique setting for an intimate and truly gourmet dinner.

Tucked in a corner of this Sheraton's restaurant is a small room used as the wine cellar. With the exception of the space taken up by a picture window and the door, the walls are lined with wine racks filled with the hotel's collection of fine wines. The center of the room is clear enough to hold a well-set table and four to six chairs (four preferred, six is tight) on which to serve a three-course gourmet dinner (appetizer, salad, entrée) with a different select wine with each course. Tight, but still romantically isolated with nothing to disturb you but the essential, brief, interruptions of your personal server.

Reservations required, of course. And when you make your reservation you can select your gourmet dinner from one of six pre-set menus of courses and wines. Package prices are by the person, the more diners the less expensive, and the six packages range from about $77 to $91 each if there are just two of you to $54 to $67 each if there are six in your party. Deserts are additional. Expensive? That's up to you. But it's definitely a dining experience.

One caution. This is a wine cellar and the wine likes it cool, so dress for a cool fall day.

ANNUAL EVENTS

MAY

GTE/BYRON NELSON GOLF CLASSIC
Wednesday–Sunday in middle of month • Four Seasons Resort and Club, 4150 MacArthur Blvd. (Mailing address: 400 South Houston #350, Dallas 75202-4811) • 214-742-3896 • Admission $40–$100 • W

About 150 top golf professionals compete in this annual classic, the only PGA Tour event named after a golfer—a Texan, of course. The four-day tournament has the largest attendance of any golf event in Texas, usually attracting more than 200,000 golf fans, and is the largest charity fundraiser on the PGA tour. Best place to see the pros come and go is around the nine-foot bronze statue of Byron Nelson at Nelson Plaza near the No. 1 tee. Some preliminary rounds played on Cottonwood Valley Course and finals on Tournament Players Course. Grassy mounds stair-step around most of the holes on the Tournament Players Course to provide excellent viewing for fans and the hill by the 17th green offers a great view of holes number 1, 17, and 18. Public parking (included in admission price) at Texas Stadium, Hwy. 183 at Hwy. 114 intersection, with shuttle buses to the course.

MAY

LAS COLINAS SOUTHWEST SHOW JUMPING CLASSIC
Five days in middle or late in month • Las Colinas Equestrian Center, 600 Royal Lane at O'Connor (75039) • 869-0600 • Admission • W Variable

Skilled riders from all over the United States compete in this event. Spectator accommodations include grandstand seating and table seating.

MAY OR JUNE

CANALFEST
Saturday and Sunday • Mandalay Canal • 556-0625 Ext. 117 • Free • W

This spring celebration on the canal walk is designed to be a true "Venetian Carnival." It features a boat parade, arts and crafts, clowns and magicians, and a variety of musicians and other performers. Free parking is available. Call for details.

SHOPPING

IRVING MALL
3800 Irving Mall (75062), at Hwy. 183 and Belt Line Road North • 255-0571 • W+

About 150 stores anchored by Dillard's, Foley's, JCPenney's, and Sears. Other strip centers around this intersection augment this mall with almost as many shops and fast food and regular restaurants. Shuttle services available from some hotels/motels.

DINING OUT

$ = Under $12, $$ = $12–$30, $$$ = Over $30 for one person excluding drinks, tax, and tip.

CAFÉ CIPRIANI
220 East Las Colinas Blvd. (75039), across from the Omni Mandalay Hotel • 869-0713 • Lunch Monday–Friday, dinner Monday–Saturday. Closed Sunday • $$ • Cr. • W+ (Elevator)

There is a bar and a few tables inside at the street entrance, but to reach the tasteful main dining room, take the elevator down one level. The menu is gourmet Italian with dishes selected from several regions of that country with the emphasis on Northern Italian cuisine. Veal and seafood are the prime ingredient in several entrees. Bar. Complimentary valet parking. Piano music at Friday and Saturday dinner.

CAFÉ ON THE GREEN
**Four Seasons Resort and Club, 4150 North MacArthur Blvd.
(75038) • 717-0700 • Breakfast, lunch, and dinner seven days.
Sunday brunch 11:30–3. • $$–$$$ • Cr. • W+**
(Note: Many of the luxury hotels in Irving have excellent restaurants. This one is just a sample. See also OFFBEAT, p. 299.)

This restaurant specializes in New American Cuisine with the emphasis on lighter, healthier fare. The dinner menu includes several pasta and risotto entrees such as risotto with wild mushroom and asparagus and shaved *parmigiano reggiano* cheese. Seafood and meat entrees include seared medallions of venison and coriander crusted sea bass as well as a selection of chicken and beef dishes. A buffet is available at all meals. The dinner buffet ($30) offers a wide selection of hot and cold items from appetizer to desserts. Sunday brunch is also a buffet featuring a lavish selection of appetizers, cold seafoods, carved items, vegetable dishes, a pasta station and a desert station. (About $25) Children's menu. Bar. The arched floor to ceiling windows of this restaurant overlook the resort's pool and landscaped grounds. Valet parking available.

I FRATELLI ITALIAN RESTAURANT
**7750 North MacArthur Blvd. #195 (75063) • 501-9700 • Lunch
and dinner Sunday–Friday, dinner only Saturday. Sunday
brunch. • $ • Cr. • W**

The name translates into "the brothers" and its owned and operated by four brothers. Pasta dishes, of course, most with tomato, marinara, or alfredo sauce, but also thin crust pizza (a local favorite), and crab claws. Children's menu. Bar.

JINBEH JAPANESE RESTAURANT
**301 East Las Colinas Blvd. (75039) east of O'Connor Road •
869-4011 • Lunch Monday–Friday, dinner Monday–Saturday.
Closed Sunday • $–$$ • Cr. • W**

Entrees include a wide selection of beef, chicken, and seafood cooked in tempura or hibachi style. And you can have these in combinations. Also *sukiyaki, sushi* and some lesser-known authentic Japanese specials like *unaju,* broiled eel served on a bed or steamed rice with special sauce; and *udon,* a Japanese favorite made of thick white noodle soup with fish cake, Japanese mushrooms, and green onions. Children's menu. Bar.

VIA REÁL
4020 North MacArthur Blvd. #122 (75038) at Northgate, in Las Colinas Plaza • 650-9001 • Lunch and dinner seven days. Sunday brunch. • $$ • Cr. • W

Southwestern is the main cuisine here with specialties like *camarones,* marinated Gulf shrimp topped with a white wine cilantro sauce served on a bed of Spanish rice with fresh vegetables and black beans. A good part of the menu is also devoted to grilled seafood, beef and chicken entrees. And this is a Mexican restaurant so all the favorite Tex-Mex entrees are here, too, like *enchiladas, flautas,* and *fajitas.* They're just prepared with a little more innovation rising them to a gourmet/fine dining class. Children's menu. Bar. Complimentary valet parking.

CLUBS AND BARS

Under the local option laws, Irving is dry. There are no liquor stores and groceries do not sell beer or wine. The only exception is you can buy alcoholic beverages with food in restaurants and they can have a bar to provide these.

LODGINGS

For a double room: $ = Under $80, $$ = $80–$120, $$$ = $121–$180, $$$$ = $181–$250, $$$$$ = Over $250; Room tax 11%.

For detailed listings see Metroplex Lodgings Section, p. 389.

DALLAS/FORT WORTH AIRPORT MARRIOTT
8440 Freeport Parkway, 75063 (Freeport Parkway exit off Hwy. 114) • 929-8800 or 800-228-9290 • $$$ • W+ 9 rooms • No smoking rooms

DRURY INN-D/FW AIRPORT
4210 West Airport Freeway (Hwy. 183), 75062 (Esters exit) 986-1200 or 800-325-8300 • $ • W+ 6 rooms • No smoking rooms

FOUR SEASONS RESORT AND CLUB
4150 North MacArthur Blvd., 75038 (two miles south from MacArthur exit off Hwy. 114) • 717-0700 or 800-332-3442 $$$–$$$$$ • W+ rooms • No smoking rooms

HOLIDAY INN SELECT—DFW AIRPORT NORTH
4441 Hwy. 114, 75063 (one mile east of north exit from D/FW Airport, Esters exit) • 929-8181 • $$ • W+ 5 rooms No smoking rooms

HOLIDAY INN/HOLIDOME SELECT D/FW AIRPORT SOUTH
4440 West Airport Freeway (Hwy. 183), 75062 (take Hwy. 183 from south exit of D/FW Airport, Valley View exit) • 399-1010 or 800-360-2242 • $$–$$$ • W+ 6 rooms • No smoking rooms

HOMEWOOD SUITES HOTEL—LAS COLINAS
4300 Wingren Road, 75039 (Wingren exit off Hwy.114) 556-0665 or 800-800-225-4663 • $–$$ • W+ 6 suites No smoking suites

OMNI MANDALAY HOTEL AT LAS COLINAS
221 East Las Colinas Blvd., 75039 • 556-0800 or 800-The-Omni (800-843-6664) • $$$$ • W+ 5 rooms • No smoking rooms

RAMADA INN D/FW AIRPORT SOUTH
4110 West Airport Freeway (Hwy. 183), 75062 (Esters exit) 399-2005 • $ • W+ 2 rooms • No smoking rooms

RESIDENCE INN—LAS COLINAS
950 Walnut Hill Lane, 75038 (MacArthur & Walnut Hill)
580-7773 or 800-331-3131 • $$–$$$ • W+ 2 suites
No smoking suites

SHERATON GRAND HOTEL AT D/FW AIRPORT
4440 West Carpenter Freeway (Hwy. 114), 75063 (at Esters
exit) • 929-8400 or 800-325-3535 • $$=$$$ • W+ rooms
No smoking rooms

WILSON WORLD HOTEL
4600 West Airport Freeway (Hwy. 183), 75062 (one mile from
south exit of D/FW, Valley View exit) • 513-0800 or
800-945-7667 • $$ • W+ 3 rooms • No smoking rooms

WYNDHAM GARDEN HOTEL—LAS COLINAS
110 West Carpenter Freeway (Hwy. 114), 75037 (O'Connor
Road exit) • 650-1600 or 800-WYNDHAM (800-996-3426)
W+ 2 rooms • No smoking rooms

MESQUITE

DALLAS COUNTY • 110,000 • AREA CODE 972

Mesquite officially became a town in 1873 when the Texas and Pacific Railroad bought 50 acres along its planned right of way for $15. The T&P plotted 40 acres for a town and 10 acres for the depot, siding, and cattle pens. This was in an area early settlers knew as the Mesquite League (a league being 4,605 acres, the usual amount given in land grants to a head of family), so the depot and town took on that name.

For a time, the depot was all that was there. But, slowly, the early settlers and new arrivals moved into the town.

It was five years later when Mesquite had its first real brush with notoriety. On the night of April 10, 1878, the infamous Sam Bass and his men robbed the west-bound train at the depot. Bass had gained fame six months earlier when he and his gang robbed a shipment of gold from the Union Pacific in Nebraska. This time the prize was slim, only $160 from the express car. The gang rode off, not knowing that the express guard had hidden close to $30,000 in an old potbellied stove in the car.

After that exciting event, the little town slipped back into obscurity. Growth remained slow. As late as 1950, the population had only reached about 1,700 and city phones still went through a switchboard operator who knew everyone in town and would take messages for those who weren't home.

MESQUITE

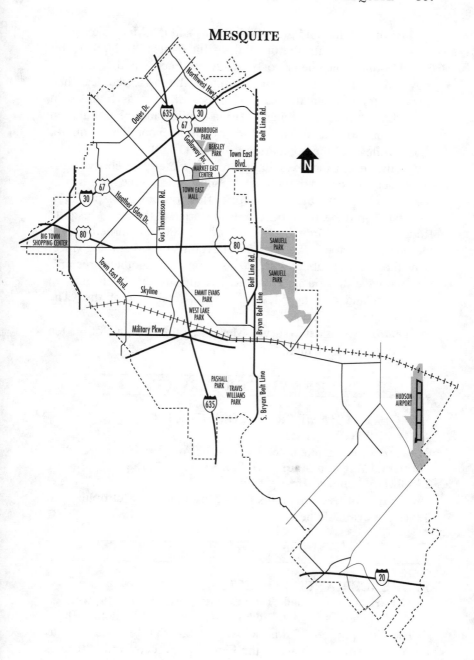

Then the vitality and growth of Dallas and the Metroplex started to spill over. With the opening of Interstates 20, 30, 80, and 635, Mesquite became a crossroads town. People and businesses moved in. In 1950, the corporate limits of the town were less than a square mile, about the same size as when it was founded in 1873. By 1960 it was almost 21 square miles and the population had zoomed to 27,256. Today the city limits encompass about 42 square miles and the population is about 110,000.

Another event that eventually brought the city celebrity status and added to its growth took place eighty years to the month after Sam Bass first gave the town its brief flash of fame. In April 1958 the first all-professional rodeo season started at the new Mesquite Rodeo Arena. According to the records, 5,000 fans turned out for the premier performance. The fans haven't stopped coming since. Now they average about 300,000 a season, plus another three million who see the rodeos on cable TV, turning this event into an institution and earning Mesquite the official title of the "The Rodeo Capital of Texas."

In a *Money* magazine survey Mesquite ranked as one of the ten safest cities in the United States.

FREE VISITOR SERVICES

MESQUITE CHAMBER OF COMMERCE AND VISITORS BUREAU
617 North Ebrite, one block west of Galloway, between Municipal Way and Main (P.O. Box 850115), 75185
285-0211 • Monday–Friday 8–5
An array of free brochures from Mesquite, the Metroplex, and Texas are available here.

HISTORIC PLACES

FLORENCE RANCH HOMESTEAD
1424 Barnes Ridge Road (Take Galloway exit from I-30, turn south, first left is Barnes Ridge) • 216-6468 • W (call ahead)
The first portion of this house was built in 1871–72. It was enlarged by the 1890s when the Florence farm covered 730 acres

and most of the furniture is from that period. The house is available for free tours the second Saturday of each month from 10-1. However, it's necessary to call ahead to arrange for a guide to be there.

OUTDOORS

MESQUITE PARKS
Parks and Recreation Department
Municipal Center, 1515 North Galloway • 216-6260

There are bicycle and jogging trails in 7 of the city's 58 parks. In addition, Parks and Recreation operates a tennis center and 24 neighborhood courts, a golf course, and an in-line-skate hockey rink at the J. Thompson School Park. Call for details.

COLLEGES AND UNIVERSITIES

EASTFIELD COMMUNITY COLLEGE
3737 Motley Dr., 75150 Off I-30 • 860-7002
W + But not all areas

Part of the Dallas County Community College District, Eastfield provides a full range of academic and technical/occupational programs for approximately 9,500 students. The architectural design of the buildings on this 244-acre campus has won several awards. Visitors are welcome to the Performance Hall programs in the college's Performing Artists and Speakers Series. This ongoing series brings in distinguished speakers as well as theater groups that put on plays for both adults and children.

MUSIC AND PERFORMING ARTS

MESQUITE ARTS CENTER
1527 North Galloway (75149), next to Municipal Center. Take Hwy 80 east to Galloway exit, then south • 216-8122 • W +

The facilities in this building include a state-of-the-art concert hall seating 492, an intimate community theater, two art galleries, and a rehearsal hall, which is also used for small recitals. It is managed by the Mesquite Arts Council (216-6444), a coordinating and support organization for several music, performing arts, and cultural organizations in the city. The council also brings in other music, dance, and theater groups for performances as well as arranging for art exhibits in the galleries.

Following are a few of the organizations that use this center as home. Each one's direct phone number for information is in parentheses.

Mesquite Civic Chorus (216-8124). In existence since 1986, this 250-member chorus has performed not only in Mesquite and throughout the Metroplex, but such prestigious places as Williamsburg, Virginia, and the Washington National Cathedral. The chorus presents several concerts each year.

Mesquite Community Theater (216-8126). This non-professional community theater group performs in the Art Center's Black Box Theatre. It usually puts on about four productions a year with ticket prices ranging from $5 for seniors and students to $8 for general admission.

Mesquite Symphony Orchestra (216-8127). A mix of both professional and non-professional musicians, this orchestra presents five or six concerts a year of mostly classical works in the Art Center's Concert Hall. They also put on an annual concert for young people that also appeals to adults and is therefore called "Not Just for Kids."

MESQUITE OPRY
Texan Theatre, 214 West Davis Street, 75149, in the Old Town Square • 285-8931 • W

You can hear traditional country and gospel music here every Saturday night starting at 8. Both professional and home-grown local talent perform. Call for ticket prices.

FAMILY FUN AND KID STUFF

CELEBRATION STATION
4040 Towne Crossing Blvd., 75150, southwest corner of intersection of I-30 and I-635 • 279-7888 • Open daily. Call for seasonal hours • W

This family entertainment park has go-karts, bumper cars, and kiddie carnival rides, plus miniature golf, batting cage, video games, shows, and a food court. Admission free, buy tokens for all rides and games. Located at what's known locally as the "Spaghetti Interchange" of the two interstates.

MESQUITE CHAMPIONSHIP RODEO
1818 Rodeo Drive (75149), exit Military Parkway (exit 4) off I-635 • 285-8777 or 800-833-9339 • Friday and Saturday evenings April–September • Adults $8, seniors $7, children (12 and under) $3 • Parking $2 • W

Most rodeos on the professional cowboy circuit last a few days or a week, then the cowboys move on to the next one. But the Mesquite rodeo goes on and on for a six-month season each year and, since its modest start in 1958, has probably become the best-known rodeo in the nation. Every Friday and Saturday night at 8, the rodeo kicks off with a colorful Grand Entry of cowboys and cowgirls on horseback riding to the tune of "The Eyes of Texas Are Upon You." From then on the show explodes with all the traditional cowboy competitions including bull and bronco riding, calf roping, and steer wrestling. Other events include ladies' barrel-racing, a calf-scramble for kids, and half-time entertainment.

Don't worry if you don't know anything about rodeo. The announcer explains each event before it starts. And to make sure you get a good view, there are TV monitors hanging from the ceiling to give you close-ups and replays of each ride.

Because this is a Professional Rodeo Cowboy Association (PRCA) sanctioned rodeo, in addition to local prizes, the cowboys compete to accumulate points. They do this in rodeos such as this all over the country during a year-long season that begins with the nearby Fort Worth Stock Show in January (See FORT WORTH/ANNUAL EVENTS, p. 228) and ends with the rodeo finals in Las Vegas in December.

The all-weather arena seats 6,000 and there are air-conditioned suites on the third level that can be leased for the season or by the night. Off-season and off-days, the arena is used for concerts, wrestling, and other events.

The gates open at 6:30, and starting at that time you can get a hickory smoked barbecue dinner in the Bull's Eye Pavilion for

$8.50 for adults and $5.50 for children. There are also pony rides and a petting zoo for kids, and a gift shop.

Plans in the works call for extending the season and making the Rodeo Arena the center of a "Rodeo City," a complex that will include a convention center with a hotel, a Texas Rodeo Hall of Fame, and shops. It's expected the Mesquite Opry will make it's home here, too.

SAMUELL FARM
100 East Hwy. 80, 75149, exit at Belt Line Road then take south frontage road • 670-7866 or 800-670-FARM (670-3276) • Daily 9–5, closed major holidays • Adults and Children 12 and over $3, Children (3 to 11) $2, under 3 free • W (no W restrooms)

Dr. W. W. Samuell, a prominent Dallas physician in the 1920s and '30s, acquired this land as payment for his services and willed it to the city of Dallas to be used as a farm park. So, although it is located in Mesquite, from its opening to the public in 1982 to today it has been operated by Dallas Parks and Recreation as a turn-of-the-century working farm. Its 340 acres offer visitors a variety of both farm and park experiences. There are five small fishing ponds stocked with bass, brim, and catfish (bring your own fishing gear). Cows, goats, pigs, rabbits, and sheep are around for close-up views and petting. Kids can enjoy climbing on antique farm tractors as well as the equipment in a playground. There are four and a half miles of hiking trails, picnic areas with grills, and a camping area. Among the many activities offered is horseback riding with horses rented for guided one hour trail rides for $12 (Reservations required 670-8551) and group hayrides can be arranged.

SPORTS

AUTO RACING

DEVIL'S BOWL SPEEDWAY
1711 Lawson Road, 75181, exit Lawson Road from Hwy.80, go south • 222-2421 • General Admission: Adults $10, Children 12–15 $5, 6–11 $2, Under 6 free • W

They hold a variety of vehicle races on this unique D-shaped one-half mile track including World of Outlaws Sprint Cars, Super Sprints, late models, and street stocks. Grandstand seating for 10,000 and more than 1,000 reserved seats available at the finish line. Races March to November. Call for meet dates.

GOLF

PUBLIC COURSES

MESQUITE GOLF COURSE AND LEARNING CENTER
825 North Hwy. 67 (75150) (I-30 and Northwest Drive)
270-7457 • 18-hole course. Call for green fees.

TOUR PLAY GOLF CENTER
2920 Gus Thomasson Road (75150) • 270-4800 • 9-hole course.
Green fees: Weekdays $7, Weekends/Holidays $11, Juniors $6.

TOWN EAST EXECUTIVE GOLF COURSE
3134 North Belt Line (75182) • 226-1959 • 9-hole par 3 public course. Call for fees.

TENNIS

WESTLAKE TENNIS CENTER
700 Gross Road, 75150 (Across from Evans Community Center)
289-5326

Six outdoor lighted courts and three covered courts. Outdoor courts $1.25 per person for 1½ hour, covered courts $6-$10 per court for 1½ hour session.

OTHER POINTS OF INTEREST

LIGHT CRUST DOUGHBOYS HALL OF FAME AND MUSEUM
105 Broad, 75149 in McWhorter & Greenhaw Hardware in Old Town Square • 285-5441 • Free • W

This band lays claim to being the longest continually performing Western swing group in America. Started in the 1930s by Fort

Worth mill magnate W. "Pappy" Lee O'Daniel as a marketing gimmick to help sell both his Light Crust Flour, which they did, and his political campaign for governor, which he won. The original band included Bob Wills who went on to become a Texas music legend. Members came and went, but the band endured, playing Western swing and country blues with only a few interruptions (like World War II) in its career. The Doughboys still perform today and the Texas Legislature has named them the official music ambassadors for the state. The small museum includes programs, billboards, and other memorabilia of the group. It's located in the front of the old fashioned hardware (and music) store owned by Art Greenhaw, one of the present members of the band. It's open during store hours Monday–Saturday.

ANNUAL EVENTS

MAY

MESQUITE MUSIC FESTIVAL
Saturday–Sunday, usually first full week in month
Mesquite Arts Center, 1527 North Galloway • 216-6444
Admission • W +

This festival normally opens with a concert by a prominent entertainer or music group. The activities include additional concerts. Call for schedule and admission. Free parking.

JULY

MESQUITE BALLOON FESTIVAL
Last Friday–Sunday in month • Paschall Park, 1001 New
Market Road (75149), one mile east of I-635 (P.O. Box 850115,
75185-0115, Mesquite Chamber of Commerce) • 285-0211
Free admission. Parking $3 • W

This has been the biggest event on the city's calendar since 1986. More than 50 colorful hot air balloons are the main attraction, but there are also arts and crafts vendors, a carnival, and almost continuous entertainment.

SHOPPING

TOWN EAST MALL
**Town East Blvd. and I-635 (75150) • 270-4431 (Mall Office) or
270-2363 (Customer Service) • W +**

There are about 200 stores and a food court in this three story
mall, anchored by Dillard's, Foley's, Sears, and Penney's. Rental
stroller and wheelchairs are available in the Customer Service
Center located on the upper level near the I-30 entrance. In the
area surrounding the mall is another large assortment of stores
including Shepler's Western Store. One advantage of shopping
Mesquite is it has a sales tax that's 1% lower than most other
communities in Dallas County.

NORTH RICHLAND HILLS

TARRANT COUNTY • 52,000 • AREA CODE 817

The history of North Richland Hills goes back to the summer of 1848 when the 600 families started to settle on the land grant of W.S. Peters. The old town of Birdville, which became the first county seat of Tarrant County, was located adjacent to what is now the southwest boundary of North Richland Hills. Dairy farming was the principal occupation of the settlers, and farms flourished.

In 1953 the North Richland Hills Civic League sought to have the area annexed into the city of Richland Hills. When the request for annexation was denied, they voted to form their own city. An election was held and the 268 acres of the Jones Farm, with a population of 500, was officially incorporated as the city of North Richland Hills. As did cities in the Metroplex, this one grew and grew, but even faster than most because it is now the third largest city in Tarrant County.

Liquor by the drink is sold in city restaurants and beer is for sale for off-site consumption.

Unless otherwise noted, the ZIP code for all the listings below is 76180.

NORTH RICHLAND HILLS

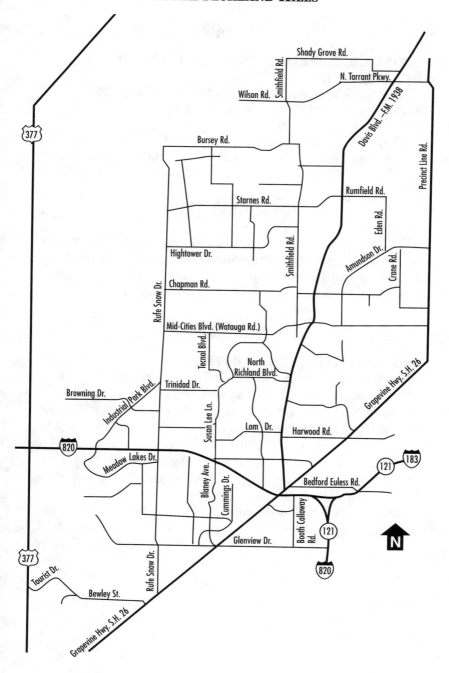

FREE VISITOR SERVICES

ECONOMIC DEVELOPMENT AND TOURISM INFORMATION OFFICE
City of North Richland Hills, 7301 Northeast Loop 820, at Holiday Lane • 581-5652 or Metro 817-498-8775
Monday–Friday 8–5 • W +

They can tell you just about anything and everything you'd want to know about the city, here. Free brochures including *Lodging, Dining & Entertainment Guide* and a city map are available.

BIRD'S-EYE VIEW

You can get a good view of the city and Fort Worth from the high ground near the intersection of Industrial Park Blvd. and Meadow Lakes Drive. If you time it right, you can see the Tarantula Steam Train crossing the bridge over Loop 820.

HISTORIC PLACES

SMITHFIELD HISTORIC DISTRICT
Main Street and Smithfield Road • Free • W Variable

In 1876, when Eli Smith donated part of his farmland to the Zion community for a church and cemetery, the residents honored him by renaming the community after him. Smith and many of his family are buried in the cemetery, which is one of places marked with historical markers. Others are the Smithfield Depot, Masonic Lodge, Cobb Barber Shop, and three churches along Main Street and Smithfield Road.

Records show that as recently as 1935 Smithfield was an independent community with a population of 137, nine businesses, and a school. In 1958 it became annexed to North Richland Hills.

MUSEUMS AND ART GALLERIES

NRH GALLERY
6515 Smithfield Road • 281-5881 • Free • W

Rotating exhibits of modern art are featured in this gallery located in the Smithfield Historic District. Hours are erratic so call first.

OUTDOORS

NORTH RICHLAND HILLS PARKS
**Parks and Recreation Department, 6720 Northeast Loop 820
581-5760**

The five parks in the city include facilities for picnicking baseball, basketball, football, softball, tennis, and volleyball. There are also hike and bike trails in several of the parks including a two-mile natural surface hiking trail in Fossil Creek Park at 6100 Onyx Dr. South. Among the several playgrounds the most notable is the 10-acre **Adventure World** which is the largest playground in Texas fully equipped for the physically challenged. Open daily, it's located at 7451 Starnes Road off Smithfield.

COLLEGES AND UNIVERSITIES

TARRANT COUNTY JUNIOR COLLEGE/NORTHEAST CAMPUS
828 Harwood Road (76054) • 515-7860 • W Variable

First opened in 1969, approximately 10,000 students now attend classes at this TCJC campus taking academic and technical programs with the emphasis on the health sciences. Visitors are welcome at the campus art gallery in the Fine Arts building, open Monday–Friday 8–5 during the academic year as well as at the small museum in the library. The performing arts department offer a spring and fall schedule of widely ranging entertainment including stage productions and musical concerts. Tickets to theatrical productions usually cost about $3 while many other events are admission free. Call for schedule.

MUSIC AND PERFORMING ARTS

NORTH CENTRAL BALLET COMPANY
6350 Glenview • 284-4431

This dance company performs on a seasonal basis in various locations. Performances include the annual *Nutcracker* in December. Call for schedule and ticket prices.

NORTHEAST ORCHESTRA
P.O. Box 821395, 76182-1295 • 283-3406

This non-profit orchestra performs at various locations several times during the year. Call for schedule and ticket information.

FAMILY FUN AND KID STUFF

NRH$_2$O FAMILY WATER PARK
9001 Grapevine Hwy., across from Tarrant County Junior College campus • 656-6500 • Mid-May to mid-September
Adults $9.95, children (3–11) $7.95, Under 3 years free • W

Truly a family park with something for every age. For toddlers it offers a water playground complete with a life-sized train engine, toddler-sized water slides, and entertainment every day. Teens and adventurous adults can try their skills in the 16,000-ft^2 wave pool, 3 twisting water slides, and a 2-person tube slide. And for the adults who want relaxation more than thrills, there's the gentle Endless River. Friday nights, June–August you can watch a Dive-In movie. Open 10 a.m.–8 p.m Sunday–Thursday, Friday–Saturday to 10 p.m. Free parking.

FAMILY ENTERTAINMENT DISTRICT
8851 Grapevine Hwy. • Admission variable • W Variable

Bunched together at the same address on Grapevine Hwy. near the Family Water Park are several other family fun attractions including:

Mountasia Family Fun Center (788-0990) includes a 36-hole miniature golf course, bumper boats, go-carts, batting cages, and video games in a large clubhouse. Separate charges for each activity. Open seven days.

Dry Ice Metroplex In-Line Hockey and Skating Center (788-1051) lives up to its name offering both hockey and public skating for in-line skaters. Skate rentals available. Open Monday-Saturday.

Mid-Cities Combat Zone Paintball (485-6364) is where you can play combat in a forested area with harmless paintball guns. Weekends only.

SPORTS

ARCHERY

SMITHFIELD ARCHERY & OUTDOOR SPORTS
6616 Davis Blvd. • 581-9400 • W

The indoor range "DART" target system here lets archers polish their skills with life-size videos of live game. Fee.

FISHING

BOB'S CAT FISHING PONDS
7712 Davis Blvd. • 428-6608 • W

Your luck should be good here because the ponds are stocked weekly (normally on Thursday). Usually open daily during daylight, but best to call ahead. Admission plus fees per pound of catch.

GOLF

PUBLIC COURSE

IRON HORSE GOLF COURSE
6200 Skylark • 485-6666 • 18-hole course. Call for green fees.

TENNIS

RICHLAND TENNIS CENTER
Loop 820 at Holiday Lane exit • 581-5763

All 16 courts are lighted. Plexipane surface. One sunken court with tournament seating. Rates: $2.50 per person for 1½ hours.

LODGING

For a double room: $ = Under $80, $$ = $80–$120, $$$ = $121–$180, $$$$ = $181–$250, $$$$$ = Over $250; Room tax 13%.

For detailed listings see Metroplex Lodgings Section, p. 400.

HOMESTEAD VILLAGE
7450 Northeast Loop 820 • 788-6000 • $$$$–$$$$$ (+13%) W + 5 suites • No smoking suites

LAQUINTA INN
7620 Bedford Euless Road • 485-2750 or 800-531-5900 (Reservations) • $ (+13%) • W + 1 room • No smoking rooms

PLANO

COLLIN COUNTY • 181,000 • AREA CODE 972

The birth of this city can be traced back to settlers who put down roots here in 1845. About a year later, William Forman started a sawmill and gristmill and a settlement grew up around it. At first the town was called Fillmore, after President Millard Fillmore, but when the post office said that name couldn't be used, the name was changed to Plano after its location on what was then open plains.

A spurt of growth came in 1872 when the railroad arrived. When major fires in 1881 and again in 1895 destroyed much of the city, the citizens rebuilt. Still as late as the 1960 census, the population of this farming and ranching community was only 3,695 and there were still working farms and ranches within the city limits.

Then in the 1970s several large firms moved in and other businesses and industry followed causing the city's population to explode to 72,331 in the 1980 census. And since then it has more than doubled again.

The city of roughly 69 square miles is divided by US Hwy. 75 (North Central Expressway). The eastern third contains the older commercial section, the revitalized and restored historic downtown area with several of the buildings that survived the disastrous fires converted to specialty shops and restaurants, and the

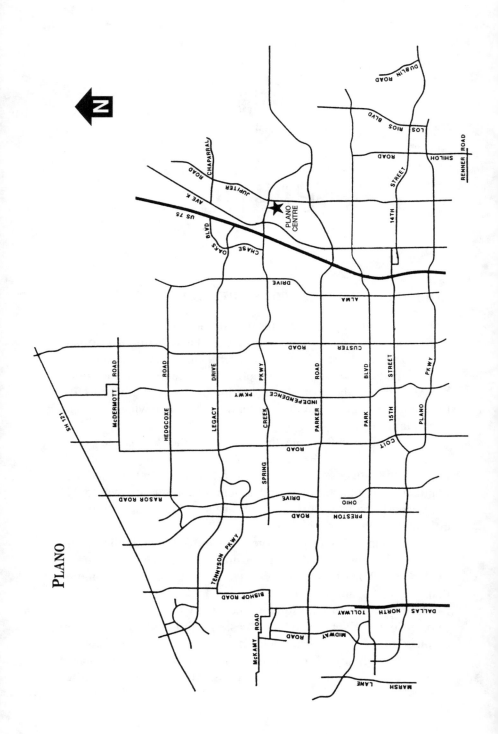

new Plano Centre, a convention center that also houses the Convention and Visitors Bureau. In the two-thirds of the city to the west of Hwy. 75 are many newer housing developments, shopping areas, and, in the far west, the Legacy Business Park, a 2,665-acre master-planned business development with the headquarters complexes of such companies as Electronic Data Systems Corp., JCPenney Co., and Frito-Lay.

The hot-air balloons that local enthusiasts fly over the city most mornings and evenings and the annual Balloon Festival held in the fall have inspired many to call Plano "The Balloon Capital of Texas."

In a *Money* magazine survey Plano ranked as one of the ten safest cities in the United states.

The commercially zoned areas of city are wet under the local options laws relating to alcoholic beverages.

FREE VISITOR SERVICES

PLANO CONVENTION AND VISITORS BUREAU
2000 East Spring Creek Parkway in the Plano Centre (P.O. Box 860358, 75086-0358), take Spring Creek Parkway east off US 75 • 422-0296 or 800-81-PLANO (800-817-5266) Monday–Friday 8–5 • W +

The Convention and Visitors Bureau is in the Sales and Booking office just inside the entrance to this convention center. In addition to details on Plano, you can get information here on most of the cities in the Metroplex.

COMMERCIAL TOUR SERVICES

HOT-AIR BALLOON TOURS
See OFFBEAT, p. 332.

SELF-GUIDED TOURS

WALKING TOUR OF HISTORIC DOWNTOWN PLANO

Tour Historic Plano, a free brochure available from the Convention and Visitors Bureau, includes a map and detailed information about seventeen properties that have been designated as local historic landmarks. Most of these properties are located within easy walking distance of the downtown area, starting from 15th Street and Avenue J. (See HISTORIC PLACES, p. 326.)

HISTORIC PLACES

HISTORIC DOWNTOWN PLANO

In 1979, recognizing that increasing development pressure would threaten historical sites in the community, the city council adopted the Historic Landmark Preservation Ordinance. As a result, several blocks of the original downtown portion of Plano has not only been preserved, but revitalized with red common brick roadways and ornamental Victorian-style street lights to enhance the historic character. Following are a few of the seventeen historic landmark buildings in this area.

The Interurban Building, 901 East 15th Street. From 1908 to 1948, this was a station on the Texas Electric Railroad's Interurban Line linking Denison and Dallas. The Interurban's impact on rural life was dramatic as it ended the isolation of distant farm families. Not only did the electric trains bring the mail, news, salesmen, and new products to small towns and their stores, but they gave rural residents a means to explore the bright lights of the big city cheaply and safely. This completely restored building is the only station remaining from the Sherman-Dallas section of the line. It is now the home of The **Interurban Railway Station Museum** displaying exhibits relating to both Plano's transportation and city history. Outside, is an electric railway car that was used as a Railway Post Office. This is being restored and is not open to the public. The museum is open for tours Saturdays from 1–5 p.m. Individual tours may also be arranged by calling the Parks and Recreation Department (461-7250) during business hours Monday–Friday. Entrance is free, but donations are welcome. It is located in Haggard Park, a pleasant park with a fountain, picnic tables, a gazebo, and restrooms, making it a good place to stop and relax when exploring the downtown area.

The Carpenter-Edwards House, 1211 East 16th Street. This 2½-story, 16-room Queen Anne style home was built in 1898. It is now a bed & breakfast offering three upstairs bedrooms (424-1889).

The Forman House, 1617 Avenue K. One of the oldest homes in Plano, built around 1867 by one of the first families to settle here.

The Matthews House, 901 East 17th Street. Built in 1888–1890 by the family that ran the general store in Plano from 1895 to 1947.

The Olney Davis House, 901 East 18th Street. A two-story Victorian style home built in 1890 by a prominent businessman and mayor.

For a complete listing of historic landmark buildings, see the free brochure *Tour Historic Plano*. Most of these buildings are private residences, not open to the public.

MUSEUMS AND ART GALLERIES

ART CENTRE OF PLANO
1039 East 15th Street at Avenue K (75074) • 423-7809
Free • W +

The three galleries in this corner building feature exhibits of the works of local, national, and international artists. Open Tuesday-Saturday 10-6. The Art Centre Theatre is co-located. (See MUSIC AND PERFORMING ARTS, p. 329.)

HERITAGE FARMSTEAD MUSEUM
1900 West 15th Street (75075), at Pitman Drive, about one and a half miles west of exit 29 off US 75 • 881-0140 • Adults $3.50, Seniors and Children (3–12) $2.50 • W (downstairs in house only)

This is a 4-acre living history museum depicting a sample of early Texas farm life on what was once a 360-acre farm that was worked until 1972. Listed in the National Register of Historic

Places, the Farmstead features the Farrel-Wilson family house, an accurately restored 14-room Victorian style home built in 1891, and 12 outbuildings including the smokehouse, a pole barn, and a windmill. The house is furnished with many original family pieces and the outdoor plants and flowers, including the heirloom roses in The Parlor Garden, are authentic to the period. Chickens roam the grounds and there is also a livestock area with a variety of sheep, hogs, horses, mules, and cows. Guides in period costumes give hour long tours beginning on the hour, starting with an audio-visual orientation on the farm. In summer the museum is open Tuesday–Friday 10–2, Saturday–Sunday 1–5. In winter it is open Thursday–Friday 10–2 and Saturday–Sunday 1–5. The last tour begins an hour before closing time. Gift shop.

OUTDOORS

PLANO PARKS
Parks and Recreation Department, 1409 Avenue K • 461-7263, Park Event Information Line 461-PARK (461-7275) • W

The city has a neighborhood park philosophy that brings at least one of its 65 public parks within blocks of most Plano homes. Park facilities include swimming pools, a tennis center, two golf courses, a playground for handicapped children, and a network of over 30 miles of hike and bike trails that link parks, recreational facilities, schools, shopping centers, and neighborhoods. The four-and-a-half-mile Bluebonnet Trail and the five-mile Chisholm Trail are designated as National Recreation Trails by the U.S. Department of the Interior. The Plano Bikeway Plan calls for expanding the current trail system to 127 miles.

COLLEGES AND UNIVERSITIES

COLLIN COUNTY COMMUNITY COLLEGE
2800 East Spring Creek Blvd. and Jupiter Road (75074) 881-5790 • W + But not all areas

The college provides about 5,000 students with both academic and technical/vocational programs on the 115-acre campus. Visitors are welcome to the **Art Gallery** (K208), which has a changing program of fine art and photography that ranges from faculty and student works to touring professional exhibits. Open Monday–Thursday 9–5:30, Friday 9–2 (881-5873). Visitors are also welcome at the five-play October–June season of the highly-regarded **Quad-C Theatre** (881-5809). The theatre offers sign-interpreted performances for the hearing-impaired the first Sunday afternoon and second Friday evening of each production (TDD 881-5950). A number of musical events open to the public are jazz concerts, including a fall concert in November and a spring concert in May, both featuring the college's jazz groups. The highlight of the jazz year is the annual Jazz Festival in March. The largest jazz festival in North Texas, it is a showcase for many of the best area jazz ensembles plus special guest musicians. The Collin County Chorale also puts on concerts here in the fall and spring. (For concert information 881-5107.) Most theatre and music performances are at the John Anthony Theatre or Black Box Theatre on campus.

MUSIC AND PERFORMING ARTS

COLLIN COUNTY COMMUNITY COLLEGE
See above.

PLANO CIVIC CHORUS
881-5653

Members of this chorus are a combination of professional musicians and amateurs with a solid background in choral singing. Its season usually includes at least three or four major local concerts at the Collin County Community College and other locations around the city. It has also performed at the Morton Meyerson Symphony Center in Dallas and with the National Symphony Chamber Orchestra in Washington, D.C. Tickets for most local performances are $5–$7 for adults and $3–$5 for seniors and children.

PLANO CHAMBER ORCHESTRA
2701-C West 15th Street, Suite 187 (75075) • 985-1983

The 35-member professional orchestra usually performs about 9 concerts in its October-April season with most featuring guest artists or guest conductors. Most performances are in the theater of the Fellowship Bible Church, 850 Lexington. Tickets for most performances are: adults $13, seniors $10, students $7

PLANO REPERTORY THEATRE
ArtCentre Theatre (Box office in ArtCentre, 1039 East 15th Street) • 422-7460 • W

The six plays presented in this community theatre group's year-round season usually include several classic American dramas, a comedy, and a musical. It also puts on a children's program and a popcorn-throwing melodrama in the summer.

FAMILY FUN AND KID STUFF

THE CLASSICS THEATRE
3015 West 15th Street (75075) at Independence • 596-8948 • W

About four national theater touring plays for children are presented in this theater each year on selected Sundays at 2 and 4:30 p.m. Tickets $6. Located in the northwest corner of a strip shopping center, the theater is part of the facilities of The Classics, a non-profit organization providing theatrical experience, dramatic training, and art classes to children and youth ages 3–16. Call for information on productions.

MOUNTASIA FANTASY GOLF
2400 Premier Drive, west off US 75 between Park and Parker • 424-9940

It's miniature golf, but not just a simple 18 hole course. There are 54 holes here taking players through caves, waterfalls, and over obstacles. Kids can also ride bumper boats. Video games in the clubhouse.

SPORTS

GOLF

PUBLIC COURSES

CHASE OAKS GOLF CLUB
7201 Chase Oaks Blvd. • 517-7777 • Two courses: a 18-hole and 9-hole courses. Green fees for 18 holes: Weekdays $47. Weekends $57.

PECAN HOLLOW MUNICIPAL GOLF COURSE
4501 East 14th Street (75074) • 423-5444 • 18-hole course. Green fees: Weekdays $13, Weekends $16.

RIDGEVIEW RANCH GOLF CLUB
2701 Ridgeview Drive • 390-1039 • 18-hole course. Green fees: Weekdays $22, weekends $30.

PRIVATE COURSES

Call for green fees.

GLENEAGLES COUNTRY CLUB
5401 West Park Blvd. (75287) • 867-8888 • 36 holes.

LOS RIOS COUNTRY CLUB
1700 Country Club Dr. (75074) • 424-8913 • 18-hole course.

PRESTONWOOD COUNTRY CLUB
6600 Columbine (75093) • 307-1508 • 18-hole course.

ICE HOCKEY/ICE SKATING

ICE BOUND ENTERTAINMENT CENTER
4020 West Plano Parkway at Coit (P.O. Box 260277, 75026-0277) • 612-8760 • W

This two-story entertainment center features two indoor ice rinks for public skating and ice hockey. It also has a gym and aer-

obics area and food concessions. Admission is free, but there is a
fee for public skating. Call for skating schedule and fees.

TENNIS

HIGH POINT TENNIS CENTER
**421 Spring Creek Parkway (just west of North Central
Expressway) • 461-7170**
Twenty-two lighted courts. Fees are $2.50 per person for one
and a half hours.

OTHER POINTS OF INTEREST

PLANO CENTRE
**2000 East Spring Creek Parkway (P.O. Box 860358, 75086),
east of US 75 off Spring Creek exit • 578-7112 (Convention and
Visitors Bureau) • W +**
Closed conventions and conferences, sure. But also events
open to visitors that range from Kick Boxing and Frisbee Championships to arts and crafts, antique, and home shows. Call to see
what's on the schedule.

OFFBEAT

HOT-AIR BALLOON FLIGHTS

IN THE AIR
**1004 East 15th Street (75074), in Historic Downtown
612-8852 • W**
Want to get a bird's-eye view of Plano? You can book a hot-air
balloon flight in this store where they also sell everything on the
growing sport of ballooning from t-shirts to books. About a third
of the 90 or so professional balloon pilots in the Metroplex live in
the Plano area and most are available to take you up to silently
float on the breeze. Because these flights depend on the winds,
they are usually scheduled at sunrise and sunset when the light
winds are best. Flights last an hour to an hour and a half and they

fly every day of the year, weather permitting. The balloons are launched from different areas, depending on wind conditions. You'll be told where the launch area is and the chase crew will bring you back to your car. All flights end with a traditional champagne toast and you'll get a flight pin and a t-shirt you can use later to brag about your adventure. Most of the balloons will carry four passengers plus a pilot. How much? About $150 per passenger. In addition to arranging your flight through this store, you can book with AirVenture Balloon Port, 1791 Millard, Suite D 75074, 422-0212.

ANNUAL EVENTS

SEPTEMBER

PLANO BALLOON FESTIVAL
Three-day weekend late in month • Bob Woodruff Park, 2601 San Gabriel, east from Park Blvd. exit off US 75 • 867-7566 Free • Park parking $6, Shuttle from remote parking $2 • W Variable

It's an unforgettable sight: a dazzling kaleidoscopic array of hot-air balloons of all shapes, colors, and striking designs filling the sky. For the most breath-taking view go to the "Mass Ascension" event when all the balloons, now up to around 100, take to the sky. This usually takes place the Saturday evening or Sunday morning of this consistently eye-filling festival. From a small beginning of a scattering of balloons and a few spectators close to 20 years ago, the festival now draws about 300,000 spectators to watch balloonists from all over the country flying the balloons.

The festival starts on Friday afternoon with ground activities that include opening ceremonies, exhibits, demonstrations, and an arts and crafts show. Then come the balloon races. The races themselves are hard to follow from the park, but the events are usually arranged so some of the flying activities start in the park and others end there. The highlight of the evening for spectators is usually the Balloon Glow in which tethered balloons are brilliantly lit up by the burning gas from their gas generators. This glowing spectacle is so popular, it's usually repeated several times during the festival, both at dawn and evenings. Most of the flying events are also scheduled dawn and dusk because this is when the winds are best for this silent flying. During all this, there's also continuous entertainment on two stages and, of course, food vendors.

Limited on-site parking is available on the north side of the park ($6). Remote-site and handicapped parking is available at the DART East-Side Transit Center on Archerwood Drive, between Park and Parker, just east of US 75. Parking is free, but to get from there to Bob Woodruff Park, you'll have to take a shuttle bus, which costs $2 round-trip.

SHOPPING

COLLIN CREEK MALL
North Central Expressway (US 75) between Plano Parkway (exit 28) and FM 544 (exit 29) • 424-7691 • W

Dillard's, Foley's, Penney's, and Sears anchor about 140 special stores in this two-story mall. Stroller rental and wheelchairs are available at the Customer Service Center on the lower level.

DOWNTOWN SPECIALTY SHOPS
East 15th Street between Avenue G and Avenue M • 423-4440

Along the brick streets of Historic Downtown Plano are over 40 specialty shops, including around a half dozen antique shops such as the Collectors Antique Mall (905 East 15th), where approximately 100 vendors offer a large selection of antiques and collectibles. Free parking on Avenue J and Avenue K north and south of 15th Street.

WHOLE FOODS MARKET
2201 Preston Road at Park • 612-6729 • W

There are several stores in the Metroplex that carry natural foods, but this is one of four in the Metroplex that are part of the country's largest chain of natural foods supermarkets. It carries what is probably the largest selection in the area of organically grown foods and seafood and meats without growth hormones or other additives. Deli/restaurant in the store.

DINING OUT

PLANO CAFÉ
1915 North Central Expressway (US 75), Suite 500, southwest corner at Park Lane • 516-0865 • Lunch and dinner Monday–Saturday, dinner only Sunday • $$ • Cr.

The management refers to this as a European style bistro, but the menu entrées range from Europe across the U.S. For example, on the European side there's grilled Norwegian salmon (everything is sauteed or grilled, nothing fried) and shrimp with red pesto pasta, but also Black Angus ribeye steak and Cajun snapper. Other entrées feature chicken, pork, and lamb. Children's menu. Vegetarian entrées available. Bar.

SEA GRILL
2205 North Central Expressway (US 75), Suite 180, west side between Park and Parker • 509-5542 • Lunch Monday–Friday, dinner seven days • $$–$$$ • Cr.

The chef-owner here prepares the fresh seafood New York style, medium-rare so as not to overcook and spoil the natural flavor. He also prepares it with a flair to produce entrees such as lobster and shrimp *rigatoni* with vodka cream sauce, grilled jumbo sea scallops with teriyaki-lime-butter glaze, and seared lemon-pepper salmon with braised leeks and whole grain mustard-dill sauce. Overall, the menu features seafood dishes that range from New American to French to Asian cuisines. Beef and chicken entrees on the menu, too, but just barely there. Bar.

LODGINGS

For a double room: $ = Under $80, $$ = $80–$120, $$$ = $121–$180, $$$$ = $181–$250, $$$$$ = Over $250; Room tax 13%.

For detailed listings see Metroplex Lodgings Section, p. 379.

THE CARPENTER HOUSE BED & BREAKFAST
1211 East 16th Street (75074) • 424-1889 • $-$$ (+13%)

COURTYARD BY MARRIOTT
4901 West Plano Parkway at Preston Road (75093) • 867-8000
or 800-321-2211 (Reservations) • $$ • W+ two rooms • No
smoking rooms

HAMPTON INN
4905 Old Shepard Place (75093), off Preston Road north of
Plano Parkway • 519-1000 or 800-HAMPTON (800-428-7866)
$ • W+ seven rooms • No smoking rooms

HARVEY HOTEL PLANO
1600 North Central Expressway (US 75), exit 29 (15th street)
578-8555 or 800-922-9222 • $$–$$$ • W+ three rooms
No smoking rooms

SIDE TRIPS

LAKE LAVON
Take Parker Road (FM 2514) east about 7 miles to St. Paul, then
St. Paul Road to Collin Park on the lake • 442-5755 • Open at all
times • Free • W Variable

There are 4 large parks with hookups for campers and several
day-use parks on this 21,400-acre Army Corps of Engineers' lake.
Boat ramps, marinas with boat rentals, swimming, fishing, water-
skiing, picnicking, and motorcycle riding trails. Caddo Park is
equipped for handicapped. For information write: Reservoir Man-
ager, P.O. Box 429, Wylie, TX 75098

SOUTHFORK RANCH
3700 Hogge Road, Parker (75002), from US 75 (exit 30) take Parker Road east about 6 miles to Hogge Road (FM 2551) then south to entrance • 972-442-7800 • Open seven days 9–5. Adults $6, seniors $5, children $4 • Free Parking • W Variable

The myths of the TV show *Dallas* live on here. This ranch was the exterior setting for that TV series, which had a 13-season run from 1978 to 1990. Because the show was seen by millions all over the world, this white, colonial-style plantation home is probably recognized by almost as many people as The White House. Tours of the mansion are available. Don't be surprised if the mansion rooms don't look familiar. All the show's interior shots were made on sets in Hollywood. You can tour the small museum featuring show memorabilia and the grounds on your own. There's a tram, if you don't want to walk. The ranch's western store is called "Lincolns and Longhorns." The Lincoln, on display in the store, is the one Jock Ewing drove in the show. The longhorns you can see in the fields as you wander around the grounds. Extensive meeting facilities cater to large groups for conferences, parties, and picnics.

RICHARDSON

DALLAS AND COLLIN COUNTIES • 78,000
AREA CODE 972

In 1842, the Jackson family came from Tennessee and settled on the land where Richland College is now located. As other settlers moved in from Tennessee and Kentucky, they clustered around the Jacksons eventually forming a town they proudly named after John C. Breckenridge, the Kentuckian who served as Vice-President of the United States from 1857-1861.

After the Civil War the railroads became the driving force in the development of the West. Unfortunately, Breckenridge was not in any railroad's plans. Then, in 1872, John Wheeler lured the Houston and Texas Railroad to the area by giving 100 acres of land northwest of Breckenridge for a right of way and a townsite. Wheeler declined to have the new town named after him and, showing his political savvy, instead named it after E.H. Richardson, the railroad contractor who built the line from Dallas to Dennison. The railroad drew the settlers like a magnet and soon Richardson was the center of activity and Breckenridge disappeared.

It was during the early years of the town that local folklore says it was frequently visited by such notorious outlaws as Sam Bass, the Younger brothers, and Belle Starr. And it's said that Jesse and Frank James often hid out in the area.

RICHARDSON

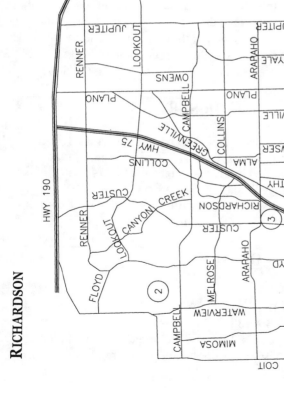

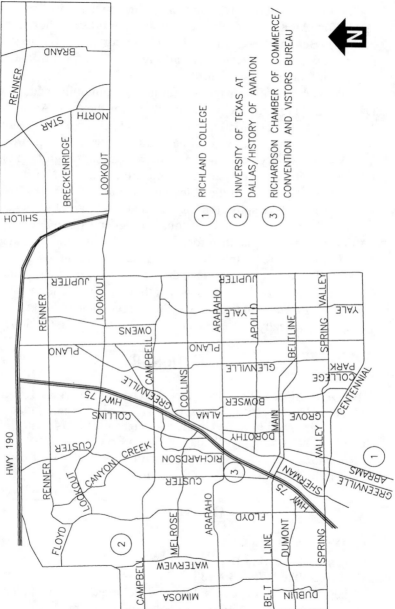

1. RICHLAND COLLEGE

2. UNIVERSITY OF TEXAS AT DALLAS/HISTORY OF AVIATION

3. RICHARDSON CHAMBER OF COMMERCE/ CONVENTION AND VISTORS BUREAU

N

Not folklore, but fact is that after the town incorporated in 1924, Tom McKamy, its first mayor and a mortician, buried the infamous Bonnie Parker. Probably more important to the citizens, however, was that McKamy was also responsible for introducing indoor plumbing to the town.

Still, Richardson remained a farming community and, after Dallas started to grow, a bedroom suburb for that city. As late as 1950, its population stood at about 1300. Then, in 1951, Collins Radio opened a Richardson office and the door to the electronic age. Today, the city is the home to more than 500 high-tech and telecommunications companies and the area along the North Central expressway is called the Telecom Corridor®.

The county line splits the city so that there are 18.2 square miles in Dallas County and 9.2 square miles in Collin County.

Richardson is dry and therefore on-premise consumption of alcoholic beverages are permitted only in certain designated areas that are zoned retail or commercial districts; e.g. restaurants, clubs, hotels. Private clubs are established in these facilities and membership costing from $.50 to $2 is required to purchase a drink. Some hotels automatically give guests memberships in the hotel club.

FREE VISITOR SERVICES

RICHARDSON CONVENTION AND VISITORS BUREAU
411 Belle Grove Drive (75080), from I-75, exit Arapaho, take South access road to Belle Grove, first right • 234-4141 or 800-777-8001 • Monday–Friday 8:30–5 • Free • W +

Brochures, maps, directions—everything you'd expect from a Convention and Visitors Bureau, and more.

OUTDOORS

RICHARDSON PARKS
Parks and Recreation Department
P.O. Box 830309, 75083 • 238-4250

The facilities in the city's 25 parks include almost 13 miles of hike and bike trails, swimming pools, and a nature area containing a unique hardwood forest. The parks department also offers a 36 hole golf course and a tennis center.

COLLEGES AND UNIVERSITIES

RICHLAND COLLEGE
12800 Abrams Road (75243) just north of LBJ Freeway (I-635)
238-6194 • W + But not all areas

One of the 7 campuses in the Dallas Community College District, Richland has an enrollment of about 13,000 full and part-time students in both academic and technical/vocational programs. The 259-acre campus features pedestrian bridges linking facilities along both sides of a spring-fed creek and 2 small lakes. Visitors are welcome at many campus activities including plays, dance and music concerts and recitals in the Performance Hall, exhibits in the art gallery, and shows at the college planetarium. There is also a greenhouse with a demonstration garden open to the public.

UNIVERSITY OF TEXAS AT DALLAS
2601 North Floyd Road (75080) at Campbell Road
News and Information 883-2293 • W + But not all areas

Established in 1969 as a graduate school only, the university added freshman through senior levels over the years until it now also offers undergraduate degrees in a variety of fields of study. Visitors are welcome at a number of cultural, intellectual, and leisure activities on the 500-acre campus. Each month concerts plays and films fill the performance spaces on campus (Arts Events line 883-ARTS 883-2787). The McDermott Library Special Collections Gallery features new art exhibits on a monthly basis. It's open Monday–Thursday 9–6, Friday 9–5 (883-2570). This library also offers stamp collection exhibits from its Wineburgh Philatelic Research Collection, one of the country's top resources on stamps and stamp collecting, and its History of Aviation Collection includes 20,000 reference volumes and 250,000 aviation periodicals, journals, and research documents tracing aviation history. Student and faculty projects are featured at the Students Visual Arts Gallery (883-2787). Class day visitors should check at the gate for the location of visitor parking.

MUSIC AND PERFORMING ARTS

DALLAS REPERTOIRE BALLET
1910 Firman #120 (75081) (Office) • 231-6883

Ballets are performed at area churches and schools several times a year. General admission to most events is about $10.

RICHARDSON COMMUNITY BAND
P.O. Box 832964, 75083 • Metro 972-851-9784

First organized before World War I, the band was broken up during both World Wars, but played in the many years between them. The present band was reorganized in 1970 and has been performing continuously since then. Composed of about 60 semi-professional and amateur musicians it performs free concerts year-round. Every summer it hosts a biweekly outdoor concert series Sunday evenings on the lawn of the Richardson Civic Center (411 W. Arapaho). Its schedule also includes performances at city festivals, a fall concert, and a Children's Concert in March

RICHARDSON SYMPHONY ORCHESTRA
333 West Campbell Road, #210 (Office)
(P.O. Box 831675, 75083) • 234-4195

Formed as a small community orchestra in 1961, now it is a well-received 70-member professional symphony orchestra performing six concerts in its regular October through April subscription season. At least three of these concerts feature internationally acclaimed artists. Usually four concerts are devoted to traditional classical selections and two are pops concerts. The subscription concerts are held at the Richardson High School Theatre, 1250 West Belt Line (W+). Single admissions range from $9 to $21. The symphony also performs other outdoor, family, and children's concerts during the year, usually in connection with city festivals or special events, and a spring concert in the Meyerson Symphony Center in Dallas.

RICHARDSON THEATRE CENTER
718 Canyon Creek Square (75080), at Custer Road and Lookout behind the supermarket • 699-1130 • W

They put on five shows a year in this small 80-seat theater converted from retail space in a strip shopping center. Each production runs five or six weeks with performances Thursday through Saturday at 8. Adult admission is $10, Senior and students $8.

RICH TONES CHORUS
P.O. Box 832978, 75083 • 234-6065

More than 125 women make up this award-winning Sweet Adelines chorus that sings four-part harmony barbershop style. They put on concerts in various locations in Richardson and the surrounding area. Call for schedule and ticket information.

RICHLAND COLLEGE
See COLLEGES AND UNIVERSITIES, p. 341.

UNIVERSITY OF TEXAS AT DALLAS
See COLLEGES AND UNIVERSITIES, p. 341.

FAMILY FUN AND KID STUFF

OWENS SPRING CREEK FARM
1401 East Lookout (75081), off Plano Road between Renner and Campbell • 235-0192 • Open daily 9–12 and 1–4 Free • W Variable

The main building on this 56-acre farm is a small museum with exhibits depicting both life in the 1920s and how the Owens family, known in Texas for sausages for well over 60 years, started out in that business. In the barn there are antique wagons and in the corrals outside are tiny Shetland ponies and, in contrast, a team of huge Belgian horses, which weigh an average of 2,300 pounds. There are also many farm animals, some of which can be petted. Guided tours are available Monday–Friday 9–3. Also on the grounds, but not open to visitors, is Miss Belle's Place, a two-story house built around 1887 which was home to Miss Virginia Bell Robberson who taught school in the town for almost 40 years.

RICHARDSON CHILDREN'S THEATRE
525 West Arapaho #20 (75080) (Office) • 690-5029

The acting company consists of a professional troupe and children and youths aged 5–16 who have successfully completed acting workshops. Six productions are put on each year at the University of Texas at Dallas Theatre (Floyd and Campbell W+). Usually three of the productions are during the summer when school is out. Plays and musicals range from time-honored children's classics to original scripts with performances scheduled for Friday-Sunday. Saturday evening performances are signed for the hearing-impaired. Backstage tours available. General admission $5, reserved seating $7.50.

SPORTS

GOLF

PUBLIC COURSES

THE PRACTICE TEE
2950 Waterview (75080), next to UT Dallas campus • 235-6540 9-hole par 3 course. Call for fees.

SHERRILL PARK MUNICIPAL GOLF COURSE
2001 Lookout Drive (75080) • 234-1416 • 36 holes. Green fees (18 holes): Weekdays $14, Weekends/Holidays $17.

Ranked as the #4 municipal course in the state by *The Dallas Morning News.*

PRIVATE COURSE

CANYON CREEK COUNTRY CLUB
625 Lookout Drive (75080) near Custer • 231-3083 • Eighteen hole course. Green fees: Weekdays $35, Weekends $50. Membership fee $47.50. Also indoor and outdoor tennis courts.

TENNIS

TENNIS CENTER
1601 Syracuse Drive (75081) in Huffhines Park • 234-6697
Ten lighted courts. Open daily 7:30 a.m–10:30 p.m. Fees: $1.50 per person for an hour and a half. (In addition to the Tennis Center, lighted courts are available at a number of city parks. Call 238-4250 for information.)

ANNUAL EVENTS

Special events Hotline 238-4021

APRIL

WILDFLOWER! ARTS & MUSIC FESTIVAL
Four nights and two days of weekend late in month • Greenway Office Park, US 75 and Campbell Road (Office: 1405 Exchange St, 75081) • 680-7909 • Admission to some events • W Variable
If Mother Nature cooperates, this festival starts with the city in full bloom with over 90 acres of wildflowers in parks, along roadsides, in street medians, and along US 75. Bus tours leave the festival area on the half hour to view many of these areas including the 25 acres of wildflowers in Breckinridge Park.

The festival itself opens with a gala "A Taste of Richardson," where several local restaurants provide the food for dining and there's dancing and entertainment. The activities for the rest of the weekend include a Battle of the Bands on three stages, with the bands made up of some of the area's top corporate executives, and non-stop music from groups on four other stages; arts and crafts booths, a car show, a carnival, a police motorcycle rodeo, a 5K run/walk, children's activities, fireworks, and a laser show. The Richardson Symphony also presents its annual concert with a patriotic theme. Total attendance at this annual event is usually around 50,000.

MAY AND OCTOBER

COTTONWOOD ART FESTIVAL
Saturday–Sunday • Cottonwood Park, 1321 West Belt Line Road, one block east of Coit Road (Office: 711 West Arapaho road, 75080) • 231-4624 • Free • W Variable

Artists from across the country participate in this twice a year show of arts and crafts. Held annually for close to 30 years, it has built a reputation for the high quality of work presented. Music, children's programs, and food. Parking is at the park and in the high school across from the park with a free bus shuttling between the school and the festival.

SHOPPING

MAIN STREET ANTIQUES
107 East Main (75080) at US 75 • 644-1558 • W

A small antiques mall with 22 dealers.

RETRO 1951
117 East Main (75080), one block east of US 75 • 479-1405 or 800-466-1951 • W

The name refers to a time when a fine pen and a writing style were important in everyday life. This store offers such pens as well as stationary and other items of yesteryear.

WHOLE FOODS MARKET
60 Dal-Rich Village (75080) at Coit and Belt Line • 699-8075 • W

There are many stores in the Metroplex that carry natural foods, but this is one of four in the Metroplex that are part of the country's largest chain of natural foods supermarkets. It carries what is probably the largest selection in the area of organically grown foods and seafood and meats without growth hormones or other additives. Deli/restaurant in the store.

DINING OUT

$ = Under $12, $$ = $12–$30, $$$ = Over $30 for one person excluding drinks, tax, and tip.

CAFÉ BRAZIL
2071 North Central Expressway (75080) • 783-9011
Breakfast, lunch and dinner seven days • $–$$ • Cr. • W

One of four in the Metroplex, this small chain serves full meals, but is famed as a real coffee-shop with coffee that has earned plaudits from connoisseurs of the java, and it features the bottomless cup. It is also consistently listed as one of the best breakfast spots in the Dallas area serving all the familiar breakfast items plus a large selection of specialties, like Brazilian Breakfast, which consists of two eggs over easy, *Chorizo Empanada,* topped with a spicy cream sauce, cheddar cheese and a jalapeno. And breakfast is available all day.

KEBAB-N-KURRY INDIAN RESTAURANT
401 North Central Expressway (US 75) # 300 (75081) at Arapaho • 231-5556 • Lunch and dinner seven days • $ • Cr. • W

They use clay-oven cooking to enhance the low-fat element of the North Indian cuisine. The popular Tandoori entrées on the menu include chicken, lamb, and shrimp, or sample all three in the Tandoori Mixed Grill. Other entrees feature a variety of authentic Indian techniques for cooking chicken, beef, lamb, seafood, and vegetarian dishes. BYOB.

SWAN COURT
2435 North Central Expressway (US 75) (75081), at Campbell
235-7926 • Lunch Monday–Friday, dinner Monday–Saturday, Closed Sunday • $$ • Cr. • W

A supper club setting with a continental menu that features seafood, including lobster and Norwegian salmon; steaks such as *steak au poivre,* a sauteed New York peppered steak with cognac; as well as veal, chicken, and pasta. Bar with live music and dancing Monday-Saturday.

LODGINGS

For a double room: $ = Under $80, $$ = $80–$120, $$$ = $121–$180, $$$$ = $181–$250, $$$$$ = Over $250; Room tax 13%.

For detailed listings see Metroplex Lodgings Section, p. 381.

CLARION HOTEL
1981 North Central Expressway (75080), US 75 at Campbell Road, exit 26 • 644-4000 or 800-285-3434 (Reservations) $$–$$$ • W + 2 rooms • No smoking rooms

HAMPTON INN
1577 Gateway Blvd. (75080), from exit 26 Campbell Road off US 75, go West to Gateway • 234-5400 or 800-426-7866 • $ W + 5 rooms • No smoking rooms

HAWTHORN SUITES HOTEL
250 Municipal Drive (75080), from US 75 exit 26, Campbell Road, take South access road to Municipal Drive • 669-1000 or 800-527-1133 • $$$–$$$$ • W + 2 rooms • No smoking rooms

OMNI RICHARDSON HOTEL
701 East Campbell Road (75081), east off I-75 exit 26 231-9600 or 800-THE OMNI (800-843-6664) • $$–$$$ W + 5 rooms • No smoking rooms

METROPLEX
LODGINGS

When it comes time to pick where you want to spend the night, the Metroplex offers an enormous bundle of choices to match just about every lifestyle and price. There are hotels and motels and hotels and motels, an occasional bed and breakfast, and then more hotels and motels. Sometimes you'll find them in clusters to meet the needs of the business centers, conventions, or in entertainment areas featuring major attractions, like Six Flags. Others are widely scattered throughout the Metroplex. You can go top dollar and luxuriate in all the amenities or go budget and get all the basics, frequently with a touch of quality.

The lodging listings we selected are just a *small sampling* of what's available in the Metroplex—a *really small sampling*. The full range of possibilities runs from The Mansion on Turtle Creek, the only hotel in Texas rated five diamonds by the AAA and five stars by Mobil, to chain budget motels. For this sample we've gathered an assortment of quality lodgings in every Metroplex city that offer you a spread of amenities and price ranges. And because city boundaries are often virtually invisible to the visitor, check the map and see if the cities around your destination city offer a better deal while still not drastically increasing the distances you have to travel to go wherever you want to go and do whatever you want to do.

Our listings are divided into the following three major groups of cities by geographical area with the listings alphabetical within each city:

Eastern Metroplex: Addison, Dallas, Farmers Branch, Plano, and Richardson.

Mid-Cities: Arlington, Irving, Grand Prairie, and Grapevine.

Western Metroplex: Fort Worth and North Richland Hills.

This sample should give you enough choices to get you started on your trip planning. We don't believe you can go wrong selecting any of these that fit your needs and budget. But, if you don't find what you want here, contact the office listed under FREE VISITOR SERVICES in the section of your destination city and/or nearby cities and ask those sources for more complete lists.

WHAT'S IN THE LISTINGS

We've tried to anticipate your needs and provide information to answer the most commonly asked questions about lodgings. If there's still more you need to know, call the numbers given in the listings and ask. Don't be shy about asking. You're buying, they're selling.

In **bold faced type** at the beginning of each listing, you'll find the following key items of basic information.

• **Property Name:** The official name of the hotel/resort/motel/B&B. The trade refers to each of these as a "property" so we'll use this all-inclusive term for convenience—at least that way you won't have to keep reading "hotel/resort/motel/B&B" over and over again. Sometimes it appears that property owners are as interested in buying and selling properties as they are in serving guests. They buy, remodel and build up occupancy rates to raise the value, then sell. Whether this is true or not, you can bet that some of the ownership of the properties listed here will change while this book is in print. What does this mean to you? At the least, probably a name change. After that your guess is as good as ours. If the location still interests you, call the new management for details.

- **Street Address:** The property's street location and Zip code. We've added the **Mailing Address** if different from the street address.
- **Directions:** If the address isn't an easy one to find, we try to add a brief note giving basic directions or, at least, the nearest cross-street or major highway to help you find it.
- **Phone numbers:** Local phone numbers and any 800 numbers and Metro numbers. Most 800 numbers are to the chain's central reservations, but some connect directly to the property. Some properties also have a Metro number that you can use to call from anywhere in the Metroplex as a local call.
- **Rates:** For comparison purposes we use what's known in the trade as the rack rate—the published standard rate for a room in each property. You might look at this as the wishful thinking price set by property management. A better way to consider it is like the published sticker price on a car; it's the base from which to negotiate because room rates depend on supply and demand and, if the demand is down, the rates are flexible and negotiable. (See "The Secret of How to Get the Best Rate," below.) The following $ symbols are used to indicate the approximate rate for a double room (two persons in a room) for one night. If two symbols are used it indicates the spread between the lowest and highest priced double room

    $ = Under $80
    $$ = $80 to $120
    $$$ = $121 to $180
    $$$$ = $181 to $250
    $$$$$ = Over $250

  We did not break out rates over $250, so the $$$$$ symbol means $251 and up—sometimes way, way up.)
- **Room tax percentage:** This is rarely, if ever, included in the quoted room rate, but it *will be added* to your bill at check-out

time. The total percentage is usually a bundle of state, county, and city sales taxes you'd pay on any purchase plus an additional percentage room occupancy tax. This total percentage is usually lumped under the term "bed tax." To reduce the shock when you get your bill, once you've fixed the exact room rate you'll be paying and made your reservation, add this in to get your total room cost per night. The only thing good we can say about the bed tax is that most cities use at least part of the occupancy tax percentage to support tourism and the arts, which can make your stay more pleasant.

- **Number of rooms equipped for guests using wheelchairs:** This information is provided with the **W+** symbol we use for full wheelchair accessibility. This specifically refers to the entrance to the property and the wheelchair accessible rooms, but implies that a guest in a wheelchair will be able to use at least some of the other key facilities. Call for details.
- **Availability of no smoking rooms:** This is just a statement of availability. If the management provided the actual number that's included in the text.

   The text portion of the listing includes details on other items the property has to offer you. This information was provided by the management of each property in response to our questionnaires. We have only included positive answers—if the management answered a question with a "No," we did not include that item in the listing for that property. For example, we asked if guests could bring pets (Pets OK?). If the answer was "No," we did not put in anything on pets. Note that there may appear to be inconsistencies in what's covered from one listing to another because some management did not answer some of our questions. We've also edited out responses that were ambiguous or incomplete. If the facility or amenity you want is not listed, it's probably not available at that property. But if that item is important to you, ask about it when making your reservation.

Most items in the text portion of the listings are self-explanatory.

- Number of floors.
- Total number of units (rooms and suites).
- Number of suites and rates.
- Number of no smoking rooms.
- Are discounts and package plans available? Our rate symbol is for the rack rate without discounts, but there are discounts! (See below.)
- Can children stay free in room with parents? If yes, we've tried to include up to what age.
- Is there a concierge floor? These offer extra amenities at a higher rate. If you expect to spend a fair amount of time in the hotel, the extra amenities (which may include extras such as breakfast, snacks, drinks, increased security, etc.) may more than make-up for the extra expense, especially for a couple on a leisurely vacation. In most of the luxury properties, even if there is no concierge floor, there will probably be a concierge on duty, usually in the lobby. As a minimum, consider every concierge a helpful walking encyclopedia of local knowledge and lore on everything from what to see to where to dine, shop, or have fun. Occasionally a property management will say they have a concierge floor when what they have is a special floor that's only open to members of their business or frequent guest club.
- Pets OK? If yes, is there a special fee and/or deposit? Check to see if it is a fee and/or a deposit and if a deposit, how do you get it back? Where pets are permitted, there are normally restrictions on size and kind. Always call first because pet policies change frequently.
- Check-in and check-out times. Most properties have set 3 p.m. as the check-in time and noon for check-out. In most cases, both may be adjusted if you ask the management.
- Inside or outside access to the rooms.

- Is there a charge for local calls or are they free? If you plan to make many local calls, this might be a factor in selecting where you'll stay. To avoid the surcharges routinely put on long distance calls, in most cases it'll probably be cheaper to use a calling card than charge it to your room.
- Is there cable TV, if so are there any free premium channels, like HBO, and any pay channels.
- Is a VCR available in the room or for rent?
- On request, can the room be equipped for the hearing impaired with captioned TV, visual or other special alarms, special phones?
- Is there an honor bar or wet bar in room? If an honor bar, check the price list carefully before you use it. They're convenient, but items tend to be extravagantly priced.
- Coffeemakers in rooms or is free coffee available in lobby or restaurant?
- Is there a modem link to hook up a computer modem in the room?
- Is there a fire intercom system where guests can be given a voice warning and instructions in case of a fire?
- Are there bellmen on duty to help you with luggage or other services? If there are none, when you check in ask for a cart or trolley to wheel your luggage to your room instead of carrying it.
- Is there room service? If you plan to use it, check the hours. Also note that a service fee is normally tacked on, and this probably does not include the tip to the person who delivers. Occasionally a property without a restaurant will have room service from nearby restaurants.
- Is there a pool? Is it indoor? Outdoor? Heated?
- Is there a sauna? Exercise room?
- Are guest memberships available (free or for a fee) for local golf, tennis, or health clubs?
- Are any business services available on the property? Many hotels now have fully staffed business centers open weekdays, while others provide just the basics in copy and fax services.

- Are there on-property: a gift shop? Barber shop? Beauty shop? Retail stores?
- Is there a self-service (free or coin) laundry on-property?
- Is one day dry cleaning service available? This normally includes laundry service as well as dry cleaning. This can be convenient, but unless you're in a real hurry, it's usually less expensive to find a neighborhood dry cleaner/laundry and drop it off yourself.
- What complimentary amenities or services are provided? Free breakfast? Cocktails? Newspaper? Shoe shine? Transportation? Consider these when comparing room rates? If you are traveling without a car, free airport, shopping, or local restaurant transportation, for example, can save you a bundle on taxi or shuttle fares.
- Are there any amenities or services for families with children? Playground? Special programs? Child care? (Although they don't advertise it, some properties have lists of local babysitters you can call. Most concierges can also arrange for babysitting.)
- Is there one or more restaurants on property? If there is more than one, combined what meals do they serve? What's the price range of the average cost of a typical dinner for one person without drinks, tax, or tip?
- Is there a bar/lounge? Is so does it offer entertainment/dancing?
- Are there meeting rooms? Banquet facilities? This information is not just for groups who might be interested in using these facilities, it's also something to consider when making a choice. Will it bother you if you're in a property with a large group holding meetings or a convention? And how will it affect your negotiations for the best rate?
- Is parking outside or inside? Park yourself or valet? If garage or valet, what's the fee (besides tip)?

> Some of the details we don't include and you might want to ask about when you make your reservation are:
>
> *What credit cards are accepted?* Most take all major credit cards.
>
> *How late can you cancel a reservation without being charged?* It used to be fairly common that you could do this up to 6 p.m. on the day of your reservation, but now that's changing to as early as noon. In some cases there may even be a cancellation fee imposed. Just as you should always get a confirmation number when you make a reservation, always get a cancellation number when you cancel.
>
> *What special security measures does the property have for guests, especially for a woman traveling alone?* We asked this, but, unfortunately, the answers were too divergent to classify.

THE SECRET OF HOW TO GET THE BEST RATE

The cost of lodgings is often the biggest part of your travel budget. Which means it'll pay you to put in a little extra work at keeping that cost as low as possible without sacrificing quality or the amenities you want. You may get this best rate through a knowledgeable travel agent, a hotel/motel half-price club, or a hotel broker or consolidator, but there's also a good chance that, if you're not shy, you can do as well by yourself.

So, what is the secret of how to get the best rate?

Ask for it!

That's it. If you ask, the odds are you'll get it.

Why? Because the hotel industry works under the law of supply and demand and each room is a perishable product on a daily basis—it's either a profit or a loss every night. When demand is high (they've booked a huge convention or there's a major event that fills all the rooms) the rates stay high. But when demand is low any room that isn't filled at night is a loss. Which means the management must be flexible on its rates to get as many rooms filled each night as possible. That, in turn, means that, at least up to a point, the rates are negotiable and if you ask for a discount or a special deal there's a good chance you'll get it.

What kind of discounts are there? There are discounts for seniors (AARP members or senior age loosely defined), AAA and other auto clubs and travel organizations, union members, teachers, students, military, clergy, frequent flier programs; if it's during a slow time, you may even get a discount if you resemble one of the desk clerk's in-laws. In general, the management doesn't care what the discount is called as long as it helps fill that empty room at a reasonable rate.

There are also special package plans that lump a room (or suite) with a number of amenities that if priced separately would cost much more. These may range from a golf or tennis package, to a Cowboys football weekend rate to a honeymoon or anniversary deal. (Honeymoon and anniversary packages are often an especially good deal, and no one is going to ask to see your wedding license to check if you're really celebrating your anniversary on the right day, or even the right month.) Properties located in the business centers of the cities that are filled with business people Monday through Thursday often offer special rates to fill those rooms on weekends. And, here again, the term "weekend" is defined differently by each hotel depending on its supply and demand; in a slow period they might stretch it for you well into the week. Conversely, resort properties that are packed on weekends may offer a good deal weekdays.

HOW TO ASK FOR THIS BEST RATE

First, from the following listings, or other sources, pick out the properties in your price range that have the location and amenities you want. You'll be dealing with sales personnel so know what you want so you can't be sold into something you don't want. Having several choices to fall back on give you a position of strength in negotiating with each one. If you're real good at negotiating, you might even play one property's offered rate against the others.

It can be one or two steps to find the best rate. One step: call direct to each property and negotiate. Two-step: call each chain property's central reservations 800 number first, then call the property direct. The questions are basically the same for each step.

If you call the 800 reservations number first, tell the clerk what you want and ask for the lowest rate. When you're given the rate, be courteous and friendly, but push without being pushy and ask, "Is that the lowest rate you have?" Each time you're given a new rate, ask the same question again. You might come up with a good deal this way, but don't expect it. Central reservation clerks can probably offer you a better rate than the rack rate, but they usually do not have the authority to negotiate anything much below the top rates. Still it's worth your time to go through the routine of questioning on all the possible discounts and package deals that interest you and any chain-wide promotional rates available.

Now, armed with these possibilities—actually these are your ceiling rates—you're ready for the real negotiations.

Call the property direct. If there's an 800 number direct to the property, fine—just make certain you are talking to someone on-site—, but even if it's a toll call, it'll probably save you much more than that small phone charge. Call during the day, but not around check-out or check-in time, and you'll have the best chance of getting someone with the authority to negotiate rates.

Once again, tell specifically what you're looking for, and ask for the lowest rate. And keep asking and exploring all the options. Be polite, but firm. This is not a conflict, it's just bargaining. The property is selling and wants to get the best price for its product which you're willing to buy, if the price is right. What you're seeking is the price point that makes both of you happy. If they won't lower the price, consider asking for an upgrade of the room or additional amenities for their asking price.

Another tack, is to figure how much you're willing to pay and then say "I was looking for something for less than (your figure)". Or even make an offer. If the demand is down, no reasonable offer will be refused.

Once you've reached the best rate you can get (meaning they are about to hang up on you) then make your reservation and get a reservation confirmation number.

And enjoy your stay!

EASTERN METROPLEX—ADDISON, DALLAS, FARMERS BRANCH, PLANO, AND RICHARDSON

ADDISON

For a double room: $ = Under $80, $$ = $80–$120, $$$ = $121–$180, $$$$ = $181–$250, $$$$$ = Over $250; Room tax 13%.

COURTYARD BY MARRIOTT
4165 Proton Drive (75244), west of Tollway, off Midway south of Belt Line • 490-7390 or 800-321-2211 • $$ (+ 13%) • W + two rooms • No smoking rooms

The 2-story Courtyard has 145 units including 11 suites ($$$) and 110 no smoking rooms. Senior, weekend, and other discounts and package plans available. Children under 18 free in room with parents. Check-in 4 p.m. Check-out noon. Inside access to rooms. Charge for local calls. Cable TV with free premium channel and pay channels. Captioned TV, visual alarms and special phones for the hearing impaired. Modem link in rooms. Outdoor pool, small exercise room. Fax and copier services available. Self-service laundry. One-day dry cleaning. Coffeemakers in rooms. Free coffee in lounge mornings. Restaurant for breakfast only (Under $10). Bar (Monday–Thursday evenings). Small meeting rooms. Free outside parking.

DALLAS MARRIOTT QUORUM
14901 Dallas Parkway (75240), Dallas North Tollway at Belt Line exit, on Tollway west access road south of Belt Line 661-2800 or 800-228-9290 • $$ (+ 13%) • W + 11 rooms No smoking rooms

This 12-story Marriott has 548 units including 15 suites ($$$$$) and 425 no-smoking rooms. Senior, weekend, and other discounts and package plans available. Children free in room with parents. Concierge floor. Check-in 3 p.m. Check-out 1 p.m. Inside access to rooms. Charge for local calls. Cable TV with free HBO and pay channels. Captioned TV, visual alarms, and special phones for the hearing impaired. In room honor bar. Modem link in rooms. Fire intercom system. Bell service. Room service. Heated indoor/outdoor pool, sauna, exercise room, two lighted tennis and two basketball courts. Free use of fitness center one block away. Business services available weekdays. Gift shop. Self-service laundry. One-day dry cleaning. Free newspaper. Free coffee in lobby mornings. Babysitting available. Restaurants serving all meals (dinner under $12 to $30). Bar. Meeting rooms. Banquet facilities for 800. Free parking in garage and outdoor. Valet parking available ($5–$9).

THE GRAND KEMPINSKI DALLAS (ADDISON)
15201 Dallas Parkway (75248), Dallas North Tollway at Belt Line exit, on Tollway west access road north of Belt Line
386-6000 or 800-426-3135 • $$$$ (+ 13%) • W + 10 rooms
No smoking rooms

The 14-story Grand Kempinski has 528 units including 32 suites ($$$$$) and 370 no smoking rooms. Senior and weekend discounts available. Children up to 17 stay free in room with parents. Concierge floor. Check-in 3 p.m. Check-out noon. Inside access to rooms. Charge for local calls. Cable TV with pay channels. Visual alarms and special phones for the hearing impaired. Modem link in rooms. Fire intercom system. Bell service. Room service. Indoor and outdoor pools, sauna, lighted tennis courts, indoor racquetball courts, health club. Business services available. Barber, beauty, gift shop and retail stores. Next day dry cleaning. Free coffee in lobby. Babysitting available. Restaurants serving all meals (dinner $12–$30). Lounge/piano bar and nightclub with dancing. Meeting rooms. Banquet facilities for 3,600. Free outside parking. Self-parking in garage($1). Valet parking ($9). A European-style hotel rated four diamonds by AAA.

HARVEY HOTEL—ADDISON
14315 Midway (75244), west of Tollway, south of Belt Line near Proton Dr. • 980-8877 or 800-922-9222 (Reservations)
$$–$$$ (+ 13%) • W + 5 rooms • No smoking rooms

The 429 units on the 4 floors of this Harvey Hotel include 18 suites ($$–$$$). Senior, weekend, and other discounts and package plans available. Children under 18 stay free in room with parents. Pets OK ($125 deposit/$100 refundable). Check–in 3 p.m. Check-out 1 p.m. Inside access to rooms. Charge for local calls. Cable TV with free premium channel and pay channels. Captioned TV for the hearing impaired. Modem link in rooms. Free coffee in lobby, room coffeemakers available. Bell service. Room service. Outdoor pool, sauna, exercise room. Guest memberships available in athletic club. Business services available. Gift shop. Self-service laundry. One-day dry cleaning. Free newspaper. Restaurants serving all meals (dinner under $12). Bar. Meeting rooms. Banquet facilities for 1,000. Outside and garage parking. Free scheduled van transportation to Prestonwood Town Center Mall and Galleria Mall and free transport to nearby restaurants available.

HOLIDAY INN EXPRESS (ADDISON)
4103 Belt Line (75244), west of Tollway and Midway
991-8888 or 800-HOLIDAY (465-4329)(Reservations)
$–$$ (+ 13%) • W + 2 rooms • No smoking rooms

The 115 rooms on the 2 floors of this Holiday Inn include 70 no smoking rooms. Senior, weekend, and other discounts and package plans available. Children 17 and under stay free in room with parents. Check-in 3 p.m. Check-out noon. Access to rooms from outside. Local phone calls free. Cable TV with HBO. Captioned TV, visual alarms and special phones for the hearing impaired. Modem link in rooms. Coffeemakers in rooms. Outdoor pool. Guest membership available in athletic club adjacent. Fax and copy service available. Self-service laundry. One-day dry cleaning. Free continental breakfast bar. Free newspaper. Charge to room privileges at nearby Humperdink's Bar and Grill. Meeting rooms. Outside parking. Free transportation within three-mile radius usually available weekdays.

HOMEWOOD SUITES HOTEL (ADDISON)
4451 Belt Line (75244), west of Tollway between Addison Rd. and Midway • 788-1342 or 800-225-5466 • $$–$$$ (+ 13%) W + 5 suites • No smoking suites

There are 120 suites in this 3-story all-suites hotel. All have a living room, bedroom (2 bedroom suites available) and fully equipped kitchen, and 97 are no smoking. AARP and AAA discounts and package plans available. Children stay free in room with parents. Pets OK ($50 charge). Check-in 3 p.m. Check-out noon. Access to 72 suites inside, to 48 suites outside. Local phone calls free. Cable TV. VCR available. Captioned TV, visual alarms and special phones for the hearing impaired. Modem link in rooms. Coffeemakers in suites. Outdoor heated pool, exercise room. Guest membership available in nearby athletic club. Business services available. Self-service laundry. One day dry cleaning. Free continental breakfast bar. Free newspaper. Social hour Monday– Thursday evenings. Restaurants nearby. Babysitting available. One meeting room. Outside parking. Free shuttle available within three mile radius. On site convenience store.

LA QUINTA INN AND SUITES DALLAS (ADDISON)
14925 Landmark Blvd. (75240), west of Tollway and south of Belt Line • 404-0004 or 800-531-5900 • $$ (+ 13%) • W + 5 rooms • No smoking rooms

This four floor La Quinta has 152 units including 8 suites and 49 no smoking rooms. Senior, weekend, and other discounts available. Children under 18 stay free in room with parents. Check-in 1 p.m. Check-out noon. Inside access to rooms. Local phone calls free. Cable TV with Showtime and pay channels. Captioned TV, visual alarms and special phones for the hearing impaired. Modem link in rooms. Coffeemakers in rooms, free coffee in lobby. Outdoor heated pool, exercise room. Self-service laundry. One day dry cleaning. Free continental breakfast. Restaurants nearby. Two meeting rooms. Outside parking.

DALLAS

For a double room: $ = Under $80, $$ = $80–$120, $$$ = $121–$180, $$$$ = $181–$250, $$$$$ = Over $250; Room tax 13%. (Note: Dallas listings include location of nearest DART Light Rail station, when appropriate)

THE ADOLPHUS
1321 Commerce Street (75202) downtown between Field and Akard (DART Light Rail AKARD Station) • 742-8200 or 800-221-9083 • $$$$–$$$$$ (+ 13%) • W + 6 rooms No smoking rooms

The 22 floors in this hotel have 431 units including 20 suites ($$$$$) and 210 no smoking rooms. Weekend discounts available. Children 11 and under stay free in room with parents. Check-in 3 p.m. Check-out 1 p.m. Inside access to rooms. Charge for local calls. Cable TV with free premium channel and pay TV. VCR available. Captioned TV, visual alarms, and special phones for the hearing impaired. In-room honor bar. Wet bar in suites. Free coffee available. Modem link in rooms. Fire intercom system. Bell service. Room service. Exercise room. Guest memberships available in nearby health club and for tennis and golf. Business services available. Gift shop, beauty shop, barber shop. Free newspaper and magazines. Restaurants serving all meals. (See also DALLAS/DINING OUT—The French Room, p. 152.) Lounge with entertainment and dancing. Meeting rooms. Banquet facilities for 800. Garage Valet parking $10. Free downtown transportation available. Afternoon tea in Grand Lobby Monday–Friday 3–5 (reservations suggested). Built in 1912 by beer baron Adolphus Busch, it still retains Old World opulence. Rated four diamonds by AAA and four stars by Mobil and one of best hotels in the United States in *Conde Nast Traveler's* magazine Readers Choice Awards. With Neiman Marcus is main sponsor of annual Children's Christmas Parade downtown.

ARISTOCRAT HOTEL OF DALLAS
1933 Main Street (75201) at Harwood, downtown (DART Light Rail ST. PAUL Station) • 741-7700 or 800-231-4235 • $$$ (+13%) • W+ 4 rooms • No smoking rooms

This 15-story hotel is a Holiday Inn. The 172 units include 72 suites ($$$) and 74 no smoking rooms. Senior and weekend discounts and package plans available. Inside access to rooms. Charge for local calls. Cable TV. Captioned TV and visual alarms for the hearing impaired. In room honor bar. Free coffee available in lobby. Modem link in rooms. Fire intercom system. Bell Service. Room service. Exercise room. Guest memberships available in health club. Copy and fax services available. One day dry cleaning. Free newspaper. Restaurant (dinner $15–$19). Bar. Thirteen meeting rooms. Banquet facilities for 240. Valet garage parking $4. Free airport transportation to Love Field. Originally built in 1925 by Conrad Hilton and the first to carry his name. Completely renovated in 1985 and again in 1994. Connected to underground pedestrian walkways that go under much of downtown (See also DALLAS/OFFBEAT, p. 132). Building listed in the National Register of Historic Places.

BEST WESTERN MARKET CENTER (DALLAS)
2023 Market Center Blvd. (75207), at I-35E (Stemmons Freeway) • $–$$$ (+13%) • 741-9000 or 800-275-7419 W+ 2 rooms • No smoking rooms

The 98 rooms in this 3-story Best Western include 47 no smoking. Senior and weekend discounts available. Children 16 and under stay free in room with parents. Check-in noon. Check-out noon. Inside and outside access to rooms. Charge for local calls. Cable TV with HBO. Captioned TV, visual alarms, and special phones for the hearing impaired. Coffeemakers in rooms. Free coffee available in lobby 6:30–9 a.m. Modem link in rooms. Fire intercom system. Bell service. Room service. Outdoor pool. Guest memberships available in health club. Business services available. Self service laundry. One day dry cleaning. Free continental breakfast. Restaurant serving all meals (dinner under $10). Bar. Meeting rooms. Banquet facilities for 80. Free outside parking.

BRISTOL SUITES HOTEL (DALLAS)
7800 Alpha Road (75240), take Coit Road Exit off I-635 (LBJ Freeway), go north to Alpha Road • 972/233-7600 or 800-922-9222 • $$$–$$$$ (+13%) • W+ 3 suites No smoking suites.

The 295 suites in this 10-story all-suites hotel include 92 no smoking. Weekend discounts and package plans available. Children 18 and under stay free in room with parents. Pets OK ($125 deposit, $100 refundable). Check-in 3 p.m. Check-out 1 p.m. Inside access to rooms. Charge for local calls. Cable TV. Visual alarms for the hearing impaired. In suite honor bar. Wet bar. Coffeemakers in suites. Modem link in Business Center. Fire intercom system. Bell service. Room service. Indoor/outdoor pool, sauna, exercise room. Business Center. Gift shop. Self-serve laundry. One day dry cleaning. Free full buffet breakfast. Restaurant serving all meals (dinner $13–$15). Bar. Fifteen meeting rooms. Banquet facilities for 280. Free garage parking. Free transportation to the Galleria and Valley View Malls.

COMFORT INN (DALLAS)
8901 R.L. Thornton Freeway (75228), take Exit 52B from I-30 East • 324-4475 • $$$ (+ 13%) • W+ 2 rooms • No smoking rooms

This 2-story inn has 42 units including 4 suites and 20 no smoking rooms. Senior, weekend, and other discounts available. Children 18 and under stay free in room with parents. Check-in 1 p.m. Check-out noon. Outside access to rooms. Free local phone calls. Cable TV. Free coffee available. Pool, sauna, exercise room. Self-service laundry. One day dry cleaning. Free continental breakfast. Free newspaper. Meeting rooms. Free outside parking.

COURTYARD BY MARRIOTT—LBJ @ JOSEY (DALLAS)
2930 Forest Lane (75234), take Josey Lane exit off I-635, then south to Forest Lane • 620-8000 or 800-321-2211 • $–$$ (+ 13%) • W+ 2 rooms

The 146 units in this 3-story Courtyard includes 12 suites ($$). Weekend and other discounts available. Children 11 and under stay free in room with parents. Check-in 3 p.m. Check-out 1 p.m. Inside access to rooms. Charge for local calls. Cable TV with HBO and pay channels. VCR available. Captioned TV, visual alarms, and special phones for the hearing impaired. Free coffee during breakfast. Outdoor pool, exercise room. Fax and copy service available. Self-service laundry. One day dry cleaning. Free newspaper. Restaurant serving breakfast only (under $10). Bar weeknights only. Two meeting rooms. Free outside parking.

DALLAS NORTHPARK COURTYARD
10325 North Central Expressway (US 75) (75231) at Meadow Road • 739-2500 or 800-321-2211 • $$ (+ 13%) • No smoking rooms

The 160 units in this 6-story Courtyard include 24 suites and 13 no smoking rooms. Children stay free in room with parents. Check-in 3 p.m. Check-out 1 p.m. Inside access to rooms. Cable TV. Free coffee available. Fire intercom system. Outdoor heated pool, exercise room. Self-service laundry. One day dry cleaning. Free newspaper. Restaurant serving breakfast only (under $10). Bar Monday–Thursday. Two meeting rooms. Free outside parking.

DALLAS NORTHPARK RESIDENCE INN (DALLAS)
10333 North Central Expressway (US 75) (75231) at Meadow Road • 450-8220 or 800-331-3131 • $$ (+ 13%)

There are 103 suites with kitchens in the 3 floors of this all-suites inn. Children stay free in room with parents. Pets OK ($50 deposit). Check-in 3 p.m. Check-out noon. Coffeemakers in rooms. Free coffee available. Cable TV. Outdoor heated pool. Sauna. Self-service laundry. One day dry cleaning. Free continental buffet breakfast. Free transportation for shopping. Free outside parking.

DOUBLETREE HOTEL AT CAMPBELL CENTRE (DALLAS)
8250 North Central Expressway (US 75) (75206) at Northwest Highway • 691-8700 or 800-222-TREE (800-222-8733)
$$ (+ 13%) • W + 8 rooms • No smoking rooms

The 302 units in this 21-story hotel include 19 suites ($$$) and 176 no smoking rooms. Senior, weekend, and other discounts and package plans available. Children 18 and under stay free in room with parents. Check-in-3 p.m. Check-out noon. Inside access to rooms. Local phone calls free. Cable TV with pay channels. Visual alarms and special phones for the hearing impaired. Coffeemakers in rooms. Free coffee available. Modem link in rooms. Bell service. Spas, exercise room, tennis court, putting green. Guest memberships available in nearby health clubs. Wine reception Monday–Thursday evenings. Free newspaper. Restaurant serving all meals (dinner $12–$30). Bar. Meeting rooms. Banquet facilities for 700. Free outside and garage parking. Diagonally across from North Park Centre Mall with free transportation to the mall. Rooms on upper floors offer view of North Dallas skyline.

DOUBLETREE HOTEL AT LINCOLN CENTRE (DALLAS)
5410 LBJ Freeway (I-635) (75075), at North Dallas Tollway 972-934-8400 • $$$ (+ 13%) • W+ 5 rooms • No smoking rooms

This 20-story hotel has 502 units that include 18 suites ($$$$–$$$$$) and 280 no smoking rooms. Senior and weekend discounts available. Children stay free in room with parents. Concierge floor. Check-in 3 p.m. Check-out noon. Inside access to rooms. Charge for local calls. Cable TV with HBO and pay channels. Captioned TV, visual alarms, and special phones for the hearing impaired. Modem link in rooms. Fire intercom system. Bell service. Room service. Outdoor pool, sauna, exercise room. Children's pool. Guest memberships available in health club. Business services available. Gift shop. Retail stores. Self-service laundry. One day dry cleaning. Free newspaper. Restaurants serving all meals (dinner $12–$30). Bar. Meeting rooms. Banquet facilities for 800. Outside parking free, garage self-parking $3, Valet parking $5. Free transportation to nearby Galleria Mall. Rated four diamonds by AAA.

EMBASSY SUITES LOVE FIELD (DALLAS)
3880 West Northwest Highway (75220), near Lemmon
357-4500 • $$$ (+ 13%) • W+ 8 rooms • No smoking rooms

The 248 suites in this 8-story all-suites hotel includes some no smoking suites. Weekend and other discounts and package plans available. Children under 18 stay free in room with parents. Check-in 3 p.m. Check-out noon. Inside access to rooms. Charge for local calls. Cable TV with free premium and pay channels. VCR available. Wet bars. Coffeemakers in rooms. Modem link in rooms. Bell service. Room service. Indoor heated pool, sauna, exercise room. Gift shop. Self-service laundry. One day dry cleaning. Free full breakfast. Free evening cocktails. Free newspaper. Restaurant serving lunch and dinner (dinner $9–$15). Lounge with entertainment. Meeting rooms. Banquet facilities for 200. Free outside parking. Free airport transportation to Love Field.

EMBASSY SUITES HOTEL-DALLAS MARKET CENTER (DALLAS)
2727 Stemmons Freeway (I-35E)(75207), take Inwood Road exit then West side access road • 630-5332 or 800-EMBASSY (800-362-2779) • $$$ (+ 13%) • W+ 4 rooms
No smoking rooms

The 240 suites in this 9-story all-suites hotel include 214 that are no smoking. Senior and other discounts available. Children under 12 stay free in room with parents. Check-in 3 p.m. Check-out noon. Inside access to rooms. Charge for local calls. Cable TV with HBO and pay channels. Captioned TV, visual alarms, and special phones for the hearing impaired. Wet bars. Coffeemakers in rooms. Modem link in rooms. Bell service. Room service. Indoor heated pool, sauna, exercise room. Fax and copy service available. Gift shop. Self-service laundry. One day dry cleaning. Free full breakfast. Free evening cocktails. Free newspaper. Restaurant serving lunch and dinner (dinner under $14). Bar. Seven meeting rooms. Banquet facilities for 250. Free outside parking. Free airport transportation to Love Field and within five-mile radius.

THE FAIRMONT HOTEL (DALLAS)
1717 North Akard Street (75201), at Ross in the Arts District (DART Light Rail AKARD Station) • 720-2020 or 800-527-4727
$$$$ (+ 13%) • W + 8 rooms • No smoking rooms

There are 550 units in this 24-story hotel including 51 suites ($$$$$) and 400 no smoking rooms. Senior and weekend discounts available. Children 16 and under stay free in room with parents. Check-in 3 p.m. Check-out 1 p.m. Inside access to rooms. Charge for local calls. Cable TV with pay channels. VCR available. Captioned TV, visual alarms, and special phones for the hearing impaired. Modem link in rooms. Fire intercom system. Bell service. Room service. Outdoor heated Olympic-sized pool. Guest memberships available in health club. Business services available. Barber, beauty and retail shops. Free newspaper. Restaurants serving all meals (dinner $12 to over $30). (See also DALLAS/DINING OUT—The Pyramid Room, p. 159.) Lounge with entertainment and dancing. Twenty-four meeting rooms. Banquet facilities for 2,000. Garage valet parking $12. Connected to underground pedestrian walkways that go under much of downtown (See also DALLAS/OFFBEAT, p. 132).

HOLIDAY INN SELECT—LBJ NE (DALLAS)
11350 LBJ Freeway (I-635) (75238), at Exit 13 (Jupiter/Kingsley) • 341-5400 or 800-346-0660
$-$$ (+ 13%) • W + 2 rooms

This 5-story inn has 244 rooms and 2 suites ($$$$). Package plans available. Children under 10 stay free in room with parents. Concierge floor. Check-in 3 p.m. Check-out noon. Inside and outside access to rooms. Local phone calls free. Cable TV with HBO and pay channels. Captioned TV and visual alarms for the hearing impaired. Coffeemakers in rooms. Free coffee available. Modem link in rooms. Room service. Outdoor pool, sauna, exercise room. Business services available. Gift shop. Self-service laundry. One day dry cleaning. Free newspaper. Restaurant serving all meals (dinner under $12). Lounge with entertainment. Ten meeting rooms. Banquet facilities for 350. Free outside parking. Free transportation within seven mile radius.

HOLIDAY INN SELECT—MOCKINGBIRD LANE (DALLAS)
1241 West Mockingbird Lane (75247), at I-35E • 630-7000 or 800-442-7547 • $$–$$$ (+ 13%) • W+ 2 rooms.
No smoking rooms

This 13-story inn has 339 units including 7 suites ($$$–$$$$$) and 211 no smoking rooms. Senior, weekend, and other discounts and package plans available. Children 18 and under stay free in room with parents. Concierge floor. Check-in 3 p.m. Check-out noon. Inside access to rooms. Local phone calls free. Cable TV with HBO and pay channels. Visual alarms and special phones for the hearing impaired. Wet bar. Coffeemakers in rooms. Modem link in rooms. Fire intercom system. Bell service. Room service. Outdoor pool, exercise room. Business services available. Gift shop. Self-service laundry. One day dry cleaning. Free newspaper. Restaurant serving all meals (dinner $12–$30). Bar. Meeting rooms. Banquet facilities for 700. Free outside and garage parking. Free airport transportation to Love Field.

HOTEL ST. GERMAIN (DALLAS)
2516 Maple Street (75201), near Cedar Springs Road
871-2516 • $$$$$ (+ 13%)

There are only seven suites on the three floors of this European style luxury hotel. Check-in 4 p.m. Check-out noon. Inside access to rooms. Charge for local calls. Cable TV with HBO and VCR. Modem link in rooms. Bell service. Room service. Guest memberships available for health club. Business services available. One day dry cleaning. Free continental breakfast. Free cocktails. Free newspaper. The reservations only gourmet restaurant serves French/New Orleans cuisine dinner Thursday–Saturday (*a la carte* over $30, *prix fixe* dinner $65). Meeting rooms. Free valet parking. Elegant Victorian home built in 1906. Each suite decorated in antiques reminiscent of a French chateaux. Rated four diamonds by AAA and four stars by Mobil.

HYATT REGENCY DALLAS
300 Reunion Blvd. (75207), downtown (DART Light Rail UNION Station) • 651-1234 or 800-233-1234
$$–$$$$(+ 13%) • W + 27 rooms • No smoking rooms

This downtown landmark hotel has 939 units on its 28 floors that include 25 suites ($$$$$) and 585 no smoking rooms. Senior, weekend, and other discounts and package plans available. Children 12 and under stay free in room with parents. Concierge floor. Check-in 3 p.m. Check-out noon. Inside access to rooms. Charge for local calls. Cable TV with HBO and pay channels. Captioned TV, visual alarms, special phones for the hearing impaired. In-room honor bar. Coffeemakers in most rooms. Modem link in rooms. Bell service. Room service. Outdoor heated pool, sauna, exercise room, tennis. Guest memberships available in health club and for golf. Business services available. Gift shop. One day dry cleaning. Restaurants serving all meals (dinner $12–$30). (See also DALLAS/DINING OUT—Antares, p. 147.) Lounge with dancing. Thirty-nine meeting rooms. Banquet facilities for 3,000. Garage valet parking $8. Excellent view of city from upper floor rooms. Includes 50-story Reunion Tower. (See also DALLAS/ BIRD'S EYE VIEW, p. 78.) Rated four diamonds by AAA.

LE MERIDIEN DALLAS
650 North Pearl Street (75201), in Arts District
(DART Light Rail PEARL Station) • 979-9000 • $$–$$$
+ 13%) W + 5 rooms • No smoking rooms

The 396 units in this 13-story hotel include some suites ($$$$–$$$$$) and 220 no smoking rooms. Weekend discounts and package plans available. Concierge floor. Check-in 3 p.m. Check-out noon. Inside access to rooms. Charge for local calls. Cable TV with pay channels. Bell service. Room service. Sauna, exercise room, ice rink. Business services available. Beauty shop and retail shops. One day dry cleaning. Free continental breakfast. Free newspaper. Restaurant serving all meals (dinner $12–$30). Bar. Outside and garage valet parking. Free transportation within three mile radius.

MANSION ON TURTLE CREEK (DALLAS)
2821 Turtle Creek Blvd. (75219) • 559-2100 or 800-527-5432
$$$$$ (+13%) • W+ one room • No smoking rooms

Once the hilltop mansion of a cattle baron, it is the only hotel in Texas to earn the highest five diamond rating by AAA and five star rating by Mobil. It is also cited as one of best hotels in the United States in *Conde Nast Traveler's* magazine Readers Choice Awards. The 9-story hotel has 141 units, which include 15 suites and 64 no smoking rooms. Weekend discounts and package plans are available. Children aged 14 and under stay free in room with parents. Small pets OK ($50 fee). Check-in 3 p.m., Check-out noon. Inside access to rooms. Charge for local calls. Cable TV with premium channel and pay channels. VCR available. Captioned TV, visual alarms and special phones for the hearing impaired. Modem link in rooms. Fire intercom system. Bell service. Room service. Outdoor heated pool, sauna, health club. Guest memberships for tennis and golf available. Business services available. Gift shop. One day dry cleaning. Babysitting available. Restaurants serving all meals (dinner $30–$50). (See also DALLAS/DINING OUT-Mansion on Turtle Creek, p. 155.) Lounge with entertainment and dancing. Seven meeting rooms. Banquet facilities for 150. Valet parking ($12 day). Epitome of luxury and service with spacious, comfortable rooms that have French doors, deep carpets, and furnishing that make you feel as if you're in your own living room.

MELROSE HOTEL (DALLAS)
3015 Oak Lawn Avenue (75219), at Cedar Springs Road
521-5151 or 800-635-7673 (Reservations) • $$$–$$$$ (+ 13%)
W+ 6 rooms • No smoking rooms

There are 21 suites ($$$$–$$$$$) and 108 no smoking rooms among the 184 units in this 8-story hotel. Weekend discounts and package plans available. Children 17 and under stay free in room with parents. Concierge floor. Check-in 3 p.m. Check-out noon. Inside access to rooms. Charge for local calls. Cable TV with free premium channel and pay channels. VCR available. Visual alarms for the hearing impaired. Wet bars in suites. Coffeemakers for rooms available. Free coffee in lobby weekday mornings. Modem link in rooms. Bell service. Room service. Guest memberships available in nearby health club. Gift shop. One day dry cleaning. Free newspaper. Restaurant serving all meals (dinner $12–$30). (See also DALLAS/DINING OUT-The Landmark, p. 154.) Bar. Five meeting rooms. Banquet facilities for 250. Free outdoor parking. Free transportation within three-mile radius.

RADISSON HOTEL AND SUITES (DALLAS)
2330 West Northwest Highway (75220), at I-35E
351-4477 or 800-254-8744 • $$–$$$(+ 13%)
W + 2 rooms • No smoking rooms

This 8-story hotel has 198 units including 31 suites ($$$) and 95 no smoking rooms. Senior, weekend, and other discounts and package plans available. Children 12 and under stay free in room with parents. Small pets OK ($50 deposit). Check-in 3 p.m. Check-out noon. Inside access to rooms, outside access to suites. Cable TV with free premium channel and pay channels. Captioned TV and visual alarms for the hearing impaired. Free coffee in lobby. Modem link in rooms. Fire intercom system. Bell service. Room service. Outdoor pool, exercise room. Guest memberships available in health club. Self-service laundry. One day dry cleaning. Free newspaper. Restaurant serving all meals (dinner $9–$19). Lounge. Eight meeting rooms. Banquet facilities for 400. Outside parking. Free airport transportation.

RESIDENCE INN—NORTH CENTRAL (DALLAS)
13636 Goldmark Drive (75240), US75 at Midpark Road
669-0478 or 800-331-3131 • $$–$$$(+ 13%)
No smoking suites

This 2-story all-suites inn has 70 suites with kitchens of which 45 are no smoking suites. Senior, weekend, and other discounts available. Children stay free in room with parents. Pets OK ($100 deposit). Check-in 3 p.m. Check-out noon. Inside access to rooms. Charge for local calls. Cable TV with free premium channel. VCR available. Coffeemakers in rooms. Modem link in rooms. Outdoor heated pool. Business services available. Self-service laundry. One day dry cleaning. Free continental breakfast. Free newspaper. Restaurant serving dinner. Free outside parking.

RENAISSANCE DALLAS HOTEL
2222 Stemmons Freeway (I-35E)(75207), near Market Center
631-2222 or 800-892-2233 (in Texas), 800-468-3571 (Outside Texas) • $$$–$$$$ (+ 13%) • W + 6 rooms • No smoking rooms
This 30-story hotel has 540 units including 30 suites ($$$$) and 350 no smoking rooms. Senior discount available. Children 18 and under stay free in room with parents. Concierge floor. Small pets OK. Check-in 3 p.m. Check-out noon. Inside access to rooms. Charge for local calls. Cable TV with HBO and Disney and pay channels. VCR available. Captioned TV, visual alarms, and special phones for the hearing impaired. In-room honor bar. Coffeemakers in rooms. Fire intercom system. Bell service. Room service. Outdoor heated pool, sauna, exercise room. Guest memberships available for nearby health club. Business services available. Gift shop. One day dry cleaning. Free newspaper. Babysitting services available. Restaurant serving all meals (dinner $12–$30). Bar. Twelve meeting rooms. Banquet facilities for 400. Free outside parking. The pink granite, elliptically shaped hotel is home of what is reportedly "the world's longest chandelier," with 7,500 Italian crystals following the winding marble and brass staircase up four floors. Excellent view from upper floor rooms. Rated four diamonds by AAA.

STEMMONS TRAIL COURTYARD (DALLAS)
2883 Stemmons Trail (75220), two blocks east of I-35E
352-7676 or 800-231-2211 • $$ • W + 2 rooms
No smoking rooms
This 3-story Courtyard by Marriott has 146 units of which 12 are suites ($$) and 20% are no smoking. Senior discount available. Check-in 3 p.m. check-out noon. Inside access to rooms. Charge for local calls. Cable TV. Captioned TV, visual alarms, and special phones for the hearing impaired. Free coffee available. Modem link in rooms. Fire intercom system. Outdoor pool,

exercise room. Self-service laundry. One day dry cleaning. Free outside parking.

STONELEIGH HOTEL (DALLAS)
2927 Maple Avenue (75201), take Oaklawn exit off I-35E to Maple, then right about a mile • 871-7111 • $$$–$$$$$
W + 3 rooms • No smoking rooms

The 11-story Stoneleigh has 153 units of which 18 are suites ($$$$–$$$$$) and 18 are no smoking. Package plans available. Children stay free in room with parents. Concierge floor. Pets OK. Check-in 3 p.m. Check-out noon. Inside access to rooms. Charge for local calls. Cable TV with pay channels. VCR available. Captioned TV for the hearing impaired. Free coffee in lobby. Modem link in rooms. Bell service. Room service. Outdoor pool. Guest memberships available in health club. One day dry cleaning. Babysitting available. Restaurant serving all meals (dinner $25–$30). Bar. Nine meeting rooms. Banquet facilities for 140. Free outdoor and garage parking. Free valet parking available. Free airport transportation.

WESTIN HOTEL (DALLAS)
13340 Dallas Parkway (75240), just north of I-635 in the Galleria Mall • 934-9494 or 800-228-3000 • $$$$ (+ 13%)
W + 8 rooms • No smoking rooms

This 20-story hotel has 431 units that include 13 suites ($$$$$) and some no smoking rooms. Weekend discounts available. Children 18 and under stay free in room with parents. Concierge floor. Pets OK. Check-in 3 p.m. Check-out 1 p.m. Inside access to rooms. Cable TV with HBO and pay channels. VCR available. Captioned TV, visual alarms, and special phones for the hearing impaired. In-room honor bar. Coffeemakers in rooms. Modem link in rooms. Fire intercom system. Bell service. Room service. Guest memberships available in health club. Business services available. One day dry cleaning. Free newspaper. Restaurants serving all meals (dinner $12–$30). Bar. Twenty meeting rooms. Banquet facilities for 1,300. Free outside and covered mall parking, valet parking $12. Built into west side of the Galleria Mall which has more than 200 shops, restaurants, a movie theater and ice skating rink. Rated four diamonds by AAA.

WYNDHAM ANATOLE HOTEL (DALLAS)
2201 Stemmons Freeway (I-35E) (75207), across I-35E from Dallas Market Center • 748-1200 or 800-WYNDHAM (800-996-3426) • $$$–$$$$ (+ 13%) • W+ 5% of rooms No smoking rooms

The complex of wings and towers that range from 10 to 27 floors of this hotel include 1620 units of which 129 are suites ($$$$$) and 40% are no smoking rooms. Senior, weekend, and other discounts and package plans available. Concierge floor. Check-in 4 p.m. Check-out noon. Inside access to rooms. Charge for local calls. Cable TV with free premium channel and pay channels. Captioned TV, visual alarms, and special phones for the hearing impaired. In-room honor bar. Coffeemakers in rooms. Modem link in rooms. Fire intercom system. Bell service. Room service. Two indoor, one outdoor pools; sauna, exercise room, tennis, health club. Business services available. Beauty, barber, and retail shops. One day dry cleaning. Free newspaper. Playground. Babysitting available. Restaurants serving all meals (dinner $12–$30). Bars/lounge with entertainment and dancing. Fifty-eight meeting rooms. Banquet facilities for 2,600. Free outdoor parking, valet parking $7. Spread over 45 acres, it calls itself a village within the city. Excellent view from upper floors. (See also DALLAS/BIRD'S EYE VIEW—Nana Grill, p.79.) Self-guided tour brochure for museum quality art collection scattered throughout hotel that includes the world's largest piece of Wedgewood china and one of the largest private jade collections in the country.

FARMERS BRANCH

For a double room: $ = Under $80, $$ = $80–$120, $$$ = $121–$180, $$$$ = $181–$250, $$$$$ = Over $250; Room tax 12%.

DALLAS MEDALLION (FARMERS BRANCH)
4099 Valley View Lane (Dallas 75244) • 385-9000 or 800-808-1011 (Reservations) • $$$–$$$$ (+12%) W + 7 rooms • No smoking rooms

This 10-story hotel has 289 units that include 7 suites ($$$$) and some no smoking rooms. Weekend discount available. Children under 12 stay free in room with parents. Concierge floor. Pets under 15 pounds OK (large deposit). Check-in 3 p.m. Check-out noon. Inside access to rooms. Charge for local calls. Cable TV with HBO and pay channels. Visual alarms for the hearing impaired. Modem link in rooms. Fire intercom system. Bell service. Room service. Outdoor pool, exercise room. Two mile jogging track next door. Business services available. One day dry cleaning. Restaurant serving all meals (dinner under $12) including deli lunch buffet and Friday seafood buffet. Bar. Meeting rooms. Banquet facilities for 900. Free outside parking.

DALLAS PARKWAY HILTON (FARMERS BRANCH)
4801 LBJ Freeway (Dallas 75244-6002) • 661-3600 • $$–$$$ (+12%) • W + 5 rooms • No smoking rooms

The 310 units in this 15-story hotel include 14 suites ($$$) and 217 no smoking rooms. Senior, weekend, and other discounts and package plans available. Children 17 and under stay free in room with parents. Check-in 3 p.m. Check-out 1 p.m. Inside access to rooms. Charge for local calls. Cable TV with free premium channel. VCR available with advance notice. Captioned TV, visual alarms and special phones for the hearing impaired. Free coffee in lobby in morning. Coffeemakers in suites. Modem link in rooms. Bell service. Room service. Indoor/outdoor heated pool, sauna, exercise room. Guest memberships available in nearby health club. Business services available weekdays. Gift shop. One day dry cleaning. Free newspaper. Restaurant serving all meals (dinner $12–$30). Bar. Meeting rooms. Banquet facilities for 250. Free outside parking. Free transportation within five miles. Located across from the Galleria Mall.

HOLIDAY INN SELECT NORTH DALLAS (FARMERS BRANCH)
2645 LBJ Freeway (Dallas 75234) • 243-3363 or 800-HOLIDAY (800-465-4329) • $$ (+12%) • W+ 4 rooms
No smoking rooms

This 6-story Holiday Inn has 374 units including seven suites and 274 no smoking rooms. Children 18 and under stay free in room with parents. Concierge floor. Check-in 3 p.m. Check-out noon. Inside access to rooms. Local phone calls free. Cable TV with HBO and pay channels. Visual alarms and special phones for hearing impaired. Coffeemakers in rooms. Modem link in rooms. Fire intercom system. Bell service. Room service. Indoor/outdoor heated pool, exercise room. Business services available weekdays. Retail stores. Self-service laundry. One day dry cleaning. Free newspaper. Restaurants serving all meals (dinner under $12). Children under 12 eat free. Lounge with DJ and dancing. Meeting rooms. Banquet facilities for 320. Free outside parking.

OMNI DALLAS AT PARK WEST (FARMERS BRANCH)
1590 LBJ Freeway (Dallas 75234) • 869-4300 or 800-460-8732 $–$$$ (+12%) • W+ 4 rooms • No smoking rooms

This 12-story Omni has 338 units that include 18 suites ($$–$$$) and 70 no smoking rooms. Senior, weekend, and other discounts and package plans available. Concierge floor. Check-in 3 p.m. Check-out noon. Inside access to rooms. Charge for local calls. Cable TV with pay channels. VCR available. Captioned TV, visual alarms and special phones for the hearing impaired. Coffeemakers in rooms. Modem link in rooms. Fire intercom system. Bell service. Room service. Outdoor heated pool, sauna, exercise room, jogging track. Membership available in hotel health club. Business services available. Gift shop. One day dry cleaning. Free newspaper. Restaurant serving all meals (dinner $12–$30). Bar. Meeting rooms. Banquet facilities for 480. Free D/FW airport transportation. Valet garage parking ($3). Located on shore of 125-acre lake.

PLANO

For a double room: $ = Under $80, $$ = $80–$120, $$$ = $121–$180, $$$$ = $181–$250, $$$$$ = Over $250; Room tax 13%.

THE CARPENTER HOUSE BED & BREAKFAST
1211 East 16th Street (75074) • 424-1889 • $–$$ (+13%)
This two-story historic home has three upstairs bedrooms. Check-in 5 p.m. Check-out noon. Breakfast included. Brunch available.

COURTYARD BY MARRIOTT
4901 West Plano Parkway at Preston Road (75093) • 867-8000 or 800-321-2211 (Reservations) • $$ (+13%) • W+ two rooms No smoking rooms
This 3-story Courtyard has 149 units including 12 suites ($$$) and 123 no smoking rooms. Senior and other discounts available. Children 17 and under stay free in room with parents. Check-in 3 p.m. Check-out 1 p.m. Inside access to rooms. Charge for local calls. Cable TV with HBO and pay channels. Visual alarms for the hearing impaired and special phone available at front desk. Modem link in rooms. Fire intercom system. Heated outdoor pool, exercise room. Guest memberships available in nearby sports club. Fax and copy services. Self-service laundry. One day dry cleaning. Coffee in lobby, special hot water dispenser for coffee in rooms. Restaurant for breakfast only (Under $10.) Free newspaper. Bar (weekday evenings). Two meeting rooms. Free outside parking.

HAMPTON INN
4905 Old Shepard Place (75093), off Preston Road north of Plano Parkway • 519-1000 or 800-HAMPTON (800-428-7866) $ (+13%) • W+ seven rooms • No smoking rooms
Eighty percent of the 131 rooms in this 5-story inn are no smoking. Senior, weekend, and other discounts available. Children under 18 stay free in room with parents. Check-in 2 p.m. Check-out noon. Inside access to rooms. Local phone calls free.

Cable TV with HBO and Disney channels and pay channels. Captioned TV, visual alarms, and special phones for the hearing impaired. Coffeemakers in rooms and free coffee in lobby. Modem link in rooms. Fire intercom system. Outdoor pool, exercise room. Fax and copy services. One day dry cleaning. Free continental breakfast. Free social hour Tuesday–Wednesday evenings. Free newspaper. One meeting room. Free shuttle transportation within five miles. Free outside parking.

HARVEY HOTEL (PLANO)
1600 North Central Expressway (US75), exit 29 (15th street)
578-8555 or 800-922-9222 • $$–$$$ (+13%) • W+ three rooms
No smoking rooms

This 3-story hotel has 279 units including 12 suites ($$$) and 186 no smoking rooms. Senior, weekend, and other discounts and package plans available. Children 18 and under stay free in room with parents. Small pets OK ($125 deposit). Check-in 3 p.m. Check-out 1 p.m. Inside access to rooms. Charge for local calls. Cable TV with pay channels. VCR available. Captioned TV, visual alarms and special phones for the hearing impaired. Coffeemakers available on request, free coffee in lobby. Modem link in rooms. Bell service. Room service. Outdoor pool, exercise room. Fax, copy, and printing services available. Gift shop. Self-service laundry. One day dry cleaning. Free newspaper. Restaurant serving all meals (Dinner under $12). Bar. Meeting rooms. Banquet facilities for 700. Free outside parking.

RICHARDSON

For a double room: $ = Under $80, $$ = $80–$120, $$$ = $121–$180, $$$$ = $181–$250, $$$$$ = Over $250; Room tax 13%.

CLARION HOTEL
1981 North Central Expressway (75080), US75 at Campbell
Road, exit 26 • 644-4000 or 800-285-3434 (Reservations)
$$–$$$ (+13%) • W+ 2 rooms • No smoking rooms

The 300 units in this 12-story hotel include two suites ($$$$$) and 183 no smoking rooms. Weekend discounts available. Children 18 and under stay free in room with parents. Pets OK (deposit). Check-in 3 p.m. Check-out 1 p.m. Inside access to rooms. Charge for local calls. Cable TV with free premium channel and pay channels. Coffeemakers in rooms. Free coffee in lobby. Bell service. Room service. Indoor/outdoor heated pool, sauna. Guest memberships available in nearby health club. Business services available. Gift shop. Self-service laundry. One day dry cleaning. Free continental breakfast. Free newspaper. Restaurant serving all meals (dinner $12–$30). Lounge. Free outside parking. Free transportation within five-mile radius.

HAMPTON INN (RICHARDSON)
1577 Gateway Blvd. (75080), from exit 26 Campbell Road off US75, go West to Gateway • 234-5400 or 800-426-7866 • $ (+13%) • W + 5 rooms • No smoking rooms

This 4-story inn's 130 units include one suite ($$) and 98 no smoking rooms. Senior and weekend discounts available. Children 18 and under stay free in room with parents. Check-in 2 p.m. Check-out noon. Inside access to rooms. Local phone calls free. Cable TV with HBO and Disney and pay channels. Free coffee in lobby. Modem link in rooms. Outdoor pool. Guest memberships available in nearby health club. Free local fax. One day dry cleaning. Free continental breakfast. Free newspaper. Free outside parking.

HAWTHORN SUITES HOTEL (RICHARDSON)
250 Municipal Drive (75080), from US75 exit 26, Campbell Road, take South access road to Municipal Drive • 669-1000 or 800-527-1133 • $$$–$$$$ (+13%) • W + 2 rooms No smoking rooms

All 72 units in this 2-story hotel are suites with kitchens and 36 of them no smoking rooms. Senior and weekend discounts and package plans available. Pets OK ($50 deposit). Check-in 2 p.m. Check-out noon. Outside access to suites. Charge for local calls. Cable TV with HBO. Coffeemakers in rooms. Modem link in rooms. Room service. Outdoor pool. Guest memberships available in nearby gym. Fax and copy service available. Self-service laundry. Free breakfast buffet. Free cocktails. Free newspaper. One small meeting room. Free outside parking.

OMNI RICHARDSON HOTEL
701 East Campbell Road (75081), east off US 75 exit 26
231-9600 or 800-THE-OMNI (800-843-6664) • $$–$$$
(+13%) • W+ 5 rooms • No smoking rooms

This 17-story Omni has 342 units of which 10 are suites ($$$–$$$$) and 294 are no smoking. Senior, weekend, and other discounts available. Children free in room with parents. Concierge floor. Check-in 3 p.m. Check-out noon. Inside access to rooms. Charge for local calls. Cable TV with free premium channel and pay channels. Modem link in rooms. Fire intercom system. Bell service. Room service. Outdoor heated pool, sauna, exercise room. Guest memberships available in health club and for golf. Gift shop. Restaurant serving all meals (dinner $12–$30). Lounge with CD Jukebox and dancing. Meeting rooms. Banquet facilities for 500. Free outside parking.

MID-CITIES—ARLINGTON, GRAND PRAIRIE, GRAPEVINE (D/FW AIRPORT), IRVING

ARLINGTON

For a double room: $ = Under $80, $$ = $80–$120, $$$ = $121–$180, $$$$ = $181–$250, $$$$$ = Over $250; Room tax 13%.

ARLINGTON COURTYARD BY MARRIOTT
1500 Nolan Ryan Expressway (76011), south of I-30 • 277-2774
or 800-321-2211 • $$ (+13%) • W+ 8 rooms • No smoking rooms

This 3-story Courtyard's 147 units include 14 suites ($$–$$$) and 120 no smoking rooms. Senior, weekend, and other discounts and package plans available. Children 12 and under stay free in room with parents. Check-in 4 p.m. Check-out noon. Inside access to rooms. Charge for local calls. Cable TV with HBO and pay channels. Visual alarms and special phones for the hearing impaired. Indoor/outdoor pool and exercise room. Fax and copying service. Self-service laundry. One day dry cleaning. Special hot water dispenser for coffee in room. Free newspaper. Restaurant for breakfast only (under $10). Bar (weekday evenings). Two meeting rooms. Free outside parking.

ARLINGTON HILTON
2401 East Lamar Blvd. (76006), north of I-30 • 640-3322 or 800-527-9332 • $$–$$$ (+13%) • W+ 3 rooms
No smoking rooms

Among the 310 units in this 16-story Hilton are 26 suites ($$$–$$$$) and 260 no smoking rooms. Senior and other discounts available. Children under 17 stay free in room with parents. Concierge floor. Check-in 3 p.m. Check-out noon. Inside access to rooms. Charge for local calls. Cable TV with HBO and pay channels. VCR available. Captioned TV and visual alarms for the hearing impaired. Free coffee in lobby in morning. Modem link in rooms. Bell service. Room service. Indoor/outdoor heated pool, sauna, and exercise room. Fax and copy services available. Gift shop. Self-service laundry. One day dry cleaning. Free newspaper. Restaurant serving all meals (Dinner $12–$30). Lounge with DJ for dancing. Sixteen meeting rooms. Banquet facilities for 600. Free outside parking.

ARLINGTON HOLIDAY INN
1507 North Watson Road (76006), take Hwy. 360 north to Avenue K/Brown Blvd., then west • $–$$ (+13%) • W+ 2 rooms • No smoking rooms

This 5-story inn has 237 rooms of which 100 are no smoking. Senior discount available. Children under 18 stay free in room with parents. Check-in 3 p.m. Check-out noon. Inside and some outside access to rooms. Charge for local calls. Cable TV with free premium and pay channels. VCR available. Captioned TV, visual alarms, and special phones for the hearing impaired. Coffeemakers in rooms. Modem link in rooms. Bell service. Room service. Indoor/outdoor heated pool, sauna, exercise room. Fax and copy service. Self-service laundry. One day dry cleaning. Restaurant serving all meals (Dinner $12-$30). Lounge with entertainment and dancing Thursday–Saturday. Six meeting rooms and banquet facilities. Free outside parking.

ARLINGTON MARRIOTT
1500 Convention Center Drive (76011), south of I-30
261-8200 or 800-442-7275 • $$–$$$ (+13%) • W + 20 rooms
No smoking rooms
The 18-story Marriott has 310 units including some suites and 150 no smoking rooms. Weekend discounts and package plans available. Children under 12 stay free in room with parents. Concierge floor. Check-in 3 p.m. Check-out noon. Inside access to rooms. Charge for local calls. Cable TV with free premium channel and pay channels. Captioned TV, visual alarms, and special phones for the hearing impaired. Wet bars in some rooms. Free coffee available. Modem link in rooms. Fire intercom system. Bell service. Room service. Outdoor pool, exercise room. Guest memberships available for golf and fitness center. Business services available. Gift shop. Self-service laundry. One day dry cleaning. Free newspaper. Restaurant serving all meals (Dinner $12–$30). Bar. Fourteen meeting rooms. Banquet facilities for 500. Free outside parking or valet parking ($5).

FAIRFIELD INN BY MARRIOTT (ARLINGTON)
2500 East Lamar Blvd. (76006), north of I-30 • 649-5800 or
800-228-2800 • $ (+13%) • W + 5 rooms • No smoking rooms
The 109 rooms in this 3-story inn include 80 no smoking rooms. Senior discount available. Children stay free in room with parents. Inside access to rooms. Local phone calls free. Cable TV with HBO. Special phones for the hearing impaired. Coffee in

lobby 24 hours. Modem link in rooms. Fire intercom system. Outdoor pool. Fax service available. One day dry cleaning. Free continental breakfast. Free outside parking.

THE SANFORD HOUSE BED AND BREAKFAST (ARLINGTON)
506 North Center (76011) at Sanford, south of I-30, in downtown • 861-2129 • $$$ • W+ one room

This two-story B&B has seven rooms, all with private baths. Check-in 2 p.m., Check-out noon. Inside access to room. Local phone calls free. Two rooms with cable TV, TV in parlor. Free coffee in dining room. Free full breakfast. Large yard with pool. No children. Antique furnishings. Free outside parking. House designed and built to be a B&B.

RADISSON SUITE HOTEL (ARLINGTON)
700 Avenue H East (76011), northeast of intersection of I-30 and Hwy. 360 • 640-0440 or 800-333-3333 • $$–$$$ (+13%) W+ 5 rooms • No smoking rooms

This 7-story all-suite hotel has 203 suites of which 150 are no smoking. Senior discount and package plans available. Children under 18 stay free in room with parents. Check-in 3 p.m. Check-out noon. Inside access to rooms. Charge for local calls. Cable TV with free premium and pay channels. Captioned TV, visual alarms, and special phones for the hearing impaired. Wet bars. Bell service. Room service. Indoor pool and sauna. Guest memberships in health club available. Business services available. Gift shop, beauty and barber shops. One day dry cleaning. Free breakfast. Free cocktails. Free newspaper. Children's programs. Restaurant serving all meals (Dinner $12–$30). Lounge with dancing. Five meeting rooms and banquet facilities. Free outside parking. Free transportation within a five mile radius.

GRAND PRAIRIE

For a double room: $ = Under $80, $$ = $80–$120, $$$ = $121–$180, $$$$ = $181–$250, $$$$$ = Over $250; Room tax 13%.

HAMPTON INN DFW AIRPORT
2050 North Hwy. 360 (75050), exit east at Carrier Parkway
988-8989 or 800-HAMPTON (800-426-7866) • $ (+13%)• W +
2 rooms • No smoking rooms

Seventy-five percent of the 140 rooms in this 4-story inn are no smoking. Senior and weekend discounts available. Children under 18 stay free in room with parents. Pets OK. Check-in 3 p.m. Check-out noon. Inside access to rooms. Local phone calls free. Cable TV with free movies. Visual alarms for the hearing impaired. Free coffee in lobby. Modem link in rooms. Fire intercom system. Outdoor pool, exercise room. Public golf course nearby. Fax and copy service available. Self-service laundry. One day dry cleaning. Free continental breakfast. Free newspaper in lobby weekdays. Restaurant adjacent (dinner under $12). Free outside parking. Free transportation to and from D/FW Airport and area restaurants within five-mile radius.

LA QUINTA INN
1410 Northwest 19th Street (75050), at I-30 • 641-3021 or
800-531-5900 • $ (+13%)• W + 2 rooms • No smoking rooms

This 2-story La Quinta has 122 units that include 2 suites ($) and 70% no smoking rooms. Senior, weekend, and other discounts available. Children under 18 stay free in room with parents. Pets OK. Check-in 2 p.m. Check-out noon. Outside access to rooms. Local phone calls free. Cable TV with Showtime and the Disney channels and pay channels. Captioned TV for the hearing impaired. Free coffee in lobby. Modem link in rooms. Outdoor pool. Fax service available. One day dry cleaning. Free continental breakfast. Restaurant adjacent (dinner under $12). Free outside parking.

HOMEGATE STUDIOS & SUITES (GRAND PRAIRIE)
1108 North Hwy. 360 (75050), at Avenue J • 975-0000
$ (+13%) • W + 7 rooms • No smoking rooms (Extended stays only. Three night minimum)

Each of the 139 rooms in this 3-story property comes with a kitchenette, and 50 are no smoking rooms. Children stay free in room with parents. Check-in 11 a.m. Check-out 11 a.m. Outside access to rooms. Local phone calls free. Cable TV with pay channels. Coffeemakers in rooms. Modem link in rooms. Exercise room. Fax and copy service available. Self-service laundry. One day dry cleaning. Free outside parking. Managed by Wyndham Hotels.

GRAPEVINE (D/FW AIRPORT)

For a double room: $ = Under $80, $$ = $80–$120, $$$ = $121–$180, $$$$ = $181–$250, $$$$$ = Over $250; Room tax 12%.

DFW LAKES HILTON
1800 Hwy. 26E, 76051, 2.5 miles north of D/FW Airport
481-8444 or 800-445-8667 or 800-645-1019 (Reservations)
$–$$$ (+12%) • W + 8 rooms • No smoking rooms

This 9-story Hilton's 395 units include 11 suites ($$$$–$$$$$) and 317 no-smoking rooms. Senior and weekend discounts and package plans available. Children free in room with parents. Concierge floor Sunday–Thursday. Check-in 3 p.m. Check-out noon. Inside access to rooms. Charge for local calls. Cable TV with free HBO and pay channels. In-room honor bar. Coffeemakers in rooms. Modem link in rooms. Bell service. Room service. Heated indoor and outdoor pools, sauna, exercise room, indoor and outdoor tennis courts, racquetball. Private stocked lake. Business services available. Gift shop. One-day dry cleaning. Free newspaper. Coffee shop. Restaurant serving all meals (dinner $12–$30). Bar/lounge with entertainment and dancing on weekends. Meeting rooms. Banquet facilities for 1,000. Free parking. Valet parking available. Free airport transportation. On 40 acres. Four diamond AAA rating.

HYATT REGENCY DFW (GRAPEVINE)
International Parkway on D/FW Airport (P.O. Box 619014,
D/FW Airport 75261-9014) • 972-453-1234 or 800-233-1234
$$$–$$$$ (+12%) • W+ 17 rooms • No smoking rooms

Located within the D/FW airport, this 12-story Hyatt offers
1,367 units that include 49 suites ($$$$$). Senior discount and
golf package plans available. Children under 18 free in room with
parents. Concierge floor. Check-in 3 p.m. Check-out noon. Inside
access to rooms. Charge for local calls. Cable TV with free HBO
and pay channels. VCR available. Captioned TV and visual
alarms for the hearing impaired. Modem link in some rooms. Bell
service. Room service. Outdoor heated pool, sauna, exercise
room. Membership available in Hyatt Bear Creek Golf and Rac-
quet Club, a 335-acre resort located at the south entrance to the
airport, with two golf courses and tennis and racquetball courts.
(See also GRAPEVINE/SPORTS, p. 275.) Free shuttle to Bear
Creek. Business services available. Gift shop. One-day dry clean-
ing. Restaurants serving all meals (dinner $12–$30.) Bar/lounge
with entertainment and dancing. Meeting rooms. Banquet facili-
ties for 3,000. Valet parking ($9). Two tower buildings, one on
each side of International Parkway, connected by covered walk-
ways. East tower also connected to American Airlines Terminal.
Four diamond AAA rating.

THE 1934 BED AND BREAKFAST (GRAPEVINE)
322 East College (76051), two blocks east of Main • 251-1934
$$ (+12%) • All no smoking

Restored single-story red brick house in downtown historic district offers three rooms each with private bath. Full breakfast in
dining room. Thirties-style radios in rooms. Children over 12 welcome. Check in 3 to 7 p.m. or by appointment. Check-out noon.
Off-street parking.

IRVING

*For a double room: $ = Under $80, $$ = $80–$120, $$$ = $121–
$180, $$$$ = $181–$250, $$$$$ = Over $250; Room tax 11%.*

DALLAS/FORT WORTH AIRPORT MARRIOTT
**8440 Freeport Parkway, 75063 (Freeport Parkway exit off Hwy.
114) • 929-8800 or 800-228-9290 • $$$ (+11%) • W+ 9 rooms
No smoking rooms**

The 491 units in this 20-story hotel include 7 suites
($$$–$$$$$) and 441 no smoking rooms. Senior and weekend
discounts and package plans available. Children stay free in room
with parents. Concierge floor. Check-in 3 p.m. Check-out 1 p.m.
Inside access to rooms. Charge for local calls. Cable TV with
HBO and pay channels. VCR available. Captioned TV, visual
alarms, and special phones for the hearing impaired. Modem link
in rooms. Fire intercom system. Bell service. Room service.
Indoor/outdoor pool, sauna, health club. Business services avail-
able. Gift shop. Self-service laundry. One day dry cleaning.
Restaurants serving all meals (dinner $12–$30). Bar/lounge.
Meeting rooms. Banquet facilities for 1,500. Outside parking.
Free airport transportation.

DRURY INN—D/FW AIRPORT
**4210 West Airport Freeway (Hwy. 183), 75062 (Esters exit)
986-1200 or 800-325-8300 • $ (+11%) • W+ 6 rooms
No smoking rooms**

This 4-story inn has 129 rooms of which 93 are no smoking.
Senior and other discounts available. Children under 18 stay free
in room with parents. Pets OK. Check-in 3 p.m. Check-out noon.
Inside access to room. Local phone calls free. Cable TV with
HBO and Disney. Modem link in rooms. Fire intercom system.
Coffeemakers in some rooms, free coffee in lobby. Outdoor pool.

Copier and fax service. One day dry cleaning. Free continental breakfast. Free cocktails Monday–Thursday 5:30–7. Restaurant adjacent. Small meeting rooms. Outside parking. Free airport transportation.

FOUR SEASONS RESORT AND CLUB (IRVING)
4150 North MacArthur Blvd., 75038 (two miles south from MacArthur exit off Hwy. 114) • 717-0700 or 800-332-3442
$$$–$$$$$ (+11%) • W+ rooms • No smoking rooms

There are 307 units in the 9 floors in this luxury resort, including 6 suites ($$$$$) and many no smoking rooms. In addition there are 50 villa-style rooms off the golf course including 6 suites. Weekend discounts and a number of package plans available. Children under 18 stay free in room with parents. Small pets OK. Check-in 3 p.m. Check-out noon. Inside access to rooms. Charge for local calls. Cable TV with pay channels. VCR available. Visual alarms for the hearing impaired. Modem link in rooms. Fire intercom system. In-room honor bar. Coffeemakers in Villa rooms. Free coffee in lounge in morning. Bell service. Room service. Four pools (1 indoor, 3 outdoor), 176,000 sq. ft. indoor sports complex adjoining, two golf courses, Byron Nelson Golf School for groups, 12 tennis courts (4 indoor), racquetball, squash, European-style spa. Business services available. Gift shop, barber and beauty shops, and golf/sports retail stores. One day dry cleaning. Restaurant. (See also IRVING/DINING OUT— Café on the Green, p. 302.) Free newspaper. Child Care Center and children's programs. Meeting rooms and conference facilities. Banquet facilities for 250. Lounge. Outside parking. Valet parking available. Top-notch resort on 400 acres of lush grounds kept colorful by plantings of close to 50,000 flowers at least three times a year. Rated four diamonds by AAA, four stars by Mobil and one of best hotels in the United States in *Conde Nast Traveler's* magazine Readers Choice Awards.

HOLIDAY INN SELECT—DFW AIRPORT NORTH (IRVING)
4441 Hwy. 114, 75063 (one mile east of north exit from D/FW Airport, Esters exit) • 929-8181 • $$ (+ 11%) • W + 5 rooms No smoking rooms

The 178 rooms and 8 suites ($$$$) in this 8-story Holiday Inn include 140 no smoking rooms. Senior, weekend, and other discounts available. Children stay free in room with parents. Concierge floor. Check-in 3 p.m. Check-out noon. Inside access to rooms. Local phone calls free. Cable TV with free premium and pay channels. VCR available. Visual alarms and special phones for the hearing impaired. Coffeemakers in rooms. Free coffee in lobby until 9 a.m. Modem link in rooms. Fire intercom system. Room service. Outdoor pool, sauna, exercise room. Business services available. Gift shop. Self-service laundry. One day dry cleaning. Free newspaper. Restaurant serving all meals (dinner $12–$30), children eat free. Bar. Meeting rooms. Banquet facilities for 800+. Outside parking. Free airport transportation.

HOLIDAY INN/HOLIDOME SELECT D/FW AIRPORT SOUTH (IRVING)
4440 West Airport Freeway (Hwy. 183), 75062 (take Hwy. 183 from south exit of D/FW Airport, Valley View exit) 399-1010 or 800-360-2242 • $$–$$$ (+ 11%) W + 6 rooms • No smoking rooms

This Holiday Inn has 409 units on 4 floors that include 7 suites ($$$) and 301 no smoking rooms. Senior, weekend, and other discounts and package plans available. Children under 18 stay free in room with parents. Concierge floor. Check-in 3 p.m. Check-out noon. Inside access to about 95% of rooms. Charge for local calls. Cable TV with free premium channel. Visual alarms for hearing impaired. Wet bar in suites. Coffeemakers in rooms. Modem link in rooms. Fire intercom system. Bell service. Room service. Holidome: indoor recreation facility includes heated indoor/outdoor pool, exercise equipment, sauna, games. Outdoor pool. Room key provides entrance to Irving Fitness Center. Copy and fax services available. Gift shop. Self service laundry. One day dry cleaning. Free newspaper. Children's play area in Holidome. Restaurants serving all meal (dinner under $12 to $30), children under 12 eat free from special menu. Lounge with DJ, dancing, and large screen TV. Meeting rooms. Banquet facilities for 500+. Outside parking. Free airport transportation, free shuttle to Irving Mall available.

HOMEWOOD SUITES HOTEL-LAS COLINAS (IRVING)
4300 Wingren Road, 75039 (Wingren exit off Hwy.114)
556-0665 or 800-225-4663 • $–$$ (+11%)
W+ 6 suites • No smoking suites

The 136 suites with kitchens on the 3 floors of this all-suite hotel include 115 no smoking. Senior, weekend, and other discounts and Dallas Cowboy packages available. Children stay free in room with parents. Pets OK ($50 fee). Check-in 3 p.m. Check-out noon. Inside access to 114 suites, outside to 22. Local phone calls free. TV with pay channels and VCR. Visual alarms for the hearing impaired. Modem link in rooms. Fire intercom system. Heated outdoor pool, exercise room and sport court. Business services available. Convenience store. Self-service laundry. One day dry cleaning. Free continental breakfast. Free beer and wine Monday–Thursday 5–7 p.m. Free newspaper. Free shuttle service within 5 mile radius. Two small meeting rooms. Outside parking.

OMNI MANDALAY HOTEL AT LAS COLINAS (IRVING)
221 East Las Colinas Blvd., 75039 • 556-0800 or 800-The-Omni
(800-843-6664) • $$$$ (+11%) • W+ 5 rooms
No smoking rooms

This 27-floor luxury hotel has 410 units that include 96 suites ($$$$–$$$$$) and 100 no smoking rooms. Weekend and other discounts and occasional package plans available. Check-in 3 p.m. Check-out noon. Inside access to rooms. Charge for local calls. Cable TV with free premium and pay channels. VCR available. Captioned TV, visual alarms, and special phones for the hearing impaired. Coffeemakers in rooms. Modem link in rooms. Fire intercom system. Bell service. Room service. Heated lake-side pool, sauna, exercise room, bicycles available for rent. Guest memberships available in local golf and health clubs. Business services available. Gift shop. Mandalay Canal shops nearby. One day dry cleaning. Free newspaper. Playground, programs for children, and babysitting available. Restaurant serving all meals (dinner $12–$30) Lounge with entertainment. Meeting rooms. Banquet facilities for 1,200. Outside and garage parking. Valet parking available ($6). On five acres of lakefront. Named on *Conde Nast Traveler's* magazine Gold List of top 500 hotels in the world. Rated four-diamonds by AAA and four stars by Mobil.

RAMADA INN D/FW AIRPORT SOUTH (IRVING)
4110 West Airport Freeway (Hwy. 183), 75062 (Esters exit)
399-2005 • $(+ 11%) • W + 2 rooms • No smoking rooms

The 142 units in this 2-story Ramada include 30 suites and about 70 no smoking rooms. Senior, weekend and package plans available. Children stay free in room with parents. Check-in and Check-out 1 p.m. Outside access to rooms. Local phone calls free. Cable TV. Captioned TV and special phones for the hearing impaired. Wet bar in suites. Coffeemakers in rooms. Outdoor pool. Free guest membership is fitness center. Self-service laundry. One day dry cleaning. Free continental breakfast. Restaurant nearby. Bar. Four meeting rooms. Free airport transportation.

RESIDENCE INN-LAS COLINAS (IRVING)
950 Walnut Hill Lane, 75038 (MacArthur & Walnut Hill)
580-7773 or 800-331-3131 • $$–$$$ (+ 11%) • W + 2 suites
No smoking suites

There are 120 suites with kitchens in this 2-story inn of which 80 are no smoking. Senior, weekend, and other discounts available. Children 12 and under stay free in room with parents. Pets OK (fee/deposit). Check-in 2 p.m. Check-out noon. Outside access to rooms. Local phone calls free. Cable TV with HBO and Showtime, VCR available. Coffeemakers in rooms. Modem link in rooms. Outdoor pool, exercise room. Self-service laundry. One day dry cleaning. Free continental breakfast. Free cocktails. Free newspaper. Two small meeting rooms. Outside parking. Free airport transportation and to businesses within 5 mile radius.

SHERATON GRAND HOTEL AT D/FW AIRPORT (IRVING)
4440 West Carpenter Freeway (Hwy. 114), 75063 (at Esters exit) • 929-8400 or 800-325-3535 • $$–$$$(+ 11%) • W + rooms • No smoking rooms

The 300 units in this 12-story hotel include seven suites ($$$–$$$$) and a majority of the units are no smoking. Package plans available. Concierge floor. Check-in 3 p.m. Check-out noon. Inside access to rooms. Charge for local calls. Cable TV with free premium channel and pay channels. VCR available. Captioned TV, visual alarms, and special phones for the hearing impaired. Coffeemakers in rooms. Modem link in rooms. Bell service. Room service. Indoor/outdoor heated pool, sauna, exercise room. Business services available. Gift shop. One day dry cleaning. Restaurants serving all meals (dinner approximately $15) (See IRVING-OFFBEAT, p. 299). Bar. Twenty-three meeting rooms. Banquet facilities for 1,000. Free outside parking. Free airport transportation.

WILSON WORLD HOTEL (IRVING)
4600 West Airport Freeway (Hwy. 183), 75062 (one mile from south exit of D/FW, Valley View exit) • 513-0800 or 800-945-7667 • $$ (+ 11%) • W + 3 rooms • No smoking rooms

Wilson's World has 200 rooms on 5 floors that include 90 no smoking rooms. Senior and weekend discounts available. Children 18 and under stay free in room with parents. Check-in 3 p.m. Check-out noon. Inside access to rooms. Refrigerators in all rooms, microwaves in some. Local phone calls free. Cable TV with pay channels. Visual alarms for the hearing impaired. Modem link in rooms. Bell service. Room service. Indoor heated pool, exercise room. Gift shop. Business services available. Self-service laundry. One day dry cleaning. Free newspaper. Restaurant serving all meals (dinner $12–$30). Bar. Meeting rooms.

Banquet facilities for 175. Outside parking. Free airport transportation.

WYNDHAM GARDEN HOTEL-LAS COLINAS (IRVING)
110 West Carpenter Freeway (Hwy. 114), 75039 (O'Connor Road exit) • 650-1600 or 800-WYNDHAM (800-996-3426) $$$ (+11%) • W+ 2 rooms • No smoking rooms

The 168 units in this 3-story Wyndham includes 45 suites ($$$) and 111 no smoking rooms. Senior, weekend, and other discounts available. Children 18 and under stay free in room with parents. Check-in 3 p.m., Check-out noon. Inside access to rooms. Refrigerators in some rooms. Charge for local calls. Cable TV with free premium channel and pay channels. VCR available. Captioned TV and special phones for hearing impaired. Coffeemakers in rooms. Modem link in rooms. Bell service. Room service for dinner. Indoor heated pool, sauna, exercise room. Guest memberships available in nearby athletic club. Copy and fax service available. One day dry cleaning. Free newspaper. Restaurant serving all meals (dinner under $12–$30). Bar. Meeting rooms. Banquet facilities for 100. Outside parking.

WESTERN METROPLEX—FORT WORTH AND NORTH RICHLAND HILLS

FORT WORTH

For a double room: $ = Under $80, $$ = $80–$120, $$$ = $121– $180, $$$$ = $181–$250, $$$$$ = Over $250; Room tax 13%.

AZALEA PLANTATION
1400 Robinwood Drive (76111) • 838-5882 or 800-68-RELAX (800-6873529) • $$ (+ 13%)

This bed & breakfast offers both four rooms with private baths and private cottages with mini kitchens. Free local phone calls. Fax and copy service available. Free continental breakfast weekdays, breakfast buffet weekends. Free outside parking.

ETTA'S PLACE (FORT WORTH)
200 West Third at Houston in Sundance Square (76102)
Metro 817-654-0267 • $$$ (+13%) • W+ elevator and some
rooms • All no smoking except for outside terraces

The 10 units in this bed & breakfast includes 4 suites. On the second to fifth floors of the building around the corner from the Caravan of Dreams. Private baths. Children and pets accepted. Check-in 3 p.m. Check-out noon. Inside access to rooms. Local phone calls free. Cable TV. Modem link in rooms. Fax and copier service. Full breakfast. Reserved spaces in parking lot across street ($5). Named after Etta Place, commonly known as the girlfriend of the Sundance Kid.

GREEN OAKS PARK HOTEL (FORT WORTH)
6901 West Freeway (76116), off I-30 at Green Oaks exit
738-7311 or 800-772-2341 (In Texas), 800-433-2174 (Outside
Texas) • $$ (+13%)• W+ 4 rooms • No smoking rooms

A 2-story hotel with 282 units including 55 suites ($$$) and 124 no smoking rooms. Senior, weekend, and other discounts available. Children 12 and under stay free in room with parents. Pets OK (deposit $20). Check-in 3 p.m. Check-out noon. Inside and outside access to rooms. Charge for local calls. Cable TV with free premium channel and pay channels. VCR available. Captioned TV, visual alarms, and special phones for the hearing impaired. Wet bar in rooms. Coffee available in lobby. Room service. Two outdoor pools, sauna, exercise room. Two lighted tennis courts and health club facilities. Public golf course adjacent. Business services available. One day dry cleaning. Free full breakfast. Free newspaper in restaurant. Restaurant serving all meals (diner under $12). Lounge with entertainment and dancing. Sixteen meeting rooms. Banquet facilities for 1,000. Free outside parking. On 11.5 acres across from Ridgmar Mall.

HOLIDAY INN FORT WORTH CENTRAL
2000 Beach Street (76103), off I-30 at Beach Street exit
534-4801 • $$ (+13%)• W+ 2 rooms • No smoking rooms

The 185 units in this 2-and-3-story inn include 9 suites, 2 with kitchens ($$$–$$$$), and 120 no smoking rooms. Senior and other discounts available. Children 19 and under stay free in room with parents. Check-in 3 p.m. Check-out noon. Inside and outside access to rooms. Charge for local calls. Cable TV with HBO and pay channels. Captioned TV and visual alarms for the hearing impaired. Coffeemakers in rooms. Modem link in rooms. Bell service. Room service. Outdoor pool, sauna, exercise room, one lighted tennis court. Business services available. One day dry cleaning. Playground. Restaurant serving all meals (dinner $12–$30). Lounge with occasional entertainment and dancing. Meeting rooms. Banquet facilities for 1250. Free outside parking. Free transportation to downtown and Stockyards.

HOLIDAY INN NORTH (FORT WORTH)
2540 Meacham Blvd. (76106) • 625-9911 or 800-465-4329
$$ (+ 13%)• W + 3 rooms • No smoking rooms

This 6-story Inn has 247 units including 6 suites ($$$–$$$$) and 168 no smoking rooms. Senior discount and package plans available. Children stay free in rooms with parents. Check-in 3 p.m. Check-out noon. Inside access to rooms. Charge for local calls. Cable TV with Disney and pay channels. VCR available. Visual alarms and special phones for the hearing impaired. Wet bar in suites. Coffee available in lobby. Modem link in rooms. Fire intercom system. Bell service. Room service. Indoor pool, sauna, exercise room. Gift shop. Self-service laundry. One day dry cleaning. Restaurant serving all meals (dinner $8–$19). Lounge with DJ for dancing. Eleven meeting rooms. Banquet facilities for 1000. Free outside parking.

LA QUINTA WEST (FORT WORTH)
7888 I-30 West (76108) off Cherry Lane exit • 246-5511 or
800-531-5900 • $ (+ 13%)• W + 2 rooms • No smoking rooms

The 3 floors of this La Quinta have 106 units that include 2 studio suites ($–$$) and 65 no smoking rooms. Senior and other discounts available. Children 18 and under stay free in room with parents. Pets OK. Check-in 2 p.m. Check-out noon. Outside access to 100 rooms, inside access to six. Local phone calls free. Cable TV with HBO and Disney and pay channels. Captioned TV and special phones for the hearing impaired. Free coffee in lobby.

Modem link in rooms. Outdoor pool. One day dry cleaning. Free continental breakfast. Free outside parking. Restaurant adjacent.

MISS MOLLY'S HOTEL (FORT WORTH)
109 1/2 West Exchange Avenue (76106), in Stockyards Historic District, just west of Main • 626-1522 or 800-99-MOLLY (800-996-6559) • $$–$$$ (+ 13%)• No smoking

This upstairs bed and breakfast has eight rooms, one with private bath ($$$), all no smoking. Free local calls on hall phone. Free continental breakfast. Free outside reserved parking. Don't expect B&B cute and cozy here. More cowboy rough and ready. Old style rooming house (once a bordello) with baths (3) down the hall. In heart of stockyards action which can be noisy until wee hours.

RESIDENCE INN BY MARRIOTT (FORT WORTH)
1701 South University Drive (76107), take University exit off I-30, go south 1/2 mile • 870-1011 • $$–$$$ (+ 13%)• W + 2 suites • No smoking suites

Sixty-four of the 120 one- and two-bedroom suites with kitchens in this 2-story all-suites inn are no smoking. Senior, weekend and other discounts available. Children stay free in room with parents. Pets OK ($5/day). Check-in 3 p.m. check-out noon. Outside access to rooms. Charge for local calls. Cable TV with HBO. Captioned TV, visual alarms, and special phones for the hearing impaired. Coffeemakers in rooms. Modem link in rooms. Outdoor heated pool. Guest memberships available in Harris Hospital Health/Fitness Center. Self-service laundry. One day dry cleaning. Free continental breakfast. Free newspaper. Free outside parking. Free transportation within 10 mile radius. Free grocery shopping service. In the Cultural District.

STOCKYARDS HOTEL (FORT WORTH)
109 East Exchange Avenue at Main (76106), in Stockyards Historic District • 625-6427 • $$$ (+ 13%)• No smoking rooms

There are 4 suites ($$$$–$$$$$) and several no smoking rooms among the 52 units in this 3-story hotel. Package plans available. Children 12 and under stay free in room with parents. Pets OK ($50 deposit). Check-in 3 p.m. Check-out noon. Inside access to rooms. Charge for local calls. Cable TV. Captioned TV for the hearing impaired. Wet bar in some rooms. Coffeemakers in rooms. Modem link in rooms. Bell service. Room service. Copy service available. Free newspaper in restaurant. Restaurant serving all meals (dinner $12–$30). Lounge with entertainment. Three meeting rooms. Banquet facilities for 425. Valet parking $5. Restored historic hotel built in 1907. Western decor includes saddle-topped stools in bar.

THE TEXAS WHITE HOUSE (FORT WORTH)
1417 Eighth Avenue (76104) • 923-3597 or 800-279-6491
$$ (+13%)• No smoking in house
The three rooms in this bed and breakfast are all on the second floor. All with private baths. No children. Free local phone calls (phone in room on request). TV in room on request. Secretarial services available. Full breakfast and afternoon snacks. Free outside parking.

THE WORTHINGTON (FORT WORTH)
200 Main Street (76102), downtown at Sundance Square
870-1000 or 800-477-8274 • $$$–$$$$ (+13%) • W+ 15 rooms
No smoking rooms
This 12-story hotel has 504 units including 44 suites ($$$$$) and 50% of the rooms designated as no smoking. Senior, weekend, and package plans available. Children 12 and under stay free in room with parents. Concierge floor. Small pets OK. Check-in 3 p.m. Check-out noon. Inside access to rooms. Charge for local calls. Cable TV with free premium channel and pay channels. Captioned TV, visual alarms, and special phones for the hearing impaired. In-room honor bar. Modem link in rooms. Fire intercom system. Bell service. Room service. Indoor pool, sauna, exercise room. Athletic club and tennis (fee). Business services available. Gift shop. One day dry cleaning. Restaurant serving all meals (dinner $12–$30). (See also FORT WORTH/DINING OUT-Reflections, p. 240.) Bar. Sixteen meeting rooms. Banquet facilities for 1,000. Garage: self-parking $7, valet $10. Hotel spans three city blocks. Excellent views of the city from upper floor rooms. Rated four diamonds by AAA and four stars by Mobil.

NORTH RICHLAND HILLS

For a double room: $ = Under $80, $$ = $80–$120, $$$ = $121–$180, $$$$ = $181–$250, $$$$$ = Over $250; Room tax 13%.

HOMESTEAD VILLAGE
7450 Northeast Loop 820 (76180) • 788-6000 • $$$$–$$$$$ (+13%)• W + 5 suites • No smoking suites

All the 133 units in the 2-story Homestead Village are suites with kitchenettes and 56 are no smoking. Children 12 and under stay free in room with parents. Check-in and Check-out 11 a.m. Outside access to suites. Local phone calls free. Cable TV with pay channels. Pets OK (Deposit and fee). Free coffee available. Self-service laundry. Free outside parking.

LA QUINTA INN
7620 Bedford Euless Road (76180) • 485-2750 or 800-531-5900 (Reservations) • $ (+13%) • W + 1 room • No smoking rooms

This 2-story La Quinta has 107 units that include 5 suites ($) and 70% no smoking. Senior and weekend discounts available. Children under 18 stay free in room with parents. Check-in and Check-out at noon. Outside access to rooms. Local phone calls free. Cable TV with pay channels. Pets OK. Modem link in rooms. Outdoor pool. Free continental breakfast. Free outside parking. Restaurant adjacent.

INDEX